Ezra Pound's Washington Cantos and the Struggle for Light

Historicizing Modernism

Series Editors
Matthew Feldman, Professorial Fellow, Norwegian Study Centre, University of York; and Erik Tonning, Professor of British Literature and Culture, University of Bergen, Norway

Assistant Editor: David Tucker, Associate Lecturer, Goldsmiths College, University of London, UK

Editorial Board
Professor Chris Ackerley, Department of English, University of Otago, New Zealand; Professor Ron Bush, St. John's College, University of Oxford, UK; Dr Finn Fordham, Department of English, Royal Holloway, UK; Professor Steven Matthews, Department of English, University of Reading, UK; Dr Mark Nixon, Department of English, University of Reading, UK; Dr Julie Taylor, Northumbria University, UK; Professor Shane Weller, Reader in Comparative Literature, University of Kent, UK; and Professor Janet Wilson, University of Northampton, UK.

Historicizing Modernism challenges traditional literary interpretations by taking an empirical approach to modernist writing: a direct response to new documentary sources made available over the last decade.
Informed by archival research, and working beyond the usual European/American avant-garde 1900–45 parameters, this series reassesses established readings of modernist writers by developing fresh views of intellectual contexts and working methods.

Series Titles:
Arun Kolatkar and Literary Modernism in India, Laetitia Zecchini
British Literature and Classical Music, David Deutsch
Broadcasting in the Modernist Era, Matthew Feldman, Henry Mead and Erik Tonning
Charles Henri Ford, Alexander Howard
Chicago and the Making of American Modernism, Michelle E. Moore
Ezra Pound's Adams Cantos, David Ten Eyck
Ezra Pound's Eriugena, Mark Byron
Great War Modernisms and The New Age Magazine, Paul Jackson
James Joyce and Absolute Music, Michelle Witen

James Joyce and Catholicism, Chrissie van Mierlo
John Kasper and Ezra Pound, Alec Marsh
Katherine Mansfield and Literary Modernism, ed. by Janet Wilson, Gerri Kimber and Susan Reid
Late Modernism and the English Intelligencer, Alex Latter
The Life and Work of Thomas MacGreevy, Susan Schreibman
Literary Impressionism, Rebecca Bowler
Modern Manuscripts, Dirk Van Hulle
Modernism at the Microphone, Melissa Dinsman
Modernist Lives, Claire Battershill
The Politics of 1930s British Literature, Natasha Periyan
Reading Mina Loy's Autobiographies, Sandeep Parmar
Reframing Yeats, Charles Ivan Armstrong
Samuel Beckett and Arnold Geulincx, David Tucker
Samuel Beckett and the Bible, Iain Bailey
Samuel Beckett and Cinema, Anthony Paraskeva
Samuel Beckett's 'More Pricks than Kicks', John Pilling
Samuel Beckett's German Diaries 1936–1937, Mark Nixon
T. E. Hulme and the Ideological Politics of Early Modernism, Henry Mead
Virginia Woolf's Late Cultural Criticism, Alice Wood
Christian Modernism in an Age of Totalitarianism, Jonas Kurlberg
Samuel Beckett and Experimental Psychology, Joshua Powell
Samuel Beckett in Confinement, James Little
Katherine Mansfield: New Directions, ed. by Aimée Gasston, Gerri Kimber and Janet Wilson
Modernist Wastes, Caroline Knighton
The Many Drafts of D. H. Lawrence, Elliott Morsia
Samuel Beckett and the Second World War, William Davies
Judith Wright and Emily Carr, Anne Collett and Dorothy Jones

Upcoming titles
Samuel Beckett and Science, Chris Ackerley

Ezra Pound's Washington Cantos and the Struggle for Light

Alec Marsh
Edited and with annotations by Archie Henderson

BLOOMSBURY ACADEMIC
LONDON • NEW YORK • OXFORD • NEW DELHI • SYDNEY

BLOOMSBURY ACADEMIC
Bloomsbury Publishing Plc
50 Bedford Square, London, WC1B 3DP, UK
1385 Broadway, New York, NY 10018, USA
29 Earlsfort Terrace, Dublin 2, Ireland

BLOOMSBURY, BLOOMSBURY ACADEMIC and the Diana logo are trademarks of
Bloomsbury Publishing Plc

First published in Great Britain 2021
Paperback edition published 2023

Copyright © Alec Marsh, 2021

Alec Marsh has asserted his right under the Copyright, Designs and
Patents Act, 1988, to be identified as Author of this work.

For legal purposes the Acknowledgments on p. xiii constitute an
extension of this copyright page.

Cover design by Jade Barnett and Eleanor Rose

All rights reserved. No part of this publication may be reproduced or
transmitted in any form or by any means, electronic or mechanical, including
photocopying, recording, or any information storage or retrieval system,
without prior permission in writing from the publishers.

Bloomsbury Publishing Plc does not have any control over, or responsibility for, any
third-party websites referred to or in this book. All internet addresses given in
this book were correct at the time of going to press. The author and publisher
regret any inconvenience caused if addresses have changed or sites have
ceased to exist, but can accept no responsibility for any such changes.

A catalogue record for this book is available from the British Library.

A catalog record for this book is available from the Library of Congress.

ISBN: HB: 978-1-3500-9655-4
       PB: 978-1-3501-8744-3
       ePDF: 978-1-3500-9656-1
       eBook: 978-1-3500-9657-8

Series: Historicizing Modernism

Typeset by Integra Software Services Pvt. Ltd.

To find out more about our authors and books visit www.bloomsbury.com
and sign up for our newsletters.

In memoriam
Burton Hatlen

Contents

List of Figures	xi
Editoral Preface to *Historicizing Modernism*	xii
Acknowledgments	xiii
A Note on the Text and Permissions	xv
Abbreviations	xvi
Intro to a Sequel	1

1 The Washington Cantos: Anagogy, Metapolitics, and the
   Warren Court   9
   Rock-Drill de los Cantares (1955) and *Thrones* (1959)   9
   Metapolitics and Politics   17
   "Four Steps to the Bughouse"   24
   The Warren Court   27

2 Obstacles to Understanding the Washington Cantos   33
   Aesopian Language and Its Problems   36
   Pound's Reading and the Poverty of Philology   40
   Trobar Clus   45
   Pound's "Late Style"   45
   The "Cleaners Manifesto"   47

3 Aesopian Language and States' Rights: Two Fables—
   John Randolph of Roanoke and Canto 103   51
   John Randolph of Roanoke   52
   Canto 103   57

4 The Aryanist Vortex: Pound's Metapolitics and White Supremacy   77
   Pound's Taxonomy of Human Types   84
   "Freedom Now or Never"   87

5 Raising Cain: The Aryan Origins of Civilization   95
   "Alfalfa Bill" Murray's *Adam and Cain*   96
   Waddell, Egypt, and the Aryan Makers of Civilization   99
   Pound's "Egyptian Problem"   104

6	Sheri Martinelli and the Paradise of Venus	113
	Ezra Pound: "a ballin' angel …"	114
	Trobar Clus	122
7	Sheri Martinelli: Right-Wing Muse	135
8	Apollonius of Tyana	149
9	Canto 97: Nummulary Moving toward Paradise	161
	Canto 97 Obverse: History as a Monetary System	163
	Canto 97: Reverse	170
10	Pound's Agrarian Bent: Physiocracy against Degradation	177
11	The Coke Cantos 107–109 as an Argument for the Defense	193
	The Connecticut Charter	201
	Pound and Catherine Drinker Bowen	203
	Four Acres	209
12	Pound at Colonus: The Poet as Oedipus	215

Afterword	229
Appendix A: A Primer of Poundian Economics	234
Appendix B: "Homage to Grandpa" by Sheri Martinelli	245
Bibliography	247
Index	257

Figures

1.1	*Ling*² 靈	20
5.1	Sargon's seal	101
6.1	"EP" by Sheri Martinelli, colored pencil on a Pound letter, Beinecke	116
6.2	"Signature" by Sheri Martinelli, ballpoint pen, Beinecke	125
9.1	Canto 97/695	162
9.2	American Social Credit Movement logo, Beinecke	163
B.1	Sheri Martinelli's "Homage to Grandpa" and letter to editor Miles Payne as printed with Payne's reply in *Light Year*, Autumn 1961	246

Editoral Preface to *Historicizing Modernism*

This book series is devoted to the analysis of late nineteenth- to twentieth-century literary modernism within its historical contexts. *Historicizing Modernism* therefore stresses empirical accuracy and the value of primary sources (such as letters, diaries, notes, drafts, marginalia, or other archival materials) in developing monographs and edited collections on modernist literature. This may take a number of forms, such as manuscript study and genetic criticism, documenting interrelated historical contexts and ideas, and exploring biographical information. To date, no book series has fully laid claim to this interdisciplinary, source-based territory for modern literature. While the series addresses itself to a range of key authors, it also highlights the importance of noncanonical writers with a view to establishing broader intellectual genealogies of modernism. Furthermore, while the series is weighted toward the English-speaking world, studies of non-Anglophone modernists whose writings are open to fresh historical exploration are also included.

A key aim of the series is to reach beyond the familiar rhetoric of intellectual and artistic "autonomy" employed by many modernists and their critical commentators. Such rhetorical moves can and should themselves be historically situated and reintegrated into the complex continuum of individual literary practices. It is our intent that the emphasis of the series upon the contested self-definitions of modernist writers, thinkers, and critics may, in turn, prompt various reconsiderations of the boundaries delimiting the concept "modernism" itself. Indeed, the concept of "historicizing" is itself debated across its volumes, and the series by no means discourages more theoretically informed approaches. On the contrary, the editors hope that the historical specificity encouraged by *Historicizing Modernism* may inspire a range of fundamental critiques along the way.

Matthew Feldman
Erik Tonning

Acknowledgments

This book has been a long time fermenting. In the meantime, versions of several chapters have been printed elsewhere. I am grateful to many old friends. Roxana Preda printed and edited essays on Sheri Martinelli in her *Edinburgh Companion to Ezra Pound and the Arts* and the essay on Pound and physiocracy in *A Companion to Ezra Pound's Economics*. Many thanks to Mark Byron for printing a part of what became the chapter on Aesopian language and John Randolph in his collection *The New Ezra Pound Studies*. Thanks to Bernard Dew for finding an elusive text. Ira Nadel and Demetres Tryphonopoulos were kind enough to edit a piece on Pound's economics for the forthcoming MLA—a version appears here as Appendix A. Steven Moore was kind enough to send me a copy of the letter Sheri Martinelli wrote to the *Light Year* attesting to Pound's extraordinary powers as a lover. It is in Appendix B.

Somewhat to my own surprise, in this book I find myself walking down a dissident path of Pound scholarship first blazed by Massimo Bacigalupo in *The Forméd Trace* (1980), followed a few years later by Robert Casillo's courageous *The Genealogy of Demons* (1988). This project has benefited mightily from very recent scholarship on *Thrones*, in particular. Michael Kindellan's lively *The Late Cantos of Ezra Pound: Composition, Revision, Publication* (2017) has been a constant source of inspiration and new insights. I'm grateful for his generous responses to my queries. The *Glossator 10* issue dedicated to *Thrones* (2018), edited by Alex Howard, is full of good things, providing a reckoning of where we stand with that intractable sequence of poems. This book is in constant conversation with the contributors to that volume. Over the years, Peter Nicholls has written more insightfully than anyone else about Pound's late work. His *Glossator* essay is one of his best. Thanks are due Gregory Barnhisel who reminded me about the Norman Holmes Pearson papers at Yale. Alex Pestell taught me that Aesopian language was no simple algebra. Archie Henderson remains for me an indispensable resource, reader, editor, and comrade: without his unstinting help this book could never have been published. Thanks to my colleagues and students at Muhlenberg, for the help I've received from our Trexler Library, and to the ever-helpful librarians at the Beinecke Library at Yale. Many thanks as well to the patient Lucy Brown and Wade Guyitt at Bloomsbury. Special thanks are due to Sarah McNamee for her editing and proof work.

I am most grateful to Mary de Rachewiltz and the de Rachewiltz family for their hospitality and all the cultural and agricultural work they do, including with my Muhlenberg College students. Pound's descendants work unceasingly to minister to a world in the death-grip of "Usura," a crisis that all the best in Pound resisted with his poem and his life.

Most of all, I need to thank my wife, Nicole, for her patience and good humor in bearing with me and my Pound obsession.

Alec Marsh
Muhlenberg College
Allentown, PA. August 2019

A Note on the Text and Permissions

Pound's spelling is eccentric and his typing erratic. Altogether, he writes an idiolect I call "Ezratic." I have not tried to regularize his spellings, but I have on occasion supplied missing letters in brackets to resolve ambiguities.

I am grateful to be permitted to use previously unpublished material by Ezra Pound, © Mary de Rachewiltz and the Estate of Omar S. Pound, used by permission of New Directions Publishing Corporation, agents. All published material by Ezra Pound used by permission of New Directions Publishing Corporation. In addition, for permission to quote from unpublished correspondence I am grateful to the New Directions Ownership Trust, which represents the estates of Norman Holmes Pearson and Sheri Martinelli. Many thanks to Christopher Wait of New Directions, for his timely help.

Abbreviations

Works by Pound

Cantos	New York: New Directions, 1996b. Sixth paperbound printing. Indicated by canto and page number: for example, 97/688.
Con.	*Confucius*. New York: New Directions, 1969.
GK	*Guide to Kulchur* (1938). New York: New Directions, 1970a.
J/M	*Jefferson and/or Mussolini* (1935). New York: Liveright, 1970b.
LE	*Literary Essays*. New York: New Directions, 1968c.
P	*Personae: The Shorter Poems of Ezra Pound*. Revised edition. Edited by Lea Baechler and A. Walton Litz. New York: New Directions, 1990.
P&D	*Pavannes & Divagations*. New York: New Directions, 1958.
P/L	*Pound/Lewis. The Letters of Ezra Pound and Wyndham Lewis*. Edited by Timothy Materer. New York: New Directions, 1985.
SP	*Selected Prose 1909–1965*. Edited by William Cookson. London: Faber and Faber, 1973.
SR	*The Spirit of Romance*. New York: New Directions, 1968b.

Correspondence and Other Texts

EPCF	*Ezra Pound's Chinese Friends*. Edited by Zhaoming Qian. Oxford: Oxford University Press, 2008.
EPCH	*Ezra Pound: The Critical Heritage*. Edited by Eric Homberger. London: Routledge Kegan Paul, 1972.
EPEC	*Ezra Pound's Economic Correspondence*. Edited by Roxana Preda. Tallahassee: University Press of Florida, 2007.
EP/JT	*Ezra Pound/Letters/John Theobald*. Edited by Donald Pearce and Herbert Schneidau. Redding Ridge: Black Swan, 1984.
EP/ORA	*"I Cease Not to Yowl": Ezra Pound's Letters to Olivia Rossetti Agresti*. Edited by Demetres P. Tryphanopoulos and Leon Surette. Urbana and Chicago: University of Illinois Press, 1998.

G   *Glossator 10: Astern in the Dinghy: Commentaries on Ezra Pound's Thrones de los Cantares XCVI–CIX.* Edited by Alexander Howard. *Glossator 10* (2018).

JK & EP   Alec Marsh. *John Kasper and Ezra Pound: Saving the Republic.* London: Bloomsbury, 2015.

Archie Henderson's many notes to this volume are marked (AH).

Intro to a Sequel

Here is the poetic evidence that Pound's right-wing ideas in the 1950s were not confined to letters or pseudonymous prose but were part of the so-called "Washington Cantos," *Rock-Drill* (1956) and *Thrones* (1959). Shut up in St. Elizabeths Hospital, the poet was not free to live or write as he pleased. Still, these installments of *The Cantos* were conceived and deployed, in part, as acts of resistance, even as "a political weapon" (Stock 1966: 91) during this troubled period. Clearly, Pound's determination to write activist, political poetry is at odds with his oft-stated project at this time, the attempt to "write paradise" and complete his forty-year epic with a grand affirmation. Mine is a political reading, so I do not spend much time on the paradisal metaphysics of these late poems. I am most interested in these poems as evidence of "civic thought," to which Pound's later poetry was dedicated. But I do address Pound's *metapolitics*: his need to align celestial and earthly politics, *kosmos* with *polis*.

Much of the material in this book was originally researched and written to serve as Part II of an earlier book, *John Kasper and Ezra Pound: Saving the Republic* (Bloomsbury, 2015), showing how Pound's right-wing, segregationist politics finds its way into *Rock-Drill* and *Thrones*, his Washington Cantos. For various practical reasons this material could not be included in the earlier volume, but this book is very much a sequel to the first. Here I place these poems in the historical context of the Cold War and the Civil Rights struggle, which the poet saw as an aspect of the Jewish/Communist conspiracy determined to subvert and subjugate the United States through specious misinterpretation of the sacred US Constitution, financial manipulation, and racial mixing. Although the poems' recondite surfaces reveal these concerns fitfully and indirectly, more explicit evidence for this view is abundant in Pound's correspondence and other writings of the time. These poems shed light on related political concerns that took up much of *John Kasper and Ezra Pound*. In the name of "civic thought," "good governance," and even civilization as such, the Washington Cantos resist developments in the 1950s. As I argued in the earlier book using the example of Canto 105, they intervene in the intensifying Civil Rights struggle that followed the Supreme Court's landmark decision in *Brown v. Board of Education* (1954), which Pound understood correctly as the rejection of white supremacy as an ideology, thereby opening the door to racial mixing and a correspondent sea-change in American culture. This is indeed what has happened. While many rejoice in this development, Pound was sure it foretold the triumph of tyrannical federal power over local custom and the end of time-honored American folkways dedicated to life, liberty, and the pursuit of happiness.

Before attempting to read and interpret the Washington Cantos, let me remind you from whence they came by recalling four claims I made in *John Kasper and Ezra Pound* that determine the concerns of these poems.

1. Pound did not believe in evolution. Pound believed in what is now called "intelligent design." Reading Louis Agassiz with John Kasper in the early 1950s resulted in the publication by Kasper of *Gists from Agassiz* (1953). The research convinced both men that the human races were created separately. Consequently, race mixing was contrary to the divine plan. Pound, like all Americans of his class and education, was quite familiar with the discourse of eugenics. Working, as he had, as an Axis radio broadcaster and propagandist, Pound knew well the eugenic arguments Hitler had learned from his enthusiastic reading of American eugenicists and repeated in *Mein Kampf*—he had taught them himself over Axis radio, so he was well prepared to accept Agassiz's compatible views. This knowledge led to or confirmed a racial taxonomy peculiar to the St. Elizabeths circle around Pound. These beliefs articulate a vision of racial destiny, of white supremacy, and of colored nonwhite inferiority that underwrites a theory of history as racial struggle, fully exposited in *Mein Kampf*, eugenicist writings, and much self-congratulatory nineteenth-century historiography concerning the West's civilizing mission.

   When the Warren Court ruled on *Brown v. Board of Education*, mandating racial integration of the public schools, Pound and his young disciples were determined to stop it. In 1956 Kasper went into the South preaching racial segregation, burning crosses, and distributing *Virginians on Guard!*, an inflammatory 32-page pamphlet advocating extreme segregation, written and edited in collaboration with Pound.

   Confined as he was, Pound was limited to anonymous articles planted in the array of dissident publications he endorsed such as *New Times* in

Australia and Bill McNaughton's *Strike*. But he also turned his cantos to counter what he perceived as a renewed threat to civilization—civilization which could only be created and sustained by specially gifted races, namely the Greeks (i.e. Europeans) and the Chinese. As we will see, Pound's Aryanism becomes, in the Washington Cantos, a significant mode of epic affirmation deployed against the constant threat of hostile Semitic pressure.

2. Pound's extensive links to right-wing figures nationally and internationally suggest that there is unbroken political continuity in Pound's politics from the 1930s forward. His eccentric Confucianism aside, Pound's political views are in basic harmony with the anti-Communist American Right of the 1950s. He admired Senator McCarthy and believed that the Roosevelt Administration was penetrated bottom to top with Soviet agents. His most important disciples became significant players on the Right, influencing American right-wing politics to this day. John Kasper, who I conclude was one of Pound's most perspicacious readers in the 1950s (*JK & EP* xii, 233), expressed what might be called its "Neo-Nazi" tendency. Kasper's ties to Admiral John Crommelin, the Ku Klux Klan, J. B. Stoner, and the National States' Rights Party link him to right-wing, segregationist terror in the South and to resurgent "Trumpist" white supremacism today. Eustace Mullins, Pound's first published biographer, authored an exposé of the Federal Reserve Bank at Pound's instigation that has become a right-wing classic. He was a rabid anti-Semite, considered a patriot and inspiration for the Know-Nothing Tea Party Movement, judging from the tributes that appeared on the Web after his death in 2010. The quietest and most mysterious of the three, Dave Horton, is connected to the military Right through the Defenders of the American Constitution (DAC), as I detailed in *John Kasper and Ezra Pound*. Later, he served Lt. Col. Archibald Roberts's Committee to Restore the Constitution in the same advisory capacity. Both these groups have strong ties to the "militia movement." As a Nevada attorney, Horton theorized resistance to the federal government's Bureau of Land Management in the name of states' rights. His ideas underpin the 2014 Bundy Ranch standoff and the takeover in 2016 of National Parkland in Oregon by Bundy followers.

3. Pound's fear of racial mixing was an extension of his long-held concern about proper nutrition—both alimentary and cultural. The adulteration of food was a practice of and a metaphor for "Usura," the predatory, corrosive theory and practice of finance capitalism. *The Cantos* were "nutriment." Pound was concerned that there be "wheat in bread"—a name he gave to

a segregationist and states'-rights faction that, under Kasper's direction, actually ran candidates for office in Tennessee. Pound's interest in grain and agrarian virtue is a pervasive theme in the Washington Cantos, putting him in a physiocratic tradition that leads back through Thomas Jefferson to the French physiocrats Jefferson knew and read and to their inspirations: Confucius and Mencius.

4. I tried to show that these beliefs, repellant as they are to most readers, were nonetheless sincerely held. *John Kasper and Ezra Pound* was not an attack on the poet but an attempt to understand him as he wished to be understood. I take the same tack here.

With these ideas in mind, we can turn to the Washington Cantos themselves with the hope of reading them the way Pound wished we would read them, as both covert activist poetry and a grand affirmation of a metapolitical cosmic order. This is "kein Week-end Spass" (93/647)—not a weekend's diversion; it takes study.

I used to approach these poems as fountains of wisdom: Pound's essential benevolence and insights were assumed. Having read and reread *Rock-Drill* and *Thrones*, however, my faith in him as a guide is shaken. Pound's economic insights are real even if they remain underappreciated, but his metapolitical vision based on bogus racial science and archaeological science fiction means that his paradisal "temple" is sited on zoological rubbish, no matter how sincerely meant. Pound scholars like me are still trying to adjust to the right-wing Pound presented in the Pound/Agresti correspondence, edited by Leon Surette and Demetres Tryphonopoulos—*"I Cease Not to Yowl": Ezra Pound's Letters to Olivia Rossetti Agresti* (Illinois, 1998), now regrettably out of print—and more recent studies like Matthew Feldman's report on *Ezra Pound's Fascist Propaganda 1935–1945* (Palgrave, 2014). This book, like *John Kasper and Ezra Pound*, is a result of that change in perspective. Pound can no longer be revered as a titan bestriding his times, a tragic Prometheus; rather, to me he is the representative man of the twentieth century. He experienced its travails; he shared (in his own way, of course) its illusions and disillusions; he tried, with all his titanic energy and talent, to write the epic of his times. Whether we view his *Cantos* as the "tale of the tribe" or as the "epic of capital," as David Moody would have it, the problems we encounter in reading them are the problems we face when trying to understand the violent century in which he lived and the convulsions of capital which shaped it.

If Pound is more representative than transcendent, one may wonder why, his technical prowess aside, he is still worth reading. It would appear that many of his political views are retrograde at best, evil at worst. But Pound is more than a reactionary technician: we may dispose of his untenable views on race, but his emphasis on content, on poetic "nutriment," is much needed. Pound realized that poetry was not at bottom an exercise in aesthetics; it is not, at bottom, about the registration of the beautiful or the expression of a fine sensibility. Poetry is vivid observation, concentrated thought, and ethical action. If those are present, beauty will come of itself like a chickadee to a bird feeder. But to be truly nutritious, he felt, poetic matter needed to be attuned to "civic thought," to the problems, contradictions, and struggle that exist under "Usura"—the regime of financialized capital.

The New Critical emphasis on poetic form at the expense of poetic matter that dominated the 1950s and 1960s until the abortive revolution we call "'68" was to a considerable extent triggered by the controversy surrounding Pound's 1948 Bollingen Prize for *The Pisan Cantos*—that and the Red Scare that accompanied McCarthyism. Openly political poetry became too hot to handle; instead, a learned, aesthetic formalism, called in the United States the "New Criticism," took hold in the academy. Aside from formal considerations, this resulted in a turn inward to the family romance, psychoanalysis, and autobiography. The confession of personal pain and pleasure is indeed a late-twentieth-century trend in American poetry since the controversy over the *Pisans*—these cantos were prize-winning only insofar as the political content Pound thought most important was repressed into irony. "Details of private life, to HIDE main ideas of ANY writer worth reading," while "Billions" are spent "to conceal 40 facts of history or 17 or even fewer / to distract from MEANING of texts, basic and auxillary," Pound groused to Norman Holmes Pearson near the time of his release (April (?) 1958).[1] In the 1940s, when Pound's more explicit politics, his notorious "agenda," was addressed by hostile critics like Peter Viereck and Robert Hillyer, it was excoriated for just that content. They reduced these marvelous, difficult poems to mere ideological statements—a trend that is more evident than ever in Pound criticism. In fact, such reductions can't be entirely avoided, insofar as, when Pound asks us to decode his verses, he encourages us to distill them into slogans. Anyone familiar with his letters knows that Pound tries out phrases that will find their way into cantos, while lines from the poems salt the letters: "Make it New" is only the most famous of these.

In an important letter to Olivia Agresti written in 1954, Pound observed that

> in the 1920s / all young men were supposed to write shapeless non-metric vers libre and have pink ideas / in the 1950s … All writers are supposed to eschew

> ALL civic thought / and the old idiots, my respected colleagues fall for it and lend their names QUITE blindly, 100 percent totally to these hoaxes ... and FUNDS, FUNDS, FUNDS, and flatter for any writer who will maintain aesthetic NON-civic attitudes. (6/22/1954, *EP/ORA* 155)

This would seem to be Pound's response to the New Critical poetics then ascendant.[2]

The result of this turn from the political was the rejection of "civic thought" by too many American poets in favor of private experience and personal pain. Funding was found for such poets by folding them into academia and lucrative Creative Writing programs, which operate today as much like group therapy as schools of poetry. The American poem of the latter half of the twentieth century is generally "shapeless non-metric vers libre" mostly devoid of civic ideas; rather, these poems typically depend on personal experience and private trauma, narrating personal journeys rather than national crises. Any political content tends to be incidental rather than programmatic.

There are important exceptions: poets we might put in the Pound tradition, such as Charles Olson and William Carlos Williams, have their gaze fixed explicitly on the *polis*. The poet most like Pound politically, Amiri Baraka, is as civic-minded as his combative black nationalism can make him, while Carolyn Forché and, above all, Adrienne Rich embrace the civic responsibility of poetry. Speaking of Shelley, Rich said: "For him there was no contradiction among poetry, political philosophy, and active confrontation with illegitimate authority."[3] Though Rich didn't read *The Cantos* for political reasons and could scarcely have found his authorities legitimate, her statement is no less true for Pound. Poetry should be engaged in the struggle for right. That Pound got much disastrously wrong in his struggle is undeniable, but that he continued the struggle while others retreated into glossolalia (viz. L=A=N=G=U=A=G=E poetry) or the interior is part of his achievement.

Rock-Drill and *Thrones* are supposed to be paradisal. Dante's threefold cosmos of hell, purgatory, and heaven continued to provide a conceptual armature for *The Cantos* till the end. Yet paradise was beyond Pound's grasp as a poet and as a person. Although he accused others of "lusting for farness" (107/782), he himself was not immune to a yen for the sublime. Throughout the 1950s he tried to push his poem up the steep and stony slope to some better, paradisal space where he might walk with Linnaeus, Agassiz, Kung, and Mozart. He found the juniper-clad Himalayas of the Na Khi a fitting image of the upward-leading trail; perhaps he glimpsed a snowy peak from time to time. That he failed to reach the summit is no disgrace. He tried his best. Thirteen long years of purgatorial incarceration in a madhouse didn't help.

The Washington Cantos demand to be read *binocularly*—as it were, with one auspicious and one dropping eye—or, to put it plainly, with one eye on Paradise and the other on the ground. A clear and clean exposition must always seem partial; it seems we must *aestheticize* or *politicize* the poems. Most commentators do both, not without some difficulty, resulting in crossed eyes and double vision. In what follows, I try to keep my eyes firmly on an earthly path. No doubt, I can't resist the occasional upward glance, to save, if I can, what beauty is still salvageable.

Notes

1   Norman Holmes Pearson papers, Beinecke YCAL MSS 899, Box 78, folder Pound, Ezra 1958. Pound wrote to Noel Stock in an undated letter (ca. June 1956) preserved at the Beinecke:

… for N.T. A recent analysis of the disease of education in the U.S.

Half century of slop re "expression", and "the personality". All in the line of "the protocols": get the public mind off specific facts of history. The yanks now start doing it young. […] Out of baby-talk into "self-expression", the poor little brats are started writing before they can read.
Secondly the flood of general texts books, about ology, any ology so long as it does not require specific knowledge of a frog, a tree, or even of grammar…
(Beinecke YCAL MSS 43, Box 50, folder 2212)

This letter, attributed to "An American scholar," was printed as "The Protocols" under the heading "perspectives" in the *New Times* 22.14 (July 13, 1956), p. 7. (AH)

2   For a succinct and informative account of the difficulties the New Critical paradigm posed for understanding *The Cantos* and for Pound criticism then and now, see Michael Coyle and Roxana Preda, *Ezra Pound and the Career of Modern Criticism* (Rochester: Camden House, 2018), pp. 110–15.

3   Adrienne Rich, *Poetry and Commitment* (New York: W. W. Norton, 2007), p. 6.

1

The Washington Cantos

Anagogy, Metapolitics, and the Warren Court

Those Poundians who, like me, came to the cantos written in Washington through Hugh Kenner's magnificent *The Pound Era* (1971) were prepared to see them as a constellation of signs and wonders. Kenner's writing is so beautiful and the poet he limns so deep that it is a bit of a shock to find on rereading that Kenner's total commentary on *Rock-Drill* and *Thrones* amounts to only seven pages, the bulk of them gnomic, if luminous, quotations (Kenner 1971: 528–35).[1] Kenner is most interested in the way similar sounds in Greek, Chinese, and English might have inflected Pound's "audile imagination," to use Robert Frost's phrase. The later cantos move toward "verbal phantasmagoria" (Kenner 1971: 532); *Rock-Drill* is organicist, about "vegetable growth": "Beatific spirits welding together / as in one ash-tree in Ygdrasail" (90/625; Kenner 1971: 530). *Thrones* is dedicated to philology and logomachy; "In *Thrones* as never before words are *exhibited*" (Kenner 1971: 532; Kenner's emphasis). That's as may be, but just what the words are supposed to signify doesn't figure in Kenner's appreciation. As he was a frequent visitor to St. Elizabeths when these poems were written and was thoroughly acquainted with Pound's circle of acolytes, Kenner certainly knew better than almost anyone what *else* these obscure poems are about, the personal and political investments hidden amongst the Delphic, oracular language. *The Pound Era* is reticent to a fault about just what these poems are supposed to mean and to what else they refer; there is virtually no trace of Pound's notorious *agenda* in Kenner's reading. A blessing perhaps.

Rock-Drill de los Cantares (1955) and *Thrones* (1959)

It is usual for Pound's Washington Cantos—*Rock-Drill* (85–95) and *Thrones* (96–109)—to be read together. This tactic makes good sense, as Canto 96, published in the *Hudson Review* in the spring of 1956, picks up exactly where Canto 95 left off, with the drowning Odysseus poet grasping for Leucothea's veil, scarf—or bikini! In Canto 96, having made landfall at the Phaecian Utopia, we enter into *Thrones*, the final authorized piece of Pound's epic. "The *Rock-Drill* cantos were published in 1954–5 and the *Thrones* cantos between 1956 and 1959," Peter Makin writes. "They are a product of the same phase of Pound's life, as the progression of poetics between them is relatively small" (Makin 1985: 252). Collected together, as they now are, we don't read these cantos one at a time; rather, we read across the two books, finding motifs and recurrences, strands and repeated dicta that may be considered as "points defining a periphery" (*Con.* 194) as Pound tries to stake out a center and define an axis or pivot around which the "great crystal" of his poem can revolve. Pound seems to know so much, seems to have so much at his mental fingertips, that if the earnest reader can hold enough allusions and motifs in one's head the effect is symphonic and exhilarating; if not, well ... the effect is merely confusing and irritating. For a few curious souls, they may act as a goad for further study.

Similarities abound between these two final books, but there are major differences of political and personal contexts that distinguish *Thrones* from *Rock-Drill*. Politically, 1954 had seen the downfall of Senator Joe McCarthy and the watershed decision by the Supreme Court of the United States concerning the racial integration of schools in *Brown v. Board of Education*. Clearly, subversive forces were in the ascendant. A second decision regarding implementation (*Brown II*) came down a year later in 1955, and 1956, with Pound at work on *Thrones*, saw the first grudging and feeble attempts to carry out the law. This was the year the United States attempted to act on what had been decided in 1954: that white supremacy was not a natural fact but an un-American ideology. The attempted integration of public schools provoked "massive resistance" throughout the South in the name of the rights of states and appeals to "local customs." A life-long believer in the America of Thomas Jefferson, Pound was firmly opposed to the vast, meddling extension of federal power at the expense of the states and their citizenry through what he and so many others saw as judicial tyranny.[2] That summer, the poet collaborated with his younger, activist cohort in composing and editing *Virginians on Guard!*, a strident document calling for a new segregationist constitution for the Commonwealth of Virginia, reasserting white supremacy and Negro inferiority in the name of natural order, justified by the racial taxonomy peculiar to the Pound circle. That summer, John Kasper and friends took the pamphlet south to Charlottesville, where they burned crosses, held rallies, and preached violence. It is in this welter of civic upheaval and political crisis that the cantos in *Thrones* were written. This was no time to be contemplating paradise.

Otherwise, much of the paradisal material in *Rock-Drill* and *Thrones* was shaped by Pound's relationship with Sheri Martinelli. Cantos 90–5 and, beyond them, 97 and 102 become paradisal because Pound was in love with Martinelli, the Bohemian muse who captured his imagination from 1954 till the winter of 1957 when these cantos were composed. Lacking a rigorous theology, lacking the "Aquinas map" that served Dante so well, Pound relies on his sensations more than his intellect in conceiving paradise. *The Cantos* are paradisal insofar as they contain elaborate, intense love poetry. The poet's gestures toward any higher paradise, realms of crystal and jade etc., are more programmatic than felt, more political necessity than paradisal revelation. Pound's poems to Martinelli alternate between extravagant claims for her goddess-like powers and Pound's agenda, presented to educate her. Just as we have the "Sacred Edict cantos" 98–9 and the "Coke Cantos" 107–109, these might be called the "Sheri cantos." Martinelli's presence is registered fitfully in other cantos too, until she is replaced by another compelling muse, Marcella Spann. Spann's arrival in Pound's life and his long-delayed release to Italy signaled the end of *Thrones* and ushered in a new post-Washington chapter memorialized in *Drafts & Fragments*.

Muses aside, Pound's paradise is otherwise a paradise of books. T. S. Eliot had once criticized Pound's "Hell cantos" as "hell for other people," and the same criticism might be made of Pound's paradise—it's a fantasy paradise, populated with authors whose books we are enjoined to read if we want to get there. Walking with Confucius, Mencius, Dante, and Agassiz in Pound's paradise is his metaphor for reading them. The exotic Tibetan material expresses a belated Romantic's wish for a paradise that is "long ago and far away"; in attitude, it has as much in common with Madame Blavatsky or with James Hilton's *Lost Horizon* (1933) and Shangri-La as it does with Peter Goullart's *Forgotten Kingdom* (1957) or the luminous details found in Joseph Rock.[3] Finally, the "Coke Cantos" 107–109 that close *Thrones* are motivated less by the desire to write paradise than to effect Pound's release from perpetual confinement. They are his brief for the defense.

Rock-Drill (1955) wants to be a book about order. Using Confucian teaching, Pound tries to establish a metapolitical foundation on which to ground his utopic vision. From Canto 90, Pound is consciously building a temple transcending commodity status, a temple that is not for sale, priceless. "Templum aedificans," Pound exhorts—build the temple—calling on Amphion, the Orpheus-like figure who built the mighty walls of Thebes (90/625). Because of the historical and personal contingencies sketched earlier and Pound's elliptical rhetoric, this foundational enterprise was far from straightforward and ultimately unsuccessful. He struggled to focus on the light.

These cantos vary widely in tone, subject matter, and decorum, much of it keyed to what Pound was reading. In fact, throughout *Rock-Drill* and *Thrones* we read along with him. *The poems themselves are to a large extent his reading notes*, as one can see by looking at his "Notebooks" at the Beinecke Library. Cantos 98 and 99, for example, were written at one go in March 1957 and barely revised for publication.[4] We are, in Peter Nicholls's useful phrase, reading Pound "reading through" other texts (Nicholls 2004: 234), as though the poet is still assembling his building materials. This technique is very noticeable in the latter half of Canto 94, a reading-through of F. C. Coneybeare's edition of Philostratus's *The Life of Apollonius of Tyana* (94/656–61); in Pound's reading-through of Alexander Del Mar's *History of Monetary Systems* in the first half of Canto 97 (97/688–95); and in F. W. Baller's translation of *The Sacred Edict* in Cantos 98 and 99 (98/710–99/732).

Rock-Drill opens as a very cryptic essay on good government. Canto 85 is an expression of civic thought but, strictly speaking, incomprehensible unless we collate it with Pound's source texts, as Carroll Terrell does in his indispensable *Companion*. More than a hundred individual Chinese ideograms that caught Pound's attention in his Chinese source decorate the pages. These too are, in effect, reading notes—ideograms that demand further attention by the poet and his readers. How Pound thought we were to negotiate this forbidding text is a good question; but he was aware of the problem, for a note at the end of the canto explains that "Canto 85 is a somewhat detailed confirmation of Kung's [Confucius's] view that the basic principles of good government are found in Shu, the History Classic" (85/579). By "detailed" Pound seems to mean "as shown by historical examples" that have occurred since the time of Shang, almost 3,000 years ago. The *Shu Jing* is one of the "Five classics" (including the *I Ching*) that supplements the "Four books" of Confucius and is traditionally thought to have been edited by him. The title may be translated as "the Book of Documents," and it is considered to be the oldest extant work of Chinese prose, complementing the *Odes*, Confucius's anthology of Chinese poetry that Pound translated as *The Confucian Odes* (1954). *Shu Jing* is not included in Pound's *Confucius*.

Rock-Drill operates under the sign of the four, a gesture looking back at Kung's Four Books, because four is the number indicating stability and order, as in the four legs of a Confucian Emperor's throne, the FOUR TUAN "or Foundations" (85/565, 86/581, 89/621), and the four staples of the Colonial American economy, "rice, cotton, indigo and tobacco" (88/604). Tim Materer has commented on Pound's use of "John Heydon's alchemical tract *Holy Guide*," lent him by Georgie Yeats, to create an alchemical "tetrad" representing "the four elements" preparatory to manifesting the quintessence—the fifth element, or philosopher's stone (Materer 1995: 65-6). All these comprise the "four altars at the four coigns" of Dante's Third Heaven of Venus (92/639), proving that "the whole creation [is] concerned with 'FOUR'" (91/636). This square form derives from nature, not culture, Pound asserts: "The four TUAN / are from nature ... not from descriptions in the school house" (99/731). *Rock-Drill* addresses the archetypal four-square natural order of all creation (88/609).

If *Rock-Drill* is about constructing the temple, *Thrones* ought to see it completed. For various reasons to be explored, however, this never happens. In Canto 97 Pound insists that "the temple is holy because it is not for sale" (97/696, 97/698, 97/699, 97/701, also 100/741), hinting that it was founded by "Sargon of Agade," the putatively Aryan founder-pharaoh of Egypt. Establishing or, like Apollonius, *re*-establishing the temple, Pound tries fitfully to concern himself with the rites to be performed there. Rites are human customs designed to keep mankind in touch with cosmos such as the Na Khi rituals that inform Canto 104; yet, *Thrones* culminates with money and the law, wholly human constructs founded on right reason and local custom—"consuetudines" (105/768). Still, insofar as laws serve justice, they too may be aligned with a profound awareness of the inchoate cosmic will that Pound calls "rightness," a cosmic imperative.

Law institutes, among much else, money, the value of which—at least classically—is determined by the state. The state is sovereign insofar as it issues all money and powerless insofar as it does not. In the Greek and Roman republics, money was "nomisma" and "nummus" respectively "because the Law (nomos) was alone competent to create it" (Del Mar 1983: 8). For these reasons, money, law, and sovereignty are braided discourses in *Thrones*. Following the historian Alexander Del Mar, Pound understood money as a legal discourse, realizing that "[v]alue is not a thing, nor an attribute of things; it is a relation, a numerical relation, which appears in exchange" (Del Mar 1983: 7). Value, for Del Mar and for Pound, is a "numerical relation" (nummus), a ratio, ratified by Law but dependent, ultimately, on Nature in toto. Ultimately, the ratios of value are sacred, because Nature just *is* value—"the abundance"—the sum and expression of all values. Nature is the referent of referents.[5] That is why, after a detailed reading through of Del Mar's *History of Monetary Systems* (1895) in Canto 97 (97/688-95) Pound reiterates that the Temple, i.e. the sacred "TEMENOS," which signifies reverence for Nature, is "not for sale."

Thrones became a very different book after Canto 106, when Pound turned his poem into a brief for his defense against the treason indictment still hanging, like Damocles' sword, over his head twelve years after World War II had ended.

Cantos 107 through 109 are the "Coke Cantos" because Pound had enlisted the great jurist as his defense attorney. Coke fought for the common law derived from the English root, "our PIVOT," the Magna Carta (107/777, 107/779). Pound celebrates English law because he believes the tradition of English law that carried on in the United States, especially regarding the basic right of *habeas corpus*, was his best defense. Determined, at last, to get out of the bughouse, Pound turned his massive poem and life's work to that end. Together, *Rock-Drill* and *Thrones* are both paradisal in that they celebrate two kinds of paradise very personal to the poet: the love he shared with Sheri Martinelli and the dream of a prisoner "thirteen years under hatches" who passionately desires his liberty to enjoy the simple paradise of moving freely about in the world.

Pound tried, famously, "to make a paradiso / terrestre" (117/822). The line break that separates the two words also separates two planes of existence requiring two modes of interpretation, two ways of writing, two kinds of reading. To read paradise, we need to read anagogically, while the terrestrial mode requires allegory. But paradise and earthly existence do not run on parallel tracks in *The Cantos*. Pound unpredictably changes register—one moment we're in an empyrean of moving crystal, the next down in the muck of history. The fact is, Pound himself can't maintain his focus on paradise. Metapolitically, Pound needs to align his utopic vision with nature, or nature's intelligence, where "The celestial and earthly process pervades and is substantial; it is on high and gives light, it comprehends the light and is lucent, it extends without bound, and endures" (*Con.* 183). He wants to "build light" and erect a sacred space, but he is forever distracted by events—including his own reading, the daily spew of news, the ward's nattering TV—and frustrated by the prospect of perpetual imprisonment. Earthly history is constantly troubling his eternity.

The same goes for readers of these poems. Critical concentration on the paradisal skews a reading one way, focus on historical particulars another. That vaunted "paradiso terrestre" turns out to be a contradiction. So far no one is quite able to square that circle. Yes, Pound told Donald Hall that in *Thrones* he was "trying to collect the record of the top flights of the mind" and recognize "those who have some part of the divine vision," adding, "The thrones in *The Cantos* are an attempt to move out from egoism and to establish some order possible or at any rate conceivable on earth." Despite the manifest failure of right reason to operate effectively in human affairs, *Thrones* "concerns the states of mind of people responsible for something more than their personal conduct" (Hall 1992: 333).[6] That's as may be, but much of the book is bitterly preoccupied with human greed and folly and the ethos of avaricious capital, the "'coil of

Geryon'" (97/689), what I call "Usura." For every glimpse of paradise there is an offsetting glimpse of hell.

It seems that *Thrones* says to us: "you takes yer choice: *polis* or *kosmos*." The reader's problem is to figure out which plane of attention or theory of reading is needed in making sense of the poems. In a recent essay on Canto 108,[7] Kristin Grogan warns:

> The danger for critics is the temptation to inflate the importance of any one concept such that it becomes the major guiding principle which risks obscuring or smoothing over the poem's many, often conflicting components; to become convinced that a single idea is the key that, with enough persistence, will unlock the rest of the poem's secret doors; to discover, in short, "the gold thread in the pattern" (116/817).

Grogan's warning applies to all of the Washington Cantos. To read them politically obscures paradisal alternatives; to read for paradise hides an unconscionable politics.[8]

Throughout these supposedly paradisal cantos, Pound is clearly making political arguments that are perforce historical. In *The Cantos* history is used allegorically for moral ends as in Dante's *Commedia*. History teaches lessons. To "Know the histories" is "to know good from evil" and "know whom to trust" (86/610). But is the poet presenting faithfully what actually happened so that we can draw the proper moral conclusions? History depends on documents, of which Pound provides many snippets. But are they used historically or polemically? Alex Pestell notes, "Pound is less than faithful to his sources when it suits him" (G 139). When it suits, Pound "weaponizes" history to score political points. *The Cantos*, he told Noel Stock, are "a political weapon," and he explained them to John Theobald as "a POLITICAL implement"—activist poetry composed to effect political change (Stock 1966: 91; EP/JT 44). *Thrones* is clearly full of errors—but *are* they errors, or are they in effect "alternative facts," visionary propaganda, disinformation unrewarding to historical or philological research?

To repeat, we need ideological bifocals to read *Thrones*—one lens focused on worldly necessity, the other on celestial imperatives—as allegory bleeds into anagogy. Writing on Canto 97, Roxana Preda uses the apt metaphor of two sides of a coin.[9] Usually the date and the face of a ruler is assigned to its "historical" obverse; whereas the reverse is keyed to potent cultural symbols, eagles, fasces, and eternal monuments (G 29). If history is contingent about action in time—about what happened—then paradise is eternal truth, constant as the gods. For those who have glimpsed the divine vision, Paradise just is; albeit, as Dante says, "above the senses"—metaphysical. Paradise is philosophical territory; it can only be read indirectly, "anagogically." As Dante had it, anagogy is "when a writing is spiritually expounded, which even in the literal sense by the things signified likewise gives intimation of higher matters" (qtd in Adams 1971: 121).

Anagogy was a key term at St. Elizabeths, although Peter Nicholls observes that it occurs only once in *The Cantos* proper[10] and in a surprising Confucian context—surprising because Confucius is not much interested in the beyond; at best, he observes the rites *as if* the otherworld of the ancestors were real. This is why the rites are means of construction, not ends in themselves (*Con.* 288; see also Chang 1957: 17). Confucianism is efficient as a "social coordinate," not revelation, according to Pound (*Con.* 19); so the exhortation to "stimulate anagogico" (99/730) must be Pound encouraging himself. Reno Odlin recalled his circle at St. Elizabeths was told that Pound's "intentions were 'paideutic and anagogical'" (Moody 2015: 399). Pound wrote Martinelli in October 1957 that "wot Ez is lookin for is the MEANING of the WHOLE picture wot comes OUT of the painter not what painter has copied or even mixed …. manus animam pinxit / hand paints the soul" and "no difference between the arts re / the URGE / merely a matter of HOW."[11] Martinelli's answer in her own bohemian idiom shows she understands fully. She closes a letter to Pound of December 17–18, 1958: "it AINT / WOT'S / ON / the paper / it is / WOT streams / FROM / it / [/] the / 'message' / as the Spades put it / [/] it EVOKES / what in turn will / re-NEW the same / [/] it is the OPPOSITE / from / the WORD."[12] This useful statement is probably what Pound and Martinelli mean when they use the term "anagogic," which occurs occasionally in Pound's letters to her and later titled her *Anagogic & Paideumic Review*.[13]

Nicholls shows that Pound's sense of anagogy goes back to Plotinus and *The Enneads*, following Peter Liebregts's *Ezra Pound and Neoplatonism* (2004), the most detailed study of Pound's paradisal metaphysics we have. Liebregts remarks Pound's particular interest in *Ennead* V, including V.8 ("On Intelligible Beauty"), which discusses the moral and anagogical beauty of art "with special reference to Egyptian hieroglyphics as 'the expression of nondiscursive thought'" (Liebregts 2004: 344), which would hold just as true for written Chinese. Moody's take is a little different but not incompatible; he finds *Thrones* to be a "composition of anagogical symbols which at times becomes a form of algebra. We might think of it, by analogy with metaphysics, as a kind of metapoetry" (Moody 2015: 399). Moody doesn't expand on this intriguing concept, but it is allied with a term I find useful in trying to resolve the split vision of *Thrones*: metapolitics. For insofar as *Thrones* is a reflection of good government, it implies a celestial politics under a transcendental signifier: Justice. Pound speaks of his own project when he writes: "That it is of Thrones / and above them: Justice" (94/660). And again:

> an interest in equity
> > not in mere terminology
>
> μετά τά φυσιχά
> metah, not so extraneous, possibly not so extraneous
> > most "*metas*" seem to be in with (97/700)

Unless "paradiso terrestre" is to remain an irreconcilable contradiction, even for a poet of Pound's powers and ambition, some other "meta" dimension does indeed seem necessary.

As Pound shoves his poem toward paradise, or at least utopia, as he tries, with Ocellus, "to build light" (98/704) and establish sovereignty, the poem nudges an ideological, "political unconscious" (to use Frederic Jameson's problematic term) that we deduce shining ominously *through* and between the words. In order to secure his "tale of the tribe" in nature, Pound needed to secure its biological, even zoological, provenance; thus Pound subtly racialized this aura, identifying light with the Arya—the noble "shining ones."[14] Pound's imaginative process allows etymology to become allegory, history to become racial and economic parables featuring virtuous Aryans and devious Semites, viz, a metapolitics with disturbing implications.

Writing on *Thrones* for the *Ezra Pound Encyclopedia*, Nicholls notes: "A few paradigmatic plots are at work beneath the surface"; the "allegorizing tendency is closely bound up … with Pound's increasingly conflicted sense of history-as-conspiracy" (Tryphonopolous & Adams 2005: 46). Dark vs light, form vs "sqush," the "manifest" vs the "abstract" (93/645), Neoplatonic light philosophy opposing the Hebraic black-out, Confucian sanity against "Bhud rot" (99/717). In short, the Manichean tendency of *The Cantos*, very marked since 1940, is the most obvious armature for allegory.[15] "Occupy yrself with *meta ta phusikaaaa* and excrete mesopotamia," Pound wrote John Theobald coarsely (9/20/1957, *EP/JT* 95), a joke that is both meta and political. Spirit over matter. Light over dark. Philosophy over the sin-racket. And, let's face it, Aryan over Semite and Jew.

Metapolitics and Politics

Metapolitics as I use it here is the key term in Peter Viereck's book *Metapolitics: From Wagner and the German Romantics to Hitler* (1941, rev. 2004) where it's used to characterize the Nazi phenomenon.¹⁶ I choose Viereck over more recent users of the term because Viereck was well aware of Pound, having listened to his broadcasts as a soldier working for Allied Intelligence and having been a severe critic of Pound's during the Bollingen controversy. His book, as revised, pays intermittent attention to Pound. But Viereck's term should not be confused with recent poststructuralist (Badiou) or current European New Right (ENR) usage, though there are numerous shared affinities between the writing of Alain de Benoist and Pound.

Metapolitik arises from a nationalist German milieu in the early nineteenth century under the sway of Hegel. It denotes the politics of the actual in Hegel's sense; that is, "the unity, become immediate, of essence with existence, or of inward with outward," as he puts it somewhere in his *Logic*. Metapolitics is to politics as metaphysics is to physics—what might be called "a first politics," an "absolute politics" that ties *polis* and *kosmos* together.¹⁷ For Viereck the term means "the semi-political ideology resulting from the intertwining of four distinct strands": romanticism; "the 'science' of racism"; on the economic front a "vague socialism" protesting capitalist materialism; and "alleged supernatural and unconscious forces of Volk collectivity" to which it is responsive (Viereck 2004: 4). All of these strands are present in the late cantos. This metapolitics can be titled "Aryanist."

Pound's metapolitics goes beyond mere racialist Aryanism, however; a full account would link it to his Neoplatonism on the one hand and his Confucianism on the other as two horizons of his metapolitical vision: on the Neoplatonic side, a route upward through various levels of vital force, through prana to crystal to jade (see 94/654); on the Confucian side, an ethics of the "four tuan" grounded in an agricultural economy in accord with nature. For Pound these became "manhood / equity / ceremonies, propriety / knowledge" (*EPCF* 67, 67n).¹⁸ This metapolitical cosmos is held together by "light," which can also be interpreted as "sincerity."¹⁹ Together these make sensibility—the sign under which the late cantos attempt to build their paradise.²⁰ John Kasper, for one, knew this. His later writings often concluded with the Confucian thought, quoted from Pound's translation: "Only The Most Absolute Sincerity Under Heaven Can Effect Any Change" (see also Pound, *Con*. 95, 175). This may be a reasonable, if Poundian, translation of "ling² 靈."

In George Kearns's copy of *Rock-Drill*, a first edition likely bought at Kasper's Make It New bookshop, which I have in front of me as I write, Kearns penciled the word "Order" over the big, black, bold character "LING² 靈", nominally "sensibility," that opens the first installment of the late cantos (85/563). The dust jacket composed by hopeful people at New Directions, probably closely following Pound's suggestions, would have us believe that love would drive "the third and final phase" of *The Cantos*, which were to celebrate "the domination of benevolence" as in Canto 94: "Beyond civic order: / L'AMOR" (94/654). At long last, *Rock-Drill* would usher in the paradisal closing movement of Pound's epic project. Beginning with Canto 90, *Rock-Drill* should be read as love poems to Pound's lover and muse, Sheri Martinelli, so there is love in these late cantos, but the domination of *benevolence* as the leading theme of these anxious, defensive poems is fitful at best. Kearns thought "order" might better describe the impulse behind them, for they are insistently metapolitical.

"The domination of benevolence" is a metapolitical premise. When it occurs it is contested, especially by capitalist materialism, i.e. Pound's "Usura"—the ideology, theory, and practice of finance capitalism used as a coercive weapon. Usura is in turn linked by Pound to a predatory and superstitious Semitic outlook that predates Judaism, represented by the Semitic penchant for bloody sacrifices, like those pleasing to YHWH performed by Abel. Grain sacrifice, by contrast, is something Pound associates with Cain, Apollonius, and Confucius, even interpolating "grain" where other translators (like Legge) do not specify what is actually sacrificed (see *Con.* 131).

If there is "something decent in the universe" (95/667), if there is "Something *there*" as Santayana said, it is occluded by "the enormous organized cowardice" of not only "the advertised literati" like Peter Viereck but the whole damned system (95/666–7). Bacigalupo stresses how Pound refuses compromise and "takes up the role of 'driller' versus the world's ignorance, becomes the exorcist of demons and the mentor of vision, covering the ground between the war to the death against usury—'Bellum cano perenne'" (Bacigalupo 1980: 219; 86/588). Nonetheless, behind all his partisan violence, Pound does have order on his mind. Perhaps only benevolence can will a proper order, like those few "sincere men willing the national good" (*J/M* 95) to whom he wished to reserve practical government.

Pound's theory of history as racial struggle is metapolitical, a politics derived from nature, not based on the *polis*. It deals with *divine imperatives as nature*. Metapolitics tries to align culture with nature in a way that is not religious in the dogmatic sense but a deep spiritual identification, a "persistent awareness" of an intelligence working through nature. This is consistent with Neoplatonic teaching, which understands nature as god's thought fallen into material existence. As above, so below. *Kosmos* is the Neoplatonic ideal of the *polis*. Pound was no Christian—indeed in the 1950s he turns violently against Christianity as a "Jew religion" under the sway of a bloodthirsty demon YHWH (see *EP/ORA* 156, 158)—but he is well aware that he needs a metaphysics to sustain the nominally "paradisal" department of his grand epic, which wants to present transcendental concepts such as justice and benevolence.

Metapolitics must be distinguished from political theory, with which it has certain affinities. If political theory is a theory of the state, of the *polis* and the relation of state to individual and vice versa, then metapolitics addresses a metaphysical dimension behind politics; that is, it is concerned with "the very nature of the state, whether political statements are propositional, whether there are political truths and whether they can be known" (Zaibert 2004: 115). Leo Zaibert posits an *ontological* dimension to a proper metapolitics. It is this other dimension that sheds light on Pound's thinking about the state, about the nature of "sovereignty," about authority, and finally about the relation of culture to nature and ultimately divinity. Pound's ideal polity is grounded in and sanctioned by permanent values guaranteed by his Neoplatonic and Confucian beliefs to derive from "the intelligence working in nature." See Canto 99: "Kung said: are classic from heaven," good manners are; "They bind thru the earth / and flow / With recurrence, / action, humanitas, equity" (99/718).[21] Likewise, in Canto 106 we learn that "Yao and Shun ruled by jade," the symbol of eternal value (106/773), which is why the "jade weathers dust swirl" in Canto 104 (104/759), the swirl being the tumult of transitory contentions and mundane politics. Yao and Shun, the quasi-mythical good emperors of Chinese history who appear at various points in *The Cantos*, bear the Mandate of Heaven, thus they serve as the link between man and nature, or *polis* and *kosmos*. This is the meaning of *ling*² 靈. *Ling*² 靈 is a complex ideogram made of three others that Pound creatively misread as heaven above three mouths over the sign for medium or witch. In Canto 104 *ling*² 靈 is partially parsed as "under the cloud / the three voices" (104/760). A large rendition of *ling*² 靈 (see Figure 1.1) dominates the opening of *Rock-Drill* where Pound appears to translate it as "sensibility": "Our dynasty came in because of great sensibility" (85/563) as though mediumistically directed by the voices from heaven.

Figure 1.1 *Ling*² 靈.

Today, metapolitics is usually associated with the European New Right (ENR). If it maintains an esoteric ontological dimension, it is ignored by Alain de Benoist and Charles Champetier in their *Manifesto for a European Renaissance* (1999), which nonetheless echoes Pound in suggestive ways:

> Metapolitics is not politics by other means. It is neither a "strategy" to impose intellectual hegemony, nor an attempt to discredit other possible attitudes or agendas. It rests solely on the premise that ideas play a fundamental role in collective consciousness and, more generally, in human history ... *History is the result of human will and action,* but always within the framework of conviction, beliefs and representations which provide meaning and direction. (qtd in Sunic 2011: 207–8; my emphasis)

This sounds more like political theory than what I mean by metapolitics. It deserves comment, however, because it is strikingly in line with Pound's "agenda." Consider Pound acolyte William Cookson's editorial stating the aims of his Poundian vehicle *Agenda*, in the summer of 1959:

> We are intended as a means of communication and to keep certain basic ideas in circulation ... We have not yet become sufficiently a forum for intelligent discussion among those who are thinking actively at the present time ... The *use* of a publication this size is to circulate ideas which are unlikely to get printed elsewhere, to form a group, to collect news and to indicate where active thinking is taking place. (*Agenda* 1[6] [July–August 1959]: 1; qtd in Coyle & Preda 2018: 190; Cookson's emphasis)

As Michael Coyle and Roxana Preda have pointed out, Cookson's agenda is his rendition of Pound's. "Ideas, usually 'basic' ones, are 'active,' they are the sediment of consciousness and attuned to what people are ready to believe. The active ideas are those that infiltrate the status quo" to ready it for change (Coyle & Preda 2018: 190). "Let us deny," Pound stressed, with Jefferson and Mussolini in mind, "that *real* intelligence exists until it comes into action" (*J/M* 18).

Likewise, in his "Preface" to Tomislav Sunic's survey of the ENR, *Against Democracy and Equality* (2011), de Benoist echoes Pound's "the history of a culture is the history of ideas going into action" (*GK* 44) when he speaks of how the ENR strives to "move forward in order to put their ideas into action" (Sunic 2011: 24).[22] Sunic claims that "the New Right concedes that the source of political power must be preceded by socio-cultural action" (69): "Culture is the most effective carrier of political ideas because culture mobilizes the popular consciousness not only by ephemeral slogans, but also by a genuine appeal to the historical memory of the people. Reversing the Marxist theorem, the New Right argues that ideas and not economic infrastructure constitute the foundation of every polity" (69).

Ironically, the New Right goes to Antonio Gramsci for authority on this matter, but Pound had learned from the Irish long before Gramsci that cultural revolution precedes social revolution. Pound's closeness to W. B. Yeats, politically an exemplary "conservative revolutionary" and a tireless cultural activist both as poet and playwright, is always metapolitical in just the way de Benoist suggests. Yeats tried by cultural means to mobilize Irish popular consciousness by a sincere appeal to the historical memory of the people—a memory he half-created and worked to shape to his own metapolitical vision. Pound knew the Irish revolutionaries personally: not only Yeats but Maud Gonne (who played Kathleen Ni Houlihan in Yeats's iconic metapolitical play and arguably never stepped out of that role). James Joyce was a friend, too, the Joyce who, as Stephen Dedalus, left Ireland "to forge in the smithy of his soul the uncreated conscience of [his] race." Then there's Arthur Griffith, founder of Sinn Féin (and later Fine Gael), mentioned so often in *The Cantos* ("You can't move 'em with a cold thing like economics"), who knew just how important convictions expressed in vivid representations that only culture could provide were to achieving social change. Interestingly, Pound liked to compare Griffith (who became president of the Irish Free State) to Mussolini, praising both for their swiftness of mind, sincerity, and frankness (*GK* 105).

It was not only Ireland that taught Pound the priority of cultural agitation to make revolution possible; it was also the United States. Pound studied and wrote extensively on John Adams and Thomas Jefferson, both profound political thinkers, activists, revolutionaries, and statesmen. Both Canto 32 (1931) and Canto 50 (1936) begin: "'Revolution,' said John Adams, 'took place in the minds of the people / in the fifteen years before Lexington'" (50/246; see also 32/157); the passage is quoted again, in part, in Canto 33 (33/161). Revolution got into the minds of the people through the ideas of Adams, Jefferson, and others. Jefferson, Pound liked to say, "governed by means of conversation with his more intelligent friends" (*J/M* 15). As well as being one of the chief architects of the United States, Jefferson's thought "informed" the French revolution by "shaping it from the inside and educating it" (*J/M* 14). Adams and Jefferson both held political office, both were politicians, but they were major political theorists as well; using de Benoist's definition, we could call them metapoliticians, although, using Viereck's terminology, we could not: to him they would be statesmen.

It is easy to link Pound to contemporary European New Right politics. Yes, Pound, like Julius Evola, was a member of the Old Right from which the ENR wishes to maintain an equivocal affinity along with a discrete distance,[23] but he has numerous agreements with ENR metapolitics. Pound shares with de Benoist an antiliberal agenda, an interest in Indo-Europeans, tradition, and historical memory. Above all, he is a forerunner of the ENR's project for a "European renaissance," a life-long project of Pound's that took on even more urgency after the Second World War. Having failed to spark such a renaissance both before and after World War I, Pound renewed his attempt at Pisa with cantos that both were a critique of the recent catastrophe and offered a way out, through saner economics and Confucius.[24]

In the 1950s Pound continued to "try to raise the cultural level" and spark a new European Renaissance via the poems he continued to write in St Elizabeths. Pound told Donald Hall in the celebrated *Paris Review* interview: "I am writing to resist the view that Europe and civilization are going to Hell. If I am being 'crucified for an idea' ... it is probably the idea that European culture ought to survive, that the best qualities of it ought to survive along with whatever other cultures, in whatever universality. Against the propaganda of terror and the propaganda of luxury, have you a nice simple answer?" (Hall 1992: 333). The "propaganda of terror" clearly means the Soviet Empire, and "the propaganda of luxury" just as clearly means soulless American materialism. This idea of the European spirit caught between the pincers of Soviet and American materialism is familiar from Heidegger's mordant remark in *Introduction to Metaphysics*: "Russia and America, seen metaphysically, are both the same: the same hopeless frenzy of unchained technology and of the rootless organization of the average man" (Heidegger 2000: 40).[25] The key term here is *metaphysical*; from that point of view both the USSR and the USA are caught up in mindless materialisms divorced from higher truths.

Rock-Drill is aptly named. It is about hammering—implying "the necessary resistance in getting the main thesis across" that European culture is threatened by two opposing forces from which Europe must be rescued with the poet's help. The remedy is Pound's unique racialized Aryanist amalgam of Confucianism, Fascism, and Jeffersonianism.

Thrones is even more obviously metapolitical than *Rock-Drill*. Liebregts comments: "In *Thrones* Pound mainly deals with what he considered the exemplary ordered societies and legal systems of the Byzantines, the Lombards, the Chinese ... and the English from Anglo-Saxon to Elizabethan times" and beyond as interpreted by the formidable legal savant Sir Edward Coke; such societies, governed by just laws with a strong ethical basis, "constituted along with the Neoplatonic-Confucian teachings, bedrocks upon which an ideal society or *paradiso terrestre* could be built" (Liebregts 2004: 329–30).

As I have written elsewhere, a long-held "Jeffersonian" ideology has everything to do with Pound's conflicted politics, which are dedicated on the one hand to individual freedom and economic justice and on the other to a conspiratorial suspicion of finance capitalism ("loan-capital"); on the one hand to local autonomy, on the other to a firm hand at the top protecting the state against rapacious financiers who use debt as a weapon to gain power over honest producers. For all of his sympathies with fascism and its centralizing imperatives, Pound shared Jefferson's suspicion of federal power and big government. Ideologically he wobbled between a centrifugal Jeffersonianism and a centripetal wish for authority. Over time, from the mid-1930s on, Pound's Jeffersonianism became first anti-Semitic and later fully racialized as he absorbed the Aryanist teachings of Hitler, Agassiz, and L. A. Waddell.

Jefferson's view that the rights of the states were a vital check on the overweening power of the federal government are expressed in the Kentucky and Virginia Resolutions of 1789 and 1799 that rejected the US Constitution as a binding contract. They were a "recipe for disunion" as George Washington called them (Chernow 2005: 587). These so-called "principles of '98" underwrote constitutional nullification, the secession of the Southern states in 1861, and resistance to the racial integration of Southern society in the century following the Civil War and Reconstruction. They were revived again by Pound's ally James J. Kilpatrick, who republished them in 1956 to resist school integration (Muse 1969: 20). As I detailed in *John Kasper and Ezra Pound*, the poet's reaction against the enormous extension of federal power mandated by the *Brown* decisions drove him into the states' rights camp of Southern "massive resistance" against this rash attempt to enforce the US Constitution in the South, which was widely seen as judicial usurpation and political betrayal leading to an unrecognizable, "mongrelized" USA.

Thus, it was inevitable that Pound would get involved in segregationist politics as a way of defending the United States against the encroachments of what he considered Jewish/Communist-inspired federal mandates to end segregation in the public schools. Pound became a theorist of states' rights and segregation, as reflected in the coded language of the Washington Cantos. During this phase of Pound's life he was, except for his Confucian preoccupations, a typical American right-winger: a firm believer in the Jewish/Communist conspiracy, a defender of states' rights, and a segregationist. He was determined to do what he could to save what was salvageable of the American republic as "Muss saved, rem salvavit, / in Spain / il salvabile" (105/766).

"Four Steps to the Bughouse"

In his book *Late Style*, Edward Said speaks of an aging artist's "social exile" due to a variety of possible factors afflicting those struggling with a variety of ailments and disabilities. Said offers Beethoven's deafness; one might also think of Adrienne Rich's arthritis. In Pound's case, social exile was no metaphor: he was locked up. The poet described this situation as a gradual process: "Four Steps to the Bughouse." Each step is a revelation, in which the mask of democratic power slips and the poet sees the cynical oppressive reality behind it. Pound gestured to this throughout his work and explained it at length in an interview given at St. Elizabeths to D. G. Bridson in December 1956.[26]

The first step was his experience with the bureaucracy of the State Department shortly after the First World War when Pound attempted to get a visa to return to London from France at the American Consulate. He overheard remarks by one junior passport officer to a superior behind a partition: "We want 'em all to go back." "*We* want"—it stuck in Pound's craw, prompting extended journalistic fulminations against the "passport nuisance." For the first time he felt the mindless weight of the state. It was "the first step," he wrote Wyndham Lewis in 1951, "toward universal bondage" (qtd in Henderson 2010: 398). As David Farley noticed, the first step even found its way obliquely into *The Cantos*— "Damn the Partition! Paper, dark brown and stretched. / Damn the partition," he wrote ominously in Canto 7 (7/25).[27]

The second step was something relayed to Pound about an immigrated Dutchman living in the United States who was called for military service. He was willing enough to fight in the US Army but protested he should not then be taxed as a foreigner. The officer in charge "leaned over the bench and said, 'Say, young feller, don't you know that in this country there ain't nobody has got any goddamned rights whatsoever.'"

The third step occurred when Pound told these stories to an American prosecutor who commented: "All I'm interested in is bunk—seeing what you can put over." In a March 2, 1942, radio speech, he was more pointed, specifying that the DA was a Jew, implying that the interest in bunk and cynicism regarding secular law was a Jewish attitude (Doob 1978: 48). When Pound relayed all three episodes to Senator Wheeler during his trip to the United States in 1939, he was told, "Well, what d'you expect? He [Roosevelt] has packed the Supreme Court, so they will declare anything he does Constitutional"—a moment memorialized in Canto 100, immediately before Pound turns to Lenin on Aesopian language. In fact, Roosevelt failed to pack the Court, though he had tried to expand the number of Justices from nine to fifteen with the hope that new appointees might endorse his New Deal. But the scheme never came to pass. FDR may have had autocratic pretentions as Pound believed, but the usurpation of the judiciary occurred not through "packing" but because FDR's long, twelve-year tenure in office gave him ample opportunities to appoint judges congenial to his outlook. Yet, FDR's strategy, in Pound's opinion, could only be to facilitate the takeover of the United States. Pound told Bridson, "[T]hat is where I took off from"; the poet claimed that was why "after two years of wrangling, when I got hold of the microphone in Rome I used it." As Robert Spoo has noted, this was a rationalization: "Pound's 'Four Steps' might have been a convenient notation for the causes that led to the radio speeches, but in 1940–5 his desire to reach war-bound listeners in other countries had been paramount." If "by taking the microphone in Rome he was seeking, however misguidedly, to bypass the flimsy and damned partition that had been created by bad laws and good wars" he had failed (Spoo 2010: 134). The partition stood—no longer sleazy brown paper but the locked wards of the Bughouse. What remained was the need to reach and educate a progressively brainwashed public.

Pound used code because his ideas were dangerous to express openly. Doing so had led to his indictment for treason that had brought him to a military prison and back to the United States in 1945, then perpetual confinement. Unconvicted of any crime, Pound could neither be pardoned nor punished. He would remain incarcerated until his keepers found him recovered sufficiently to aid in his own defense. In 1945 Pound was understandably ambivalent about going on trial for his life and so had acceded to the court's judgment that he was insane. Nonetheless, part of him wished for a trial so he could stage his exposé of the great betrayal of the United States. But to be successful his trial would require an educated jury. Raising the "cultural level" was a prerequisite for a trial envisioned as a great lecture on civic awareness; "way you spring Ez / is to raise cultural level of the country," he wrote his supporter Professor Giovanni Giovannini in 1954.[28] However, another part of Pound was understandably averse to risking his life in such a manner—to the point when those working for his release were frustrated by his apparent indifference. As part of his self-censorship—his melodrama, as Alex Pestell calls it—Pound refused to sign many of his letters at this time for fear they could be used to prove his essential sanity. Still, because he believed his country was in danger, Pound wanted to remain politically active. This was his responsibility as a poet and a citizen. So he involved himself in the Civil Rights struggle as a states' rights segregationist, part of his effort to rescue the United States and its Constitution from a Jewish/Communist cabal fronted by the Warren Court. Pound's own fate, he thought, proved that it would stop at nothing to pervert, weaken, and ultimately subjugate the United States.

The Warren Court

For Pound and his young friends—Kasper, Dave Horton, his personal lawyer Bob Furniss, his muse Sheri Martinelli, and others—the Warren Court was the vanguard of the Jewish/ Communist conspiracy working tirelessly to subvert the Constitution and "mongrelize" the United States in its quest for world domination. This view was widely shared throughout the country. The solidly Democratic South believed it; J. Edgar Hoover of the FBI believed it. School integration would lead to racial amalgamation and the end of white supremacy. It is too easy to forget that a century ago "White Supremacy" was the slogan of the Democratic Party, at least south of the Mason-Dixon Line. In the South the so-called American way of life was explicitly built on Jim Crow racial segregation; in the North, this unhappy American way was tacit, not explicit, but it was real enough for people of African descent, ghettoed in certain neighborhoods and too often illegally "Jim Crowed" out of public places, restaurants, and theatres.

Although it took until 1965 and the Civil Rights Act for the rights promised by the Constitution to black citizens to acquire some overarching statutory basis and begin to be fitfully enforced; although racism remains, the rejection by the Warren Court of white supremacy as a credible ideology has changed America entirely. Racial integration has succeeded brilliantly in cultural terms. Even in the shadows of Trumpism, contemporary racial problems in the United States are much better explained as problems of assimilation in tension with rather desperate attempts by many whites and blacks to maintain distinct cultural identities; or even in terms of class struggle, rather than race. But, because cultural identity and racial solidarity are crucial to minority politics and because the concept of class struggle is ideologically beyond the pale in the United States, these issues are talked about in racial terms; "systemic racism" proceeds via channels long carved into the culture at large and quite evident in our daily politics as I write.[29]

Pound worried about the Warren Court. A meditation of 1957 gives the flavor of his thinking:

> Never since 1628 when the corrupt Charles Stewart [sic] and the illustrious Buckingham tried to extinguish English liberties [has] there been a more crucial mo[men]t. never a more dastardly [at]tempt against all constitutional law and all justice than now under [Wa]rren, the tall aspiring student of the Talmud and father in law to jews, along with the rump of Roosevelt's nominees, [ap]pointed as Senator Wheeler noted and was punished for mentioning, [to?] declare anything he does constitutional, the rump of Dexter-White [...]

> [It r]emains to be seen whether we have the stuff in us that our English [f]orebear had in the days of Coke and Selden, or whether we have [b]een miscegenated, bastardized, mixed and brain washed until we can [n]o longer resist executive, quasi-[r]oyal encroachments or the [c]orruption of jus [sic] judges working to uproot all our heritage.[30]

This untitled piece of prose is filed with the Coke material at the Beinecke written in 1957–8. Its themes can be found in the Coke Cantos (107–110). The fear of executive "encroachments" helps explain, too, why Coke and acceptance of the Petition of Right are chosen to close the authorized *Cantos*. Again, we find "the fourth step to the bughouse," Senator Wheeler's objection to FDR and his attempt to pack the Supreme Court. Wheeler's punishment must have been that he was smeared as profascist for becoming an isolationist spokesperson for "America First" and a supporter of Charles Lindbergh. The main thrust of this document, however, is the attack on the Warren Court and Warren himself as "the tall aspiring student of the Talmud and father in law to jews," which together with the reference to Dexter White points to the Jewish/Communist conspiracy.

Harry Dexter White, the Soviet spy and asset, was an important FDR advisor attached to the US Treasury and one of the architects of the postwar financial order. White is largely responsible for the invention of the International Monetary Fund, which he later headed, and the World Bank. Pound believed, correctly, that White was a Soviet agent (see *EP/ORA* 164). He often uses White to stand metonymically for the large group of Soviet spies and agents of influence he saw surrounding Roosevelt, including the subversive Quakers Alger Hiss and Harry Hopkins as well as the sinister Jews Bernard Baruch and Felix Frankfurter. Serving Stalin, White developed the "Morgenthau Plan" that would have deindustrialized Germany and exposed Western Europe to Soviet aggression. Under investigation by HUAC in 1948, after a day of testimony White died suddenly of a heart attack that many conjecture was suicide. White and the allegedly Communist-infested Treasury department were investigated by McCarthy in 1953, so Pound, who was a great admirer of the Wisconsin senator, would have been quite familiar with White's case and the subversive milieu it stood for.

Pound's obvious right-wing orientation is only so helpful in considering the poetic problems posed by Pound's hoped-for "paradiso" of late Washington Cantos. By now, we know only too well what Pound opposes, but what does he stand for? Dante had Catholic Christianity; he had Aquinas's "star-map." Pound had an ethical program in Confucius and, eventually, a legal advocate, Coke; he had a metapolitical theory of history as racial struggle and an economic one of class conflict between debtors and creditors; he had the US Constitution, or what was left of it. He also had his indubitable debunking poem that conveyed, however darkly, his understanding and critique of what was really happening.

Notes

1 Kenner's path-breaking *The Poetry of Ezra Pound* (1951) appeared prior to any "Washington Cantos."
2 "E.P. was opposed to SOCIALISM, and to the socialist elements IN fascism," Pound explained to Olivia Agresti. "He wanted what was best for Italy at a given time. He did NOT concede an inch of his Jacksonian principles." His economic program "fitted in [with] Jeffersonian belief in the MINIMUM government" (11/9/1955, EP/ORA).
3 Both Hilton and Goullart were indebted to Joseph Rock. Hilton's novel was inspired by Rock's *National Geographic* articles, while Goullart knew Rock personally in China. Pound was steered to Tibet by L. A. Waddell's richly illustrated *Lhasa and Its Mysteries* (1905), a source for Canto 105. He may have known Waddell's *Among the Himalayas* (1899) as well.
4 Beinecke YCAL MSS 43, Series IV, Notebook 107, March–April 1957, Box 121, folder 4975. See *Sacred Edict*, pp. 3–18 and 99/720–28.
5 Pound, like Del Mar, believed in the "quantity theory of money." "To wit," as he wrote Agresti: "the monetary UNIT [is] the total volume of nation's money / [I believe with Del Mar] That new issue cd / be made ONLY by the govt. and wd diminish the value of each buck already in circulation" (3/18/1955, *EP/ORA*).
6 For political implications of this, see Nicholls (2004: 240–1).
7 Kristin Grogan, "Three Ways of Looking at a Canto: Navigating Canto CVIII," *Glossator* 10 (2018): 329–53.
8 Compare, for example, the difference in tone of two of the few indispensable books on *The Cantos*: Massimo Bacigalupo's urbane skepticism in his politically orientated *The Forméd Trace* (1980) and Peter Liebregts's earnest tracing of the Neoplatonic strand through the epic in *Ezra Pound and Neoplatonism* (2004).
9 Roxana Preda, "Gold and/or Humaneness: Pound's Vision of Civilization in Canto XCVII," *Glossator* 10 (2018): 27–49.
10 Peter Nicholls, "Hilarious Commentary: Ezra Pound's Canto XCVIII," *Glossator* 10 (2018): 51–82.
11 Ezra Pound to Sheri Martinelli, October 4, 1954 (Beinecke YCAL MSS 868, Box 12, folder 9 "Pound, Ezra"). "Manus animam pinxit" is the key line from Dante Gabriel Rossetti's short story and parable of anagogy "Hand and Soul" (1850), one of the most influential reads of Pound's youth. He told Agresti: "Hand and Soul / very applicable to Sheri / that being modus operandi" (2/1/1956, *EP/ORA* 225).

12 Sheri Martinelli to Ezra Pound, December 17–18, 1958, p. 4 (Beinecke YCAL MSS 43, Box 33, folder 1392).
13 *The Anagogic & Paideumic Review* was a mimeographed affair of fifty copies each. It was begun in 1959 and was for sale at City Lights bookstore, publishing in it such poets as Charles Bukowski, Bob Kaufman, Clarence Major, Charles Richardson, and others. By 1960 Martinelli would announce to Bukowski that she was the "Queen of the Beats" (Moore 2001: 54). Copies are among the Martinelli papers at the Beinecke.
14 All sources agree that "Arya" means noble, distinguished, etc.; hence, "aristocrat." Waddell (2013: 5) posits "shining ones" in *Makers of Civilization in Race and History*, where Pound would have seen it.
15 The other is Neoplatonism. See Liebregts (2004), *passim*.
16 Peter Viereck's father George Sylvester Viereck was a registered German agent and an outspoken partisan for the Nazis. In the 1950s, he wrote Pound and sent him a touching elegy of his older son's death fighting against the Axis at Anzio. His younger son Peter was politically opposed to his father. Part of Peter Viereck's job in World War II was to listen to Pound's broadcasts. Young Viereck, who won a Pulitzer in 1949 for the book of poems *Terror and Decorum*, seems one of the likely targets of those lines from Canto 95 railing against "all these twerps and Pulitzer sponges" (95/665). He took part in the "Bollingen Controversy" as one of the more principled critics of the award to Pound. Viereck began to write *Metapolitics* as a very young graduate student at Harvard; it was published when he was only twenty-five years old, going through several revisions with additions later. Pound's deep hostility to Peter Viereck is registered in a letter to Agresti (8/17/1954, *EP/ORA* 162).
17 Metapolitics is thus well suited to describe "esoteric fascism" although that is not our purpose here. Francis Parker Yockey's concept of "absolute politics" tries to capture the same vision and may derive from *Metapolitik*. Alain Badiou's "metapolitics" comes from the Left, although it must also derive from Hegel or his epigones. I have not read Badiou. See Alain Badiou, *Metapolitics* (New York: Verso, 2005).
18 Eustace Mullins (1961: 325–6) tells us that in 1951 Pound scribbled the key to the four as: 1) love; 2) duty; 3) propriety; and 4) wisdom. But Pound's correspondence with Achilles Fang reveals something rather different. Fang told Pound that the Chinese never thought of duty or justice as abstractions; they are practices. Justice is part of etiquette and good manners (*EPCF* 83). Pound, naturally assumed the Confucian "four *tuan*" usually translated as benevolence, righteousness, propriety, and knowledge were *virtues*. Fang insisted that the *tuan* were not virtues at all but aspects of an "ethical outlook" and felt "at a loss to suggest any sensible translation" (*EPCF* 82)—one reason that Pound does not translate them in *The Cantos* (see 85/565). Pound then suggested the four *tuan* might be rendered "decent impulse,

limits to which, modus to which and horse sense acquired by action" (*EPCF* 85), a formula that explains lines from Canto 85: "Praecognita bonum et ut moveas [pre-know the good to move yourself] / and then consider the time" (85/569). In Canto 99 he says that "the four TUAN / are from nature / jen, I, li, chih / Not from descriptions in the school house" (99/731), which suggests they are innate, possibly racial, and certainly not "culturally constructed." Eventually Pound settled on "manhood / equity / ceremonies, propriety / knowledge" as close to the four *tuan* (*EPCF* 67, 67n). This choice matters for the late cantos, especially *Rock-Drill* (1955), because he posits the "THE FOUR TUAN / or foundations" (85/559) as their philosophical support. In Pound's revised formula, the four—"manhood / equity / ceremonies / propriety / knowledge"—makes five (an all-important number in China as there are five cardinal directions: North, East, South, West, and center, where is the capitol). For us, the concept four signifies order—that's why "the whole creation [is] concerned with FOUR" (91/636), therefore "ceremonies / propriety" must be run together.

19 In light of Hegel's definition of "the politics of the actual" given earlier (note 4), it is interesting that Pound's translation of "Chung Yung, The Unwobbling Pivot" shows that "sincerity" interacting with self-fulfillment and knowledge gained by "perfecting things outside himself" "constitute[s] the process which unites outer and inner, object and subject, and thence constitutes a harmony with the seasons of heaven and earth" (*Con.* 179).

20 In his *Guide to Ezra Pound's* Selected Cantos (1980), Kearns spends a few pages unpacking what this ideogram meant to Pound—for it does not usually mean "sensibility" but rather "marvelous" or "benevolence." Kearns glosses Canto 85 roughly as "the spiritual forces registered by the Emperor I Yin provide a point of reference for sincere and intelligent action." Kearns sums up Canto 85 by addressing its metaphysical dimension: "Pound, putting together everything he knows about the character—a rejected reading from Legge's notes, Karlgren's analysis, Couvreur's translation, all other appearances of ling^2 靈 in the Confucian canon, and what he sees just by looking at it—decides that the character attracts to itself the meaning of the entire ode [Ode 3.I.8], a lyrical presentation of a Tory paradise in which king, people, nature, and music are in constructive harmony and where pond-park-tower [all terms modified by ling^2 靈 in the Ode] appear not to be a 'real' place but to be a symbol of a civilization informed by the spirits of the ancestors, or by 'Heaven'" (Kearns 1980: 199).

21 Pound connects the seemingly political exhortation to cosmos (heaven) and nature (earth) by riffing on Baller's "The peace of the Empire depends entirely on good manners and customs" in his translation of the *Sacred Edict* (Baller 1979: 99).

22 Perhaps de Benoist is unwittingly quoting Pound—after all, "Knowledge is NOT culture. the domain of culture begins when one HAS forgotten which book" as Pound pointed out in his *Guide to Kulchur* (*GK* 134).

23 De Benoist does not mention Evola's service in the SS in his biographical/critical essay included in *Aus rechter Sicht* (1983–4).
24 Like Pound, de Benoist has good things to say about Confucius. See *Aus rechter Sicht*, Band II, "Confucius."
25 Sunic quotes Ralph Manheim's translation, which is a little different: "From a metaphysical point of view, Russia and America are the same; the same dreary technological frenzy, the same unrestricted organization of the average man" (Martin Heidegger, *Introduction to Metaphysics* (Delhi: Motilal Banarsidass, 1999), p. 37, quoted in Sunic 2011: 186).
26 Beinecke YCAL MSS 43, Box 103, folder 4318.
27 David Farley, "Damn the Partition! Ezra Pound and the Passport Nuisance," *Paideuma* 30(3) (2001).
28 Beinecke YCAL MSS 43, Box 19, folder 831.
29 Even now, from the reactionary Right's point of view, racial "mongrelization" and the bastardization of the Constitution have weakened the United States domestically and internationally—one sees it in the unreasonable hatred of President Obama and the persistent Trumpist fantasy that he is somehow not American, nor even Christian.
30 Beinecke YCAL MSS 43, "Coke on Principles," Box 83, folder 3642.

2

Obstacles to Understanding the Washington Cantos

The Washington Cantos show the effects of Pound's incarceration. Pound is like a fly trapped in a bottle—his poetry against an invisible barrier, buzzing fiercely, hitting some points over and over, making uncanny music in an attempt to bust through to some free space—while each canto can be labeled and classified: there are "Coke Cantos" (Cantos 107–109), Thomas Hart Benton cantos (Cantos 88–9), and those written for Sheri Martinelli (Cantos 90–5, 97, 102). No canto is self-contained: in practice they bleed into each other, with references showing up like musical motifs in several cantos, demanding they be scrutinized together. As his notebooks show, Pound did not set out to compose cantos; he composed and divided up what he had written into cantos during the revision process. Nothing in process or result could be further from the New Critical ideal poem. To make sense of these cantos, one needs to make use of them all; a question raised in one canto may be answered in another, but often enough a remark made once is contradicted somewhere else.

So, how to read *Rock-Drill* and *Thrones*? Notoriously difficult, cryptic, and confused by strange editorial decisions and outright carelessness by Pound, these poems have caused too many critics to throw up their hands, finding them largely unreadable. All treatments of these books begin with a survey of the many disparaging critical judgments against them. Randall Jarrell famously called *Rock-Drill* "notes on the margins of the universe" but concluded his *Yale Review* notice shaking his head in regret: "What is worst in Pound and what is worst in the age have conspired to ruin the Cantos, and have not quite succeeded" (*EPCH* 439, 441). Donald Davies declared *Rock-Drill* a "write off" (*EPCH* 443) and *Thrones* "largely rubbish" and, most crushingly, "a bore"; Yvor Winters worried, prophetically, about *Rock-Drill* that we would need guidebooks "more awkward" than *The Cantos* themselves (*EPCH* 446). It seems downright delusional that Pound told Sheri Martinelli he was writing *Rock-Drill* "to save you some strength, from 30 years war" so that "the descent into hell is not wasted."[1] And yet, as Michael Kindellan points out, because the poetry is "written in flagrant contravention of normative standards of attention, diligence and care," it demands so much *more* care from its readers that we're forced back to check his sources (Kindellan 2017: 2–3). Far from the wisdom book Pound imagined, the poems seem more like the poet's unsifted library, demanding to be unpacked, organized, collated, and checked for accuracy.

If *Rock-Drill* was not a critical success, reaction to *Thrones* was worse. Daniel Pearlman's dim view of *Thrones* was "altogether despairing" (qtd in *G* vii); Peter Makin can barely contain his irritation with the tendentiousness of the Coke Cantos (Makin 1985: 285–7); Ronald Bush found *Thrones* "unreadable" (qtd in Nicholls 2004: 51). Richard Sieburth finds the paratactic "economy of the text virtually autistic" in *Thrones*. George Kearns put it more gently: the book was "ineffective as poetry" because—and this is crucial to *Thrones's* problems— "no amount of extracurricular reading will help" (*G* vii). Kearns's reasoning is important, because, despite what Pound told Martinelli, the one thing these cantos obviously demand is a hell of a lot of extracurricular reading. Many readers of this book will have taken Pound's references and allusions back to their sources and as a result looked into literatures and fields we would never have otherwise known: Confucianism, troubadours, Apollonius of Tyana, Byzantine history, Egyptology, Tibetan anthropology, money forms, eccentric Aryanist archaeology, English legal history; and we've had to reread with closer attention the *Odyssey* and Dante's *Commedia* as well.

Condemnation was not universal, of course. People close to Pound and aware of his mode of thought, including Noel Stock, David Gordon, and Hugh Kenner, all found much to praise. Kenner eulogized the "great work" of *The Cantos* drawing "to a close with undiminished elan," finding that "beginning with canto 90 some forty pages of unfaltering lyric brilliance initiate us" into a realm of eternal values (Kenner 1956: 457).[2] Even those put off by Pound's late mode are elated by certain lines and images.

Still, what do these poems mean? Can any one of us explain *all* of any of these poems *as though every word matters*?

Thrones is the most difficult; even Moody, who is all but indefatigable in his readings of almost every canto in his three-decker biography and does yeoman's work with *Rock-Drill* (Moody 2015: 349–64) is forced to skate lightly over *Thrones*, for the ice is thin, the connections fragile, and the whole intelligible only by means of what we might call "creative philology." As both books seem to demand exhaustive research into Pound's recondite source-texts, the experience is not exactly *reading*, Moody admits (2015: 353); it's study. First we explore the printed curriculum indicated by Pound's poem, then his correspondence, and then, with persistence, the archives, those notebooks, etc. After all that, there's the imaginative effort to make Pound's notes cohere—for many of these cantos just *are* notes, pretty much—and finally we must muster the creative will to make sense of it all. Readers must become philological questers and students "reading with the mind of a grandson" (85/570), undertaking research, observation, and training. All that plus 50 percent Techne! In short, a graduate school-like curriculum is recommended by Pound (85/570). But those of us who have taken the courses, read the scholarly literature, and written the papers still remain too much in the dark. The suspicion remains that these poems fail us, not that we fail them.

In search of coherence, earnest readers are forced to invent a Pound consonant with their own needs. Since Pound is a polarizing, contradictory figure, these cantos are usually regarded as cryptic or Delphic, evasive or prophetic, depending on each reader's temperament, predilections, and politics. On the whole, skeptical readers are prone to hand-wringing over Pound's repellant politics while more hopeful souls remain receptive to his fitful glimpses of paradise. Most of us are both: wishing to segregate Pound's paradise from his political profanations or, as the mood strikes, to somehow align Pound's utopian Confucian-Jeffersonian fascism with tolerable and beneficent celestial imperatives underwritten by his own sincerity. To get anywhere with these poems we need to confront and overcome several obstacles.

1. The poems are prison literature that might at any time be used against their author as evidence for his basic sanity and treasonous intent.
2. Confined as Pound was, these poems rely heavily on the poet's wide and eccentric reading; the real world filters in via his correspondence and reactions to newspapers or the ward's blaring TV. Part of their difficulty is that they feature works no one has ever heard of—and that seems to be part of the point.
3. Pound was steeped in troubadour poetry and conventions. He used *trobar clus*, the hermetic love code of troubadour poetry, to disguise his affair with Sheri Martinelli.
4. The Washington Cantos are classic examples of what Edward Said called "late style," a difficult mode of composition that certain artists undertake nearing the end of their lives. Said's examples are musical, but a kind of "impatient shorthand" (Said 2006: 7) can be seen in artists working in every field, including poetry. Pound seems to be one of them.

5. Another, broader difficulty is Pound's dissident economic program evident here in the poems on money and monetary ratios. It is tempting to reject Pound's economic thinking as the work of a crank. In fact, his thinking about money is no more difficult than his thinking about literary theory— and no easier! Pound thought deeply about economics, especially money, the language of exchange. He was more aware than most of the major structural contradictions of capitalism, including the basic opposition of capital and labor, the sacred cow of the labor theory of value, and the relationships between progress and poverty, profit and loss, debt, interest, and time. He saw how these contradictions are expressed and embodied in the form of money, which, as the language of capital, had become so confusing that it was—and remains—incoherent. Part of Pound's project is to make money talk sense.[3]

6. Finally, there is Pound's problematic metapolitical, racialized theory of history that lies near the heart of this book. After all, the dust jacket of *Thrones* explains that the purpose of *The Cantos* is to "give the true meaning of history as one man found it" (qtd in *EPCH* 450). Delmore Schwartz quoted this in a useful 1960 review essay titled "Ezra Pound and History," finding Pound wanting as a historian "in two important ways: he has an intense tendency to overinterpret and overgeneralize from his own experience and his undisciplined and very often uninformed abstraction; that is, his wobbly deductions" (*EPCH* 448). Pound's historical premises and resulting judgments are eccentric at best. Earlier Pound's theory of history was "Jeffersonian": history was a class struggle between a clique of creditors and a mass of debtors. By the 1950s, Pound has thoroughly racialized this struggle as between Semitic destroyers and Aryan culture-builders.

Aesopian Language and Its Problems

The Washington Cantos are prison literature, subject to perusal by the state apparatus, that might at any time be used against their author as evidence for his basic sanity and treasonous intent. Therefore, they are written partly in "Aesopian language (under censorship)" (100/733), as Pound signals in Canto 100, so it behooves us to read these cantos as Aesopian parables and allegories designed to mislead unauthorized readers who lacked the key to the code. The key is no simple thing: only a reader steeped in Pound's writing and familiar with his thinking could ever hope to locate it, much less turn it in the lock these poems present. Finally, there are *codes*, plural. The poems demand to be read as Aesopian allegory *and* anagogic prophecy.

At first glance it appears that the Aesopian mode is predominantly nominative ("where I wrote 'Japan,' you may read 'Russia,'" as Lenin put it). In Canto 100, where Pound indicates that we factor in Aesopian language as his mode of writing, we are given permission to read the poems as code; where Pound writes Roosevelt on that same page, we may read Eisenhower. But simple Aesopian readings can take us only so far. We have already figured out that elsewhere when he contemptuously gestures to Roosevelt, as he too frequently does, he is calling out the Jewish/Communist conspiracy for which FDR was, in the poet's view, the figurehead. In Canto 104, Pound may have had the burgeoning Suez crisis on his mind when he picked up the thread (broached in Canto 86) about Disraeli extralegally buying the Suez Canal for England via the Rothschilds— although, significantly, Pound will not say this out loud. In fact he doesn't even mention Disraeli and censors the Rothschilds out of the canto, only implying that someone sold "England / for four million quid to ... (deleted[)] ... / Suez Canal shares ... " steering us to "Hollis (Christopher)" where, with a little work, we can look up the reference to Disraeli in his book *The Two Nations: A Financial Study of English History* (1935) (see 104/762, 86/584, and Hollis 1935: 169).[4] A political prisoner, pretending to be crazy, Pound wrote darkly because if he said what he meant he feared he might be tried for his life.

Moreover, the historical situation in the mid-1950s, amidst the Cold War and after the disastrous Chinese Civil War (1947–9) and the indecisive Korean War (1950–3), lent itself to conspiratorial interpretation of recent history. Pound's dark view of the scene, in terms of his personal situation, US foreign policy, the Civil Rights struggle and the "subversive" Warren Court, was by no means eccentric. Thanks to Senator McCarthy and his allies, the Communist conspiracy was a dominant trope in contemporary discourse. Pound was a great admirer of the Wisconsin senator, as were his circle of young right-wing disciples. John Kasper disseminated McCarthy's reports at his Greenwich Village Poundian bookshop, the Make It New, and Eustace Mullins claimed to have been a researcher for McCarthy. In Canto 100, Pound quotes Lenin on Aesopian language, partly because Aesopian language was much in the air as the result of publicity surrounding the McCarthy hearings (Henderson 2010: 355–8). But Pound's use of Aesopian language throughout the late cantos is in fact a practice of long standing in his writing, a politicized derivative of his "personae" strategy.[5]

Alex Pestell's richly informed *Glossator* essay on Canto 100, "'In the Intellect Possible': Revisionism and Aesopian Language in Canto C," is particularly helpful regarding Aesopian language and Pound's drama of censorship, which he shows is far more complex than simple nominative or algebraic substitution; rather, it involves a whole range of winks and nods between the writer and the two readerships addressed, the censors on the one hand and a sympathetic coterie on the other.

Unsurprisingly, the theory and practice of Aesopian writing has been dominated by Russians. Pestell cites Ilya Kutik's definition of the Aesopian mode as "writing designed to appear orthodox to the censor but betraying itself to the reader in the know" (qtd in *G* 124), which fits quite well with Pound's practice at St. Elizabeths. But there is more to it than that. Irina Sandomirskaja points out (again quoted by Pestell) that "Aesopian language ... is a skill, in speaking as well as listening ... '[T]he initiated' are expected to be skillful enough to understand that it has to be interpreted in some other sense" (qtd in *G* 124).[6] Clearly, Aesopian language demands a specific social context to be intelligible. Pestell comments on the importance to *Thrones* of Pound's circle of intimates at St. Elizabeths, "a community that is both aware of Pound's position in the recent course of history (as he sees it) and is trained to recognize the relevance of recondite texts to the contemporary situation" (*G* 125). Pestell suggests we use a terminology of "screen" and "marker" developed by Lev Loseff in yet another study of Russian literature; "the former is 'bent on concealing the Aesopian text,' while the latter 'draws attention to that same Aesopian text'" (*G* 125), a strange confluence of concealment and exposure that is easily seen in the frequent use of ellipses throughout *Thrones*. Taking note of the provoking ellipses concealing the name of Sumner Welles in Canto 100 (100/733), Pestell remarks on these "conspicuous, indeed often melodramatic markers of omission" (*G* 127).

Likewise, in his important article on Canto 107, Peter Nicholls speaks of a "sense we may have here of conspiratorial powers at work which compel the text toward a kind of self-censorship" (Nicholls 2015: 10), which makes melodramatic if not logical sense. How could such powers, should they exist, compel a text to censor itself? But Pound did censor himself, as one can see from his notebooks. The very instance from Canto 108 that Nicholls brings up in his article—the obscure line "was 15 000 three score" (108/785), which Nicholls (following Bacigalupo) shows refers to Jews banished from England in Edward I's "Edict of Expulsion" (Nicholls 2015: 11)—is no more explicit even in the original jotting (see Notebook 112). Pound *was* censoring himself, even in his unpublished notes. The gesture is, even in the privacy of a notebook, melodramatic, "a strategy of mystification" with a "theatrical component" (*G* 128; see also Kindellan 2017: 44). Pestell detects "an almost hysterical air to Pound's pantomime of censorship, as if he can't help drawing attention to his transgressive speech in spite of all counsels to the contrary" (*G* 144). This tone of beleaguered urgency is a typical feature of right-wing texts and tracts, which, like *The Cantos*, pose as presenting detailed covert research exposing vast, nefarious conspiracies.

But Pound's "Aesopian" method does not help us much with the Chinese ideograms, Confucius, and higher matters. Despite his faulty grasp of the language, when Pound cites Kung, he cites Kung. So there is another way to read these cantos: anagogically. If Aesopian allegory helps decode the Washington Cantos on the political plane, an anagogical approach helps with the paradisal or metaphysical plane of the cantos. Pound always goes in fear of abstractions, hence his famous "ideogrammic method" that tries to analyze the Chinese ideograms as rebuses—as concatenations of particulars. But the many ideograms that take up Canto 85 just are abstract; one doesn't know how to grasp them. Ripped out of context as they are, even native Chinese readers feel nonplussed as to how they are to be assembled in a way that makes any sense, much less the sense Pound wants us to make (Kindellan 2017: 6–7). Feng Lan refers to Pound's method as "etymographic reading" that, in his informed view, "is responsible for the largest and most polemical group of misreadings in Pound's translations of Confucius" (Lan 2005: 29). Hopeless as Chinese, these signs must be read otherwise—anagogically—as hieroglyphs: sacred signs.[7] For Pound, these signs are not abstractions but "radiant gists." As I've mentioned, anagogical reading is usually associated with Christian readings of the Old Testament, in which events of Jewish history are read as anagogical foreshadowings of the Christian messiah.[8] Pound demands that we use a similar technique when reading cantos dedicated to Confucian ethics. If, as Pound claimed, Confucius's value is that he "gives what a man can believe without kidding himself" (c. 1949–50, *EP/ORA* 40), his very practical ethical advice still "intimates higher matters" because his ethics are aligned with *kosmos*. At a more personal level, the cantos celebrating Pound's love for Sheri Martinelli can be read in an anagogical spirit. Pound's sublime feelings for his muse make it silly for us to take Pound's imagining of Sheri as Diana, Artemis, Flora Castalia, or their confected goddess "Ra-Set" in Canto 91 as Aesopian. These are not cover names but spiritual attributes demanding a spiritual (if eroticized) response.

Pound's Reading and the Poverty of Philology

The Cantos were always recondite. The poet as muckraking archivist became more pronounced in St. Elizabeths. Pound seemed to revel in their difficulty, pretending that the work was perfectly clear and that his sources ought to be common knowledge. The Washington Cantos delight in featuring works no one else has ever heard of. Through his academic friends Professors Giovanni Giovannini and Craig LaDrière at Catholic University, John Kasper's connections to the used book trade, and Eustace Mullins's willingness to delve into the Library of Congress, Pound had access to out-of-the-way texts: Paul the Deacon's eighth-century history of the Lombards, *The Eparch's Book* of Leo the Wise, Senator Thomas Hart Benton's nineteenth-century memoir *Thirty Years' View*, lives of obscure American Presidents Franklin Pierce and James Buchanan, revisionist histories of World War II, the neo-Confucian *Sacred Edict* by the "salt commissioner" Kuang-Tzu, the Aryanist fantasies of L. A. Waddell, Philostratus's *Life of Apollonius of Tyana*, Joseph Rock's accounts of the threatened Na Khi way of life, Sir Edward Coke's *Institutes*, and Alexander Del Mar's *History of Monetary Systems*, among others. Altogether it makes for a strange blend of Neoplatonism, Confucianism, archaeology, and law picked up from the margins of history—recovered, Pound believed, from the historic blackout imposed by the usurers and the Jews; "ALL Byzantine history," Pound wrote to Olivia Agresti, in reference to *The Eparch's Book*, "part of black out" (*EP/ORA* 174). It is as though marginality certified each text's importance: they are marginal *because* they are important. Pound even quotes from the footnotes of texts in his poem, showing a preference for the margins of the marginal. This mirrors Pound's own marginal position exiled in the bughouse; the world's margin is his center. Decades of scholarship have been devoted to discerning and then learning Pound's myriad source texts, some of which undoubtedly still remain unknown.

Even when the text is well known, Pound's codes are not always a simple encryption. As Michael Kindellan has recently argued in his *Late Cantos of Ezra Pound* (2017), an impressive philological study of Pound's "anti-philology" in *Rock-Drill* and *Thrones*, there are distortions, reversals, and editorial decisions that defy any straightforward decoding. The drafts of these poems are betrayed by strange contradictions, which make nonsense in the printed poem. And errors: in Canto 105, for instance, Old Gallagher's remark about British "loans to Tibet" (87/596) becomes the opposite, "loans *from* Tibet" (105/767); and something said to Anselm in a typescript draft, "And we biJayzus *respect* your damn bishops," is printed as its opposite, "we biJayzus *reject* your damned bishops" (105/767). Typo or poet's error, the poem's argument about Anselm preserving local laws and customs ("consuetudines")—a coded response to the threat of federal power unleashed against Jim Crow folkways—is muddied considerably.

There is the matter too of Pound's tenuous, certainly idiosyncratic, hold on the many languages involved in his poem. Pound warns at the outset that he is not operating according to philological protocols—"No that is *not* philological," he snaps early in Canto 85 (85/564)—and he famously sends philologers to the chopping block in Canto 93. But why? It would seem that we are to believe that Grandpa knows best and that philology is unhelpful because the tradition has been "blacked out" and corrupted. As Kindellan (2017: 158) warns, "We have yet to come to terms with the extent to which the most important of Pound's textual influences were written in languages he could not properly understand."[9]

This is especially true of Chinese, which saturates much of these late cantos as a result of the poet's prior immersion in his Confucian translations. There are "a full 104 ideograms in the first *Rock-Drill* canto alone," Kenner notes (1971: 529), making that poem unintelligible without recourse to generations of scholarship, which nevertheless still fails to entirely enlighten us because, well, the Chinese is not exactly Chinese![10] Though generous in his appreciation of Pound's use of Chinese in his thought and writing, Feng Lan patiently concedes that the primary source of Pound's misreading of Chinese is primarily his "insufficient and inadequate knowledge" of the language (2005: 17).[11] Lan also zeros in on Pound's anxious need to challenge the decisions of the famous translators Pauthier and Legge, supplanting their idioms with his own, ostensibly to "get nearer the original meaning." Too often, this meant merely meanings of his own invention (Lan 2005: 27–9). Pound's "maverick sinology" (Kindellan 2017: 160), his turn to notional Chinese *sounds* rather than Chinese *sense*, evident in Canto 99, produces babble. As Kindellan points out, this sort of willful misprision is a characteristic of many of Pound's most salient key terms—like Aristotle's *metathemenon* (or *xreia*, which Kindellan does not address), Frobenius's *Paideuma*, and even the great *ling*^{2} 靈 character, which (as George Kearns has shown) had *not hitherto* meant "sensibility"—that are simply misappropriated by Pound for his own polemical purposes in the manner of Humpty Dumpty, to show who is master.

Kindellan's work is unsettling, to say the least. Kindellan prefers the term "errancy" to "error" in discussing Pound's late cantos because Pound's misquotations, errors of fact, and idiosyncratic translations are not so much mistakes as *decisions*.[12] Having studied the Notebooks intently, Kindellan is adamant that Pound was quite sure about what he wanted to say. "Pound's texts are unstable not because he was unsure about his meanings; they were unstable because he *was* sure" (2017: 247; Kindellan's emphasis). To read Pound properly, Kindellan concludes, "we have to allow his misconceptions to unfold according to the logic of their errancy" (2017: 249); that is, we have to accept them. It's pointless to contest them. "The model for understanding *The Cantos* tries to realize is one where philological difficulties can be overcome by belief" (2017: 18–19). In fact, "what Pound's anti-philological attitude is designed to facilitate is a staunchly author-centric conception of literary production" (2017: 21).[13] We believe Pound sincerely meant it all, or we don't. Intention, it seems, is everything.

Kindellan's *Glossator* essay "'Tinkle, Tinkle Two Tongues': Sound, Sign XCIX," on Canto 99,[14] is indicative of the problems with Poundian philology because the canto ought to be amenable to a traditionally philological approach as the poem appears to be derived almost entirely from a single text, F. W. Baller's 1924 translation of *The Sacred Edict*, that eighteenth-century redaction of the emperor K'ang Hsi's sixteen practical maxims. The canto seems to be relatively easy to read, at least as *Thrones* cantos go, as it works as a "reading through" of Baller's translation.

Kindellan's research is nothing short of devastating; from a philological point of view, Canto 99 is simply a disgrace. The overwhelming realization, which Kindellan has culled from many sympathetic readers of Pound's "Chinese," is that Pound's knowledge of the language was rudimentary at best. Despite all those many years spent poring over the Chinese dictionary, his ingenious rebus readings have next to nothing to do with the Chinese written language. Despite warnings by his informants Achilles Fang and William Hawley that, in effect, he didn't know what he was talking about, Pound persisted in imagining his own idiolect, one which we can call "Chinese" only by courtesy. Their demurrals have been seconded by readers of *The Cantos* who should know, Zhaoming Qian and Feng Lan to name two (see especially Lan 2005: 21–3). Pound's vaunted turn to the *sound* of Chinese, his wished-for "tone-charts" to go along with his translation of the *Odes*, should not be confused with actual noises intelligible to Chinese speakers; Pound's "Chinese" is all his own. This wouldn't matter so much if he wasn't constantly in *Thrones* steering us toward notionally Chinese words and sounds, all the while hectoring us to open dictionaries and "learn the meaning of words" (98/709, 100/739). The meanings Pound may have in mind are not to be found in any books outside his own.

Kindellan has dutifully attempted to track down some of the renderings of Chinese syllables (with their fiddly little tone-indicators) in the dictionaries

Pound used, especially *Mathews'*, but has had little luck. Dictionaries of Chinese are organized around the written signs, sorted by "radicals" (which indeed have important sound values); they are not organized sonically. Though we think of Baller's *Sacred Edict* as the source text here, "it could be more correct to say, technically speaking, *Mathews' Chinese-English Dictionary* is every bit as much a source as Baller" because, with a few exceptions, "Baller offers no transliterations" that make up so much of Pound's poem. Kindellan adds that "the exclusively phonetic exhibition of words in canto XCIX in fact contravenes the central tenet of Pound's ideogrammic method" (*G* 107), which is based on written signs where, crucially, verbal transactions are made *visible* (Fenollosa n.d.: 8–9). "Attending exclusively to sound," as Pound wants to do here, "frequently deletes the actual meaning of the character being spoken/heard when the word being exhibited is removed paratactically from the larger context of its use" (*G* 108). Nonetheless, Pound deploys these noises because they mean something to *him*. Kindellan argues that "since at least 1952" (when he completed his Confucius translations) "Pound had begun to think of Chinese (at least in part) as *a network of ciphers* as much as a system of graphically unambiguous and therefore ethically virtuous ideograms" (*G* 108; my emphasis). Pound reads Chinese as if they are (to quote H.D.) "anagrams, cryptograms, / little boxes, conditioned // to hatch butterflies" (1998: 53). Pound's ideograms are, effectively, magic words. The "Chinese" in Canto 99 is a code known only to the poet himself. To be sure, if you suspected that the "paltry yatter" on the bottom of 99/722 was written onomatopoetically to suggest the barking of dogs or the chattering of monkeys, you'd be right (*G* 101). We can live with that; "paltry yatter" just *is* noise. And the duple intensifiers Kuang/Kuang/Ming/Ming noises above on the same page *do* comport with Chinese usage to mean brightest, most intelligent. OK: but what are we to do with the four tintinnabulating, notionally Chinese sounds "tien t'ang^2 hsin^1 li$^{3-5}$"? "Heaven's temple is in the heart," Terrell says, noting that li$^{3-5}$ should be li$^{3-4}$—i.e. a different word. No surprise, Cookson parses it a little differently, observing that Pound has "rearranged [the original] sentence" (2001: 235).

But philologically? A mess. And without those invaluable handbooks? Ting, tang tinkle two tongues indeed. As Kindellan notes: "there is a fine line between Pound's mock-castigations of Buddhist yatter and some of this canto's own verses … so that discerning a proper difference comes down to either intuiting his intentions or looking for extra-textual explanations" (*G* 102), which, I might add, comes to the same thing. We are forced to examine Pound's fortunately copious correspondence to figure out what the poem meant to him, if not to us. This necessity goes beyond Pound's Chinese cipher to the rest of *The Cantos*.

All of this puts Pound's stated interest in *cheng ming*, "right naming," in a new light. It would seem that his insistence on right naming is all too often wrong naming. One of the poet's best critics, Peter Makin, argues that Pound's earlier ideogrammic method contradicts his increasingly legalistic insistence on *cheng ming*, which in Makin's view is "un-Poundian, an aberration" (2003: 120)—albeit one with a long life, beginning around 1935 and pervasive in the late cantos. Makin shows that Pound's passion for "precise terminology" waxes as his interest in the ideogrammic method wanes. That must be, for the ideogrammic method is by its nature indirect, never nominative, but never abstract either; it is always a cluster of concrete examples bracketing a precise state.

But by insisting on "right naming" Pound seems to be promoting mere "verbalism." Makin points out that statements Pound made in the 1940s—"Without the definition of words knowledge cannot be transmitted from one man to another" and "thought hinges on definitions of words"—show "a very limited conception of knowledge" that would make "language and thought … a closed field" (Makin 2003: 135). Fortunately, Pound is quite wrong about the way language works, or we could have no poetry. Indeed, Pound's hopeless method of parsing Chinese characters as rebuses is impossible under this regime. I stress "regime," for Makin links Pound's verbalism to his "authoritarian streak," his rage for totalitarian order based on legal statutes amidst economic disorder. Linking "definition" to "sincerity," Pound arrives at the center of his Confucianism, forgetting, seemingly, that sincerity is most often nonverbal, not about words at all.

Independently, Peter Nicholls also notes this "increasingly contradictory" problem (2004: 240) in *Thrones*. He reminds us that the ideogrammic method was designed to be "excessive"—that is, in Ernest Fenollosa's famous (and fictional) confection of rose, cherry, rust, flamingo, the "'ideogram' for 'red'" there is "a kind of remainder which always exceeds the process of adequation" (Nicholls 2004: 240), whereas Pound's "two doits to a boodle" and other monetary equivalences "produce only a moment of reified identity in which being—the 'is' of equivalence—can express itself only as a quantity" (240). "We find in *Thrones*," he writes, "an insistent emphasis on mere correspondence or adequation, a kind of inert lexicography which parallels the circularity of monetary ratios: 'an askos is a leather bag' (96/682), 'θόλος a round building' (96/682), '8 stycas: one scat' (97/690)" (Nicholls 2004: 240). In Canto 94 adequation becomes tautology: we learn that that Apollonius "wanted to keep Sparta, Sparta … not a melting pot" and that he told Vespasian "the king shd / be king" (94/661). But tautology might be considered the trope of purity—everything is exactly itself, unmixed, unmongrelized, and purebred. This is the language and thinking of apartheid, like Pound's famous complaint that everyone deserves the right to have their ideas examined one at a time.

Pound's translation of "Chung Yung" or "The Unwobbling Pivot" closes with two passages from the *Book of Odes* and explication. We are told that "The Hidden meaning of [the first] lines is: thus heaven is heaven." The sense of the second passage quoted is that King Wen was perfect: "The *unmixed* functions {in time and space} without bourne. / This unmixed is the tensile light, the Immaculata. There is no end to its action" (*Con.* 187; Pound's emphasis). "Heaven is heaven": perhaps tautology is a "paradisal" trope. Didn't the voice emanating from the burning bush announce "I am what I am"?

Trobar Clus

A close student of Romance literature, especially of the Troubadours, Cavalcanti, and Dante, Pound had long been interested in the "'*trobar clus*,' which means 'enclosed,' perhaps hermetic" composition. "'Trobar clus' is the name given to the art of those troubadours who put hidden meanings in their songs," as Peter Makin explains in *Provence and Pound* (1978: 160). Pound's important talk to the Quest Society that centered later editions of *The Spirit of Romance* is concerned with the "love code" that lurks within certain poems by Arnaut Daniel and in Cavalcanti's "Donna mi Prega," a work with which Pound was obsessed. Because they are concerned with the love code, these poems are not Aesopian, but for that very reason, because it is the mode of adulterous love poetry and not politics, *trobar clus* operates in the "Sheri cantos," where this mode of concealment will be discussed more fully.

Pound's "Late Style"

To compound their problems, the late cantos are classic examples of what Edward Said called "late style"—the style of some artists late in life, confronting death and their audiences with a kind of impatient compositional shorthand marked by "intransigence, difficulty and unresolved contradiction" (2006: 7). Said evokes a dissenting spirit of lateness, a "late style that involves a nonharmonious, nonserene tension, and above all a sort of deliberately unproductive productiveness going against" (2006: 7). Nicholls wonders if the "desire for an ending may explain the impatience that so often attaches to Pound's handling of his materials" in

Thrones (2004: 235). This speaks, I think, to our problems getting a grip on these late poems, which are "marked by reticences, lacunae, curtailments, and suppressions of grammatical and semantic sense," as Kindellan notes, considering *Thrones* specifically (*G* 143). Why? And why can't we help feeling that there is something very important there, if only they weren't so damned cryptic? But what? And if there is something there, why doesn't Pound just come out and say it? Our ambivalence seems to be shared by the poet himself. On the one hand, he can write in a late Pisan Canto "in / discourse / what matters is / to get it across e poi basta" (get it across and be done with it) (79/506);[15] on the other, he confronts us with stacks of Chinese ideograms, as in Canto 85, or in Canto 94 his reading notes (half in Greek) of Coneybeare's bilingual edition of Philostratus's *Life of Apollonius of Tyana* (2013). Nicholls wonders: "Even as Pound wants to expose the malign forces at work in history his language recoils from direct statement, characteristically beginning in media res, giving the verb, and holding back the subject" (2004: 237). Examples abound: "'By the conquest,' said Picabia, 'of Alsace-Lorraine'" (97/698)—i.e. exhausted, Europe is ... Such formulations "encode a deep anxiety, twisting language against itself and withholding that which it yearns most to deliver" (Nicholls 2004: 237). In no way is Pound getting across much of anything except a record of his own remarkable curiosity.

Still, if Said is correct and if we can call these late cantos an example of late style, then at least Pound is not alone: Ibsen did it; Beethoven is Adorno's example. One might also recall late John Coltrane or, thinking of poets, late work by Jay Wright and Adrienne Rich. Concerning "late style," Adorno discerned "a moment when the artist who is fully in command of his medium nevertheless abandons communication with the established social order of which he is a part and achieves a contradictory relationship with it. His late works constitute a form of exile" (qtd in Said 2006: 8). Pound, of course, had been literally exiled from the social order by his indictment for treason and perpetual incarceration in St. Elizabeths, to say nothing of the loss of his "legal-personhood" attesting his legal incompetence (see Moody 2015: 247–50). This is one reason why the exile of Ovid to Pontus is a strand through these poems: "Winter in Pontus distressing," Pound/Ovid remarks near the end of Canto 103, bracing himself by recalling that "the lion-heads," those monuments to noble ideals, still remain at Sulmona, Ovid's birthplace (103/756; see also 104/762, 105/766). Writing on Canto 107, Nicholls, the most insightful critic who has dared to tackle *Thrones*, finds that "a powerful sense of finitude infects much of the writing here"; he wonders if this contributes "to the poet's fetishistic fondness for the words of dead languages"

(Nicholls 2015: 12). If the voices of the dead persist in speaking in their own language, perhaps Pound's will too.

Pound's intransigence and impatience come through loud and clear in the irascible asides that spot these poems but also in gaps and silences, elisions and repressed passages. Speaking of Canto 107, Nicholls has noted that "the writing is increasingly turning in on itself, and almost literally so, as Pound habitually inverts the propitional logic of his broken phrases." He calls this "classic late Pound, unsettling the reader by beginning at the end of the story, folding back bit by bit, but never quite getting to the heart of the matter." This is a "mannerism that reflects [Pound's] impatience with any narrative contextualization"; he notes, too, "the sense of imminent ending—Pound's own" (Nicholls 2015). Nicholls's observations chime suggestively with Said's connection of "late style" to "the last great problematic … the last or late period of life, the decay of the body" (Said 2006: 6). He thinks that, for certain great artists, the end of life requires "a new idiom" (2006: 6). Perhaps this is what we encounter in the Washington Cantos.

The "Cleaners Manifesto"

Sublime or merely politic, Pound's coded language—saying one thing while meaning another—and what I think of as late-style intransigence are disturbing because they are more or less at odds with a poetic program the poet was publicizing through his acolytes from 1948, when Dallam Flynn promulgated the following manifesto[16] in his short-lived Pound vehicle, "Four Pages":

1. We must understand what is really happening.
2. If the verse makers of our time are to improve on their immediate precursors, we must be vitally aware of the duration of syllables, of melodic coherence, and of the tone leading of vowels.
3. The function of poetry is to debunk by lucidity.

Flynn republished the manifesto in his prolix preface of Basil Bunting's *50 Poems*, which he printed via his Cleaners Press in 1950. Cleaners Press was later taken over by Dave Horton and John Kasper to become Square $ Books, but it lent its name to the manifesto. The Cleaners Manifesto was republished in Noel Stock's *New Times* (January 13, 1955) and by Bill McNaughton in *Strike* 9 a year later (February 1956). Stock wondered whether these tenets might be "the logical successor of the original three-point IMAGIST manifesto" and whether any current poetry might had been written to it (1/13/1955, *New Times* 7). But Stock changed the manifesto slightly, writing that "debunking by lucidity" was only *a* function, not *the* function, of poetry; that slip was not made by McNaughton who was located closer to the source.

Surely Pound himself thought he was adhering to these principles he was so anxious to instill in others. Arguably he achieved everything but the most important: the third precept. He debunked—and how!—but building a light-questing late style did not automatically include transparency of meaning. The Washington Cantos remain stubbornly obscure. Either Pound thought he was a lucid debunker, as his impatience with readers might have us believe, or he wrote darkly on purpose; lucidity, when and if it came, would dawn only on the initiated few. Nonetheless, assuming, which we must, that Pound knew what he was doing, perhaps the critical power of lucidity is not so much related to Imagism but harks back to Pound's "New Method" of his New Age period, his "luminous details" and "radiant gists." Lucidities do twinkle fitfully in these late cantos: "Their mania is a lusting for farness / Blind to the olive leaf / not seeing the oak's veins" (107/782-3). In debunking mode, we should identify "their mania" with those who wish to "drive truth out of curricula" (107/780) and who invade the rights of subjects (107/781) like the Stuart monarchy, likely Aesopian language for the current usurping usurocracy. Pound sheds light on this paradise of finance that sees the planet not as an abundance of particulars to be cultivated with care but as natural resources to be exploited, as commodities to be exchanged, often as credit ("the future tense of money") and commodity "futures"; a virtual reality, far from the here and now, far from vine and leaf.

"Understanding what is really happening" for Pound means locating the conspiracy—economic and political. Dark conspiratorial speculations bubble uneasily just beneath the "benevolent" civic thought of these cantos, erupting frequently in rage and resentment, expressing all the difficulties attendant on late style. After a marvelous if incomprehensible line—"Two doits to a boodle, 13 ½ bawbees: 160 doits" that turn out to be measures of Scots money, culled, characteristically, from one of Del Mar's footnotes (1896: 258n)—Pound bursts out: "Will they get rid of that Rooseveltian dung-hill / and put Captain Wadsworth back in the school books?" (97/691). But, since FDR had been dead a dozen years, it's hard to say what brought on this eruption of spleen.[17]

The poet's feeling that his own ancestor has been usurped by FDR in the pantheon of American history gives us one clue as to what is going on in Canto 97 and in the Washington Cantos generally. By establishing his own family's place in America, Pound asserts his authority to comment on US history and, covertly, current events. In Canto 109, the final canto of *Thrones*, Pound interrupts his notes on Coke to gesture to Wadsworth while reading through the Connecticut Charter (109/793)—all part of his presentation of his bona fides as a real American, as well as a way of offering tantalizing glimpses of key documents retrieved from the official blackout. The obscure texts chosen for *Thrones* are often books of laws, money forms, and rites. They are "measures" in every sense, and their function is to govern *The Cantos* as a whole and to educate readers, with the poet himself as unacknowledged legislator and executive.

Notes

1. Ezra Pound to Sheri Martinelli, June 10, 1954; Beinecke YCAL MSS 868, Box 12, folder 4 "Pound, Ezra June 1–10."
2. Hugh Kenner, "Under the Larches of Paradise" (review of *Rock-Drill*), *Hudson Review* 9(3) (Autumn 1956): 457–65.
3. Leon Surette has argued that Pound was an incompetent economist: in over his head, naïve, "muddled," and therefore prey to conspiracy theories. The fundamentals of Pound's economic thinking are treated in Appendix A. See also Leon Surette, *Pound in Purgatory: From Economic Radicalism to Anti-Semitism* (Champagne: University of Illinois Press, 1999), *passim*.
4. As Archie Henderson has shown in his *Glossator* essay, Hollis's source is Count Corti's *The Reign of the House of Rothschild 1830–1871*, translated into English in 1928, where the anecdote quickly became "a staple of Anglophone anti-Semitic literature" (*G* 240). Pound read the book in 1950. See Henderson, "Exploring Permanent Values: Canto CIV," *Glossator* 10 (2017): 231–68. Incidentally, the 1928 translation of Corti's work (in two volumes, including *The Rise of the House of Rothschild 1770–1830*) was republished in the United States by the John Birch Society, Western Islands Press, Belmont, MA, in the 1970s.
5. See Casillo (1985: 68). For example: as Anne Conover has shown, and Olga always knew, the obscure homage to Dotto Aldo Walluschnig, a fifteenth-century physician, in Canto 28 is Pound's way of registering the difficult birth of his daughter Mary Rudge on July 9, 1925, although the poem deliberately falsifies the date. See Conover (2001: 60–1) and 28/133.
6. "There were," Nicholls writes, "some readers skilled in the arts of Pound's obscurantism; they, he knew, would quickly fill in the missing text" (2015: 10). An age-old tactic: "he that hath ears to hear, let him hear," as the Scripture says (Matt. 11:15).
7. "Ideograms carry, for Pound, a special talismanic weight, seeming to situate verbal performance outside the grammar of normal exchange" (Nicholls 2015: 7n).

8   Dante's example is the people of Israel coming out of Egypt to Judea, making it holy. Anagogically, this intimates the soul's progress from bondage to earthly matters to salvation in Christ.
9   Pound wrote to Olivia Rossetti Agresti on May 7, 1956: "I am not a classical philologist. I have small greek and very promiscuous latin, which matter I read to find out what I want to know etc." (*EP/ORA* 231).
10 Achilles Fang's letter (*EPCF* 153–4) with corrections and queries regarding Canto 85 is instructive about Pound's wayward limitations and Fang's patience—and not only concerning Chinese!
11 In an informative chapter in *Ezra Pound and Confucianism* (2005: 14–44), Feng Lan details "five types of misreading" in Pound's Confucian translations. Naturally these five misreadings also inform his deployment of Chinese in *The Cantos*.
12 See Nicholls on Carl Schmitt's "decisionism" (2004: 241).
13 Speaking of the Washington Cantos, Bacigalupo writes: "Now a captive in Washington, D.C. he responds to the violence of his community with the violence of his uncompromising poem, of which he is sole master" (1980: 219).
14 Kindellan (2018), entitled "'Tinkle, Tinkle Two Tongues': Sound, Sign XCIX" and including images of notebook pages, is a version of a subchapter of Kindellan (2017).
15 Kindellan (2018: 3 and note).
16 The manifesto was signed by "We, the CLEANERS, D[allam]. Simpson, L. C. Flynn [i.e. Dallam Simpson], and Igon Tan [i.e. Ezra Pound]." (AH)
17 Michael Reck (1967: 115) reported that Pound's "Hatred of Franklin Roosevelt was out of all right proportion … [H]e could and did talk for twenty minutes straight on this subject."

3

Aesopian Language and States' Rights

Two Fables—John Randolph of Roanoke and Canto 103

"The Unprintable part of my writing is what deals with ANYthing of importance"
                    Ezra Pound to John Theobald, September 24, 1957 (J/T 98)

In the summer of 1952, Ezra Pound told Guy Davenport that "the poet looks forward to what's coming next in the poem,"[1] as though the poem not the poet dictated the work. Since that can't happen, one way of interpreting this Delphic remark is to suppose that Pound meant pending events, whether in the poet's head or out in the world, would determine the content of the later cantos. Noel Stock called the late cantos "the diary of a mind" (Stock 1966: 104); if so, they also comment on current events.

From 1945 to 1958—during which time virtually all of the later cantos, from Canto 74 on, were written—Pound was a prisoner, his correspondence subject to censorship.[2] He rarely signed letters while in St. Elizabeths, for fear it might compromise him.[3] Paranoia? Pound considered himself a political prisoner.[4] For all his gestures toward paradise, Pound is most interested in a "paradiso / *terrestre*" (117/822; my emphasis); therefore, these poems are political. He told Noel Stock that the cantos were a "political weapon" (Stock 1966: 91). John Theobald was apprised that "None but the commies had sense to observe that *Cantos* are a POLITICAL Implement like the *Div. Com*" (6/17/1957 J/T 44). Pound and even James Laughlin worried that "Jews" and unnamed political "enemies" in the printing plants—presumably Communists—stood ready to ruin the poem in production in order to block its political message; "A fear of sabotage in the printing presses might help explain the rampant obscurity of Pound's late cantos," Michael Kindellan suggests (2017: 111). Fear of censorship, sabotage, and the Jewish "blackout" meant that their radical political content would appear in coded form. Pound acknowledged the situation in Canto 100. As discussed, the famous lines about "Aesopian language" taken from the "Preface to the Russian Edition" of Lenin's *Imperialism* are crucial to understanding how to read *Rock-Drill* and *Thrones*.

> And Lenin: "Aesopian language (under censorship)
> Where I wrote 'Japan' you may read 'Russia'" (100/733)

Lenin actually refers to "that *accursed* 'Aesopian language'" (my emphasis) and remarks how "painful it is in these days of liberty to reread the passages" written in exile, now published in revolutionary Petrograd, "which have been distorted, cramped, compressed in an iron vice on account of the censor" (Lenin 1917: 7). Just so, the unhappy reader often finds late cantos "distorted, cramped and compressed" as well as heavily coded. Read "Aesopianly" as directed, the phrase "'not a trial but a measure' committed Danton" (100/733) just a few lines down this same page of Canto 100 can be taken as referring to Pound himself: for Danton, read Pound. Likewise, we are free to read the opening of Canto 100 where Senator Wheeler criticizes FDR for "packing the Supreme Court" as code for Eisenhower's practice of using "recess appointments" to bypass Congress and get his own judges on board—most glaringly and fatefully, Governor Earl Warren of California, his foremost rival in the Republican party.[5] Once installed, Warren and the "Warren Court" became notorious in right-wing circles for making public policy.[6] Pound and his fellows on the Right saw Warren and the rest of the court as taking direction from Moscow and ultimately the Jews.

One of the problems with the kind of self-censorship Pound engaged in is determining which code is in play. A comparison of notebook drafts and final printing shows that Pound himself sometimes got mixed up. Add in the frequent errors, most by Pound, some by his printers, in these late poems and you get a textual surface that is unusually distorted, cramped, and compressed, making them even more difficult to read.[7]

The code we are most concerned with in these late cantos conceals resistance to the racial integration of schools and the inevitable "mongrelization" of society once racial equality was achieved. The Warren Court's rulings directed by the Jewish/Communist conspiracy fulfilled its long-term desire to destroy the white race and the "American way of life." Resistance required an appeal to states' rights.

John Randolph of Roanoke

The arch-republican John Randolph of Roanoke is something of a leitmotif from Canto 88 onward. He figures prominently in Cantos 88 and 89 as a figure lifted from Senator Thomas Hart Benton's recollections of Andrew Jackson's "bank war." Pound links Randolph with his then-allies Benton, Martin van Buren, and Andrew Jackson (89/616) as a proponent of the rights of the states. In Canto 107 Pound remarks that Randolph has been a victim of the historic "blot-out,"[8] listing Randolph with Alexander the Great (because he paid his soldiers) and Antoninus Pius (who kept marine insurance to a minimum) as historical nonpersons for practicing economic sanity. Why Randolph?

Randolph surfaces in *The Cantos* for three reasons. One, he was a radical republican of the Jeffersonian persuasion, a firm believer in "the principles of 1798," as expressed in the Virginia and Kentucky resolutions that interpreted the US Constitution to be a voluntary compact, not a binding contract, between the states that could be repudiated at the states' discretion, the position underlying all states' rights interpretations of the Constitution. Pound would know that James Kilpatrick of the *Richmond News Leader* had revived these resolutions and published them in "lengthy excerpts" in the autumn of 1955 to support resistance to *Brown* (Muse 1964: 70–1).[9] Second (and consequently), in Canto 100 Randolph becomes an Aesopian figure for more contemporary states' rights agitators reacting to the Supreme Court's "encroachments" onto state sovereignty. Pound deploys Randolph's states' rights creed as both critique of the Warren Court and the *Brown* decisions of 1954 and 1955 and support for the "massive resistance" then being organized in Virginia to defy federally mandated integration of schools, which would lead, Pound thought, to the destruction of the United States.

Harry Meacham, the poetry reviewer for Kilpatrick's paper, became interested in Pound the poet and later wrote a book about their relationship featuring their correspondence—*The Caged Panther: Ezra Pound at St. Elizabeths* (1967)— that is a main source for this section. Meacham corresponded with Pound, visited him at the hospital, and agitated for his release. To look ahead, briefly, Meacham persuaded Kilpatrick to write a significant editorial about Pound's situation—"EZRA POUND: SET HIM FREE!" published in February 1958— that concluded, "No possible useful purpose is served by keeping Pound locked up in St. Elizabeths. To all intents and purposes, he remains a political prisoner— in a nation that prides itself on political freedom. What does it take to get him free" (qtd in Meacham 1967: 68). The editorial may have helped secure Pound's release in April that year.

In October 1955 the second *Brown* decision on implementation (*Brown* II) threatened to put the federally mandated integration of schools into practice. In response Kilpatrick reprinted in his editorials the 1798 Virginia and Kentucky Resolutions, the anti-federalist creed of Randolph, Jefferson, and James Madison.

Advocating resistance to the federal government through the doctrine of "interposition" drawn directly from the "legacy of Jefferson and Madison and the 'principles advocated so forcefully' by the two, Kilpatrick argued that they had 'great validity today' in the present school crisis" (Lewis 2006: 63). "Interposition" "was the doctrine once held by Southern leaders that a state had the right to 'interpose its sovereignty between the federal government and its people'" (Muse 1961: 20). "Interposition" is akin to antebellum legal strategies of constitutional "nullification" and other discredited states' rights doctrines, which were revived in the 1950s as part of the South's resistance to integration. Kilpatrick's editorializing was designed to influence the Virginia legislature, which in September was considering revising its Constitution to preserve its dual school system at any cost, including abolishing the public schools altogether. As we know, Pound was also to be involved in efforts to revise the Constitution of Virginia through *Virginians On Guard!* distributed in Virginia by Kasper and his Seaboard White Citizens Council in August of 1956 (see *JK & EP* 133–49). So Randolph's radical brand of Jeffersonian politics made him useful as an Aesopian cover name for Pound's own politicking via his *Cantos*.

There is a third reason John Randolph is important. He is an ancestral connection of Dorothy's, so he stands as a tribute to her perseverance during the years of his incarceration, helping to certify Pound's authority. Randolph was a close cousin of Dorothy's maternal great-grandfather, St. George Tucker, who married Randolph's widowed mother and raised the boy, a fact alluded to in Canto 88 (88/599).

In his mock autobiography *Indiscretions* (1923), Pound bragged that "one could write the whole history of the United States from one's family annals" (*P&D* 6), an important strategy in *The Cantos*, which make regular references (often in Aesopian code) to family and friends. In *Rock-Drill* Pound attends the appearance of Randolph with a shout-out to Dorothy, interrupting the narrative of Randolph's duel with Secretary of State Henry Clay to remind us that "His (R's) stepfather / brought out a 'Blackstone'" (88/599), an edition of the British legal bible in 1803 (Meacham 1967: 156). This is St. George Tucker; on the next page, Pound quotes from this edition, establishing Tucker's work as part of the source-field for *The Cantos*.

"My wife's connections go back to that Tucker who married John Randolph's ma and brought out a Blackstone," Pound noted in a September 1957 letter to Meacham (1967: 51). Dorothy explained more fully to Meacham about Tucker (1752–1827), a Virginia notable and patriot who fought against Cornwallis in the Yorktown campaign and later became a distinguished judge (Meacham 1967: 156).

Her own branch of the family returned to England before the American Revolution, but Dorothy's connection to one of Virginia's first families—"The Tuckers are to Virginia what the Lowells are to Massachusetts," Meacham remarks (1967: 155–6)—was important enough that one of the first things the Pounds did together after Ezra's release from St. Elizabeths was to visit the Tucker house at Williamsburg in Meacham's company on May 1, 1958.

St. George Tucker married John Randolph's mother when John was five years old, and John was raised on the Tucker plantation—wonderfully named "Bizarre"—which he inherited. A direct descendent of Pocahontas, Randolph became an extreme republican and anti-federalist and an explicator of states' rights doctrine. He was a slave-owner who, as Pound notes twice in his poem, freed his slaves after his death ("liberavit masnatos" [90/626; see also 89/616]).[10] Randolph was aristocratic, charming, brilliant, bad-tempered, in constant ill-health (possibly from syphilis or some unknown genetic disorder), and, by the end, of doubtful sanity. An owner of enormous estates and hundreds of slaves, like Jefferson he preached the virtues of agriculture. Like Jefferson, he was burdened by debt, and like all Virginians he hated banks and bankers. In his biography of Randolph, Henry Adams marked his politics:

> Dread of the Executive, of corruption and patronage, of usurpations by the central government; dread of the Judiciary as an invariable servant of despotism; dread of national sovereignty altogether, were the slogans of this creed. All these men foresaw what the people of America would be obliged to meet; they were firmly convinced that the central government, intended to be the people's creature and servant, would one day make itself the people's master, and, interpreting its own powers without asking permission, would become extravagant, corrupt, despotic. (Adams 1882: 56–7)

These same fears define American populism to this day. They are in line with Pound's own views in the 1950s. He was a devoted Jeffersonian from early on and, as I have shown in *John Kasper and Ezra Pound*, influenced by anti-Reconstruction pro-Southern revisionism. Pound wrote Meacham of his life-long interest in Virginia and Jefferson, even enquiring of Meacham if the stables at Monticello might be available as living quarters (Meacham 1967: 83).[11]

Randolph first enters *The Cantos* through Senator Thomas Hart Benton's memoir of his public life, *Thirty Years' View* (1854), part of which Pound redacted to form the hearts of Cantos 88 and 89 published in the *Hudson Review* in the summer of 1955. His source chapters appeared as a Square $ publication, *Bank of the United States* (1954), obviously intended as a useful gloss on the poems. These cantos are concerned with the recharter of the Bank of the United States, which Benton, a true-blue Jeffersonian, opposed. Nonetheless, Canto 88 begins with an extensive account of Randolph's inconclusive duel with Secretary of State Henry Clay on April 8, 1826, caused by Randolph's abuse of the secretary in Senate debate.[12] Pound uses the action to show Randolph asking for his money at the local bank preparatory to crossing the Potomac for his combat. Randolph refuses the paper bills offered him and demands hard money, real money: gold.

This extended story, which takes up much of Canto 88, is the Aesopian parable of the Virginian resisting the federal government: Randolph vs Clay. It shows that the Virginian has a Jeffersonian concept of money,[13] as opposed to the bank's and the government's view. The federal government is corrupt, Pound implies, because of its financial arrangements. Randolph liked to refer to his opponents as "white slaves" doing their master's bidding, their masters being the money power of the north-east: Philadelphia, New York, and Boston. Pound argues in *The Cantos* that the Civil War was caused by northern financial machinations, not slavery. "J[ohn] Q[uincy] A[dams] objecting to slavery," he complains in Canto 89 (89/613), leaving his real meaning unsaid, which is, "when he should have been objecting to usury." Later, in Canto 103, he will tell us, "The slaves were red herring / land not secure against issuers" (103/752) of bonds and mortgages who prosper by enslaving others through debts.[14]

In Canto 100 Randolph comes in under Aesopian cover when Pound coyly assigns to Andrew Jackson language Terrell shows is Randolph's. "'That Virginia be sovereign,' said Andy Jackson, 'never parted with'" (100/735). At the end of his life John Randolph offered some resolutions in the Charlotte courthouse to the effect "**That Virginia** is, and of right, ought to **be**, a free **sovereign** and independent state ... [W]hen Virginia joined the other twelve colonies ... she **parted with** no portion of her sovereignty" (qtd in Terrell 1984: 648).[15] Ironically, as Eaves and Kimpel noted years ago, these resolutions were made *against* Jackson, but from the 1930s on Pound preferred ideological consistency to historical accuracy in his rendition of history, especially American history. He found these resolutions in Martin Van Buren's *Autobiography* (1983: 424–5) and alludes to them in Canto 88 (89/618). They were part of the states' rights talk at St Elizabeths.

Cantos 88 and 89, about Benton and the Bank War, were designed to call attention to the Jeffersonian interpretation of the United States at precisely the same time and for the same reasons as Kilpatrick's editorials espousing states' rights. This can be seen in two ways, by the publication by Kasper & Horton's Square $ Books of the chapters from Benton's *Thirty Years' View* from which the cantos are redacted and by the invention of the "Benton Award" given by the DAC to honor the member of Congress who had best defended the US Constitution from judicial and executive usurpation (see *JK & EP* 105–113). The point is that Cantos 88 and 89 were composed not as historical curiosities but as activist poetry.

Canto 103

In 1960 Pound told Donald Hall that in *Thrones* he was "trying to collect the record of top flights of the mind" (Hall 1992: 332), so it's tempting to smile at Pound's Quixotic attempt in Canto 103 to rehabilitate Millard Fillmore (comically misspelled "Fillimore" on 103/754), Franklin Pierce, and James Buchanan, three of the most obscure American presidents. None of the three were intellectual or political high flyers, so why is the better part of Canto 103 devoted to quoting them?

Canto 103 has resisted would-be commentators. Bacigalupo, Wilhelm, and Makin have next to nothing to say about it except for nodding to its obvious Americanness; Moody avoids it. Canto 103 doesn't fit the paradisal paradigm, so it is not relevant to Liebregts's Neoplatonic project. Moody merely acknowledges the canto's existence. Kindellan spends time on Pound's mistaken claim "Talleyrand started / no war in Europe" (103/753) that the poet went to such neurotic lengths to correct to the present "one war," including insisting on the introduction of errata slips, causing the elimination of the lines altogether from the Faber & Faber *Thrones*. What's perplexing is Pound's refusal to address other mistakes that were just as glaring (Kindellan 2017: 189–202). In any case, Kindellan's detailed philological approach to Pound's antiphilology in *The Late Cantos* did not allow him to dilate on the overall meaning of Canto 103.[16]

Kimpel and Eaves's "American History in *Rock-Drill* and *Thrones*"[17] devotes a few trenchant pages to the sources of the canto, and Carroll Terrell's valuable commentary reads as "notes toward" a latent, unwritten essay. Other than these, James Dowthwaite's reading of Canto 103 in *Glossator* 10 is a rare, almost unique, and thereby commendable attempt to read the whole poem. Dowthwaite concludes that the canto is "perhaps best seen as a recapitulation of *The Cantos*' dominant political and economic theses. Its specific central theme is that rulers with good intentions have had their plans or legacies ruined by external forces beyond their immediate control" (*G* 216). He divides the canto into three— maybe four—parts: US politics c. 1850; the European balance of power as seen through the memoirs of Talleyrand; and finally a return to US politics and

President Buchanan, concluding or perhaps scattering into readings of Paul the Deacon and Del Mar (*G* 216). Dowthwaite doesn't mention Pound's closing gestures toward Hitler's resistance to finance via the Nazi term "Leihkapital"— Loan-capital—and the (then) unpublished "Mensdorf [sic] letter" written in 1928 from Vienna in concert with Count Mensdorff asking the Carnegie Endowment to look into the causes of war with a view toward outlawing it (103/757; see also Pound 1960b: 281–2). In fact, these last lines, added in 1958 to a canto that had been gestating since at least 1953, are an essential aid in reading the poem.

Dowthwaite is not wrong, but he could have been more specific. The "external forces" are in every case financial speculators—the Mensdorff letter calls them "interested cliques"—who in Pound's reading of nineteenth-century history ("the age of usury" *GK* 26) work behind the scenes to foment wars so as to create debts from which they profit. As this is one of the poet's hobby horses, perhaps it is not worth getting into here—what we really wish to know is *why* Pound takes this sudden interest in all-but-forgotten US presidents and *why* the deliberations and effects of Talleyrand and Metternich's reconstruction of Europe in the 1830s and beyond is suddenly important. There are two reasons. First, Pound wants to inject states' rights ideology into his poem in order to support Southern resistance to racial integration. Second, he wants to show how history is *made* (it doesn't just happen) behind the scenes by those "interested cliques."

For the American side of Canto 103, Pound uses three presidential biographies: William Elliot Griffis's *Millard Fillmore: Constructive Statesman, Defender of the Constitution* (1915); Roy Nichols's *Franklin Pierce: Young Hickory of the Granite Hills* (1931); and George Ticknor Curtis's two-volume *Life of James Buchanan* (1883). Pound weaves together these three Democratic prewar administrations in a way that seems to have frightened off most commentators, especially as these American references are counterpointed by adventures into European— and obliquely even Caribbean—politics. The European side of the canto is mostly derived from the five volumes of *Memoirs of the Prince de Talleyrand* (trans. 1891),[18] continuing a strand that is present in Canto 101. Let's take it from the top:

> 1850: gt objection to any honesty in the White House (103/752)

The reason Pound suddenly turns to 1850 to open Canto 103 is because he believes in the "repeat in history."[19] He thinks that the political struggle that led to the American Civil War of 1861–5 is instructive about the current struggle between North and South, white and black in the USA in the wake of *Brown*. "1850" points to the Compromise of 1850 that maintained a shaky balance between Southern, strict Constitutional constructionist, proslavery expansionists and Northern Constitutional moralists, who saw slavery as a curse upon the country and a betrayal of its ideals. States' rights doctrine, the mainstay of Southern recalcitrance from the very birth of this nation,[20] is a significant strand in the late cantos and marked in Canto 103. The assertion of the rights of states to resist "encroachment" of their sovereignty by the federal government was the argument used by the Southern states to justify their secession from the Union in 1861 and was being deployed again as part of the massive resistance intended to uphold Jim Crow folkways in the face of the school integration mandated by *Brown*.

"The Compromise of 1850" was regarded by President Fillmore, who signed off on it on September 18, 1850, as having delayed the Civil War for a decade (Griffis 1915: 76). A century later, Pound seeks guidance from that far-off but profoundly relevant compromise that, for a time, repressed the "irrepressible conflict" and put off disaster. Pound was well aware of the violence accompanying school integration; it was not all that extreme to think that the Civil Rights struggle might lead to another civil war.[21] Fillmore may be said to rhyme with others Pound celebrates who did their best to forestall warfare, like Edward VIII. Beyond delaying the inevitable, what's difficult for the reader to assess is just where Pound stands on the 1850 Compromise; just because it *is* a compromise, Pound's position is, at first, unclear.

In one sense it's surprising that Pound does not present the protracted and pyrotechnic debate that eventually birthed the famous 1850 Compromise, which featured the greatest orators and most powerful and charismatic senators of the nineteenth century: Henry Clay, Daniel Webster, Stephen A. Douglas, William Seward; the dying architect of Southern nationalism, John C. Calhoun; and Pound's hero, Thomas Hart Benton, who features so strongly in Cantos 88 and 89. The speeches made at these debates are among the greatest in American history; the passions ran high, the stakes were existential. Yet none of these towering figures are even named in Canto 103. Why *not* give us Benton facing down the drawn horse pistol of Henry Foote of Mississippi on the floor of the Senate, shouting "Let him fire! ... Let the assassin fire!" (qtd in Bordewich 2012: 220). But Pound is not Stephen Vincent Benét: he's not engaged in writing a narrative; he's engaged in polemic. The fact of the Compromise, its success in delaying and its ultimate failure to prevent a civil war, is what concerns him.

The opening line of Canto 103 is difficult to construe historically, as there were two presidents in 1850. President Zachary Taylor (a tough-minded Louisiana slaveholder but a dedicated Unionist) died in July of that year while the Compromise was being hammered out in Congress. He was succeeded by his able vice-president, Millard Fillmore, who signed the bill into law in September. Franklin Pierce, to whose administration Pound turns in the next line, "'56, an M.C. from California" (103/752), was elected in 1852. So in his opening Pound can only have Fillmore, not Pierce or Taylor, in mind.

The part of the great compromise that is bitterly remembered is the Fugitive Slave Act that enforced Southern property rights over their enslaved labor, even when these "fugitives from service" (as Buchanan biographer Curtis puts it, euphemistically [Curtis 1883: vol. 2, 268]), found their way north to "free-soil." They now could be brought back by US Marshals detailed for the purpose; moreover, anyone who helped these fugitives could be charged for being accessories and accomplices and even rebels. The imposition of this law and several notorious violent renditions of fugitives, notably of Thomas Sims and Anthony Burns, further radicalized an already agitated North.[22] Despite upholding the all-but-sacred right to private property, Fillmore is forever tarred with supporting the bill, as is his successor, Franklin Pierce, who said in an 1857 speech at Boston's Faneuil Hall (ironically, given Pound's point, his first public oration *after* his presidency) that Northerners must be "respectful of our own rights and the rights of others," for which "decent view," Pound tells us, he was ousted from office. The "gt objection to any honesty in the White House" must mean that Fillmore and, by extension, Pierce were vilified by antislavery agitators for upholding the US Constitution and his oath of office (Fillmore) and upholding the law of the land (Pierce).

Elected vice-president under Zachary Taylor, Millard Fillmore became the thirteenth president of the United States following Taylor's unexpected death. Fillmore did not stand for reelection and remained president until Pierce's inauguration in March 1853. If he is remembered at all today it is usually because he signed the Fugitive Slave Law. But that infamous law was but one part of the great Compromise of 1850 that brought California into the United States as a free state, outlawed the buying and selling of human beings (but not slavery) in the District of Columbia, and settled the problematic western boundary of the new State of Texas (which had threatened to metastasize into as many as four different slave-states) while organizing New Mexico and Utah as vast territories that included present-day Nevada and Arizona. These territories would decide through "popular sovereignty" whether to become slave or free states once they gained statehood, which fortunately did not occur until decades after slavery was abolished. As part of this territorial compromise, the US government paid out substantial sums, in large part to eliminate the Texas debt by buying up money and bonds issued by that short-lived former republic. These were now mostly held by speculators who lobbied Congress relentlessly because they stood to profit if these bonds were redeemed at even a fraction of their stated value (see Beard & Beard 1930: 597–9). How much of this latter aspect of the Compromise Pound may have known or guessed at is unclear; it does not appear in Griffis, nor does Curtis mention it.[23] What does appear in Griffis is a report of

> the Act fixing boundaries, granting a civil government to New Mexico and to Texas a bonus of ten millions of dollars in United States bonds bearing interest of five percent on condition of all land exterior to those boundaries as well as all claims on the United States and of a territorial government in New Mexico, whose four years of military rule were now over. (1915: 68)

This passage may have influenced Pound's observation that "the land is not secure against issuers" (103/752), possibly holders of Texas paper, using their influence to pervert legislation in their favor—a recurring theme in American history from the "Scandal of the Assumption" (otherwise the "Compromise of 1790") to modern-day bank bailouts.

Though it does not appear in the canto but remains behind it, so to speak, "popular sovereignty"—a concept associated forever with Stephen Douglas as part of the Kansas-Nebraska Act—must have struck Pound. His own slogan, "local control of local affairs," was similar. The difference was that Pound knew there was no local control without some form of local purchasing power (preferably Gesellite currency), as he had proposed in *Virginians on Guard!* (see *JK & EP* 134, 141). He knew that "there was no sense of quiddity" (103/752) in merely popular sovereignty. Following Alexander Del Mar, he knew that "sovereignty inhered in the power to issue" money; that is, currency creditably backed by actual production, a power liable to be usurped by private bankers and perverted by speculators.

Millard Fillmore unexpectedly takes his place in *The Cantos* as one of the country's best executives thanks to Pound's source, William Elliot Griffis's 1915 laudatory biography. Fillmore is praised in Canto 103 for his honesty and for his work in the New York legislature abolishing prison for debtors (Griffis 1915: 5; 103/754); when in Congress, Fillmore pushed for the construction of a warship to deter British aggression in the Great Lakes. The innovative iron ship *Wolverine*, built in Pittsburgh, effectively "dismantled every fort and dismounted every gun, American and British, along a frontier of three thousand miles" (Griffis 1915: 18–19; 103/754) without firing a shot, inaugurating an epoch of peaceful relations between Britain, Canada, and the United States that obtains till now. Pound no doubt felt there was a lesson there. Also, while in Congress Fillmore was instrumental in securing funding for Samuel Morse's world-changing invention of the telegraph (Griffis 1915: 24–9; 103/754). As president (1850–2) he directed Commodore Matthew Perry's "opening" of Japan (see 88/602) and tried to reassure the Japanese that the USA was interested in trade, not plunder (Griffis 1915: 95; 103/755). Like Fenollosa (whom he may have known) Griffis lived and taught in Japan (1870–4), and he later wrote many books about the Far East. The lines in the canto having to do with the Rev. Beecher and the Bunker Hill cannonballs (103/755) derive from Griffis and refer to the great public enthusiasm for the Hungarian freedom-fighter Lajos Kossuth, the flamboyant hero of the failed revolutions of 1848 (Griffis 1915: 81). Pound even quotes the biography and Griffis by name in Canto 103, citing his judgment re: "the colossal conceit of Americans" (103/755) in imagining that "Commodore Perry virtually created the New Japan." In that same passage Griffis notes prophetically how, as a result of the Japanese expedition, Fillmore

> helped to bring before the American people a social and racial problem, that is destined to shake the world. The "white man" must now descend from his exalted throne to consider the claims of intellectual equality of Asian men of color. The American—spoiled by the experience of red and black men—the conquered and enslaved—has, very naturally, considered the men of Asia inferior ... Now he is compelled by the men of [Asia] to think, study, read history and acquaint himself with much of which he is ignorant (Griffis 1915: 95)

Pound would have sincerely endorsed this view, which agrees with everything he ever wrote about Japan. All in all, Griffis's Fillmore is a paragon: sober, judicious, firm, and statesmanlike,[24] far from the symbol of obscurity he has now become.

Using selective quotations from Roy Nichols's biography of the fourteenth president, Pound gives the impression that Franklin Pierce was "ousted" from the presidency in the opening lines of Canto 103; although, typically, Pierce is not mentioned by name. Thus:

> '56 an M.C. from California
> > killed one of the waiters at the Willard
> 22nd. Brooks thrashed Sumner in Camera Senatus
> "respectful of our own rights and of others"
> > for which decent view he was ousted (103/752)

Somehow, Pound manages to praise South Carolina Congressman Preston Brooks for all but clubbing to death the abolitionist Senator Charles Sumner of Massachusetts in 1856 for telling the truth about slavery (103/752). These lines, derived from a single page of Nichols (1931: 464), are deliberately garbled so that words spoken by Pierce supporting states' rights and the Fugitive Slave Law urging antislavery and proslavery hotheads to be "respectful of our own rights and of others[']" (103/752) seem to be ascribed to Brooks (who manifestly did *not* support the rights of others), thereby giving the impression that Pierce, not Brooks, was "ousted" from office much like Edward VIII. In fact, the unpopular Pierce could not stand for reelection; the nomination fell to James Buchanan because the Democratic party had shattered over the slavery issue, its free-soil faction splitting off to become the new Republican party. Meanwhile, to *avoid* being ousted, Brooks resigned from Congress after a farewell speech upholding the South, making him wildly popular in his home state, South Carolina, which promptly reelected him (see Terrell 1984: 663). At the same time Pound insists that "the slaves were red herring" as cause of the Civil War (103/752) because the Civil War was fomented by "issuers" or, as Pound put it in the Mensdorff letter, "[t]he intrigues of interested cliques" (1960b: 281; 103/757), who encouraged the federal coercion of the several states in order to create debts and roil the financial markets. "Still market, no use to brokers," Pound warns darkly (103/753). Part of the remedy, as will be seen, is the assertion of the rights of the states because "the Union" is "a grant from States of limited powers" (103/756)—the states' rights position revived by Southern resistance to *Brown*.[25]

Near the end of Canto 103, Pound quotes from President Buchanan's inaugural address, given March 1857, which was directed at the issues of his day. Pound's extract focuses on the issue of expansion of slavery into the western territories of Kansas and Nebraska. Thanks to the Kansas-Nebraska Act of 1854, the question was to be decided by the voters of the new states themselves (when they became states), not by the federal government—an unfortunate extension of Douglas's "popular sovereignty" idea that had been bruited but never tested in the Compromise of 1850. Pound merges passages from two places in Buchanan's "inaugural":

> That men have sunk to consider the mere material value
>   of the Union
> a grant from States of limited powers (103/756)

Buchanan used this states' rights formula to defend the Kansas-Nebraska Act. The catastrophic Act, the brainchild of Stephen Douglas seconded by President Pierce, effectively abrogated the "Missouri Compromise" of 1820, which had served for a generation to keep slavery confined to the Southern areas of the country below the Mason-Dixon line at longitude 36°30′. The 1854 act reopened the possibility of slavery north of the line by making it a local issue. The concept of "popular sovereignty" used to postpone addressing the question of slavery in the new territories of New Mexico and Utah in 1850 was now to be applied to territories ready for statehood. It was like pouring gasoline onto a hot stove.

Predictably, proslavery and antislavery elements moved into the Kansas and Nebraska territories hoping to influence the popular vote, eventually resulting in two territorial governments, one legal and proslavery, the other illegal and antislavery. Soon Kansas was involved in a violent civil struggle earning the title "Bleeding Kansas."[26] Guerrilla warfare between rival pro- and antislavery factions continued for months, including the burning of Lawrence, Kansas, and hundreds of extrajudicial killings.[27]

Quoting Buchanan in support of states' rights, Pound implicitly holds up the Kansas-Nebraska Act of 1854 as a model for how to handle the current crisis of the 1950s. The states should decide if they wish to integrate themselves, not the federal government. For Pound, the *Brown* decisions abrogating *Plessy v. Ferguson*, with its "separate but equal" formula that had served to contain the racial problem in the United States for half a century by providing cover for Jim Crow laws, were equivalent to the Kansas-Nebraska Act. Equivalent—but opposite. Kansas-Nebraska did the right thing, Pound thought, by returning power to the states, whereas *Brown* was usurping the rights of states to govern themselves. Were he voting in 1860, it is probable that Pound would have voted for Stephen Douglas, whose mantra was the sovereign rights of states.[28]

We see by now why Buchanan, Pierce, and Fillmore get so much space in Canto 103. They all interpreted the Constitution as strictly limiting federal power to interfere in the "domestic relations" of the states. Kimpel and Eaves were correct that "the three neglected presidents of Canto CIII had tried to preserve the Union by compromise, not arms, and had been more influenced by their respect for the legal rights of the states than by their dislike of slavery" (Kimpel & Eaves 1980: 435). The historical record seems to say that they were, on the whole, morally indifferent to slavery; to them, it was a business like any other—except for its explosive political ramifications. Still, these men worked to avoid, to delay, and if possible to stop a civil war between North and South. In this they are like King Edward VIII, who, in Pound's view, bought "three years' peace" by negotiating with the Germans in 1936 (86/583, 89/621). For that, not because of Mrs. Simpson but because the warmongers feared the King "would balk and not sign mobilization," Pound tells us, Edward was forced to abdicate (109/793), just as were all three Unionist compromisers and appeasers of the slave power.

Pound's rather conventional judgment of Buchanan—"nec Templum aedificavit / nec restituit rem"; he "neither built the temple nor restored anything"—is tempered by his conclusion that it was "not his fault by a damn sight" (103/756), which raises the question just whose fault it may have been. "External forces," Dowthwaite says, but the canto is quite clear: "Leihkapital" (103/757)—loan capital and the creditors who profit from it.

Pound ties the American situation in the 1850s and the narrative present a century later to European conditions then and now when he follows the Pierce/Brooks tangle with a kind of equation:

Homestead versus kolschoz
Rome   versus Babylon (103/752)

Homestead and Rome are assigned to the realm of virtue where coexist the American dream of individual independence and Roman (including fascist) order. These are opposed to Soviet agricultural collectives and "Babylon," a consistent metonym for "the Jews" and therefore financial scheming, from *The Pisan Cantos* forward. In brief: freedom and order versus a Jewish/Communist tyranny.

The key term "Homestead" also recalls Sumner Welles, who appears in censored form in Canto 100 as "S ... W ... fished out of a duck pond—" (100/733). This is certainly Roosevelt confidante and former undersecretary of state Sumner Welles. Pound remembered that Welles was found all but frozen to death near his Maryland home December 26, 1948, after a mysterious late-night walk. He had apparently fallen into a nearby stream, then crawled ashore, to lie out all night in temperature well below freezing.[29] The connection is obscure, but the name of Congressman Brooks's victim, Senator Charles Sumner, is echoed by Sumner Welles's first name because it happens that Welles is a direct descendant of the noble abolitionist senator. Moreover, Pound was a cautious admirer of Welles's May 9, 1943, speech at Toledo, Ohio, in which Welles condemned "economic aggression" and praised the homestead. Their mutual interest in the homestead probably explains Pound's signal about Welles in Canto 100. Pound devoted five radio speeches in May 1943 to considering Welles's Toledo speech. He must have concluded that Welles's sudden and, at the time, baffling resignation from the government later that year in August had to do with that speech, which Pound interpreted as a critique of US "dollar diplomacy" and its usual aggressive way of doing global business. In fact, Welles resigned from the government because of a sex scandal, but neither Pound nor anybody else except a very few administration insiders knew of this. Pound thought that Welles's resignation from the government in 1943 rescued him from further contact with the muddy "duck pond" of the Roosevelt administration.

In his first radio speech on Welles's Toledo talk, Pound noticed that Welles "quite clearly and definitely mentioned the common man's desire to have a house of his own for his own family. That is what we believe National Socialism stands for in Germany. It is what Italy stands for. It is quite emphatically what Communist Russia does NOT stand for, and would not stand for by program" (5/11/1943; Doob 1978: RS #85).[30] By the 1950s, Pound was reading *Hitler's Table Talk* in the fall of 1953, so he knew that the Germans, had they been victorious, planned to repopulate the decimated East with farmsteads given to military veterans by a grateful Reich. This Roman practice was also emulated by the United States in Pierce's time. Pound quotes from Nichols's biography Pierce's approval of a bill offering "land to all veterans: Mommsen [the celebrated historian of Rome] / 160 acres, 33rd Congress" (103/752; Nichols 1931: 379). Pound elaborated in the Bridson interview: "Lack of local government is an effect not a cause. The contest between the homestead and the *kolkhoz*." He continues: "Mommsen noted that the Roman Empire endured longer than oriental tyrannies because they settled veterans on the land. Civilization is from the homestead. The Russian revolution was a fake: it pretended to attack capital—the general understanding that that was loan capital—and it merely attacked peasant property down to the peasant's cow" (qtd in Cookson 2001: 243). This is what Pound means in Canto 103.

Just as the then-unprinted radio speeches illuminate this canto, Noel Stock observed that "we are better able to follow what is going on in *Thrones*" if we know something about the numerous "unsigned or pseudonymous items Pound contributed" to dissident publications directed by his acolytes when they were being composed (Stock 1966: 104). Carroll Terrell's notes elucidating the "Homestead versus kolschoz" passage above are exceptionally useful because they draw on remarks Pound published in Bill McNaughton's *Strike* 5 (October 1955).[31] In his *Strike* piece, Pound used Mencius's "nine field" system to criticize Soviet land policy (Terrell 1984: 663–4) and asked, in regard to American China policy, whether the Voice of America was using Mencius's "idea in the fight against Communism in China. Bolshevism started off as an attack against loan-capital and quickly shifted into an attack against the homestead" (qtd in Terrell 1984: 664). Although Joe McCarthy had lost his power by this time, it is significant that, in the *Strike* article, Pound attacks two of the senator's favorite targets, the Voice of America and the State Department "China hands," as well as using Hitler's term "loan-capital" (*Leihkapital*) to score against the Bolsheviks. Again, loan capital signifies the preferred mode through which economic imperialism as practiced by Anglo-American finance works; loan capital seeks investment opportunities abroad, leading, Lenin argued, to inevitable global conflict.

Pound correctly saw Lenin's heirs trying to exacerbate global tensions by dumping goods abroad while enslaving the Soviet masses at home—it is a recurrent theme in his Axis radio speeches and a primary cause of war according to the Mensdorff letter (Pound 1960b: 281). The temporary alliance between Great Britain, the USA, and the USSR (1941–5) remains one of the most unlikely events of the time, fertile ground for the worst sort of speculation about an immense global conspiracy invoked by McCarthy. So, with this passage from *Strike* in play, we may revisit the cryptic lines about Sumner Welles (100/733) and judge that Pound intends to rehabilitate Welles on McCarthyite grounds. Pound is thinking of Welles's exemplary career in the Department of State, otherwise that nest of traitors and spies, culminating in his honest but ill-advised criticism of economic aggression.

Returning to Canto 103, we can see that Pound's historical equation, homestead versus *kolkhoz*, provides a schema for reading the canto as a whole. There is a dialectic throughout that poses the homestead as the manifestation of social order, "civilization," epitomized by Rome, which can be connected to the Compromise of 1850 and the effort by the three presidents "willing the national good" to prevail against the nineteenth-century version of the Jewish conspiracy later manifest in the oppressive Soviet collective farm.[32] Economic anarchy stirred up by profit-seeking Jews (Babylon) who pull the strings behind the scenes created a civil war to destroy the USA in the 1860s. Now they were doing it again. After a digression addressing the funeral of Nathaniel Hawthorne, Pierce's closest friend,[33] Pound turns back to political questions:

> names of the principal bond-holders
> —persuade Spain to sell Cuba
>   via Belmont, not Sickles (103/752)

Pound's poetic telegraphy gestures to the feelers put out by the Pierce administration to Spanish bondholders with an offer to "persuade Spain to sell Cuba" to the USA in order to raise cash to pay off its debts. Pierce's agent was August Belmont, who Pound could see was an agent for the Rothschilds (Nichols 1931: 357).

Buying, or alternatively invading, Cuba was a lively geopolitical fantasy of Southerners who dreamed of a New World slave empire. Slavery was already legal in Cuba, so acquiring the island would have greatly augmented the slave power, economically, politically, and geographically. By 1850, rumors were about that the Spanish were mulling ending slavery in their empire as the British had recently done (1834). In Cuba the result would be "Africanization," as had happened to Haiti, which would encourage abolition efforts in the United States, so there was pressure from the slave power to act fast. An invasion of Cuba by armed "filibusters" in August 1851, supported by the governor of Mississippi and other prominent Southerners, was a fiasco similar to the Bay of Pigs 110 years later (Bordewich 2012: 230–8). However, indiscreet Dan Sickles made Pierce's approaches to European bankers public just before the 1854 midterm election, dismaying the Northern Democrats, who were Pierce's principal base of power, thus further eroding Congressional support for any Cuba intervention. Pound's anti-bank ideology makes unlikely any support for Pierce's underhanded scheme to buy Cuba so that Spain could pay its debts. "It's hard to believe," Kimpel and Eaves write, "that Pound approved their plan, which originated with Belmont, an agent of the Rothschilds." On the other hand, at the time Pierce could be said to be using purchase as an alternative to war; in any case, "no disapproval is indicated in Pound's lines" (Kimpel & Eaves 1980: 431–2).

If the ideological schema—Homestead/Rome versus *Kolschoz*/Babylon—is one way to approach Canto 103, another is to take the hint Pound gives from *The Analects* just a little further down the page. Confucius asks Tze-Kung who comprehends most, and the student modestly replies: "I see its relation to one thing, / Hui sees its relation to ten" (103/752). Pound's translation in *Confucius* is a bit clearer: "Hui hears one point and relates it to ten, I to one only; I hear one point and can only get to the next" (*Con*. 210). This is Pound's definition of genius: "Genius ... is the capacity to see ten things where the ordinary man sees one" (*J/M* 88).[34] The canto is written as a genius might have done—each point is related to many others. Still, by looking at the Mensdorff letter we are able to guess at the "one point" centering the network of relationships the canto presents. That point is the danger posed by loan capital, the debt weapon wielded by the external force sensed by Dowthwaite.

The Mensdorff letter urging a comprehensive investigation of the causes of war was composed by Pound and Count Albert Mensdorff in Vienna in 1928. It was sent to Nicholas Murray Butler, who was the director of the Carnegie Endowment for Peace (and president of Columbia University 1902–45). Count Mensdorff was the very distinguished Austro-Hungarian diplomat whom Pound had got to know in London. He is the "Albert" mentioned in Canto 19 (19/87).[35] An Anglophile, Mensdorff worked steadily to maintain peace in Europe, so much so that he was kept in the dark by his own government about belligerent Austro-Hungarian intentions toward England in August 1914. Mensdorff's connections reinforce a strand in Canto 103 that runs through Vienna with all the European machinations and tensions "Vienna" implies.[36] Mensdorff, Metternich, even Kossuth (hidden behind Rev. Beecher's Bunker Hill cannonballs) twine together.

The burden of the Mensdorff letter was that the Carnegie Endowment should explore these several causes of wars. First: "Intense production and sale of munitions; the whole of the trade in munitions and armaments might be subjugated to contemporary, not retrospective investigation via trade channels." Pound himself would undertake this investigation in Canto 38 (1933). Second: "Overproduction and dumping, leading to trade rivalries and irritation." Lenin explores just this dimension of warmongering in *Imperialism*. Finally, "the intrigues of interested cliques" justifies Pound's conspiratorial view of history and much of the didactic thrust of *The Cantos* as a whole.

Nothing ever came of the Mensdorff letter initiative, which is the reason Nick Butler becomes one of the whipping boys in Pound's prose and correspondence. Pound assumed, not without cause, that the Carnegie Endowment was part of the problem; it was merely cover for a liberal capitalist financial system that uses *Leihkapital* to cause "one war after another," loading the lavish festive table for "a usurer's holiday" (76/483).

Although our main interest is the domestic US racial politics running through Canto 103, it is instructive to glance at the equally salient presentation of nimeteenth-century European politics, largely culled from the five volumes of *Memoirs of the Prince de Talleyrand* (trans. 1891). Though the transition from domestic to foreign politics may seem abrupt—on page one of the canto we're mostly in the USA c. 1850s, on the next page we're in the midst of negotiations over Belgian neutrality c. 1830s—this too can be read as Pound's Aesopian method at work. Terrell's perceptive remarks on the "digression" about "Mme de Genlis" and her "gifts of paintings" (103/754) help: "During the decade in which these cantos were written, the same nations of Europe were struggling for position and power, as they always had been, only now the tentacles of intrigue reached into every corner of the world" (Terrell 1984: 668). The effort to restore the balance of power in Europe by creating neutral buffer states links these seemingly different moments. Belgian neutrality was proclaimed first at the Congress of Vienna in the aftermath of Napoleon's defeat in 1815 then reaffirmed in a five-power accord that Pound alludes to here.

For Belgium 1831, read Austria 1955 (see 103/753). In May 1955 the Austrian Independence Treaty was also negotiated and signed in Vienna, with Soviet Foreign Minister Molotov and the American Secretary of State John Foster

Dulles, as well as Britain's Harold Macmillan, officiating. These contemporary names do not appear in the Canto—but there is a reference later to "Buchanan getting a treaty out of the hRooshians" (103/756), which echoes somewhat events of 1955, as the object of the negotiations was to get the USSR to withdraw from its part of occupied Austria. Pound was skeptical of this treaty, publishing some of its more objectionable articles in *Strike* and getting Noel Stock to reprint them in *New Times* with the note that Senators Malone, McCarthy, and Jenner—all Pound favorites—had voted against ratifying it, because it seemed to give too much away to the Soviets.[37] As with Belgium in 1830, Austria declared itself "permanently neutral." In the canto we read "Protocol Jan. 1831: Belgium neutral / in perpetuity" (103/753). Austrian neutrality went into effect on October 26, 1955, around the time when the canto was being written. Pound is only too aware that Belgian neutrality had not been respected, neither in 1914 nor in 1940; nor were the various compromises with the slave power that punctuated US history from its founding. The final confrontation, as Pound saw it, was the Civil Rights struggle egged on by those "interested cliques" bent on "mongrelizing" the United States. Without a thoroughgoing attempt to explore, analyze, and reject the causes of war, all the diplomatic creativity in the world, whether expressed in Congressional debates or in European Conferences, will come to nothing.

* * *

When indictments against Pound were dismissed on April 18, 1958, he was released as incompetent, in the charge of "the Committee" (his wife Dorothy). Harry Meacham was one of the first to see Pound—they went out for Chinese food the next day—and on April 30 Meacham brought Pound (though not Dorothy) down for drinks and dinner at the exclusive Rotunda Club in the Jefferson Hotel in Richmond.[38] Present, among others, was James J. Kilpatrick, Meacham's friend and editor, who wrote up the evening in a sympathetic and touching article for William F. Buckley's *National Review* (May 24, 1958; reprinted Meacham 1967: 137–42). Kilpatrick admits they did not talk serious politics—"it is useless," he conceded, "to talk serious politics with Ezra Pound. He is the last statesman of a lost cause—a cause lost a thousand years ago—and most of his enemies are dust" (Meacham 1967: 137). Pound's political table-talk, in short, was much too much like *The Cantos*. Nonetheless, Kilpatrick does mention in passing that Pound brought him a personal message of greeting from "Mrs. Lane of Arlington," a segregationist member of the Arlington, Virginia, school board and an acquaintance of Dave Horton,[39] which, if it is the only nod to contemporary politics, does suggest the direct ideological linkage between past and present that Virginia was, as embodied by Randolph and theorized as "states' rights" in these late cantos.

Notes

1. See Leary (1961: 33).
2. Mullins says Pound was not subject to censorship—but only because he entrusted his outgoing mail to Dorothy, not to the hospital mail room (Mullins 1961: 331).
3. "SHUT UP," he chided Louis Dudek in December 1956. Dudek had tried to be helpful by urging Pound's release in his journal, *CIV/n*, No. 4. "You are not supposed to receive any letters from E.P. They are UNSIGNED / and if one cannot trust one's friends to keep quiet re / the {supposed} source / whom can one trust" (Dudek 1974: 105–106).
4. Casillo writes: "Apart from whether he had committed treason, there is no doubt that Pound suffered a degree of persecution during his confinement, which coincided with his post-war anxiety, a climate of political suspicion, McCarthyism etc. At this point in his career it was highly imprudent for Pound, seeking exoneration or pardon, to express too openly many of the political or cultural views for which he had originally been brought to trial." He adds: "In order to include Fascist and anti-Semitic themes in the poem, Pound had to 'encrypt' them" (Casillo 1985: 67). Similar reasons mandated the encryption of his segregationist, states' rights arguments.
5. Governor Earl Warren of California was appointed Chief Justice while Congress was in recess, September 30, 1953. Justice William Brennan (September 29, 1956) and Justice Potter Stewart (October 13, 1958) were also "recess appointments" (see Nichols 2011: 57, 80, 82).
6. "Chief Justice Earl Warren was appointed to that post by Eisenhower for the specific job of ratifying the anti-segregation decision." See Eustace Mullins, "Communism Hits South with Non Segregation. Jewish Marxists Threaten Negro Revolt in America! Communists Plan Black Republic in South," *Common Sense* (Union, NJ), 8(209) (July 1, 1954): 1–4 (at 2). (AH)
7. For example, in Canto 100, Pound records the 1828 electoral vote as "Jackson 83; 83 Adams" (100/736). He should have recorded it as he had earlier, in Canto 88 (88/604), as Jackson 183, Adams 83. Actually, both figures are wrong; the vote was Jackson 178, Adams 83 (see Terrell 1984: 508). In Canto 90 Pound writes: "'Mother Earth in thy lap' / said Randolph" (90/626); but Randolph didn't. The line comes from John Greenleaf Whittier's elegy *on* Randolph, "Randolph of Roanoke."

8   This despite a recent biography of Randolph: Russell Kirk, *Randolph: A Study in Conservative Thought* (Washington, DC: Regnery, 1951). Kirk's publisher Henry Regnery was one of Pound's correspondents and later the publisher of *Impact*. Pound's main source besides Benton's *Thirty Years' View* is the definitive two-volume biography (Bruce 1922).

9   "For six weeks beginning on November 21, 1955, Kilpatrick reprinted lengthy excerpts from both sets of resolutions on the editorial page of the *News Leader* along with other states' rights tracts, solemn editorials, and large portraits of states' rights heroes such as John C. Calhoun" (David John Mays, *Race, Reason, and Massive Resistance: The Diary of David J. Mays, 1954–1959*, edited by James R. Sweeney [Athens and London: University of Georgia Press, 2008], 79). These materials were reprinted in Kilpatrick, *Interposition; Editorials and Editorial Page Presentations, 1955–1956* (Richmond [1956]), where the Virginia and Kentucky Resolutions appear on pp. 1–5. Also included is "Senate joint resolution no. 3, interposing the sovereignty of Virginia against encroachment upon the reserved powers of this State… [Feb. 1, 1956]," pp. 51–4. Senate Joint Resolution 3 was reprinted in "Interposition of Sovereignty of State of Virginia Against Encroachment upon Reserved Powers of That State-Joint Resolution of Virginia Legislature," 102 *Congressional Record*—Senate, Monday, February 6, 1956, pp. 2020–1, online at https://www.govinfo.gov/content/pkg/GPO-CRECB-1956-pt2/pdf/GPO-CRECB-1956-pt2-7-1.pdf. See also *The Doctrine of Interposition, its History and Application: a Report on Senate Joint Resolution 3, General Assembly of Virginia, 1956 [Interposing the Sovereignty of Virginia Against Encroachment upon the Reserved Powers of this State] and Related Matters* ([Richmond]: Commonwealth of Virginia Division of Purchase and Print, 1957), online at https://www.scribd.com/doc/51233647/Doctrine-of-Interposition. Kilpatrick mentions Randolph when he writes: "The right of interposition, as enunciated by Jefferson, Madison, Calhoun, Hayne, Randolph and many others, is seen historically as the States' right to interpose their sovereignty between the Federal Government and the object of its encroachments upon powers reserved to the States. This right rests in the incontrovertible theory that ours is a Union of sovereign States; that the Federal Government exists only by reason of a solemn compact among the States; that each respective State is a coequal party to this compact; that if the compact is violated by the Federal government, every State has a right to judge of the infraction; and that when an issue of contested power arises, only the States themselves, by constitutional process, may finally decide the issue" (Kilpatrick, *Interposition; Editorials and Editorial Page Presentations, 1955–1956*, p. 16). (AH)

10 Randolph not only freed his slaves but provided money in his will for their resettlement in Ohio territory. In all, 383 people were rescued this way, founding the now vanished town of Rossville in Miami County, Ohio.

11 "What to do with Ezra Pound [?] If this country had any imagination they would give him living quarters in the stables at Monticello. seeing he has done more to excite interest in American history. Than any other 3 men living" (EP note to Sheri Martinelli, ca. April 1958, Beinecke YCAL MSS 868, Box 12, folder "Pound, Ezra 1958").

12 Randolph's most colorful insult regarding Clay is that he was "so brilliant yet so corrupt, which like a rotten mackerel by moonlight, shined and stunk" (qtd in Bordewich 2012: 74), but this was not the remark that provoked the duel. The provoking insult seems all but incomprehensible except to devotees of Fielding's *Tom Jones*; Randolph complained on the House floor that he had been defeated "by a coalition of Blifil and Black George—by a combination unheard of till then of the Puritan with the blackleg" (Sawyer 1844: 130). Apparently this is an Aesopian reference to the "corrupt bargain" Clay was reputed to have made with John Quincy Adams in the presidential election of 1824. In exchange for the post of secretary of state, Clay was supposed to have swung his electors in the Electoral College to Adams and away from Andrew Jackson, whom Clay despised. Pound, of course, is a Jackson man (see Cantos 34 and 37).

13 The Jeffersonian attitude toward paper money versus gold and silver is complex, in part having to do with the near unavailability of gold and even silver in the early republic. See Marsh (1998: 26–9).

14 The Crash of 2008 is just the latest in a series of avoidable financial crises caused by these same issuers of bonds, mortgages, and other instruments designed to put people in debt so they can be foreclosed and ruined. Trump's Secretary of the Treasury Steve Mnuchin is a classic representative of this type of usurer.

15 Kimpel and Eaves (1980: 417–39) discuss this and cite Bruce.

> Benton naturally reminded Pound of his earlier source for the Bank war, Martin Van Buren, and there are a good many references to Van Buren's *Autobiography* [16] in Canto 89. On pages 458–59 the *Autobiography* has a flattering picture of Talleyrand, who also appears as one of the heroes of the later cantos: "Van Buren already in '37 unsmearing Talleyrand" (p. 597). Actually it was five years before 1837 that Van Buren formed his favorable opinion. He has a full account of the resolutions which Randolph of Roanoke got adopted at a meeting in 1833 at Charlotte Court House, resolutions against Jackson's opposition to South Carolina's Nullification Act (pp. 424–25), and Pound alludes to these in "Randolph of Roanoke: Charlotte Court House, '32" (p. 598). In Canto 100, page 735, part of Randolph's resolutions ("That Virginia 'is, and of right, ought to be, a free, sovereign and independent state'… when… Virginia entered into a strict league of amity and alliance with the other twelve colonies…, she parted with no portion of her sovereignty" [17] strangely gets assigned to the man they were directed against. (425)

Pound's lines are meant to recall Virginia Senate Joint Resolution 3. Resolution interposing the sovereignty of Virginia against encroachment upon the reserved powers of this State, and appealing to sister States to resolve a question of contested power. (AH)

16 Canto 103 was composed over a long period. Kindellan reports that the groundwork for the canto was sketched out as early as the latter half of 1953 (with the Talleyrand business dating from September 1952). He guesses that the whole was reworked and took canto form in the winter of 1957–8. Kindellan notes that Canto 103 is the only poem in *Thrones* not published separately beforehand and sees it as closer to *Rock-Drill* in spirit rather than to *Thrones* (personal communication 7/20/2019).

17 See Kimpel and Eaves (1980).

18 Terrell suggests that Pound must have used the translated *Memoirs* rather than the original French because his quotes from it are all in English.

19 As Pound tried to explain to his father in a letter of April 11, 1927; see Moody and Moody (2010: 625).

20 Consider Virginia Governor Patrick Henry's objections to the US Constitution in his anti-federalist papers and Virginia speeches. One of his concerns was that federal power would be used to liberate enslaved people. In fact, prior to the Civil War, federal troops were often used to recapture fugitives. The Seminole War was fought, in part, because the Seminoles welcomed refugees from slavery. See Finkelman (1984: 189).

21 Hugh G. Grant, head of the States' Rights Council in Georgia, stated: "Although the front lines in this race war are centered in the South, where the bulk of the Negro population is located, the contest is not sectional, but is national in scope" ("Supports Segregation. States Rights Leader Hits Party Chieftains," *Daily Times News* [Burlington, NC], Wednesday, August 15, 1956, pp. 1 B, 11 B). (AH)

22 The Fugitive Slave Law produced reactions ranging from Harriet Beecher Stowe's *Uncle Tom's Cabin* (1852), the most influential novel ever written in the United States, to Walt Whitman's *Leaves of Grass* (1855) to John Brown's campaign of righteous antislavery terror, bankrolled by prominent New Englanders, "the Secret Six."

23 Pound was a great admirer of Charles Beard, to whom he wrote and hoped to meet on his 1939 visit to the United States. The Beards (Charles and Mary) wrote about the scandal of Texas paper in their *Rise of American Civilization* (1930: 597–9), where Pound could have seen it had he been curious. The problematic Texas bondholders would not be treated in depth until Hamilton Holman's *Prologue to Conflict: The Crisis and Compromise of 1850* (1963: 118–32).

24 Griffis gushes: "Fillmore's foreign policy when he became president [was] fully equal to Washington's in prudence or to Grant's and to [Theodore] Roosevelt's in firmness or to Taft's or Wilson's [in] wisdom" (Griffis 1915: 18).

25 "The Southern Manifesto" of March 12, 1956, deplores the "trend in the federal judiciary undertaking to legislate in derogation of Congress, and to encroach

upon the reserved rights of the States and the people" (qtd in Martin 1998: 220). Incidentally, *Virginians on Guard!* attacked "The Southern Manifesto" as so much senatorial bluster that needed to be backed up with violent action (13).

26 The most famous figure in this savage, guerrilla-style war was the bearded prophet John Brown. Brown is not mentioned in Canto 103, nor elsewhere in *The Cantos*. Incredibly, he is only mentioned *once* in Pound's source, George Ticknor Curtis's *Life of James Buchanan*, and is absent from the index, as is Harper's Ferry. Curtis was the federal commissioner in the Sims case—the first test of the Fugitive Slave Law. Curtis remanded Sims (reputed to be the son of a senator) back to slavery over the protests of a dangerous Boston mob. He was also Dred Scott's cocounsel. Curtis consistently argues that the Civil War was precipitated by Northern aggression—legislative and actual—against the South. Franklin Pierce's biographer Roy Franklin Nichols also sees Northern provocations, not Southern intransigence, as the primary cause of the war. So Pound's "Southern" orientation in the canto is entirely consistent with that of his sources.

27 See Etcheson (2004).

28 Douglas's refusal to compromise on "popular sovereignty" is what split the Democratic Party in 1860 in the face of the Republican threat and Abraham Lincoln. The South was for enforcement of the law—both the Kansas-Nebraska Act and the Fugitive Slave Law. They wanted protection of their slave property over the protests and nonacquiescence of the free states. That is what the Dred Scott case was all about. Thus the South seceded from the Democratic party before seceding from the Union. By refusing to accept Douglas, the "Northern" Democratic nominee, in 1860 they fatally split the party along sectional lines, guaranteeing a Republican victory solely through Northern votes.

29 "Welles, Stricken, Lies in Field For Hours in Icy Weather," *New York Times*, December 27, 1948, pp. 1, 18. The article, by Jay Walz, reports that Welles was "deeply upset by the tragic death of Laurence Duggan, a former State Department official who was a close personal friend. Mr. Duggan died in a sixteen story fall from his office window Dec. 20." Duggan was suspected, correctly as we now know, of being a Soviet spy. Welles had defended Duggan, just as Dean Acheson had defended Alger Hiss. Like those of others under investigation by Congress, Duggan's "suicide" was convenient. His defenestration has long been the subject of conspiracy theories. Eustace Mullins said of Duggan: "Many eunuchs who became a liability to the World Order have been eliminated without mercy. When Hiss, White and others faced Congressional investigation, many of their acquaintances became casualties. A lawyer named Marvin Smith, a close friend of Hiss, fell out of a window. Laurence Duggan, an intimate of both Hiss and White, was slated to testify when he fell out of a twelfth story window. Duggan was an official of the Institute of International Education, of which his father was founder and president,

but these family ties offered him no protection. In his haste to get to the window, he tore off one shoe, and left his office in a shambles as he fought his way across it. The verdict was 'suicide.' The Canadian diplomat, Herbert Norman, and the Harvard Professor F. O. Matthiessen, also went out the window before they could be made to testify about their associations. The phenomena became so common that it gave rise to a new term 'defenestration,' meaning the avoidance of testimony, and a suitable warning to others who might think of talking." See Eustace Mullins, *The World Order: Our Secret Rulers* (Staunton, VA: Ezra Pound Institute of Civilization, 1992), pp. 194–5). (AH)

30 Welles: "If we are going to give a man who has never worked a pension of $40 a month when he is 65, then we should give practically the same pension to the man who has worked and saved enough money to build himself a home or provide his family with a small income." (AH)

31 October 1955 is the month that *Brown* II regarding implementation of school integration was promulgated.

32 In Canto 104 he repeats "Homestead versus kolschoz," arguing that government should offer "advice to farms" not assert "control" over them (104/765).

33 Pound deliberately leaves out his direct maternal ancestor, Henry Wadsworth Longfellow, who is among mourners named by Roy Nichols (1931: 525). This melodramatic instance of self-censorship may explain why the funeral is mentioned at all.

34 Pound may be speaking of himself as well as Jefferson and Mussolini; if the genius sees ten things, "the man of talent sees two or three, PLUS the ability to register the multiple perception in the material of his art" (*J/M* 88). (AH)

35 See Alec Marsh, "Ezra Pound: Muckraker; Cantos XVIII and XIX," in *Readings in The Cantos: Vol. 1*, edited by Richard Parker (Clemson, SC: Clemson University Press, 2018), 165–86.

36 For Pound, "Vienna" means Freud, "kikiatry," and the Jews. See *Strike* (September 1955): "the sewage from Vienna has for 45 years distracted the attention of the Occident from the divine light and the great tradition, focusing in on particular bits of putridity" etc. (Gallup C 1765; also La Pira and Watson (aka Ezra Pound), "Academia Bulletin 2," *Paideuma* 3(3) (Winter 1974): 392.

37 See extracts from the summary of Article 22 of the Austrian State Treaty in *Strike* reprinted as "Washington Report. Austrian Peace Treaty," *New Times* 21.24 (Dec. 2, 1955.P. 6 on line at https://alor.org/Storage/New_Times/pdf/NT2124.pdf. (AH)

38 I've been unable to determine if the Rotunda Club admitted women guests in 1958. Possibly not.

39 A letter dated November 11, 1958, from Horton to Pound details her appearance on his segregationist radio show as well as her support for John Kasper and George Lincoln Rockwell, Führer of the American Nazi Party (Beinecke YCAL MSS 43, Box 23, folder 853).

4

The Aryanist Vortex

Pound's Metapolitics and White Supremacy

The project that Pound set John Kasper, *Gists from Agassiz*, completed in 1953, is a condensation of Louis Agassiz's teaching that had a profound and unfortunate impact on Pound. Agassiz's views on race confirmed what Pound had already learned from Hitler about history as a drama of racial struggle. Agassiz did not believe in evolution, nor did Pound; rather, all creatures, including the different races of humankind, were created separately—each had their proper domain. Agassiz and Pound believed in an "inspired creation," what some call "intelligent design."[1] Though he predates eugenics proper, Agassiz's scientific racism is one of its rationales and in this way confirmed for Pound Hitler's eugenic outlook. When, in 1954, the Supreme Court decided *Brown*, Pound realized it implied racial mixing and the end of both white and black races, which he thought a disastrous turn of events completely at odds with nature and its creator. By 1957 Pound was telling others that racial equality was a "disease of thought." Zoologically different, each race had its own gifts, strengths and weaknesses, and proper place in a racial hierarchy, with Greeks (Europeans) and Chinese inventing civilization while other races fulfilled other functions. Africans were agriculturalists in Pound's schema, while the hopelessly mixed Jews were seen as, effectively, destructive parasites on the rest of humankind.

Pound's hierarchical taxonomy of races is discussed in my *John Kasper and Ezra Pound* (2015: 63–72), but here we will read a different document, "Freedom Now or Never," written not by Pound but by someone of his circle that links this taxonomy directly to the school integration crisis and to *The Cantos*.

Pound's racial taxonomy explained a development in his theory of history. If all history is the history of racial struggle, an idea Pound had encountered before in *Mein Kampf*, then Pound needed to push his "poem including history" back beyond the Bronze Age, past the Homer of foundational Canto 1, into nearly prehistoric time to discover the origins of his own racial tribe, the Aryans. He found them in Sumer, thought by some to be an Aryan civilization, and in the supposed Sumerian pre-dynastic rulers of Egypt. This is the function of "Sargon's seal" in Cantos 97 and 99.

Unlike Hitler, Pound believed that the Chinese were also a culture-bearing race, since they had produced Confucius, mankind's most effective ethical teacher. "Civilization comes from the Med / basin and from the Middle Kingdom," he wrote Agresti, "TWO founts of light," and a few years later, "Civilization comes from the Med / basin and Middle Kingdom" (2/14/1951, 4/3/1954, *EP/ ORA* 58, 147). Thanks to L. A. Waddell and his Egyptologist son-in-law Boris de Rachewiltz's more sober researches, throughout the Washington Cantos China and Egypt are routinely linked. Pound's typically modernist preoccupation with origins, visible since Canto 1, is now corrected and enlarged to include India, Egypt, and Africa.

Pound's research took him to some remarkable books: *Adam and Cain* by Governor William "Alfalfa Bill" Murray of Oklahoma, an American populist and staunch defender of Jim Crow, treated in the next chapter; and the Victorian adventurer L. A. Waddell, translator (some might say inventor) of the "Indo-Sumerian" signs, traveler throughout India and Tibet, an Aryanist and an anti-Semite. Waddell saw world history as a struggle between Aryans and Semites who were a problem long before Judaism. Taken together, the works of Murray and Waddell seem like archeological science fiction, but when Pound came to these writers in the summer of 1954, they confirmed his trust in Agassiz.[2] Aryans founded civilizations, then, succumbing to their own sensual nature, interbred with local "brown-skins" till civilization foundered. Pound even read Shakespeare's *Antony and Cleopatra* as one version of this tragedy. Again and again, Aryan priority, miscegenation, and consequent racial degradation was the broad picture of human history, from Sumer to ancient Egypt, India, and elsewhere. Was America next?[3]

Since the prospect of court-mandated racial integration enforced at the point of the bayonet at Clinton, Tennessee; Clay and Sturgis, Kentucky; and later at Little Rock, Arkansas (1956–8), threatened the race-integrity of white people, it also threatened civilization as such. Pound's late cantos deploy imagery of floods, dykes, and dams to suggest racial flood control, citing laws and edicts, prohibitions, warnings, duties, and responsibilities. They are a handbook of Jeffersonian, fascist, and Confucian precepts preaching a sense of order to be achieved through the proper study of history and ethical indoctrination. Since Pound had learned that the Aryan civilizing mission was innate, such study requires the recovery of the hidden Aryan core within all civilizations. These cantos explore the history of the Ara, "the exalted or noble ones," shining in their glory (Waddell 2014: 5). Their "whiteness" is brightness.[4] Only with whiteness can one "build light."

Pound's metapolitical investments and his sense of the epic as the "tale of the tribe" require an Aryanist viewpoint if only because his tribe is Aryan. Therefore, a unique racial politics explained by Pound's peculiar taxonomy of human types is a major strand in these late cantos. Since Pound clearly thinks the Chinese are a master race as much as white people, he brings his Aryanism and sinophilia together by constantly linking China and Aryans. He does this via Egypt, which Pound, following Waddell and other speculative "hyper-diffusionists," considered to be founded by Aryans.[5] Pound implies this by his constant equivalences between East and West, as when he interjects Chinese ideograms into a Western text and vice versa. In his "Chung Yung" he translates Legge's rendering of Confucius's question "Do you mean the energy of the South or do you mean the energy of the North?" into a question about Southern and "Nordic" energies, subtly racializing Confucius's query. "Nordic energy" means "To sleep on a heap of arms and untanned skins"—such energy is clearly barbaric—but Nordics also "die unflinchingly and as if dying were not enough, that is Nordic energy" (*Con*. 112–13). A renewed version of Pound's Italian text, burned by the Allies but published in James Laughlin's *Pharos* in 1947, this passage retains an unmistakable Axis resonance despite the publisher's precautions (see Barnhisel 2005: 116–17), suggesting deep-rooted affiliations between Nordics (i.e. Aryans) and China.

L. A. Waddell's books inform several important cantos in *Rock-Drill* and *Thrones* because Pound took his racialist thinking very seriously. Scots, born in 1854, Laurence Waddell took medical degrees at Glasgow and "became a medical officer for the Indian medical service, working in India, China, Burma and Tibet." He took part in the Boxer Rebellion (1899–1901) and the English invasion of Tibet (1903–4). He read Sanskrit and, maybe, Tibetan. He wrote widely on Tibet and Tibetan Buddhism, on Indian archaeology, and on ancient civilizations (Waddell 2013: n.p.). He was particularly interested in the ancient Aryans, the people from whom, in his view, all civilizations worthy of the name descended, including Sumer, Egypt, India, Persia, China, and even the Americas.

This "Aryanist" viewpoint supports the "paradisal" dimension of Pound's poem by establishing a metapolitical order extending from the origins of civilization to the present. The concept "civilization" has, in the Aryanist view he adopts, a materialist racial essence. There is, in the words of Waddell, an innate relationship "of Civilization to the Aryan Race." Conversely, any "racial impoverishment" through interbreeding "tends to the weakening of Civilization" (Waddell 2013: xxi). The measure of civilization is its Aryan-ness. White supremacy means white priority—unless Aryans got there first, civilization cannot occur. Civilizations fail when the culture-bearing Aryan group is genetically drowned in the nonwhite masses.

Waddell's thoughts cannot be separated from words Pound had read in Italian in the 1940s: "All the human culture, all the results of art, science and technology that we see before us today, are almost exclusively the creative product of the Aryan." They, and they alone, are "the true-culture-founders of this earth." The author also noted that "once the actual and spiritual conqueror lost himself in the blood of the subjected people, the fuel for the torch of human progress was lost!" Adolf Hitler had not read Waddell, nor had Waddell read him; but Hitler's thoughts must have made Waddell's far-out historical speculations easier to accept. Pound found Waddell basically "sound"—but I anticipate.

Before we embark on this rather dodgy subject, two studies are of special importance here. First is Massimo Bacigalupo's *The Forméd Trace: The Later Poetry of Ezra Pound* (1980), which remains one of the very best books on the poet, astute and remarkably unimpressed. Bacigalupo was the first to recognize and explicate Pound's commitment to fascism and anti-Semitism, famously stating that *The Cantos* were "the sacred poem of the Nazi-Fascist millennium, which mercifully never eventuated" (Bacigalupo 1980: x). In other words, his was the first reading of Pound's later poetry that tried to take the poet's political investments seriously. Bacigalupo refuses to sympathize with Pound's views, but he understands they cannot be ignored if we wish to understand him.

Whereas Bacigalupo only touches on Waddell and Pound's Aryanism briefly (1980: 326, 366–7), Robert Casillo's important book *The Genealogy of Demons: Anti-Semitism, Fascism and the Myths of Ezra Pound* (1988)—begun, I believe, as a dissertation under Hugh Kenner at Johns Hopkins—is a richly documented exposé and rejection of Pound's metapolitics.[6] Long before anyone else except Bacigalupo, Casillo cracked the codes of the late cantos, learning to read them as a kind of metapolitical manifesto. From the opening sentence of his book, Casillo introduces a poet "fascinated by two vast, disparate, and incommensurable orders of being: the luminous realm of divine wisdom, beauty, and order" and its "dark, confused" other, a microbial world, Casillo says, signified by the Jews (1988: 1). Given the state of Pound studies at the time, which focused almost exclusively on Pound's luminous vision rather than its anti-Semitic shadow, Casillo's book functions as its own kind of rock drill, educating us about the hostile other in Pound.[7] If, looking out the barred windows of St. Elizabeths or into Sheri Martinelli's eyes, Pound could sense "Beyond civic order: l'AMOR" and "Above prana"—the vital force of Hatha Yoga—"the light, / past light, the crystal. / Above crystal, the jade!" (94/654), below he found a world of undifferentiated ooze, if not worse. His war was "la Guerra di merda" (72/425). Pound's task was to maintain solidity against liquidity, to construct a throne that would not "sqush" based solidly on "THE FOUR TUAN" of Confucius as on legs (85/565).

Casillo's work is of special relevance here as it includes not only a chapter on Pound's Aryanist cantos called "Waddell and the Aryan Tradition"[8] but also several other relevant chapters, each entitled "Nature, Race and History." In what follows I walk in his footsteps but with a slightly different end in view. The "race" that Casillo is particularly interested in is the Jews, not people of African descent; whereas I am most interested in Pound and the Civil Rights struggle. Casillo sees his task as elucidating "systematically the connection between Pound's work and the historical ideologies he embraces"—ideologies, he states in no uncertain terms, that were among "the most brutal and dehumanizing" of his time (Casillo 1988: vii). The task that needed doing in the late 1980s was to confront a critical view of Pound that ignored or downplayed his anti-Semitism and fascism. To this end, Casillo's focus is not much on the United States but on Pound's English and Continental sources. My task here is allied to Casillo's, but the focus is on Pound's defense of the US Constitution in relationship to the Civil Rights movement and Afro-America.

In his chapter on Waddell, Casillo stresses the anti-Semitism that accompanies Waddell's Aryanism in accord with his main argument. He concedes that "it might be argued that Pound's borrowings from Waddell imply only Aryanism rather than anti-Semitism, although the two are rarely if ever very far apart"; Casillo quite rightly finds it "probable that Waddell serves an anti-Semitic purpose in Pound's poem" (Casillo 1988: 99). No question. Waddell's premise is "the innate relationship of Civilization to the Aryan Race from the earliest period" onward (Waddell 2013: xxi; Murray 1951: 511). On that same page Waddell reports in italics that *"no Semitic dynasty whatsoever is to be found in Mesopotamia throughout the whole period of recorded history from the Rise of Civilization downwards until the Semitic Assyrians period of about 1200 B.C."* (Waddell 2013: xxi; Murray 1951: 511–12; Waddell's emphasis).[9] For Pound, Waddell's Aryanism is more than just anti-Semitic polemic. It has a *constructive* purpose: Waddell's fantasies could be used to ground the earthly pole of the poet's metapolitics. Seemingly everywhere at the beginnings of historical time, Waddell's Aryans are used by Pound to bring West and East together, grounded on the premise of white Aryan supremacy and cultural priority—never on grounds of racial equality, the premise of the Civil Rights movement.

Agassiz had been able to discover cosmic order in earthly nature as divine "intelligence." Current events in the United States meant that a "thinking being's" system of careful distinctions superintending "the whole development of nature from beginning to end" (Kasper 1953: 95) was under attack.

Cosmic catastrophe aside, the social implications of school integration were instantly recognized by people worried about "race-mixing." Once young people began to treat each other as equals, they would inevitably socialize, then go to dances, and before you knew it the laws of lower nature would overcome those "higher" laws that protected race integrity, and you could say farewell to the ideology of white supremacy that had sanctioned Jim Crow. As the Christian nationalist Don Lohbeck, editor of G. L. K. Smith's *The Cross & the Flag*, put it in a talk, "Race contact *always* breeds race mixture" (Murray 1951: 108). He was not wrong; that is what has happened. An exasperated Pound wrote Norman Holmes Pearson: "The dance from the beginning of time: courtship toward copulation / Now Elvis Rock an Roll / [...] do none of our obviously god DAMNED contemporaries ever notice anything!" (5/24/1957).[10]

The inevitable result would be an "amalgamated" America or, to use the term popularized by Mississippi Senator Theodore G. Bilbo in his 1947 book *Take Your Choice: Separation or Mongrelization*, "Mongrelization"—the very image of unnatural disorder. The distinguished senator and Klansman Mr. Bilbo was of course a "white supremacist" although, like Pound and Kasper, he avowed deep respect for black people, impugning to them the same need for race integrity that he pretended white people maintained. For Pound, "mongrelization" applied not only to the Negro problem but to the discrimination of ideas. If ideas be not properly "dissociated," Pound thought, the result would be the "bastardization of everything," the end of political, economic, intellectual, ethical, and philosophical legitimacy—the end, in short, of the actual and its submergence in the general "dung-flow" of mere existence without essence.

This metapolitical ideology was shared by the St. Elizabeths group, although with different emphases. For the activist Kasper, it meant risking life, limb, and his freedom to defend civilization in its segregated American form, even if that meant resorting to terroristic methods: cross burnings, KKK rallies, and bombings. For Dave Horton it meant radio exhortation, legal research, and steady appearances before Congress. It informed Sheri Martinelli's muse-like powers to inspire the poet in his work and see through to the poem's cosmic energy. At the same time, it imbued her with a deep pessimism about the immediate future of the white race.

"Segregation or Death," Kasper's essay published alongside William Faulkner in the 1957 "Segregation Issue" of the *Virginia Spectator*, not only means that as a "white nationalist" he pledged to die rather than accept racial amalgamation; it was also a warning: without the bulwark of segregation, the white race will drown in a rising tide of color.

> In the Seaboard White Citizens' Councils and as nationalists, we view government as an organic construction which takes unto itself the highest duty of protecting the various racial components which make up the nation, allowing each to develop according to its highest destiny, without at anytime interfering with the unimpeded development of any other. The government also makes and administers law under the Constitution. It does not interfere with the racial composition of the United States, except insofar as to protect the highest, most energetic racial energies from parasites and secondary, less virile racial energies, which would tend to unnaturally alter, even prevent, a wholesome continuous development of the entire nation according to its highest destiny.[11]

"Racial destiny" is a metaphysical concept with metapolitical implications. It implies a divine plan. Each race is capable of attaining its "highest destiny" insofar as it assumes its proper place in the divine order. It is understood that the "most energetic racial energies" belong to white people, the less virile energies inhere in the other nonwhites, and that the parasites—it almost goes without saying—are the Jews.

Given the particular political situation in the mid-1950s—the Republic menaced from without by the red hordes of barbarous Asia, from within by the Jewish/Communist conspiracy; the Constitution under attack by the Communist Warren Court; the historical order of white supremacy under siege by African Americans politicized by Jewish agitation—Pound's political prescriptions to preserve decent metapolitical order are scattered liberally throughout the late cantos. They account for these poems' obsession with law and measure. When he coopts *The Sacred Edict* in Canto 99, writing that "Thru the ten voices of tradition / the land has been ploughed ... & there have been taxes in kind and by ... measure" (99/727) he consolidates this assertion by asking us to "consider the complications; / Dykes for flood-water, someone must build 'em, / By the ten mouths of the tradition: / have peace / Meaning get rid of criminality. Catch 'em!" (99/727). This is not only about taxation and public works projects but about the maintenance of a white supremacy and race integrity. Pound's solution is "INCORPORATE" (99/727)—i.e. his heterodox fascism—but also he is asking us to protect our bodies, our very selves, from the threat of racial mixing, loosed when the legal dams holding the races apart were sabotaged.

The paradisal aspirations of Pound's poem require that, beyond earthly politics, the cosmic order itself must be maintained against a hostile, integrationist, "mongrelizing" force that is out to abolish all distinctions, all hierarchies, and any semblance of a natural, and therefore rational, purpose.

Pound's Taxonomy of Human Types

In *John Kasper and Ezra Pound* I detailed Pound's "taxonomy of human types," an important ideological formula shaping Pound's thought in the 1950s, noticeable in the Washington Cantos (*JK & EP* 151–60). Pound's taxonomy, synthesized from his understanding of Agassiz and Frobenius, is a unique signature of the racial ideology promoted at St. Elizabeths, frequently alluded to in Pound's correspondence and *The Cantos*. It inspired the quirky phrase "butchers of lesser cattle" in Canto 87, where Pound admits mysteriously that "the hunting tribes require some preparation" (87/594). These are two of his own taxonyms.

This was a "secret doctrine"; using the pseudonym J.V., Pound laid it out under the title "Organic Categories" in *Agenda* (3 [1959]: 1):

> There are six basic psychologies or types of mind. 1. Hunters 2. Agriculture 3. Butchers of lesser cattle 4. Magicians 5. Exploiters 6. Creators. Hunter: priest who takes it on himself to fight bulls, requiring courage and skill. Butcher: Shepherd who fattens for kill, or to fleece. Ethics are from agriculture, religion is in hunters. Magicians or shamen have a code, not ethics, for the purpose of exploitation.

As expressed to William Cookson, these categories do not, at first seem racial; they are "psychologies"—perhaps a matter of different *paideuma*—inherited cultural styles. Pound seems, although ambiguously, to follow Frobenius, who thought he observed two different cultural styles in Africa: a "Hamitic" hunting culture, with knightly conceptions of honor but otherwise tough-minded, materialistic, and [contra Pound] irreligious; and the other that he called "Ethiopian," "marked by the piety of the men in service to the plants they tend" (Frobenius 1928: 160; *JK & EP* 53)—an outlook associated with sub-Saharan Africa.

Frobenius's distinction is not racial in the thoughtless American sense, which imagines all Africans as essentially the same. Frobenius was not American and did not share its national pathologies. Pound, however, was not immune to them. In other places Pound will talk loosely of a racial "paideuma," using Frobenius's term, that becomes, as the poet's thought crystallizes under the influence of Hitler and Agassiz, innate, "zoological" characteristics, even destinies, as Pound pointed out to a number of correspondents (*JK & EP* 155–8). The other distinctions, if not quite species, are elaborations of this basic duality. "Butchers of the lesser cattle" are, as Pound makes abundantly clear in myriad places, nomadic Semites and, latterly, the Jews. The magicians might be thought of as the ideologists—professional economists and their jargon, their "laws" and pseudoscience, and the "Kikiatrist" shamans at St. Elizabeths. Secular exploiters justify their depredations by deferring to the authority of these experts.

In opposition: the creators, although artists are not Pound's first thought here. He means the Aryans, as Hitler did: "All the human culture, all the results of art, science and technology that we see before us today, are almost exclusively the creative product of the Aryan"; they, and they alone, are "the true culture-founders of this earth" (Hitler 1999: 290).[12]

Perhaps creators can also mean artists, which is not a racial category for Pound since, besides the Chinese poets he translated, he recognized non-Aryans like Louis Zukofsky and Langston Hughes as true poets. Pound certainly saw a benign conspiracy of creative intelligence as the counter to the Jewish conspiracy to degrade mankind (*GK* 264; Marsh 2011: 142–3). In a piece called "Values" printed in the *British Union of Fascists Quarterly* (1937), Pound quotes something he heard from Constantin Brancusi: "One of those days when I would not have given fifteen minutes of my time for anything under heaven" (*SP* 253). Pound comments on this phrase, which is repeated in Canto 85 (85/579): "There speaks the supreme sense of human values. There speaks *work* unbartered. That is the voice of humanity at its highest possible manifestation" (*SP* 253; Pound's emphasis). The artist at work shows humanity at its most. Such labor is not for sale, thereby allying it to the motif in the late cantos of the Temple that is not for sale accompanied by a temple sign derived, tellingly, from the hieroglyph naming the Aryan/ Sumerian culture-hero King Sargon (97/699, 701).

In an important note sent to Jack Stafford in the 1950s—"Note Against Degradation," which worries about messing up the divine plan through racial mixing—Pound argues that,

> Each race has its own qualities. Any attempt to obscure racial character is antiscientific.
> No race can fully perform the functions of another.
> The howl for equality comes from a bastardizations of words, though it started in a righteous fight in the law courts.

Pound explained:

The fight against variety is a fight against the laws of nature as manifest in all animal and vegetable life.
If you believe in God it is a fight against the laws of God. If you are a scientist, not a shyster, it is a fight against the manifest facts of nature.
No one ever advocated melting all things down to one pattern save in lust for domination, and in hatred of all qualities the tyrant had not in himself.[13]

He concluded: "We are against diseases of THOUGHT,[14] not against individuals seeking to rid themselves of infections." Given his hierarchical metapolitics, Pound interpreted "racial equality" as a "disease of thought." Racial integration was, effectively, "racial *dis*-integration." The ideal of racial "diversity," to use the current term, meant its opposite, the end of racial and cultural difference in a slave-state of sameness, a sort of universal biological Soviet. He tried to explain to John Theobald "[t]he PRINCIPLE OF DEGRADATION of bastardization and mélange[.] It is good that Hindoos be MORE Hindoo / that chinks be more chink each rising to its own height and not a *mélange adultère de tout*" (9/11/1957 *EP/JT* 84). The envious promoters of this racial sludge were the "butchers of the lesser cattle," the Jews (qtd in Stock 1970: 397; *JK & EP* 153).[15]

This viewpoint was taught at St. Elizabeths and filtered down to his acolytes. John Kasper explained his racial politics in similar fashion in his long Poundian letter to the *New Amsterdam News* (November 16, 1956), rebutting the September 29, 1956, article headlined "RACIST EXPOSED" rehearsing much of what he had already written (though not yet published) in "Segregation or Death" (see *JK & EP* 191–6). Kasper exhorts the *News* to teach its African American readers about different racial gifts, "talents and abilities" endowed by "the Creator"—the god of Agassiz. He closes by saying:

> The wisdom of the Chinese and Greek has been in moderation, balance, and proportion. ... The genius of the Hindu is for tolerance for every living thing. ... The African genius is for agriculture .... The Anglo-Saxon-Nordic white man envisioned and carried out (for the benefit of ALL) a concept of free government which has given the maximum of personal liberty and the minimum of tyrannical irresponsibility.[16]

Greek, of course, means European, i.e. "white," as much as "Anglo-Saxon-Nordic" does. Hindu tolerance is registered in Canto 88 as "respect for vegetal powers / Or life however small (Hindoustani)" (88/602). It is clear that "moderation balance and proportion" as well as their desire for good government is the blessing bestowed on whites and Chinese; for Pound, whites and Chinese are the bearers of civilization—the culture-bearing races. Remember, "Civilization comes from the Medit / basin and from the Middle Kingdom" (4/3/1954, *EP/ORA* 147). Given this, Pound in his world-epic needs to bring whites and China together in order to provide a truly global basis for his metapolitical project. The Africans, being best suited for agriculture by the intelligence operating in Nature, are compensated by the ethical outlook that comes from growing grain. In this they are like the Chinese, also agricultural, also ethical, as Confucius and Mencius proved.

So just because Pound believed in racial segregation doesn't mean that he *crudely* promoted white supremacy; he saw a cosmic hierarchy, with each race in its proper place. It was proper, even divinely ordained, that Pound, an Aryan, should be concerned with civic thought and preoccupied with good government; if he had been of African descent he might have happily penned farming manuals or, like George Washington Carver (one of Pound's minor heroes), made known the virtues of peanuts and sung the blues. After all, "[e]ach race has its own qualities. Any attempt to obscure racial character is antiscientific. No race can fully perform the functions of another."

"Freedom Now or Never"

While we can piece together a reasonably coherent "St. Elizabeths Tendency" regarding race and politics from Pound's "Note Against Degradation," his letters, Kasper's writings, and *The Cantos* themselves, as I tried to do in *John Kasper and Ezra Pound*, its fullest expression in the Civil Rights context is in an anonymous piece called "Freedom Now or Never," probably drafted to be distributed as a broadside by the SWCC, found in the David Gordon file at the Beinecke.[17] Because much material by Dave Horton is mixed in with the Gordon letters, it is not possible to say whether David (Gordon) or Dave (Horton) or, indeed, someone else might have written it. It is not Pound's, but that is precisely its value, for it shows that there was a common ideology, a racial metapolitics, shared by Pound's group. It is long, but stay with it, for it epitomizes a worldview while placing it in a concrete hstorical situation. In a communication to me, Archie Henderson located in Pound's work similar or identical statements for all ten points in "Freedom Now or Never."

> FREEDOM, NOW OR NEVER
> Concerning the knotty problem that seems to be serious involving the entire country: the integration of the negro, let us devote five minutes of sharp thinking on the subject to clarify the haze which seems to have enveloped us.

1/ The negroes that were brought over to this country were already slaves in their native Africa. Frobenius assures us of this.

2/ Mussolini's "ruthless attack" on Abyssinia put a stop to a type of slavery that allowed the cutting off of limbs and more grotesque kinds of mutilation.

3/ Just as the naturalist [Agassiz] points out that the Chimpanzee, Orangutan and Baboon are three members of the ape family that are ONLY separated by a slight lengthening of the cartilage of the nose, or our own observation tells us that the Black Maple leaf is short and squat in comparison to the longer and more slender Silver Maple leaf, or the Mountain Maple leaf is comparatively simple and uncomplicated next to the large and spectacular Broadleaf Maple leaf, so our candid observation might differentiate between the following psychological types among humanity:

(1) The hunting tribesman
(2) The killer of lesser cattle
(3) The killer of bulls
(4) The agriculturalist
(5) The exploiter magician
(6) The artist

4/ Now let[']s see who the REAL slaves and masters are today.

5/ We can ascertain that the Luce owned Time, Life, Fortune; the Meyer owned Washington Post, the Saltzburger [sic] owned New York Times are all centralized under the powerful leadership of Bernard Barauch [sic]. We can see this press use the insidious communist party line: race against race, class against class, group against group, religion against religion with the same old weapons: dissension, strife, filth, demoralization and always IGNORANCE.

We have seen this press put 6 American presidents in office, starting with Wilson, and all advised by the "omnipotent" Mr Barauch.

We have seen since 1912 centralized money power take over all questions of great importance concerning where our money is coming from, how much it is worth, how much it will buy, prices going up, DEPRESSIONS; in short the most important security we have, and that money power called itself THE FEDERAL RESERVE BOARD[,] which has the power over and above congress and the president, and all of this power in the hands, for all practical purposes, [of] Mr Barauch.

We have seen Mr Barauch's friend take over the Supreme Court. David Lawrence has helpfully pointed out how much Felix Frankfurter has tyrannized over the Supreme Court.

We have seen Mr Barauch's money power, press, and supreme court put this country is wars that have caused a National debt that it is not foreseeable how even the unborn can pay off.

6/ In other times and places we might have called this man a tyrant, dictator.
7/ Let us now answer the question: What % of the 'integration problem' is being used to "cover" Mr Barauch's "business"?
8/ How much complaining would be valid if some of the money for income tax, war, foreign aid, etc, etc, were used for schools and other necessaries in this country?
9/ Let us assume that the question [answer] to #7 is 100% and the question [answer] to #8 is NONE!
10/ Since it is established that we, negroes and whites, are the slaves and Mr Barauch is the master let us now send Lehman's ADL & Naacp back to the communists[.][18]

Concerning slavery in Africa, Pound wrote Agresti about a fellow patient at St. Elizabeths, an African American actually named Booker T. Washington[19] who was "surprised to learn that the slaves imported had already been slaves in Africa" (5/20/1957, *EP/ORA* 246). As Henderson points out, it appears that Pound has been reading Kasper's essay "Segregation or Death," recently published in the *Virginia Spectator* (May 1957), in which Kasper writes that Frobenius "recorded accurately all the different cultural manifestations of DIFFERENT KINDS OF NIGRAS, their habits, ways of making a living, beliefs, arts, religions etc." (see Kasper 1957a: 21, 34–37; Henderson 2010: 556–7).

As for the second point, that "Mussolini's 'ruthless attack' on Abyssinia put a stop" to slavery there, the author of the broadside seems familiar with Cyril Rocke's "The Truth about Abyssinia, by an Eye Witness. An open letter to the Archbishop of Canterbury, the Lords Cecil, Craigmyle and Snowden, etc." (1935), which detailed the horrors of the Ethiopian slave trade, especially the castration of children.[20] Pound used Rocke's report to justify the Italian "acquisition" of Ethiopia.

Point 3: The naturalist in question is Louis Agassiz. He claimed that "the Chimpanzee, Orangutan and Baboon are three members of the ape family that are ONLY separated by a slight lengthening of the cartilage of the nose." The phrasing here might seem to make the case for the basic similarity of these different creatures—and thus betray the point it wants to make about their immutable differences. But in the fifth of thirty-one summary points Agassiz made as published in Kasper's *Gists* we find: "The correspondence, now generally known as special homologies, in the details of structure in animals otherwise entirely disconnected, down to the most minute particularities, exhibits thought, and more immediately the power of expressing a general proposition in an indefinite number of ways, equally complete in themselves, though differing in other details" (Kasper 1953: 92). In other words, close correspondences between diverse species do not point to adaptation to local conditions through natural selection but rather to divine foresight: the "premeditation, power, wisdom, greatness, prescience, omniscience, providence" of the all-wise Creator (Kasper 1953: 96). Pound used the maple leaf comparison with a similar intent, writing to Agresti in favor of Agassiz's arguments against materialism that "anybody who has looked at a maple-leaf can do without further demonstration that Marx didn't make the world, and that mud is an unlikely origin" (*EP/ORA* 42). In Canto 87 he writes, "In nature are signatures / needing no verbal tradition, / oak leaf never plane leaf" (87/593). In "Freedom Now or Never" and even in the canto these Agassizan remarks lead immediately to the poet's taxonomy of human types.

Before returning to Pound's taxonomy, however, we can understand the obsession with Bernard Baruch in "Freedom Now or Never" as being consistent with Pound's wry name "Baruchistan" for the United States. It means that the Elders of Zion, among them the seemingly all-powerful and ubiquitous Baruch, advisor to six presidents, control the country through underlings such as the Jewish Senator Lehman of the banking Lehmans, who supported racial integration. Pound believed their rule was enforced by the Jewish Anti-Defamation League that aggressively pointed out perceived anti-Semites, while front organizations like the NAACP actively subverted the Constitution. This is why the first terror action of the SWCC was to burn crosses in front of Senator Lehman's Washington residence as well as that of an NAACP organizer (*JK & EP* 138–43). Pound used the title "Baruchistan" frequently in letters to correspondents like Agresti, in a paragraph where, ironically enough, he demands "honest and thoughtful" definition of words. For Pound, calling the United States "Baruchistan" is telling it like it is (*EP/ORA* 91): that America is becoming a Jew/Commie slave state. At Pisa, he'd already envisioned the poor devils, both black and white, "sent to the slaughter / Knecht gegen Knecht [slave against slave] / for a usurer's holiday to change the / price of currency" (76/483). The true victors of World War II were the international bankers, not the United States or the already enslaved USSR.

The international bankers were the international Jews. According to "Freedom Now or Never" the Jews were the masters and everyone else their slaves, destined to become "mongrelized"—"chaff," as Hitler said, apt to be molded into a Soviet-style mass. Though not written by the poet himself, "Freedom Now or Never" is altogether too helpful as a guide through certain obscure moments in the Washington Cantos and in Pound's correspondence.

Notes

1. For example, see William Cookson's (2001: 201) comment on Agassiz, citing Michael Behe's *Darwin's Black Box* (1998).
2. Kindellan (2017: 159) writes that Pound "recognized Waddell's racial biases but did not consider them important problems for scholarly endeavor." To the contrary! "'Waddell hel fer leather Aryan ... '" Pound wrote Mary July 27, 1954.
3. Though not on Pound's reading list so far as is known, this is the thesis of Mississippi Senator Theodore Bilbo's historical polemic *Take Your Choice: Segregation or Mongrelization* (1947).
4. Most definitions of "Aryan" indicate nobility or exalted status. Waddell, who sees the word as a root for "aristocrat," adds "brightness," which must have struck Pound (see Waddell 2013: 5–6).
5. John Harvey wrote in *The Heritage of Britain* (1941), a short book reprinted in William Murray's *Adam and Cain*, that "Gothic [i.e. Aryan] culture probably reached China shortly before Troy fell," adding that "the works of Confucius himself and his followers are models of Aryan wisdom" (Murray 1951: 581). Murray himself, at the beginning of the same book, claims that one "Twanghi who was *Gothic Aryan* and ruler of China" destroyed Chinese libraries to eradicate an unnamed "fanatical religion and verify Confucius" (19; Murray's emphasis), a claim that must have caught Pound's eye. In an issue of the *New Times* that Pound sent to Norman Holmes Pearson, Bedrich Hrozny's *Ancient History of Western Asia, India and Crete* is quoted: "There is documentary evidence proving strong influence of the Sumero-Akkadian culture upon Egypt, the Hittites, and the ancient culture of India. Sumero-Akkadian influence upon far-off China is somewhat less tangible but still obvious. The same can be said about the cultures of the Mediterranean Sea. Thus, the Sumero-Akkadian culture became a lighthouse whose rays fell upon whole of the ancient cultural world" (*New Times*, January 13, 1956, p. 7). Hrozny, too, sees the Aryans as shining brightly. Like Waddell's, Hrozny's scientific reputation is poor. Though his decipherment of the Hittite language is a genuine accomplishment, his later work with Minoan scripts and the enigmatic Indus seals that fascinated Waddell is, like Waddell's readings, regarded as fantasy, if not mad.
6. Robert Casillo, "The Parallel Design in John Ruskin and Ezra Pound" (PhD, Johns Hopkins University, 1977).
7. I remember reading it and resisting it all the way. I even wrote a dissertation trying to show that Pound's anti-Semitism was not integral to his worldview, populism was; regardless, anti-Semitism *became* integral to the poet over time as his views crystallized.
8. A concise version of Casillo's Waddell chapter titled "Pound, L. A. Waddell and the Aryan Tradition of 'The Cantos'" appeared in *Modern Language Studies* 15(2) (Spring 1985): 65–81.

9   Pound first read these remarks in William Murray's *Adam and Cain* (1951).
10 Norman Holmes Pearson papers, Beinecke YCAL MSS 899, Box 79, folder "Pound, Ezra 1957".
11 In his contribution to the "Segregation Issue" of the *Virginia Spectator* (118[8] [May 1957]), Floyd Fleming, Kasper's comrade in the SWCC and later an American Nazi, issued a warning that "desegregation had led to white flight and an impossible teaching situation in integrated schools, due to the wide disparity in mental ability to learn and educational achievement between the white and negro students." Fleming concluded that "intermarriage ... is what integration in the schools leads to and as that comes to pass, the white race becomes a mongrelized race and history records that the breeding is downward instead of upward."
12 Hitler suggested that "[i]f we were to divide mankind into three groups, the founders of culture, the bearers of culture, the destroyers of culture, only the Aryan could be considered as representative of the first group." For this reason, in the preceding paragraph, Hitler argues that, as the "founder of all higher humanity," the Aryan "represents the prototype of all that we understand by the word 'man'" (1999: 290). These ideas may underlie Pound's last words in *The Cantos*: "To be men not destroyers" (117/823).
13 Beinecke YCAL MSS 43, Box 49, folder 2190.
14 In a poem sent to Pound in 1957, David Wang, quoting Pound himself, includes the line "Attack disease of thought, not of mind" (Beinecke YCAL MSS 43, Box 54, folder 2486). (See *JK & EP* 212.)
15 Pound to Douglas McPherson (aka D. D. Paige): "The melting pot has been tried and FAILED. Some blends are O.K. but the others rot in three generations, even when the mulatto happens to be good ... We want our Italians Italian; French French; ang/sax ang/sax Dutch dutch. That is enough for everyman, with an occaisional hybrid" (1/18/1940; qtd in Redman 1991: 196). (AH)
16 Kasper makes a nearly identical claim in "Segregation or Death" (1957a): "The genius of the Greek and Chinese is moderation, proportion, and balance. The African genius is in agriculture. The Hindu is tolerance for every living thing. The Nordic peoples have developed representative government" (*Virginia Spectator*, May 1957).
17 Beinecke YCAL MSS 43, folder 851.
18 Beinecke YCAL MSS 43, folder 851.
19 "Booker T. Washington, with sense of humour that his family had saddled him with that celebrated pair of prenoms, conversation at table has degenerated since he got OUT of bughouse" (5/20/1957, *EP/ORA* 246).
20 Rocke: "Does your grace of Canterbury realize that, in Abyssinia, countless little male children are mutilated every year to qualify them for the slave market of the ruling race of that fair but unhappy country? The mutilation takes the form

of the crudest surgery, after which the wounds caused by the act of abscission are cauterized by the application of red hot irons. The Abyssinian experts who perform this operation do not use anaesthetics. This happens to countless unfortunate little children every year, of whom the writer has seen and spoken to a considerable number. The horrible sufferings of every day life in large parts of Abyssinia are such as would make every sanctionist shudder with repulsion were these idealists to be brought face to face with them." Pound sent Rocke's "Letter" to Senator Borah in November 1935 (see Holmes, *Correspondence of Ezra Pound and Senator William Borah* [Urbana: University of Illinois Press, 2001], 47). Henderson quotes from the *Gale Concise Dictionary of American Literary Biography*: "'After Abyssinia [Pound] carried photographs of alleged Abyssinian "atrocities," which he eagerly presented to people as explanation of Mussolini's change of policy'" ("Ezra Pound," *Concise Dictionary of American Literary Biography: The Twenties, 1917–1929* [Gale Research, 1989]. Reproduced in Biography Resource Center, Farmington Hills, MI: Gale, 2008, http://galenet.galegroup.com/servlet/BioRC). (AH)

5

Raising Cain

The Aryan Origins of Civilization

Writing to Olivia Rossetti Agresti on December 1, 1953, Pound expanded on "the one valid myth of Xtianity," that

> the kikes crucified …. And by myth I mean a relation that recu[rs], time and again / true myth is something that repeats / and is figured by a great metaphor. nacherly yr / kikery crucifies. Age old opposition of butchers of lesser cattle to the growers of grain. The agriculturalist the villain in their fable. And none of the skill needed to bull-kill for Mithra. Or the bravery of the hunting tribes. (*EP/ORA* 135)

The agriculturalist Cain killed the hunter Abel in the Jewish fable, so it seems that the conflict between farmers and herders goes back quite literally to the beginnings of human time, well before Judaism. To Pound, the conflict between Cain and Abel is the conflict between the agricultural Aryan, Cain, and Semitic shepherds, represented by Abel. The biblical myth is the ur-story of Semitic nomads victimized by civilized Aryans, who, in the tribal propaganda that is the book of Genesis, are eternally cursed by the vengeful Jews. The "crucifixion myth" is the same story. A virtuous Aryan is betrayed and tortured to death by malevolent Jews of Pound's fifth exploiter magician type, the Pharisees, who harbor a primordial resentment of Aryan constructivity. Though Pound was not Christian enough to care about the reactionary notion that "Christ was not a Jew" already central to the Christian Identity Movement in the 1950s[1]—a doctrine preached by his one-time disciple Dallam Flynn when he became a Baptist minister in Texas—the crucifixion only makes sense as a "true myth" if this racial component is assumed. This "exploiter magician" has "a code, not ethics, for the purpose of exploitation." These show up in Canto 97 across the page from the Aryan culture hero Sargon's seal as "those who have a code and no principles" (97/698). The "magicians" gestures toward the Kahal, a group Pound had long accused of running a religious racket by levying fines for various breaches of Jewish law. "The bulk of jewish law is nothing but a wheeze ... to jerk fines out of the populace for the benefit of cohens and levis," Pound insisted to Agresti. Insofar as Christians followed suit they were just as bad: "The Xtn is basically dishonest from the minute he starts professing belief in a formula which he either does not believe, or does not understand" (*EP/ORA* 40).

What does this idea do for Pound? To what does it commit him? First, there is the absolute rejection of, even revulsion toward, the God of Genesis: "JHV figliocide demon who chose a foul race to do evil" (*EP/ORA* 158). The Jewish crime against the worshipper of the grain god (or gods) is simultaneously the rejection of ethics. The Cain and Abel story lurks deep within Pound's agrarian ideology—something Pound himself recognized when he writes Agresti complaining about the "damKike who divorced the idea of divinity from agriculture ... And the agriculturalist Cain, the villain in mystery Ersat'z by the butchers of lesser cattle" (*EP/ORA* 88).[2] When Cain's offering of "the fruits of the ground," his grain sacrifice, was rejected by the Jewish god, who preferred "the firstlings of Abel's flock and their fat portions" (Gen. 4), the meaning is not about jealousy and fratricide but obscene acceptance of a bloody-minded YHWH and the rejection of the "grain god" who wished no blood on his altar, an important theme in the "Aryan" Cantos 94 and 97: "Was no blood on the Cyprian's altars" (94/655); "no blood on the altar stone" (97/700); "Flowers, incense, in the temple enclosure / no blood in that TEMENOS" (97/701). This is based on information derived from Waddell. The rejection of blood sacrifice also explains Pound's identification with Apollonius, who "made peace with the animals" (94/655) and is thus on the side of Cain and Waddell's Aryans in these poems. All this, we may add, is completely at odds with the incessant sacrificial barbecue that constitutes religious observance in Homer, where meat and blood dominate virtually all social interactions among the indisputably Aryan Greeks.[3]

"Alfalfa Bill" Murray's *Adam and Cain*

The rehabilitation of Cain would have been confirmed for Pound through an amazing book called *Adam and Cain* published in 1951 by William H. "Alfalfa Bill" Murray, the former governor of Oklahoma. He's the "Alfalfa" "no longer in Who's Who" mentioned in Canto 93 (93/647). Murray, born in 1869 in euphonious Toadsuck, Texas, comes straight out of American populism. A one-time member of the Farmers' Alliance, he was a Democratic politician who played a major part in the appropriation of Oklahoma, formerly Indian

Territory. He was that state's first Speaker of the House, as well as its ninth governor. Unsurprisingly, as a populist Southern Democrat he was a staunch upholder of Jim Crow. He wrote and published prolifically. Reading the list of titles at the back of *Adam and Cain*, Pound would have approved of the first listed publication, *Agriculture for Beginners*. The list also includes, besides a three-volume history of Oklahoma, diatribes against Roosevelt and the New Deal, as well as *The Negro's Place in Call of Race*, which must be a defense of white supremacy and an argument for Negro inferiority.

Adam and Cain amazes because it is a "symposium" of extreme right-wing, anti-Semitic, white supremacist material with ongoing commentary by Murray. It has an English slant. *Adam and Cain* is dedicated to L. A. Waddell, John H. Harvey, Arnold Leese, and H. H. Beamish and uses extensive excerpts from Waddell's *Makers of Civilization in Race and History* (1929). Leese, Beamish, and Harvey simply *were* the Imperial Fascist League, a Nazi sect founded by Leese in 1929. Beamish was its secretary; his photo can be found amidst an article by G. L. K. Smith (Murray 1951: 33). Waddell, who died in 1938, is not known to have been a member of the IFL, but his vision of the ancient Aryan world is clearly a projection of the British Empire five thousand years back in time. His Aryanist and anti-Semitic views could only have provided useful ideological support for the IFL, as Harvey's work reveals. Noel Stock correctly considered *Adam and Cain* a source for *The Cantos* (see Stock 1966: 102), and Pound's letters reveal that he was led to Waddell's work by Murray's obscure book.

It had been sent to Pound by Sheri Martinelli, then staying with John Kasper in New York (EP to NHP 1/15/1956, Beinecke YCAL MSS 899 Section V). Kasper's Make It New Bookshop carried Meador Books, the Boston Press that published *Adam and Cain*. Pound was reading it with enthusiasm in July 1954, at the height of his passion for Martinelli, asking Olivia Agresti that month if she'd ever heard of "'Alfalfa Bill' who has read Waddell (and a LOT of other stuff that the wops OUGHT to read and Digest)," finding him "a SOUND man re / all except xtianity" (*EP/ORA* 162, 161, 163). Late in the month he wrote his daughter Mary: "Waddell hel fer leather Aryan" (qtd in Kindellan 2017: 159). Pound must have brought Waddell to Boris de Rachewiltz's attention as well, for in August Boris sent him his own recent translation from Ancient Egyptian, his *Massime degli antichi Egiziani* (1954), perhaps as an antidote (Hesse 1969: 180). In mid-November, Pound alerted Wyndham Lewis to *Adam and Cain*: "alzo Wad[d]ell (du[g] up fer yanks by 'Alfalfa Bill' Murray / who alzo did chapter on Swabey's fight fer local school[)]"[4] (*P/L* 281). Pound reminds Lewis about him again in January 1955 (*P/L* 288). Months later Pound was still thinking about

Murray, telling Agresti, "It took a Greenwich Village dope [doll?] to drag in a volume (of a rather crude mixture) by Alfalfa Bill of Oklahoma, to restart hunt for Wad / 's lost vols" (5/22/1955 EP/ORA 190). In response to a request, Kasper reported on June 1, 1955, that he would get some Waddell for the young poet Mary Barnard, who was at that time working in a New York publishing house (JK to EP 6/1/1955). Pound put Noel Stock to reading Waddell too; Stock recalled that "at Pound's suggestion I read L. A. Waddell's works on Sumer as a civilizing influence. Some of the details I sent him were later used in *Thrones*."[5] This proves that *Adam and Cain* was no passing fancy and also that Murray's book led Pound to Waddell and eventually to Waddell's prominent place in two cantos, 94 and 97, as well as a reference in Canto 105 derived from one of Waddell's books on Tibet, *Lhasa and Its Mysteries* (1905). It is possible that Waddell's richly illustrated Tibet book led to Pound's interest in that remote country and thus that Waddell led Pound to more respectable writings he treasured—Peter Goullart's *Forgotten Kingdom* and Joseph Rock's research on the Na Khi people, which takes up several very late cantos.[6]

I also suspect that Murray's belief in "Gothic" Britain took Pound back to a number of books on ancient Britain including John Harvey's *Heritage of Britain* (1941) (reprinted in full in Murray 1951); Waddell's translation of *The Eddas* (excerpted in Murray); Layamon's medieval poem *Brut*, invoked beautifully in Canto 106 (106/774-5); and Alexander Del Mar's *Ancient Britain: In Light of Modern Discoveries* (1899),[7] a source for Canto 100 (see Stock 1966: 112-13).

Adam and Cain is in part a eugenic text, featuring generous selections from eugenicists Madison Grant and Lothrop Stoddard and making frequent reference to Luther Burbank's eugenic *The Human Plant* (see esp. 92-120). Murray's book also reprints *The Protocols of the Elders of Zion*, articles from G. L. K. Smith's *The Cross and the Flag*, and Arnold Leese's *Gothic Ripples*. Along with Beamish, Leese and Smith's photos grace the text. As we read these others, Murray interjects comments and encouragement throughout. He exhorts readers to become "Jew-wise" (Murray 1951: 8), denies evolution, and decries race-mixing: "No animal has ever evoluted upward greater than human-kind; each race of men in the beginning, created by The All-Wise, just as they are today, before the races become mixed and 'messed-up' because of man himself" (Murray 1951: 69). Overall, the book is a compendium of American fascism of the "Old Right" variety: Aryanist and Christian, plus eugenics. Of particular interest here, however, are the long excerpts from Waddell and the sixty-page reprint of John H. Harvey's *The Heritage of Britain* (1941).[8]

Aside from the general assault of Jewry throughout, the main argument of Murray's compilation is that what Christians call the Old Testament is Jewish propaganda. Pound's letters to Agresti at this time are especially full of bile about the Bible ("the jew-book"), particularly Genesis and "that mass of corrupting incoherence forgery, fakery / the O[ld] T[estament]" (*EP/ORA* 162). Murray, too, parades his skepticism about the Old Testament—"the whole of Genesis and Exodus is pure fable" he wrote (1951: 19). To refute the propaganda of the Jews, Murray "intends to prove" through his generous selection of sources "that Adam was the first known King; that he founded the city of Troy"—the world's first city, according to Murray; that Adam "established Gothic civilization in the mental twilight of all the dark races, whether yellow, or brown, or red, or black; and that this civilization was the first known by any physical or documentary evidence known to the world. Adam and Eve were parents of Cain but not of Abel, whose parents were "El," a "*superstitious cult*" priestess (Murray's italics), and "Woden" (Murray 1951: 17–18). This is just the beginning of Murray's "sound" (!) if admittedly "crude mixture" of racial fantasy, amateur archaeology, and wild etymologies, based, as Murray happily admits, on Waddell and John Harvey (Murray 1951: 18).

Waddell, Egypt, and the Aryan Makers of Civilization

The first of these Aryan "Goths," as Waddell invariably styles them, were the Sumerians, whose writing Waddell found he could read far better than the trained Assyriologists who came at the Sumerian problem (who they were, what kind of language they spoke) from the Assyrian—i.e. Semitic—point of view rather than the proper Aryan one. Today we know the unique language of Sumer (long thought to be Indo-European by various cultural chauvinists like Waddell) was assimilated and preserved for ceremonial purposes by the Akkadians, their Semitic-speaking northern neighbors, and hence by the succession of Semitic empire-states that followed, including that of the Assyrians. But Waddell does not admit that Semites are capable of civilization. It's worth repeating that for him "*no Semitic dynasty whatsoever is to be found in Mesopotamia throughout the whole period of recorded history from the Rise of Civilization downwards until the Semitic Assyrians period of about 1200 B.C.*" (Waddell 2013: xxi; Waddell's emphasis); the impressive succession of civilizations following Sumer were imitations at best.

The opening paragraph of Waddell's *The Indo-Sumerian Seals Deciphered* (1925)—like *Egyptian Civilization, Its Sumerian Origin* (1930), both main sources for Cantos 94 and 97—suggests Waddell's single-minded obsession with an Aryanist view of human and especially British history:[9]

> In my recent work on British Origins, I proved by a mass of new historical evidence that the "Sumerians"—those foremost civilized and civilizing ancient people whose monuments and high art of five thousand years ago are the wonder of the modern world—were the long lost Early Aryans; that the Phoenicians were not Semites as has been hitherto supposed, but Aryans and the chief colonizing branch of the Sumerians; and that the people who colonized and civilized the Mediterranean, North-western Europe and Britain and who were the ancestors of the Britons, were likewise Aryan and belonged predominantly to the Phoenician branch of that race. (Waddell 1980: v)

This paragraph goes far to explain Pound's use of Waddell in Cantos 94 and 97. Despite his claim that Waddell's books had been hidden from view by interested parties, they were not difficult to get.[10] Pound collected a range of Waddell's writings. *Egyptian Civilization* remains in Pound's library at Brunnenburg along with *The Indo-Sumerian Seals* and *The Aryan Origins of the Alphabet* (1927). Waddell's massive (646 pages plus plates) *Makers of Civilization in Race and History* (1929) is excerpted in Murray's book, as is his introduction to *The Eddas*. Pound probably saw *Makers* proper, not only the long passages excerpted in Murray; but, whatever the case, virtually the same material can be found in *Makers of Civilization* as in *Egyptian Civilization, Its Sumerian Origins* (1930). Both Boris de Rachewiltz and Casillo concentrate quite properly on Waddell's later book, because a drawing in it (taken from Egyptologist Flinders Petrie) is a source for Sargon's seal (Waddell 2013: 245; 97/699; see Figure 5.1) and the Phoenician lion-head (97/701) in Canto 97.

The baffled reader, already subjected to many Chinese ideograms and Egyptian hieroglyphics, now is confronted with these cruder, more primitive signs. Pound appears to be reaching back to the origins of writing itself. We have seen the first element of this array already in Canto 94 (94/655) and concluded it must be Egyptian. Now we learn it is the personal sign of Sargon the Great, the first conqueror of the ancient world (Waddell 2013: 247–8; 1930: 21–2), a "white king" according to Murray (1951: 20), and that the language signified is not Egyptian at all but Sumerian! In Canto 94 Pound had called him "the hawk-king" for the hawk (Horus) standing atop the figure. Here we see that Pound's temple sign is derived from the marks in the box directly under the hawk.[11] Closely following Waddell, Casillo (1988: 98–9) comments:

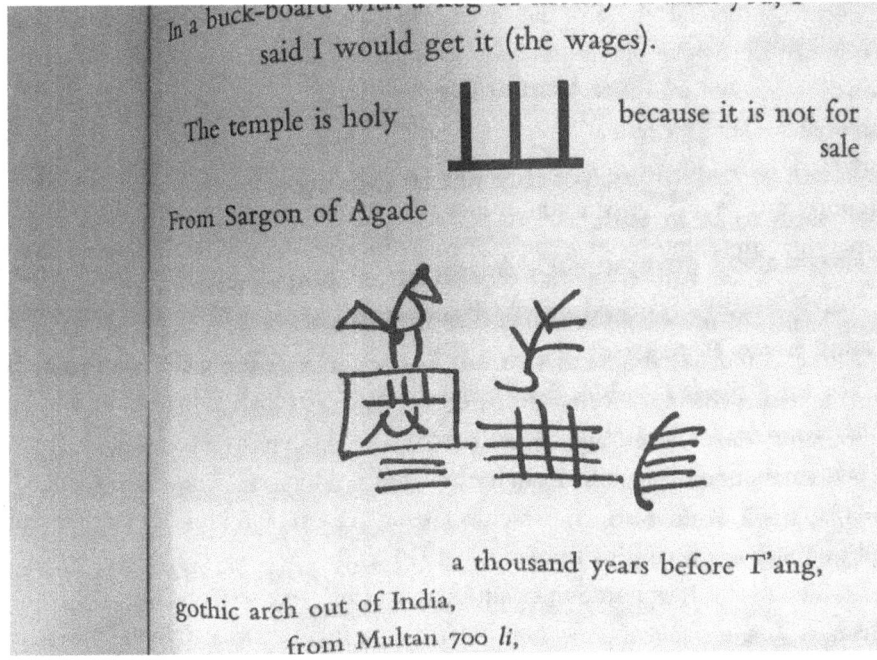

Figure 5.1 Sargon's seal.

Sargon's seal contains three signs: the lower sun sign [those double x's] and the middle temple sign, both enclosed in a cartouche or "shield," and the upper hawk sign. The sun sign is Sargon's "solar title," indicating that he is not only a king and sun-worshipper but representative and son of the Sun-God. It thus testifies to a solar religion which the Sumerians (Aryans) originated and spread from Mesopotamia to Egypt and then to Europe.

I would point to the "vegetation signs" to the right of Sargon's seal that Casillo ignores. These might be interpreted as a field, or fields, and would have reminded Pound of Mencius's nine-field system with the crop indicated above it. On the far right we see a river with irrigation canals running into the hinterland, imagery abundant elsewhere in the *Rock-Drill* sequence.[12] Casillo concludes that "Pound repeatedly relies on Waddell in order to weave into his 'arcanum' elements of a far-diffused and Aryan religion, a religion of agrarianism and *hence* anti-Semitic" (Casillo 1988: 99; my emphasis). Pound is promoting not only Aryan religion and economy here but a whole way of being. In a word: "civilization." Aryans build civilizations; Semites destroy them.

Waddell's *Indo-Sumerian Seals* relies on descriptions by a Chinese pilgrim, Hiuen Tsiang, "the remarkably accurate geographer" who made a Buddhist pilgrimage through India in the seventh century BC (1980: 104).[13] Pound uses Tsiang at a crucial moment in Canto 97, directly under Sargon's seal. He seized on the Chinese connection, making poetic telegraphy of Tsiang's rich description of the temple to the Sun at Multan: "torchlight, at Multan, perfume" (1980: 109; 97/699). In *Indo-Sumerian Seals* the full passage of a note citing Waddell's early reports on "Indo-Scythian" antiquities tells us that he discovered "the *Gothic* arch there in sculptures of second to third centuries A.D. *i.e.*, about a thousand years before its supposed origin" in Northern Europe (1980: 103n; Waddell's emphasis). In his poem, Pound fuses two Waddell citations, from two books, making Waddell's "thousand years" refer back to Sargon's inscription as well as the arch, which according to his dating was c. 2700 BC. This would be "a thousand years before T'ang," founder of the Shang dynasty, appeared in China (97/699). Pound uses Waddell's dating in Canto 94 too, as "somewhere about 2 7 0 4," (94/655; Pound's stress), which is the date of Pharaoh Menes's accession to power in Egypt, according to Waddell (1930: x).

Much of the Egyptian/Sumerian references on page 655 of Canto 94 come from a single page of *Egyptian Civilization, Its Sumerian Origin and Real Chronology* (Waddell 1930: 31). There, Waddell argues that "Menes, the founder of the First Dynasty of Egypt … Sargon's Queen, the Lady Ash, and probably" Menes himself "were buried at Abydos … [B]y these discoveries is found the first synchronism between Egypt and Mesopotamia by which is now fixed with comparative certainty the date of Menes … at no earlier period than 2704 B.C. and that *the civilization of Egypt was of Sumerian or Aryan origin*" (Waddell 1930: 31; my emphasis). Like Waddell, Pound's point in stressing the date of 2704 is to establish Aryan priority, without which, they agree, civilization could not occur. It means that Egypt, with its allegedly Aryan/Sumerian/Goth founders Sargon and his son Menes, has priority over China.

Pound's purpose is to show that the foundational culture of Waddell's Aryan Sumerian Goths underwrites Egypt *and* China—implicitly, *all* world civilizations. John Harvey, who bases his work on Waddell (Murray 1951: 536), stresses the "racial disparity between rulers and ruled" in ancient Sumeria and China where in both places "the subjects were referred to as the 'black-haired people' showing that the rulers were conscious of their racial difference"; ergo the Aryan rulers must have been fair (Murray 1951: 536–7). Murray himself speaks of a Chinese Emperor Twanghi "who was a *Gothic Aryan* and ruler of China" (19; Murray's emphasis).

Among Waddell's eccentric theories was that the Phoenicians (Waddell's "Panch"; see Waddell: 1980: 9), were Aryans, not Semites (97/700), because of their seafaring prowess, evidently an Aryan trait that conveniently placed Aryans in ancient Britain. He had already determined the incredible range of Phoenician nautical feats in his 1924 book *The Phoenician Origins of the Britons, Scots and Anglo-Saxons*,[14] where they were imagined undertaking long dangerous voyages to Britain for tin (94/656). Among them was the ubiquitous Menes, Sargon's son, who died there, Waddell tells us, of a bee sting and is buried in Ireland (not Abydos, as he had hinted earlier) (1930: 96)—a moment Pound celebrated in Canto 97: "By Knoch Many now King Minos lies" (97/700).

A trained Egyptologist who could read hieroglyphics, Boris de Rachewiltz scoffs at Waddell, finding his inspired research preposterous and gently shaking his head at Waddell's "fanciful identifications of historical personages, particularly Sumerian and Egyptian, made in support of his strange theories [that] have crept their way into the late Cantos" (Hesse 1969: 187); "Agdu, Prabbu of Kopt, Queen Ash are all purely arbitrary" inventions (Hesse 1969: 187–8; see 94/655). Nonetheless, Boris forgives Pound's pseudohistory for "the hieroglyph and the interpretation that Pound gives to it under Waddell's false guidance might be said to retain some value as [a] personal ... vision of ideal cities that reappear throughout the epic" (Hesse 1969: 189). But it's not personal for Pound; ideal cities demand Aryan origins. Pound's adoption of Waddell's Aryanism is a constitutive aspect of Pound's metapolitics, with deep roots and a constructive purpose. He returned to the Aryan roots of civilization to renew it on its proper racial basis.

Through Murray, Waddell, and Boris de Rachewiltz, Pound realized the importance of Egypt in any comprehensive account of culture. The poet came belatedly to admire Ancient Egypt; intrigued, Pound began to see Ancient Egypt as grist for the grand mill of *The Cantos*. "Kati and Antef as Kung and Mang [Tsze i.e. Mencius] ... King KATI is the bright light of that collection ... A Man's paradise is his good nature. I should like that in hieroglyphs ... Cantobile [Canto-izable]" (8/15/1954, qtd in Hesse 1969: 180).[15] The hieroglyphs with their translation duly appear leading off Canto 93 (93/643). They function as a kind of Egyptian equivalent to the grand Chinese ideogram $ling^2$ 靈 that opens *Rock-Drill* (85/563).

"Congratulations," he wrote Boris, "you have / humanized the Egyptians / and Budge didn't." Boris's translations returned Pound to his British museum phase in the years before World War I. His lively early poem on Egyptian themes, "The Tomb of Akr Çaar" (*P* 56) was inspired by the artifacts in the British Museum and the popularizing Egyptology of E. A. Wallis Budge. Pound would have read his version of *The Book of Coming Forth By Day*, based on the Papyrus of Ani, which

Budge misleadingly called *The Egyptian Book of the Dead* (1895) because the text is often found in Egyptian tombs. Although Budge argued that the cult of Osiris must have come from black Africa, he also wrote in the introduction to *Egyptian Religion* (1900) that "the genius and structure of the Egyptian language are such as to preclude the possibility of composing in it works of a philosophical or metaphysical character in the true sense of the words" (Budge 1900: 10). This view of the Egyptians as thorough-going materialists incapable of "higher" thinking served to insulate the Greeks from the possibility that they had borrowed heavily from the Egyptians—most especially in philosophy, metaphysics, and religion—as the Greeks themselves repeatedly and happily attested![16] Nonetheless, Budge's views were too generous to Africa for Sir Flinders Petrie, England's other most distinguished Egyptologist, who decided that Egyptian civilization could only have been instated from outside by a non-African "dynastic race" of superior people gradually swamped by interbreeding with the darker races they ruled.

On one hand, the equivalence Pound would like to draw between Kung and Mencius, Kati and Antef could not be more favorable to Egypt; on the other, in agreement with the leading Egyptologists of the first half of the twentieth century, Pound's sense of order could not admit the culture-founding potential of African people. Thus Waddell's solution to this entirely factitious "Egyptian problem" recommended itself. To make Ancient Egypt "cantabile," Kati and Antef must be Aryan "Goths." It helped that Waddell finds the term "Khaiti" or Khati, Khatti, and Catti to mean "Hittite," an "Aryan ... people" (1980: 100, 106; see also Murray 1951: 520). In this reading the historical Kati of Canto 93 could be closely related to Aryans; in the Waddellian argot, his name might plausibly signify "the Aryan." Later, in *Thrones*, Pound will write "Kati to Kang H[s]I / two 1/2s of a seal" accompanied by the ideograms for the Emperor ideograms for the Emperor K'ang[1] (康, peace) and Hsi[1] (熙, bright) (98/710), the same idea as that behind the Ara—the lordly shining ones.

Pound's "Egyptian Problem"

Pound's Aryanism led him into a twentieth-century impasse caused by the influential majority of contemporary scholars who accepted what Martin Bernal calls "the extreme Aryan model" of ancient history, which simply meant the denial of any Semitic or African influences on Greek culture, positing a pre-Classical Greece completely insulated from its near geographic neighbors Phoenicia and Egypt. By their account, invading Aryans from the north overran the Peloponnese, subjugating the darker matrilineal aborigines and birthing a culture. This "Aryan model" was posed against "the ancient model" that simply accepts the abundant testimony of the Greeks themselves that they derived massive sectors of their culture—especially their high culture, religion, political concepts, etc.—from Egypt; and their palace culture and alphabet from the Levant.

In its most extreme form, "hyper-diffusionism," the "extreme Aryan model" could be applied to a variety of historical moments and regions as it was by Waddell, Harvey, Murray, and even Senator Bilbo of Mississippi. Invading Aryans create civilization, dominating a darker, weaker group, then disappear as they interbreed with the subject peoples. The Aryan strain survives only in a variety of cultural artifacts, ceremonies, a few lighter individuals, or indirectly through toponyms. Hitler lamented how "once the actual and spiritual conqueror lost himself in the blood of the subjected peoples, the fuel for the torch of human progress is lost! Just as, through the blood of the former masters, the color preserved a feeble gleam in their memory, likewise the night of cultural life is gently illumined by the remaining creations of the former light-bringers" (1924: 292). Pound makes a slogan of the thought: "maintain antisepsis / let the light pour" (94/655).

Egypt has always posed a problem from the Eurocentric point of view, which since the Enlightenment until recently has begun the story of civilization with Greece and Homer, as do *The Cantos*. The nineteenth-century discovery of a variety of Mesopotamian civilizations, urban, literate, and powerful, as well as the new view of Egyptian civilization afforded when the window of hieroglyphics was opened by Champollion and others, threatened the fable of Greek originality. For those who think that race is *the* determinate factor in human potential and development—and there were many such in Europe and America in the twentieth century—the race of the Egyptians and of the oldest known Mesopotamian culture, the Sumerians, became the object of obsessive study. Who, or rather what, were these people?

Pound had landed in what has been called "the Egyptian problem," an artifact of nineteenth-century imperialism and the racism that justified it. Martin Bernal explains:

> *If it had been scientifically "proved" that Blacks were biologically incapable of civilization, how could one explain Ancient Egypt—which was most inconveniently placed on the African continent? There were two, or rather three solutions. The first was to deny that the Ancient Egyptians were black; the second was to deny that the Ancient Egyptians had created a "true" civilization; the third was to make doubly sure by denying both. The last has been preferred by most 19th—and 20th—century historians.* (Bernal 1986: 241; author's italics)

The leading Egyptologist of his time, the discoverer of the Abydos tomb cited by Waddell and Pound, Sir Flinders Petrie chose option one. He posited a "dynastic race" of non-Africans as the founders of Egyptian civilization in his *History of Egypt* (1923). Waddell took Petrie's illustrations as his main source, including the photo of those signs supposed by Waddell to be that of Sargon of Akkad that Pound appropriated for Canto 94 (see Figure 5.1). Since Waddell admired Ancient Egypt as much as Petrie, he differed only in boldly identifying the dynastic race, arguing that the creative impulse behind Ancient Egypt came from his Sumerian Aryan "Goths" and that the pre-dynastic inscriptions were in Sumerian. Egyptian civilization had been created by the Sumerian Menes, rebellious son of the Sumerian monarch Sargon I. This Menes is the Manis of Canto 94 (94/655) and also King Minos of Crete and the same Minos that "by Knoch Many ... lies" in Canto 97 (97/699). Pound would have learned this first in Murray's book, before reading Waddell (Murray 1951: 554). For the record, forensic DNA analysis proves that Petrie's dynastic race hypothesis is a myth necessitated to preserve the Aryan Model followed by Waddell and Pound. Contemporary scholarship concludes: "Egypt was a distinct North African culture rooted in the Nile Valley and the Sahara" (Lefkowitz & Rogers 1996: 67).[17]

From a Eurocentric perspective using the Aryan model, however, it was self-evident that Egyptians were not African—racially at least. They could not be, as Africans were incapable of civilization. Egypt is still conceived as part of the Middle East—"Oriental" in the old sense of the term—not part of Africa connected to the "black" interior through the umbilicus of the Nile. Since Egyptian civilization is undeniable, its influence has posed a problem for Eurocentrists and especially for classical studies, which has been invested in Greek priority from its very beginnings as a discipline. A few decades ago, Bernal's massive and compelling three-volume study *Black Athena: The Afroasiatic Origins of Classical Civilization* (1986–2006) caused a disciplinary crisis,[18] sparking the liveliest academic debate of the 1990s. Redeeming Egypt for Africa is a major part of the Afrocentric project as well, as the work of Cheikh Anta Diop[19] and many African American poets (Askia Touré, Jay Wright, Ishmael Reed) and musicians (Sun Ra) testifies.

For Pound and his epic poem, Afrocentricity is not an option, but by 1954 he does see the need to get Egypt into *The Cantos*. Waddell's sweeping vision coupled with Boris's expert knowledge of the ancient Egyptian language and books on the subject virtually placed Egypt in his hands. The problem is how to make it "cantabile." In facing this problem Pound followed the then-dominant Eurocentric view that the founders of Egypt could not be African; they weren't Chinese; ergo they must be European: Aryan.

The narrative of a creative but foreign minority of aristocratic white masters gradually dissolving in the broader darker stream of subject peoples obsessed those of a racialist persuasion, who took a eugenic attitude toward race. Flinders Petrie was an avid eugenicist and collaborated with Frances Galton, who invented eugenics as a science.[20] So was Senator Bilbo of Mississippi who, in *Take Your Choice: Separation or Mongrelization* (1946),[21] joined Waddell in claiming the Phoenicians as Caucasians. For Bilbo, all of the great civilizations had been founded by white people—Bilbo's survey includes Egypt, India, Phoenicia, Carthage, Greece, and Rome. He warned that all these civilizations had been lost through race mixing:

> Civilizations, the product of race, have been maintained only so long as the race which created them has maintained racial integrity. The Caucasian has founded all great civilizations, and this race, so long as it remains white, has not lost civilization. But when the blood of the white man has become mongrelized, civilization has not been maintained. The mongrel can neither create nor continue civilization. The record of written history offers the proof. (Bilbo 1947: 22)

Bilbo's judgment would have earned the fervent assent of Governor Murray. In comments throughout *Adam and Cain*, Murray argues that "mixing with native dark races" caused the fall of the early Aryan nations, like Sumer (Murray 1951: 569–70). He continues later: "[I]t may be observed that every time the Aryan Royalty mixed his blood with a kinky or curly haired race he produced a baneful and despotic ruler; when the people did so in large numbers, culture and civilization went down. Will America follow that here?" (Murray 1951: 572).

Pound did not disagree. Indeed, I think this horror of blood-mixing is part of Murray's basic "soundness." Skimming *Antony and Cleopatra* sometime in 1957–8, perhaps in aid of the "Spannthology" project that became *Confucius to Cummings* (1964), Pound was struck by the very opening of the play, where Philo introduces the dramatic situation, explaining to Demetrius that "this dotage of our general's / O'erflows the measure" (I. i. 1–2): we learn that Antony's warlike eyes

> now bend, now turn
> The office and devotion of their view
> Upon a tawny front; his captain's heart,

>   Which the scuffles of great fights hath burst
>   The buckles on his breast, reneges all temper,
>   And is become the bellows and the fan
>   To cool a gypsy's lust. (I. i. 4–9)

When Cleo and her attendants enter, Philo continues under his breath: "Take but good note, and you shall see him / the triple pillar of the world transform'd / into a strumpet's fool" (I. i. 11–13). Rereading this, Pound suddenly understood that the tragedy was not about Antony and Cleopatra, Rome and Egypt, but about the tragic temptations confronting the white race in a world of racial struggle. In notes he scribbled to himself, he paraphrased: "<u>Philo</u> falling for a miscegenation / with a brownskin / fucks now and fibs not / ugh—may as well a dog from that breed." Concluding "but Tony + Cleo highly moral work,"[22] Pound never followed up on these notes directly, but his realization that Shakespeare produced a "highly moral work" because he read Mediterranean geopolitics in the Roman period as a racial struggle may account for the nods to Shakespeare in contrast to the Stuart Monarchs in Cantos 105 and 107 (see 105/769, 107/777).

Pound's metapolitics demanded race integrity as the expression of cosmic order. But in the pessimistic master narrative of eugenics instanced by the fall of Antony, racial degeneracy is inevitable. The ancient civilization of Egypt, the Aryan masters of India, and soon those people Madison Grant called "Native Americans"—the members of the WASP ascendency like himself and Pound—were in danger of similar amalgamation into an undifferentiated and mediocre mongrelized mass. Coming to Waddell through Murray meant that Pound read Waddell as being an advocate of racial purity, Aryan priority, and its corollary, white supremacy. This formed the constructive side of Waddell's extravagant thesis for Pound and grounded his poetic "vision."

To conclude, the function of Aryanism generally and Waddell specifically in *Rock-Drill* and *Thrones* is not fundamentally to "get the kike," as Reno Odlin (formerly of the St. Elizabeths' cenacle) wrote to *Paideuma* (qtd in Casillo 1988: 96), but, more than that, to found and establish Pound's metapolitics in what he took to be the concrete reality of zoologically different human races. In this view only the Aryans, with the assistance of the Chinese, were capable of creating and maintaining "culture at its *most*"—of "building light." Pound's paradise is a white paradise. For even Confucius and Mencius, Pound's master teachers, are essentially white. As he wrote to begin his *Pisan Cantos*:

>   What you depart from is not the way
>   And olive tree blown white in the wind

> Washed by the Kiang and Han
> What whiteness will you add to this whiteness
>   What candor? (74/445)

What indeed, if not whiteness?

Notes

1. Pastor Wesley Swift preached this doctrine in the 1950s and beyond. Admiral Crommelin, John Kasper's other mentor, preached to Swift's congregation on these themes in sermons available to this day online.
2. Pound wrote in *The Townsman* "only a WHEAT GOD can save Europe" ("The Inedible," *Townsman* III.10 [February 1940]). He wrote to Roger Sharrock that "the butchers of the lesser cattle will always gang up on any agricultural holiness" (9/20/1955; qtd in Henderson 2010: 175). (AH)
3. Aryan horse sacrifice is attested in Waddell, though grudgingly, because he wants to assign animal and human sacrifice to "Chaldee semites," practices abhorred by Aryans as Devil-worship (Waddell 1930: 37; 2013: 90, 369). Interestingly, Pound justified animal sacrifice on eugenic grounds. This explains the lines on horse sacrifice at the end of Canto 97: "& Spartans in Mount Taygeto / sacrifice a horse to the winds" (97/702). Pound ranted to Norman Holmes Pearson that "while bastardization, mongrelism rages elsewhere, no sense of race / no sense of eugenics / sacrificial animals probably to keep up breed, like hoss in Ky" (6/23/1957; Beinecke YCAL MSS 899, Box 79, folder "Pound, Ezra 1957").
4. It is unclear who wrote the chapter Pound refers to. Not Murray, who merely comments on it: "The only way we can check Communism in U.S.A. is to challenge the Jew promoting the Ism" (1951: 488). Rev. Henry S. Swabey's "fight for local school" can be found on pages 486–8. Swabey was an English Social Creditor, a Pound correspondent, and a political ally.
5. Stock (1983: 177).
6. They are first hinted at in Canto 98, dominate Canto 104, and pervade *Drafts & Fragments*, especially the shard of Canto 112.
7. This book was published as *Ancient Britain Revisited* by the Christian Book Club of America (Hawthorne, CA) in 1973. This publisher reprinted several Square $ titles, so *Ancient Britain* may have been projected for the Square $ list at some point.
8. Murray claims to have adopted Harvey's book "in full" (1951: 536).
9. Waddell's view of Cain and Abel (as well as Harvey's later elaboration on it) is the mirror opposite of a book highly influential in Anglo-Israelite circles and later in Christian identity theology: Ethel Bristowe's 1927 life of Cain, *Sargon the Magnificent*.

Here, Cain just is Sargon and Sargon is evil, not good. For Bristowe, see Michael Barkun, *Religion and the Racist Right* (Chapel Hill: UNC Press, 1997), 162–72.

10 Earlier, and independently of Pound, Charles Olson became interested in Waddell through his lover Frances Boldereff. Waddell informs *Maximus*. See *Charles Olson and Frances Boldereff: A Modern Correspondence*, edited by Ralph Maud (Middletown, CT: Wesleyan University Press, 1999).

11 The hawk sign links Sargon to Frederick II Hohenstaufen, author of the first book of ornithology, *The Book of the Falcon*. The name Frederick may also be an Aesopian shout-out to *Frederick* John Kasper, who had hawklike features. Kasper is nowhere mentioned directly in *The Cantos*.

12 Casillo continues: "Waddell also connects solar religion, patriarchal authority, and agriculture; the Sumerian sun-worshippers, he says, with their father gods, introduced agriculture into the ancient world" (99). He uses these common attributes to link Waddell and the Nazi ideologue Alfred Rosenberg.

13 This journey to India links Tsiang to Apollonius of Tyana, who also went to India to learn about Indian religion. See Mead (1901).

14 Casillo points out this had the added effect of erasing the problem of the Greek adoption of a Semitic alphabet (Casillo 1988: 98), a problem Waddell had "solved" in his *Aryan Origins of the Alphabet*.

15 Pound wrote Boris that "it is not the bare 16 points of the Edict, or the Yong Tching but Wang's expositions that gets up to Khati / 'the flaming light in the heart is one's heaven'" (9/27/1955, qtd in Kindellan 2017: 164–5).

16 See Bernal (1986), chapters 1 and 2, *passim*.

17 That said, a standard textbook, *A History of the Ancient Near East Circa 3000–323 BC* (2nd ed.) (Hoboken, NJ: Blackwell, 2006) by Marc Van de Meiroop, hints at contacts between ancient Uruk (the earliest civilization known today) and the Nile Valley early in the third millennium (38).

18 The disciplinary counterblast, *Black Athena Revisited*, edited by Mary R. Lefkowitz and Guy MacLean Rogers (Chapel Hill: University of North Carolina Press, 1996), required a fourth 500-page response, *Black Athena Writes Back: Martin Bernal Responds to his Critics* (Durham, NC: Duke University Press, 2001) that should be read as integral to the rest of his study.

19 Two of Diop's books that appeared in French in the 1950s were combined and translated as *The African Origin of Civilization: Myth or Reality* in 1974. This was followed by *Civilization or Barbarism: An Authentic Anthropology* (1981, trans. 1991). Both argue that the Egyptians are proper Africans and thus that the origins of civilization are at bottom African.

20 Petrie worked closely with Galton, providing him with thousands (!) of skeletal remains dug up during his excavations in Egypt. See Kathleen Sheppard, "Flinders Petrie and Eugenics at UCL," *Bulletin of the History of Archaeology* (online) 20(1) (2010): 16–29.

21 *Take Your Choice* is a substantial book of 330 pages, not a polemical pamphlet. In it Bilbo shows a wide familiarity with black intellectuals like W. E. B. DuBois, George Schuyler, and Richard Wright, as well as Franz Boas, Gunnar Myrdal, and eugenicists. Bilbo's "Greater Liberia Act" introduced in the Senate in 1939 is a detailed plan for the "voluntary" resettlement of Afro-Americans in their "fatherland, West Africa" (298–317). One would think that Murray would use Bilbo in *Adam and Cain*, but he does not. Although Pound's use of "mongrelization" might be traced to Bilbo's book and Senate speeches, Pound shows no interest in him—perhaps because Jews just don't come up in the senator's racial theory of history. See Bilbo (1947).

22 Beinecke YCAL MSS 43, Box 122, folder 4981, Notebook 113 (*Thrones* 24) 1957–8 Mar., p. 16.

6

Sheri Martinelli and the Paradise of Venus

As though swimming up from the depths, Sheri Martinelli is now surfacing in the midst of Pound's Paradise. That's because for a time she *was* Pound's paradise, its center of attraction, "Centrum circuli" (87/590), "the center of the circle," the object of contemplation, the focus of desire. Without her, there are no Cantos 90 through 95 as we know them; without her, the latter "paradisal" half of Canto 97 makes little sense and the Homeric tropes in Canto 102, which reprises the end of Canto 97, are unaccountable. We must now understand that these cantos were inspired by her, written *with* her, *specifically for her to read*. To underscore that claim, in what follows, I will call them the "Sheri Cantos."

Over the past several years, Martinelli has been brought in from the Bohemian suburbs of *The Cantos* to its paradisal center, at least as far as Dante's Third Heaven, the Heaven of Venus, of Spirits inclined to Love. I believe it was Wendy Flory who first brought attention to Martinelli's importance in *Ezra Pound and the Cantos: A Record of Struggle* (1980): "Once we have read canto 94," she writes, "we realize that Isis-Kuanon is, in large part, Sherri [sic] Martinelli herself." Flory points us to Martinelli's picture of that goddess in *La Martinelli* (1956), which Pound had published by Vanni Scheiwiller in Italy, the same printer who would first print and set *Rock-Drill* and *Thrones*: "The poet sees her as more than an individual." Martinelli "comes to represent for him the very idea of love as inspiration. Set against the bleak and stultifying reality of the asylum ward, her youth, enthusiasm and spontaneity" meant life and love. Flory quotes from David Rattray's sensational *Nation* article of November 16, 1957, where Martinelli told the young Dartmouth undergrad that Pound loves her "because I symbolize the spirit of Love to him" (Flory 1980: 246). Since Flory's book, Pound scholarship has only grudgingly followed up.

Still, Martinelli has been emerging into the collective critical consciousness. Though she was once dismissed by scholarship as a kind of groupie, it is now admitted that the love was deep and real. David Moody writes in his authoritative biography that "Pound certainly delighted in La Martinelli, and was joyfully in love with her for a time," concluding that Pound was no "fond and foolish old man." Despite the thirty years' difference in their ages, "the sexual attraction was there for all to see" (Moody 2015: 312). The implication is that the two did enjoy some kind of sexual relationship. It now seems clear that they did. In other words, for a time—three years—Sheri Martinelli was the most important woman in Pound's life and had a major, even determining influence on the cantos he was then composing, the Sheri Cantos, 90 through 95, which record (among much else) the progress of their love.

Born Shirley Burns Brennan (1918–98) in Philadelphia, "La Martinelli" was an important late-twentieth-century muse and minor painter who inspired, before Pound, Anatole Broyard and William Gaddis and, after him, Charles Bukowski. She went to art school in Philadelphia and married the successful painter and sculptor Ezio Martinelli; they had a daughter and moved to New York City. When the marriage broke up, Martinelli became part of Anaïs Nin's circle of devotees, and she figures in Nin's diaries of the late 1940s. Martinelli lived in Greenwich Village, hung out with Charlie Parker and the Modern Jazz Quartet (one of her best things is a portrait of bassist Percy Heath), and shared their interest in drugs. An alcoholic, like many models she used heroin (which is why "dope" is a major theme in the Washington Cantos); she painted and wrote. Martinelli is a classic, almost archetypical muse.[1]

Although they knew each other from 1952, when Sheri first visited the incarcerated poet, Martinelli began serving as Pound's muse at St. Elizabeths from 1954, after a blitz of letters from him persuaded her to move down to Washington. Her influence on him was strongest from that summer of 1954 to late 1957,[2] when he was writing *Rock-Drill* and *Thrones*. Martinelli was supplanted in Pound's affections by Marcella Spann in the months before Pound's release in the spring of 1958 and finally, just weeks before, sent off to Mexico to paint and write.[3] What we are just now realizing is the profound effect she had not only on the poet but on Pound's poetry.

Ezra Pound: "a ballin' angel ..."

Scholars like me have long been skeptical that an actual sexual relationship between Pound and Martinelli was possible given the lack of privacy at St. Elizabeths. I had decided that their relationship was consummated on the astral plane only. Still, the rumor has been about for decades. According to Fuller Torrey, "by Martinelli's own admission, she and Pound were lovers" (qtd in Carpenter

1988: 802–803). In 2005 Steven Moore, the scholar along with Richard Taylor who has most appreciated Martinelli's importance, was alerted to an item taken from a letter defending Pound that Martinelli had written to Miles Payne, editor of an ephemeral little magazine called *Light Year*. Payne published a redacted version of it in his Autumn 1961 issue. Moore transcribed it and appended it to his important *Gargoyle* article on Martinelli, originally published in 1998 (see Appendix B).

As Moore says, it "seems to put to rest the question of whether she and Pound were lovers" (Moore 2005).[4] Indeed, "Homage to Grampa" is a five-star review of their sexual relationship, which states baldly that Pound "could fuck better than any man and that includes men of many colors." Addressing "Grampa" as "a great stud," Martinelli marveled at "the ideas he flows through a woman's mind whilst he flows through her body" (Moore 2005). In her account she and Pound are literally engaged in the poet/muse relation. These lines from Canto 90 are about them: "Beatific spirits welding together / as in one ash-tree in Ygdrasail / Baucis, Philemon" (90/625); Ezra, Sheri, intertwined as one tree of life. Years before, Pound had written: "Sex is of a double function and purpose, reproductive and educational" (*SR* 94). In 1960, Martinelli explained to Charles Bukowski about "'education' in the way gramps meant it … he had one hand on my breasts & one eye on me … & one hand on Ovid's metamorph & one eye on th' book & his mouth on mine … dear Educational Gramps" (Moore 2001: 54). The poet is physically transmitting his poetic knowledge to her; she is physically offering aid and comfort and inspiration to him.

Pound makes this oblique comment in a December 1954 letter: "Damn it ALL physical contact should be ART @ level of Flora Castalia. You know that. " (EP to SM).[5] Love, even in a relationship as sexually fulfilling as Pound's and Martinelli's evidently was, aimed toward ecstasy, not only orgasm (think: "beatific *spirits*"), as Sheri tried to explain without success to Bukowski in her letters (Moore 2001: 52, 352; see also Moody 2015: 312–13).[6] Still, as Pound wrote to her, "absolute purity does NOT require castration. BUT on the contrary. That don't now concern us" (EP to SM 9/25/1954). In an August 1954 letter the poet preens: "Test tube eZamination of st{u}ds: put 'em near a chick" (EP to SM)—sounds like Ez passed the eZam!

"Ezra Pound is the ONLY man I'd ever met," Martinelli told Payne, "in the full sense of being a man." To her, "Grampa ain't a fallen angel—he's a ballin' angel." She insists, and I repeat: "I'd like to record this fact … that Ezra Pound, agish 69 to 72 could fuck better than any man" (Moore 2001: addendum 23). Pound was age sixty-nine to seventy-two from 1954 to 1957, when she and he were having deep sexual communion together; she knew from experience that Pound was "a good & benevolent man / and a great stud / and a Shape Changer—a maker of Souls" (Moore 2005: 23). Martinelli's Ezra is a virile demigod (see Figure 6.1).

There are fascinating gender issues involved in their muse/poet relationship of which Martinelli was fully aware: "I am IMAGINATION," she wrote to Pound on May 1, 1957, "I cannot AFFORD TO BE A LADY. I have too much work to do. Also I was born OUTSIDE of CLASS ... SEX ... OR POLITICS. I SEE what I SEE. I AM as I AM." (SM to EP).[7] Echoing Canto 94, Sheri told Bukowski: "I never die Buk because I am Spirit acting thru Matter or that Energy made by Prana / I am of the Crystal beyond Prana & I never die; just have many names" (Moore 2001: 125–6; see 94/654). To Pound and his circle, she was Isis, Kuanon (Gwanyin), Flora Castalia (after the spring at Delphi), the synthetic goddess Princess Ra-Set, Gea and Sybil—all images or avatars of Martinelli that permeate Pound's paradise in *Thrones*.

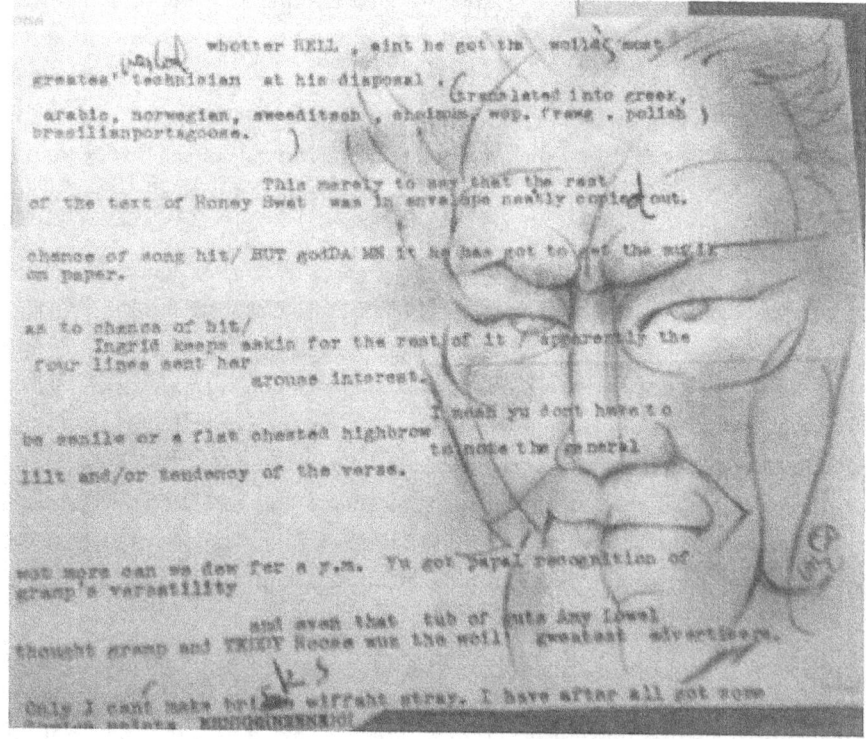

Figure 6.1 "EP" by Sheri Martinelli, colored pencil on a Pound letter, Beinecke.

Sheri's coded epiphany opens Canto 90, attended by a plethora of avatar goddesses, from Kuthera Aphrodite to Leucothea. Moody states flatly that "Pound's 'Paradiso proper' starts here" (Moody 2015: 357). "The importance of Martinelli can hardly be overstated when it comes to an understanding of Pound's paradise," Kindellan concurs. "Martinelli ... figures as these cantos' first and perhaps only intended audience ... Readers, so far as they existed, were invited to peruse a recondite sub-suite of cantos, that, despite superficial sense, were little more than a concatenation of personal references." Cantos 90 through 95 are *"really* about him and Martinelli" (2017: 103; Kindellan's emphasis).

If so, we have to change our approach to these poems. Canto 93, read as a message to Martinelli, takes on a new and refreshing inflection, to be read as a lovers' secret. We have long recognized that the poem has a special relation to Martinelli because two of her paintings, "Lux in diafana" and "Ursula benedetta," figure in it (93/648). But let's listen to the poem as if we were overhearing it whispered into Martinelli's ear. Take it from **"Came then Flora Castalia"** (93/650)—who we now know is Martinelli herself—to the end of the canto. (The poet's whispers are bolded). Thus:

"Came then Flora Castalia" (93/650) means she responded to Pound's call. Flora Castalia is a goddess invented by Pound, says Peter Liebregts, who does not mention Martinelli in his brilliant, Neoplatonic reading of these cantos (Liebregts 2004: 299–328). The goddess in Sheri has been revealed, not *by* Pound but *to* him, by their love. Only the name is invented by Pound: Spring (the season of flowers) plus the Delphic spring, source of poetic inspiration. She has arrived, summoned by the poet whose tone has drawn her like the dolphin, **volucres delphinasque vad auditum**—swimming up as though from his unconscious life, like the "undine" Sheri is figured as in Canto 91. Now, the poem modulates to Pound's memory of lines by the Roman poet Sulpicia, whose verses to her lover Cerinthus Pound had long ago worked into Canto 25; it was Sulpicia who told her lover not to worry, **Pone metum,** the gods protect lovers **Nec deus laedit** (25/117).

Pound tells Sheri she is also **"the Lorraine girl,"** Joan of Arc, who saw the angel in the fields of defeated France; she has given the poet a new life, **"nuova vita,"** as Beatrice did young Dante; she has spoken to him as Beatrice speaks to Dante in the opening of *Paradiso* Canto V, **"e ti fiammeggio"**—"for you I burn"—and *sub voce* Sheri is to hear the rest of the line: "nel caldo d'amore"— from the warmth of love. In the *Paradiso* Beatrice tells the poet that the light within her proceeds from perfect sight attracted by the good in him. Good to good, as if commenting on the lines from Richard St. Victor bracketing Canto 90 "UBI AMOR IBI OCULUS EST"—where there is love, there is the eye.

Yes, **Such light is in sea-caves,** the light-flecked womb-space of the beautiful Cyprian, **e la bella Cipriana,** where the lovers look into each other's eyes, their eyebeams twining like flames, rising as heat "**to fade / in green air**" that will leave somewhere a "**foot-print**"—probably in this poem—"**alcun vestigio,**" a trace to last five thousand years, like the love poems of the ancient Egyptians: **Thus saith ... (Kati).**

So yes, **philologers** will have a difficult time making sense of this. And to hell with **biographers,** off with their heads! They'll never understand the essential nature of this thing between us, this intense sexual **quiddity**! They'll never catch up, following us in **the dinghy astern there**—the famous line from *Paradiso* Canto II that will close *Thrones.* No: "**there must be incognita,**" unknowns, in the private sea cave of our intimacy "**un lume pien' di spiriti**", "a light filled with spirits" and of our private memories. The Italian is a line from a Cavalcanti ballata that Pound translated as early as 1910 (Ballata V; see *Translations* 106). You have come this far, beloved, "**You who dare Persephone's threshold,**" the doors of hell here at St. Elizabeths. Don't be afraid, "**Beloved, do not fall apart in my hands**"; no, no, she is to put aside her doubts, **E "chi crescera"** others will be drawn to and confirm our love, we flourish through attraction, that's how it begins, even as Swedenborg had it, even whole **societies** begin this way, "**by attraction.**" The Italian is from *Paradiso* V.105, where Dante's intellectual doubts and fears are allayed and the strength of human will affirmed and acclaimed.

Now, Pound harks back to another early poem from *Canzoni* (1911), "Ballatetta," much influenced by Cavalcanti and the Troubadours, that begins: "The light became her grace and dwelt among / **Blind eyes and shadows** that are formed as men" (*P* 36). These blind ones, distracted by the wrong things and transitory triumphs, are the ones with the "**trigger happy minds,**" "**going six ways a Sunday,**" fumbling their ways "**amid stars / ... dangers, abysses**" that they can't even sense, because they are distracted, so busy running down rabbit holes (perhaps philological) that they can't see what is right in front of them—including this poem.

> **to enter the presence at sunrise**
> **up out of hell, from the labyrinth**
> **the path wide as a hair** (93/652)

Terrell has an elaborate note on these lines; scholarship has been attracted to the notion that they point to the "bridge between worlds" of the last fragment of

Canto 117, claiming that the upshot is metaphysical. Cookson thinks so (2001: 203). I think Martinelli would have read it as a description of their lovemaking. "The presence" is the quiddity, *their* thing itself. There is an imperative here, the desire to enter a sacred space.

& as to mental velocities: Pound always praised Sheri's instant uptake that proved their shared intuitive understanding. He found Martinelli's mind quicker than others: "after 9 years among people [in] whose minds NOTHING happens (and I do not mean patients, I mean visitors[)] E.P. has COMFORT when a mind is full of fish and birds / But imagine those whose minds merely WALK, trying to follow the dive and flight" (EP to SM 7/3/1954). "Who the hell else can collaborate?" he wondered in a letter written next day. Pound complained that everyone else has to be "TOLD, TOLD TOLD" what to do; their minds were mechanical, and they expected him to "blow their nozez"—everything he wanted done had to be tediously explained (EP to SM 7/4/1954).[8]

Quickness of mind is something Pound associated with the divine. Liebregts notes that "communicative mental swiftness fits the context of *Thrones*, which, both in terms of its philosophy and its textual strategy, is a poetry of intuitive understanding rather than of rational discourse" (Liebregts 2004: 339; see also Kindellan 2017: 145). In Canto 93, slow **Ian Hamilton** (the General who commanded at Gallipoli) is supplied to contrast Pound's judgment of Martinelli's extraordinary "mental velocity"—something only she would know. Velocity, "**duration**"—i.e. concentration, sensitivity, hence "**antennae**" ("artists are the antennae of the race," Pound had written long ago [*LE* 58]) as opposed to stupidity or **malevolence**, another kind of stupidity.

But Pound closes by worrying about his beloved, his Sheri. He knows she is "**tender as a marshmallow**" and vulnerable. She has stirred his mind out of the dust of despair; she has lifted him "from under the rubble heap … from the dulled edge beyond pain" (90/626); because of her "**the wind is ½ lighted with pollen**," the blown seed (93/652), "semina motuum" (92/638) of the fertile universe; she makes him remember the glories of love, Cavalcanti and his "**Monna Vanna**," Cavalcanti's love name for Madonna Giovanna, another "Lady Sapientia"—a name not so different in feeling from "Flora Castalia."

"The wind ½ lighted with pollen" is, Pound sees, a "**diafan**," a key term in Pound's *phantastikon* psychology, derived from his reading of medieval "light philosophy" and explored in his work on Cavalcanti in the 1920s (see Canto 29). Pound liked to think that Cavalcanti had read Grosseteste on "the Generation of Light" (*LE* 149)—that light comes *from* the body; we don't simply receive it from outside. At times of peak intensity, as when energized by sexual love, Pound believed, we radiate light, which creates a diaphanous radiance, a kind of halo. In his essay on "Cavalcanti" published in the 1930s, Pound describes the diafan as "Formed there in manner as a mist of light" (*LE* 155). This diaphanous quality of the corporeal substance of light seemed to Pound to become a paradox of crystal in motion: "Crystal waves weaving together toward the gt / healing"; "Light & the flowing crystal / never gin in cut glass had such clarity" (91/631).[9]

If we accept Martinelli and Pound as lovers in the full sense, then it behooves us to read the Sheri Cantos as I have here. Read this way, as by, for, and about Sheri Martinelli, odd references gain more meaning. The nod to "The Baroness," Elsa von Freytag-Loringhoven, a famous Bohemian figure in Manhattan in the 1910s (she is said to be the subject of Duchamp's "Nude Descending a Staircase") where she famously intrigued and tormented William Carlos Williams,[10] comments on Sheri's situation as a beauty who attracted a lot of unwanted attention from men. The Baroness is called "Cassandra" because she said several true things that were not believed about the difficulties confronted by women artists who wished to "adhere to "the principle of non-acquiescence" (95/666); that is, resistance to a lascivious patriarchy bent on controlling women, the same situation faced by Martinelli half a century later.

Or, to take another instance that has a personal valence: Martinelli herself explained to Bukowski that the lines from Canto 90 "Grove hath its altar / under elms, in that temple, in silence / a lone nymph by the pool" (90/627), refer to a time "in 1954 [when] Ezra prayed for an 'altar in the grove' for me" (12/11/1960; qtd in Moore 2001: 115).

In his philological dissection of Canto 97, Kindellan spends time on Pound's curious substitution of EROS for EPOS in Canto 102, another "paradisal," Martinelli-saturated canto. As others (Bacigalupo and Rabaté) have noted before him, Kindellan focuses on a curious error in the line of Romanized Greek: "OIOS TELESAI ERGON ... EROS'TE" that ends the first page of that canto (102/748). The Greek comes from *Odyssey* II l. 272, where Athena, disguised as Mentor, is praising Odysseus to Telemachus. The full line, including the words Pound has elided, is translated by Richmond Lattimore as "such a man he was for accomplishing word and action" (Lattimore 46, l. 272; qtd in Kindellan 2017: 187). One can see that Pound has mistranscribed the Greek, substituting EROS for EPOS, "love" for "word," so that the poem reads "such a man he was for accomplishing love and action." Kindellan has assiduously explored this crux in Pound's notebook and drafts, the "genetic dossier" documenting the evolution of the poem (2017: 188). He finds that Pound originally transcribed the Greek correctly and that "epos" survived until the first typescript, becoming "eros" only from the second typescript. The question is whether "eros" was a conscious poetic decision by the poet or one of the many "inadvertent errors of transcription" that confuse these poems. Kindellan is interested primarily in showing the "textual indeterminacy" that justifies his careful genetic approach, so he defers any final judgment on the meaning of this error, which Jean-Michel Rabaté saw as an inspired misquotation from Homer (Kindellan 2017: 187). Now that we've seen the thoroughly erotic nature of Pound's paradise, it seems clear that, at the very least, the transition of epos to eros was a true Freudian slip, but it is much more likely that it was a decision, that Pound was describing himself, and that he was speaking as another kind of mentor, not to Telemachus but to Martinelli.

Martinelli was fully invested in the poetry: "yr poetry truly superior" she wrote Pound, "one has the inner knowledge/conviction/sense wotever—that you are not so much watching yr emotional system ... as looking at wot things are doing, so your eye is on the real world & not on any impression of it" (SM to EP 5/3/1960).[11] She was most interested in Pound's poetic process in which she saw herself as a spiritual partner. As she wrote to Bukowski:

> When Ezra was in his room writing "you are as tender as a marshmallow my love" I was in a car ... & suddenly touched my soft bozum—being so intelligent—I've never done it before in my life—the only time I realize I'm a female is when I'm impassionately [sic] in love ... it was a strange thing for me to do &I said "why I'm as tender as a marshmallow" ... was of course astounded when Ezra handed me my poem with those words in / It happened several times. (Moore 2001: 131–2)

Writing to Bukowski, Martinelli understandably forgets the implicit criticism of the context: "You are as tender as a marshmallow, my love, / I cannot use you as a fulcrum" (93/6521). A fulcrum to lever Pound where, exactly? Where else except Paradise? Where Pound and his poem need to go. Despite his devotion to her, Pound seems to realize that Martinelli could only take him and his poem so far.

More than a lover, Pound also saw Martinelli as his goddess rescuer. Early on, Pound had written her, wondering, "Am I tempting Providence by committing this statement to writin?"

> Supposed line (bagged from Odyssey)
> yet he doubted till the raft brast
> + came to Phaecians (EP to SM 10/22/1954)

Sheri was to be Leucothea, the sea goddess who rescued Odysseus when his raft was destroyed by unforgiving, relentless Poseidon in Book V of *The Odyssey*. By giving him her veil, Leucothea preserves the epic hero safely ashore at Phaecia. Scholarship agrees that Leucothea is Sheri, probably because, keeping with her Bohemian ways, Pound has her offering, instead of a veil, her bikini, the skimpy bathing suit invented in 1946 and named, ironically, after the first H-bomb test, which obliterated the Pacific atoll of that name. "My bikini is worth your raft" becomes Pound's jaunty way of putting Leucothea's offer—possibly the first use of the word "bikini" in a literary context (91/636, 95/665).[12] Leucothea is the deified Ino, daughter of Cadmus, who in *The Odyssey* surfaces from the briny deep to become a compassionate seabird: "Leucothea had pity," Pound writes in closing the Sheri Cantos, "mortal once / who now is a sea-god" (95/667). Odysseus relied on Leucothea's help to reach the land of the Phaecians, a utopian *paradiso terrestre*. Pound had similar visions of Sheri doing the same for him, escorting him to the *paradiso terrestre* that inspired *Thrones*.

Trobar Clus

Scholars have long noticed the Provençal influences throughout Cantos 90 through 95; Massimo Bacigalupo knows that the most important gloss on these poems is "Psychology and Troubadours" (1912), where the young poet makes a rare prose foray into the psychosexual origins of poetry (see Bacigalupo 1980: 282–4). Originally a talk given to the Quest Society, "Psychology and Troubadours" is about *trobar clus*—the "closed" form, the "close ring" (*SR* 90) that had something to do with a chivalric "love code" (*SR* 87). The problem, as Pound conceived it in 1912, was this:

> Did this "chivalric love," this exotic, take on mediumistic properties? Stimulated by the color or quality of emotion, did that "color" take on forms interpretive of the divine order? Did it lead to an "exteriorization of the sensibility," and interpretation of the cosmos by feeling? (*SR* 94)

I take these to be rhetorical questions: the answers are yes, yes, and yes. Pound had read about and probably personally experienced such things. He wrote about them in Canto 29. In 1954 Pound's love for Martinelli brought these phenomena to the forefront. Mediumistic properties? Check. Martinelli claimed telepathic contact with Pound when he was composing. The color of emotion and the divine order? Check. Kindellan shows that the first line of Canto 90, "From the colour the nature / & by the nature the sign," though attributed to John Heydon (and consistent with his thinking), were in fact the words of Martinelli (90/625;

Kindellan 2017: 103). "Exteriorization of the sensibility"—i.e. the *Phantastikon*? It's virtually defined in Canto 91: "that the body of light come forth from the body of fire" (91/630)—the body of fire being the body of lovers in their passion.

The whole sequence of Cantos 90 through 95 is one of the most elaborate love poems of the twentieth century.[13] Bacigalupo claims that "the forty pages of cs. 90–95 may be taken as a single new *Canzone d'amore*" on the model of Cavalcanti or Dante (Bacigalupo 1980: 259). These cantos are shot through with lines from Arnaut Daniel, quotes from Dante, and nods to Cavalcanti, helping us locate the poem in the Provençal tradition of "*trobar clus*," of encoding secrets in a song, usually the illicit desire of the singer for a Lady. Peter Makin opens his chapter on Arnaut in *Provence and Pound* by asserting:

> Arnaut Daniel's work contains the main reasons for Pound's later interest in the troubadours. These can be called "*trobar clus* as rite" and "woman as focus of the poet's intelligence." To explain these two concepts is to explain Pound's whole view of the troubadour poetic, and perhaps most of Pound's own poetic effort. *Trobar clus*, which means "enclosed," perhaps hermetic composition, is the name given to the art of those troubadours who put hidden meanings in their songs … [Pound] saw this *trobar* as an act of worship. He believed that Provence's discovery was the way in which the love of a woman and the effort to "get across to her" raised the artist's perception to the divine. The artist became a priest. The connection between these two ideas is religious but not particularly Christian, and comes from the benevolent, divine, and ordered nature of the universe, which it is the whole purpose of the Cantos to show. (Makin 1978: 160)

That Pound has such stuff in mind is signaled by the opening lines of Canto 91, "ab lo dolchor qu'al cor mi vai," "with the sweetness that goes to my heart" (91/630), a confected line of Provençal music and lyrics (Terrell 1984: 545–6).[14] But just because they are such an intimate, esoteric document, the Sheri Cantos rustle with exoteric references hiding personal meanings. The human situation, the lovers' drama, is well concealed in a thicket of private allusions, foreign languages, and inspired blather.[15] As well, consistent with the rest of *The Cantos* these poems have a didactic purpose; they are to educate Martinelli as well: Roman law, Kung, Mencius, Dante, and Agassiz for "Gestalt seed" (94/655) and Apollonius as Aryan paragon. Once we accept that these are love poems written with, by, and for a real flesh-and-blood lover, some of the tropic underbrush is cleared. Thus one of Martinelli's love-names for Pound, "Fuss-cat," appears after a citation of Roman law, which interestingly enough has to do with the rights of illegitimate children and thus bears on Pound's own difficulties in protecting his own daughter, Mary, from abuse by his wife (see Terrell 1984: 574; Moody 2015: 246–50).

Martinelli saw herself as Pound's spiritual partner in making *The Cantos*. Pound thought of her as a "collaborator." Richard Taylor argues that she "can be said to have had almost as much influence on Ezra Pound as he on her" (Taylor 2000: 98). Likewise, Steven Moore observes that Pound found ways to weave Martinelli's paintings into the cantos he was composing: "she would show Pound her works in progress and often he would give them titles"; these, in turn, worked their way into cantos. Moore instances her paintings "Lux in diafana" and "Ursula benedetta" in Canto 93:

> Lux in diafana,
> >Creatrix oro [I pray].
> Ursula benedetta,
> >Oro (93/648)

Both of these paintings are "idealized self-portraits" (Moore 2005: 19–20).[16] In other words, Sheri's paintings did not only "illustrate" Pound's poem but also inspired it (Moore 2005: 21–2)—each lover drives the other to kindle paradise. Mary de Rachewiltz has shown me another idealized self-portrait, featuring Sheri's magical magnetic eyes drawn in ballpoint pen on the flyleaf of Pound's copy of *The Cantos* that he used at St. Elizabeths, so that the poet could draw inspiration and encouragement from them as he worked. Painted over and over in different contexts, Martinelli's portraits were crafted to project paradisal energy—love. What this means is that Cantos 90 through 95 should be read as the two lovers' collaboration. Kindellan shows that Pound campaigned to have a small deluxe edition of *Rock-Drill* printed that would include reproductions of Martinelli works as frontispiece and final colophon. Her "Gea Mater" "accompanied" Canto 85 in its initial *Hudson Review* publication. "Gea Mater," rather than *ling*² 靈, is the opening of *Rock-Drill* Pound preferred (Kindellan 2017: 108–109). Under the sign of the Earth Mother, rather than a hieroglyphic rebus, *Rock-Drill* would naturally be read differently. *Paradiso terrestre* indeed! Sheri and Ezra must have been in intense, intimate conversation about these poems, which are constantly cited in Pound's letters to her and, later on, in Martinelli's letters to Bukowski.

Big-eyed, erotic sylphs—Martinelli's dream of herself—peer out in pastel colors from her paintings and drawings. Martinelli was in the habit of drawing her own muse-eyes in closing letters to Pound, as in the accusatory letter shown in Figure 6.2, complaining about Pound's rejection of her—although the eyes are surprisingly mild.

Martinelli was uninterested of painting the world as it appears; instead she painted what for her was the real world, the invisible, anagogical world of poetic

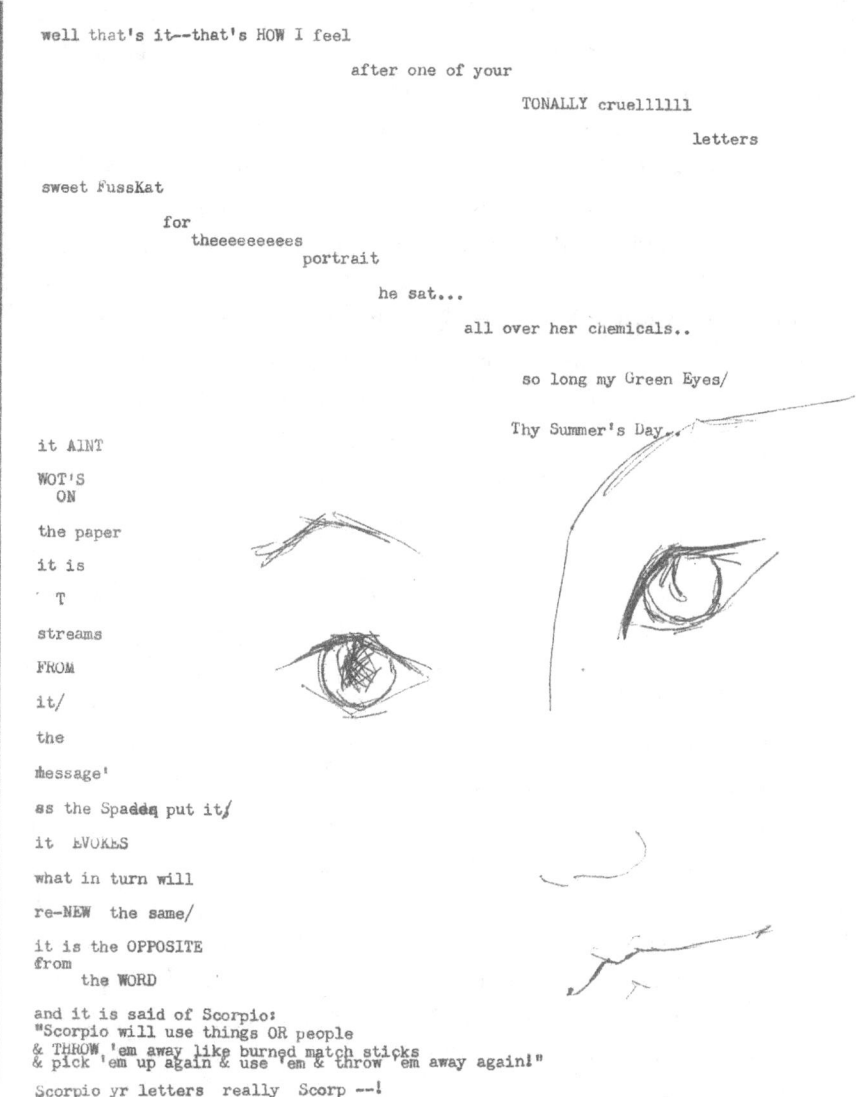

```
well that's it--that's HOW I feel
                    after one of your
                              TONALLY cruellllll
                                         letters
 sweet FussKat
             for
                 theeeeeeeees
                            portrait
                          he sat...
                              all over her chemicals..
                                  so long my Green Eyes/
                                Thy Summer's Day
it AINT
WOT'S
   ON
the paper
it is
  T
streams
FROM
it/
the
message'
as the Spades put it/
it EVOKES
what in turn will
re-NEW the same/
it is the OPPOSITE
from
     the WORD
and it is said of Scorpio:
"Scorpio will use things OR people
& THROW 'em away like burned match sticks
& pick 'em up again & use 'em & throw 'em away again!"
Scorpio yr letters really Scorp --!
```

Figure 6.2 "Signature" by Sheri Martinelli, ballpoint pen, Beinecke.

meaning and idealized essence. This anagogical poetics (as in Provençal *trobar clus*) sends messages to readers already on the same wavelength, as lovers usually are (SM to EP 12/18/1958, p. 4). As Pound put it, "the meaning comes out of the poet," through (almost in spite of) the words on the page (EP to SM 10/4/1954). This statement helps explain a positive aspect of Pound's codes technique: code can be constructive, like the prayers to the Goddess that Pound breaks into from time to time in these cantos, most famously in Canto 90 "Sibylla ... m'elevasti" (90/626) and the gesture toward Layamon's *Brut* in Canto 91 "Leafdi Diana" (91/632). This is probably what Pound and Martinelli mean when they use the term "anagogic," which occurs occasionally in Pound's letters to her and later titled her *Anagogic & Paideumic Review*. In the reproduced letter, both in the words and most especially in the drawing, one can see that Martinelli is riffing on the passage from Richard St. Victor that frames Canto 90: "Animus humanus amor non est, sed ab ipso amor procedit" ("The human soul is not love but love flows from it") (90/625). Pound himself plays changes on the Latin at the end of that canto—"Not love but the love that flows from it"—ending the poem "UBI AMOR IBI OCULUS EST" ("WHERE LOVE IS, THERE IS THE EYE"), the phrase that Martinelli alludes to in her many drawings of her huge-eyed, hypnotic, goddess self (90/629; see also Terrell 1984: 540, 541, 544).

In "Psychology and Troubadours" Pound mentions (without quoting) Richard St. Victor's "one very beautiful passage on the splendors of paradise" (*SR* 96) that must be a reference to one of Pound's key touchstones, the trinity of "cogitation, meditation and contemplation," states of mind that correspond, in Pound's view, to hell, purgatory, and heaven (see 87/590). "Richardus" is a recurrent reference in the Sheri Cantos.[17] A Churchman, Richard would not have expressed it this way, but "copulation" properly considered, properly practiced, might be a worthy adjunct to his philosophical trinity as a path to cosmic consciousness. Pound had no such inhibitions: "Sacrum, sacrum, inluminatio coitu" (36/180) – "The rite, the rite, illumination in coition" (Makin 1978: 202). The aptly named Alexander of Aphrodisias, a Peripatetic philosopher active in Athens at the turn of the third century, "believed that 'our supersensible knowledge' comes about 'by the copulation of the possible and active intellect'" (qtd in Makin 1978: 246). Makin: "The lady has a very precise philosophical function as the Lady Sapientia in a whole body of medieval writing" underpinning the twelfth-century poets Pound knew so well.

> She is the active intellect that pours light into the "passive intellect" which is shared by all men; which is why Pound says that the cult of Eleusis "will also shed a good deal of light on various passages of theology or of natural philosophy re the active and passive intellect (*possibile intelleto*, etc.)" ["Terra Italica" *SP* 59]. This concept of course is very important in Cavalcanti. Pound further remarks, much later, that familiarity with the idea of Philosophy as a woman "would have saved several barrels of speculation re Dante's visions" [*Confucius to Cummings* 69]—because it can be applied both to religious anthropology and to personal sexual relations. (Makin 1978: 246)

One might add that scholarly acceptance of Pound's "personal sexual relations" with Sheri Martinelli might have saved Pound scholarship "several barrels of speculation" as to what is happening in Pound's paradisal cantos.[18]

In "Terra Italica" (1932) Pound noted: "For certain people the *pecten cteis* is the gate of wisdom" (*SP* 56). In an illuminating note Makin explains what is hiding behind the polyglot Classical figleaf: "*Pecten kteis* are, respectively Latin and Greek words, apparently cognate, both meaning 'hair,' 'comb,' 'pubic hair'; Callimachus and others use *kteis* for the female pudenda" (Makin 1978: 384n). In Canto 93 Pound says simply "That love is the 'form' of philosophy" (93/646), and he has a certain woman in mind. Arnaut might have thought as much. Arnaut understood "the lady"—whoever she might be, and "La Martinelli" is certainly such a lady—to be a "source of wisdom" (Makin 1978: 175): "So clear the flare / That first lit me / To seize / Her whom my soul believes" ("L'Aura Amara," *LE* 128). Pound says much the same thing in Canto 91, again with Martinelli on his mind: "that the body of light / from the body of fire / And that your eyes come to the surface / from the deep wherein they were sunken" (91/630). Sheri herself, as the form philosophy took, certainly led Pound to the third heaven of Venus, which is where we find ourselves at the end of Canto 91: "O Cythera / che'l ciel movete" (91/637).

Once we understand the emotional context here, it is obvious that the brazenly life-loving Cunizza, a principal in Dante's Third Heaven, is the very type of Sheri Martinelli. He refers to her with affection from as early as "Provençal" Canto 6 (6/22), then in the *phantastikon* canto, Canto 29 (29/141–2), and in *The Pisan Cantos*, Canto 74 (74/458, 463) and 78 (78/503). Though she is not named openly in these later cantos, both Bacigalupo and Peter Makin have detected Cunizza's pervasive, if all but subtextual, presence. Makin marks her haunting Canto 90, because "like the woman of doubtful fame in Luke 7, 'she loved much' / said Randolph / ἠάπησεν πολύ" (90/626). In the poem, the Greek is folded into a reference to "Mother Earth in thy lap," a poem about (not by) John Randolph (Dorothy's ancestral connection), who, like Cunizza, liberated his slaves (Makin 1985: 273; see Liebregts 2004: 302). If Cunizza is hiding behind Randolph, as Martinelli may be said to be hiding behind "Mother Earth" (Gea Mater) then "liberavit masnatos" may refer as much to the sexual fulfillment of those enthralled by the Lady's charms as to liberation from actual slavery. For the canto continues in lines not quoted by Makin—"Castalia like the moonlight / and the waves rise and fall"—where the inspirational spring at Delphi is also Flora Castalia, Sheri Martinelli. Just as in Dante's heaven of Venus, we quickly turn to another similar, if disturbing, figure: "Evita, beer halls …" Bacigalupo thinks the primary reference is to Eva Braun, for surely those "beer halls" point to the "Beerhall Putsch" of 1923, Munich, and the Nazis, though the poem openly gestures to the somewhat more sympathetic Evita Perón. One line later, though unnamed, stands Hitler, "not arrogant from habit / but furious from perception" (90/626; see also 104/761). Eva Braun, and Evita, like Martinelli could be seen as undines, swimming up—"actresses," party girls, "loving much"—from the bottom of society to partner with men of power. The poem's veer to starboard is alarming,[19] but it may suggest the extent to which Martinelli was positioned in Pound's mind as a partner to his own ambitious project—and secret sharer of his politics as well as his body.

Makin then takes us to Canto 92, where we find "Folquet"—aka "troubadour turned bishop" Folco de Marseille (Dante 2007: 364)—"nel terzo cielo," in the third heaven. Folquet is clearly a stand-in for Pound himself, gesturing to his neighbor "In questa lumera appresso" (92/639), a woman whom Makin reads as Cunizza but who Dante indicates is Rahab, another honored, life-loving harlot; regardless, it scarcely matters who—these are the kind of spirits who populate the third heaven.[20] So too is Helen of Tyre in Canto 91, a temple prostitute in thrall to a mage—not Apollonius, but Simon Magus. All of these, it should be clear by now, are figures for Pound and his lover.

Pound's oeuvre shows that his imagination was prepared for Sheri long before he knew her, from long before she was born. So does his biography. The fact that H.D. and Sheri recognized themselves in each other is not coincidental. Pound was always drawn to fey, "New Age," artistic women; the women we know or suspect to have been his lovers have that in common. The imago of the Dryad-type imprinted by Hilda Doolittle in his youth never lost its power. Seeing this in retrospect, as Pound himself must have, we can sense the true nature of Pound's paradise and why Pound thought these cantos, really an extended Ode to Martinelli, might serve as *The Cantos' paradiso*, but a rather more specific, carnal paradise than chaste scholars prefer. Pound's paradise is not an abstraction; paradise sat beside him and breathed with him in Sheri's person. "Pound's paradise *is literally within reach*," as Liebregts writes, but it is not (or not only) the *nous* within our grasp (Liebregts 2004: 318; my emphasis).

Clearly, Martinelli spoke to Pound from the depths of his unconscious life when he had called her in that blitz of passionate letters in May and June of 1954, and she had swum up, "that your eyes come to the surface / from the deep wherein they were sunken," an undine to share some time on the rock (91/630).[21]

In a remarkably ardent letter of September 23, 1957, Pound tells Martinelli, "at first {3 years gap}"—i.e. when they first met in 1952—"didn't see her face or body at all, just look in her eyes once not notice eternal beauty till one day by little pine tree. # only <u>her</u> sometime after June 16th (a holy day) ... might be approx. in cantos. = that wd be re / Drake and the Eliz verses."[22] In Canto 91, Pound figures himself as Francis Drake (who shared the poet's red-gold color) and Martinelli as Queen Elizabeth:

> Miss Tudor moved them with galleons
> from deep eye versus armada
> from the green deep
> > he saw it.
> In the green deep of an eye:
> > Crystal waves weaving together toward the gt /
> > > healing (91/631)

Using Sir Francis Drake as a mask for himself, Pound continues: "That Drake saw the splendor and wreckage /. In that clarity / Gods moving in crystal / ichor, amor" (91/631)—blood of the gods, love. Love under threat, love in the face of the Armada; something heroic in it, confronting the massive, alien power of the state, facing the "the splendor and wreckage." And Queen Elizabeth is, even Liebregts admits, "one of the women of Amor, such as Helen of Tyre ... Artemis and Princess Ra-Set ... etc." (Liebregts 2004: 307), i.e. "Elizabeth" is Sheri. These lines are about lovers facing their all-but-impossible existential, emotional, legal, and historical situation: Pound married, incarcerated, thirty-plus years older, constantly attended by his wife; Martinelli having her own problems with drugs and money and her brother's suicide in September 1954, just when she and Pound were bonding tightly.

Inevitably the great molten crystal of their love cooled and congealed. Pound and Martinelli had lovers' difficulties, misunderstandings, and differences. Canto 95 may indicate some anxiety about this. Pound figures Martinelli and himself as the great stars, as comets:

> LOVE, gone as lightning,
> > Enduring 5000 years.
> Shall the comet cease moving
> > Or the great stars be tied in one place! (95/663)

In a typescript fragment, written for Martinelli's eyes only but printed by Michael Kindellan, Pound had written:

>   Like comets
>   to hell's deep,
>   then emergent,
>   unstable,
>   hurled.
> Sheri has seen it.   (qtd in Kindellan 2017: 105)

In 1956 Martinelli married (Moore implies she was married off to) Gilbert Lee, a supportive and—judging from occasional frustrated letters to Pound—long-suffering Chinese American, later an auto mechanic, who was an enormous practical help to her. Lee must have known of and tolerated Martinelli's affair with the poet, which preceded his own claims. After marrying Lee, whom she clearly felt strongly about, Martinelli sometimes jokingly signed herself in letters to Pound, as "Po-Li," i.e. Poor Lee, also a play on the name of the immortal Chinese poet, a lover of wine, like herself.

In March 1958, just before his release, and perhaps because Dorothy Pound knew it would come soon, Martinelli was suddenly dismissed from Pound's court and encouraged to go off to Mexico to paint, a trip that turned into a fiasco when a promised fellowship and place to stay failed to materialize.[23] In April, when she heard of his release, Martinelli wrote bitterly to Pound from Guadalajara about how meanly she was "Repaid with ingratitude" for her faithfulness to him:

> does it not grieve you a little that the day of your freedom comes and I am not there to share it..when I worked hard to keep your heart light.. I beg of you do not ask me to return in any way.. for I hold you in such contempt it would disease my soul to show you favor.. break my mind's clarity.. pity. Trifling man twisty Breaker of word Liar and dishonorer it was for speaking truth you abandoned me. Can you recall your written words? Deny the paintings? They were builded with shining energy & clarity of vision.. Truth.[24]

Then she added: "I was promised canto 99. If it has my drawing on or perhaps it hasn't, I expect it by mail" (4/10/1958),[25] more evidence of their collaboration.

The poet in these last months of captivity was deeply engaged with Martinelli's rival, Marcella Spann, in the production of "the Spannthology" (*EP/JL* 259) *Confucius to Cummings*. In the same letter, Martinelli blasted the "sneaky and silent Marcella" who had stolen the poet's love from her. If Martinelli was his Leucothea, Spann was his Nausikaa, a type of Artemis, as she figures in *her* cantos, 110 and 113. In the spring of 1958, having served her purpose, having "elevated" Pound into another, higher sphere (90/626–7), to the Paradise of Venus, but not qualified to provide the fulcrum to vault the poet into the

Paradiso terrestre represented by Phaecia and the promise of Nausikaa/Marcella, Sheri was returned from whence she came. And Pound returned to Italy with Marcella—not to Phaecia, as it happened, but a rocky Ithaca.

> On May 6, 1958, Pound wrote to her, formally telling Sheri it was over:
> Her Highness the Martinelli,
>   That two comets cannot remain tied together, therefore go with the sea gods, be blessed,
> The myths are recurrent, you can refer to Leucothea, return to the seagods in the unplumbed depths ADITON THALLASES (possibly spelled wrong) of ocean...

He signed it "B" for "Bun," adding the Greek letters for *Aditon Thallases* in green pen with *temenos*, also in Greek, then closed: "the sacred an inviolable depths of the sea / as Temenos for temples on terra firma."[26]

Even after the poet's rejection of her, Martinelli still felt she was his guide. Cast as Cunizza, or as Leucothea, she'd rather be Beatrice. "I return from Paradise," she wrote stoically to Bukowski; "—had I gone to Italy with Ezra we'd have had some Paradisal Art ... as it is we shall have a Paradisal Spirit" (qtd in Moore 2001: 133). At the same time, she tried to reassert herself as Pound's muse, disparaging the poems in *Thrones* inspired under the influence of "Texas," Marcella Spann, because they "lacked the paradisal spirit," and complaining to Pound that he was being "smothered in breasty hens / that AINT PARADISE and the THRONES shows it—face it Mon—you need your Paradisal Spirit back again" (SM to EP 2/1/1960).

Notes

1   Her correspondence with Bukowski, published as *Beerspit Night and Cursing: The Correspondence of Charles Bukowski and Sheri Martinelli 1960–1967*, is a very substantial volume edited by Steven Moore and is a major source of information about the Pound/Martinelli relationship. Pound's letters to her are at the Beinecke Library at Yale: YCAL MSS 868, Box 12, seventeen folders. Her letters to Pound are contained in two collections among the Ezra Pound papers, YCAL MSS 43, Box 33, folders 1389–93, and in addition YCAL MSS 53, Box 12, folder 277 "1962–1963" (in fact these letters begin in 1961, not 1962 as stated) and folder 278 "1964–1969." These contain the continued correspondence after Pound's removal to Italy. Presumably they were in Olga Rudge's possession and only got to Beinecke with her papers. There are no replies from Pound. Folder 277 has many clippings sent by

Martinelli to Pound. Martinelli's papers, containing Pound's many letters to her, are also at Beinecke YCAL MSS 868, Box 12, a dozen folders "Pound, Ezra (year)."

Moore's biographical essay "Sheri Martinelli: A Modernist Muse" in *Gargoyle Magazine* #41, available online, is essential reading and supplied much of the biographical information. Moore's essay was reprinted and supplemented with Martinelli's invaluable addendum, rescued from a 1961 issue of *Light Year*, "Homage to Grampa," in 2005. See stevenmoore.info/martinelli/index/shtml. Richard Taylor's "Sheri Martinelli: Muse to Ezra Pound," published in *Agenda* 38(1–2) (2000–2001), contains his memories of meeting with and speaking to Martinelli.

A version of this and the next chapter, with an emphasis on Martinelli's art and illustrations, is published as "Sheri Martinelli: The White Goddess" in *The Edinburgh Companion to Ezra Pound and the Arts*, edited by Roxana Preda (Edinburgh: Edinburgh University Press, 2019), 463–76.

2   According to a Kasper letter to Pound dated April 26, 1954, she had not seen Pound for almost two years (Beinecke YCAL MSS 43, Box 26, folder 1126).
3   From Katherine Heyman (who saw herself as Pound's lover on the astral plane) to Margaret Cravens to Hilda Doolittle and onward, Pound was drawn to fey, artsy women projecting a New Age vibe, including Dorothy, Nancy Cunard, Ingrid Davies (a correspondent), and Olga Rudge.
4   See Moore's 2005 update, with Martinelli's "Homage to Grampa."
5   Beinecke YCAL MSS 868, Box 12, "Ezra Pound 1954."
6   Martinelli's ringing endorsement—that he was "a stud"—goes far to explain the strong feelings he elicited in experienced women like Nancy Cunard, who knew Pound had rare gifts as a lover.
7   Beinecke YCAL MSS 43, Box 33, folders 1389–93.
8   Beinecke YCAL MSS 868, Box 12, folder "Ezra Pound 1954."
9   Thus at the end of Canto 23, when Aphrodite makes love with Anchises he "saw"—i.e. experienced—"as of waves taking form, / As the sea, hard, a glitter of crystal, / And the waves rising but formed, holding their form. / No light reaching through them" (23/109). If no light reaches through the crystallized wave forms, then how does Anchises "see"? Obviously, "light comes from the eye"—Grosseteste's idea. In Anchises' sexual epiphany with Love herself, the *phantastikon* crystallizes—a magic moment—outside of time and space: the "coitu illuminatio" of the Eleusinian mysteries.
10 Pound would have heard about the Baroness from Williams himself, among others. In his *Autobiography* (1951) Williams devotes a chapter to "The Baroness" and the New York scene c. 1918 that is not much different from the New York City scene of the 1950s. The parallels between the Baroness's situation and Martinelli's are striking. See *The Autobiography of William Carlos Williams* (New York: New Directions, 1967), 163–9.
11 Ezra Pound papers, Beinecke MSS 43, Box 33, folder 1392.

12 In the second instance Leucothea is called Leucothae. Although something can be made of this, it is probably a printer's error (95/665).
13 It seems Pound thought so. Charles Bukowski's poem "Horse on Fire" tells us what Martinelli must have told him about Canto 90 in a letter (unfortunately not preserved) sent to Bukowski in August 1960 (see Moore 2001: 79):

> and reading canto 90
> he put the paper down
> Ez did (both their eyes were wet)
> And he told her
> "among the greatest love poems
> ever written."

14 From Charles Bukowski, *Rooming House Madrigals: Early Selected Poems 1946–1966* (Los Angeles: Black Sparrow, 2002).
15 Bukowski was unimpressed: "Pound? Part of Pound is all right, of course, but much circus and blather, maestro maestro throwing spagetwopchink and rolling with the punch, *effect* of doing, appears walking straight while lying down" (6/8/1960, CB to SM; Moore 2001: 39).
16 Both are reproduced (in black and white) in *Beerspit*.
17 Pound's *Collected Early Poems* (99); and see Liebregts (2004: 300–301).
18 Unconscious of Pound's personal situation, Liebregts (2004: 318) writes, "Pound claims that paradise is literally within our reach, that is, that the *Nous* is within our contemplative grasp, by referring to the phrase 'agitante calescimus'" (XCIII/628), taken from Ovid's *Fasti* VI 5–8:

> Est deus in nobis; agitante calescimus illo:
> Impetus his sacrae semina mentis habet,
> Fas mihi praecipue voltus vidisse deorum
> Vel quia sum vates, vel quia sacra cano.

["There is a god in us: when he stirs us, we grow warm. This impulse contains the seed of inspiration ('sacred mind'). I especially have a right to see the faces of the gods, either because I am a poet or because I sing of sacred things" (Liebregts's translation)]. Liebregts reads Neoplatonically what I read erotically.

19 In his notes to *Paradiso* Canto 9, translator Robin Kirkpatrick observes that "Dante cannot long restrain himself from political controversy" as "canto 9 constantly depicts the relationship of love as the point of principle which is offended by political corruption" (Dante 2007: 362). The same may be said for Pound in these nominally paradisal cantos.
20 Makin has a good note re: Dante Gabriel Rossetti's 1840 book *Il mistero dell' amor platonico nel Medioevo*. "Rossetti believed that the *Fedeli d'amore,* the 'loyal servants

of love' as these Tuscan poets called themselves, were adepts of a secret doctrine which they referred to variously as 'Rosa,' 'Beatrice,' 'Giovanna,' 'Lagia,' 'Selvaggia,' and so on, by an obvious trick: they are all supposed to be the names of their ladies, but the ladies are all identical. Rossetti, as [Luigi] Valli says, came to consider the *Fedeli d'amore*, as 'the continuers of a secret Pythagorean worship of the initiatory Wisdom, and haters of the Church and its doctrine'" (Makin 1978: 243).

21 A sketch by Martinelli on the back of an envelope that Roxana Preda discovered and printed with my essay on Martinelli in *The Edinburgh Companion to Ezra Pound and the Arts* conveys Sheri's sense of her role as undine/L. Leucothea. See p. 463.
22 Beinecke YCAL MSS 868, Box 12, "Pound, Ezra 1954."
23 Sheri and her husband Gilbert Lee had gone there in expectation of a scholarship, which didn't materialize. Then they were surprised by the early return of Mexican host José Amaral, who threw them out to make their way back to the United States as best they could on borrowed money and sleeping in the car (SM to EP 11/11/1958).
24 Moore observes that "it was her quest for truth, rather than celebrity worship, that led Sheri to apprentice herself to writers like Nin and Pound" (Moore 2005: 3).
25 Ezra Pound papers, Beinecke YCAL MSS 43, Box 33, folder 1391. Martinelli probably means Canto 98, which begins under the sign of the boat of Ra-Set.
26 Beinecke MSS 868, Box 12, folder "Pound, Ezra 1958."

7

Sheri Martinelli

Right-Wing Muse

> Civilization
> The children of Moses take pleasure in breaking
> What the children of Ovid take pleasure in making.
>
> (SM to EP 2/11/1958)

This little poem, recalled by Sheri Martinelli in a letter to Pound in February of 1958, had been scribbled four years earlier in one of the notebooks in which *Rock-Drill* was drafted. Martinelli felt that she was one of Ovid's children—Leucothea, literally the white goddess[1]—that Pound was Ovid, "a shape shifter," as well as a great stud, and that they had written the latter half of *Rock-Drill* (Cantos 90 through 95) together. The couplet could stand as an epigraph for the politics of *Rock-Drill*—even its metapolitics. The title "Civilization" brings back all the issues raised in previous chapters.

Besides her roles as muse and lover, Martinelli was a child of Ovid who acquired a racial politics by absorbing Pound's "agenda." "Before Ez & After Ez man! the change—he tuned me in clear & LOUD—but it's still me," she wrote the poet Charles Bukowski in December 1960 (Moore 2001: 132). Martinelli was remade by Pound into a muse very much aware of the peculiar terrors of the world-historical struggle between Ovid and Moses, vision versus materiality, light versus darkness, creators versus destroyers, Aryan versus Jew, and black versus white.

Despite this, one feels reading her letters that Martinelli was not by nature a racist; rather, Pound's agenda made her so. Her friendships show constant contact with a diverse group of people; she wrote to Bukowski of her "three husbands," each of different races. These might be her first husband the Italian, Ezio Martinelli; Anatole Broyard (who may have admitted to her that he was legally black); and her current husband, the Chinese/American Gilbert Lee. Of course, Pound, a special sort of husband, counted too as the ultimate white man, as "Merlin the High Priest of White Magic" as she told Norman Holmes Pearson (qtd in Kindellan 2017: 104n).

When she moved there after being "kicked out of the nest" of St. Elizabeths, Martinelli's contacts in San Francisco were equally various. She published her *Anagogic & Paideumic Review* with help from the African American poet Clarence Major, she "loved" Allen Ginsberg despite his left-wing politics, and she took a Jewish lover about whom she writes to Bukowski; perhaps the person she respected most in San Francisco was the biracial poet Bob Kaufman— "Bomkoff" she called him fondly in letters to Pound and Bukowski. She enjoyed being called "the Mother of the Beats"; Martinelli is the main link between Pound and the San Francisco scene.

We know, too, that John Kasper and his intimates saw her as she wished herself to be seen, as a Goddess, or high priestess to the goddess (Moore 2001: 215). Like Pound himself, St. Elizabeths initiates Edward Stresino and Bill McNaughton were besotted with her. Dave Horton corresponded with Sheri till the 1980s. Many of Kasper's early letters to Pound concern Martinelli and her problems, especially with heroin. When Pound finds himself "mid dope-dolls an' duchesses" in Canto 97 he has in mind Martinelli and Dorothy respectively (97/700–701).[2] In 1953–4 Sheri was struggling with her addiction, and in 1955 she was busted for marijuana,[3] which is one reason Kasper let his bookstore be used for yoga classes (yoga was thought to cure addiction and provided an alternative high) and why dope becomes a theme in the later cantos. Pound himself composed a sign advertising these classes that, copied by Florette Henry, duly appeared at the bookshop (*JK & EP* 8–9). Pound and his friends were convinced that drugs were part of a wider conspiracy to stupefy and control the masses.[4]

In June 1954, just when Pound was bent on getting Martinelli to come to Washington and, not incidentally, to kick drugs, he wrote to Olivia Agresti a long letter about heroin, characterizing dope as a Jew/Commie plot, wanting

> every detail possible / both as to sources of supply, AND methods of treatment. The definite drive here is not only to produce violent irresponsibility at the bottom / blacks used for the mass attack, supplied by the friends of Dexter White and his coreligionists / BUT everything done to get at the TOP sensibilities.
>
> Start with marijuana, which one jazz player said all of 'em tend to use, because it magnifies TIME, which means they can gain precision. (*EP/ORA* 154)

This information about jazz musicians may have come from Willam French or Martinelli herself. Pound continues: "duration of an experience depending on the velocity of the mind during the experience. Same applies to sense of space

/ vid / canto whatever" (*EP/ORA* 154). Henderson speculates that Pound had Canto 49 in mind regarding "the dimension of stillness" (Henderson 2010: 339). I'd suggest a canto he was working on at the time that may not yet have been numbered. What of those cryptic lines in Canto 87 about Monsieur F. who "saw his mentor / composed almost wholly of light" and "Windeler's vision: his letter file / the size of two lumps of sugar, / but the sheet legible," then mentioning "Santa Teresa" (87/593) before the thought slips away into a rant about "the butchers of the lesser cattle"; that is, Dexter White's Jewish "coreligionists." Tim Materer discovered that Monsieur F. is in fact William French, who wrote Pound about his vision in January 1954 (Materer 1995: 189n). In his subchapter on Martinelli, Moody expands on this, telling us French was a jazz musician and his wife was a heroin addict (Moody 2015: 317), but he doesn't link this information to Canto 87. Windeler's vision of the whole of his letter file and every letter therein, "the size of two lumps of domino sugar laid flat, side to side," along with St. Teresa "who 'saw' the microcosmos, hell, heaven and purgatory complete 'the size of a walnut'" are recounted in Pound's "Translator's Postscript" to *The Natural Philosophy of Love*. There, Pound calls these phenomena "hyper-aesthesia," a "new form of genius," which affect space—and time—for Pound also mentions the faculty of hearing four parts of a fugue simultaneously, a genius associated with one of his heroes, Mozart.[5] These visionary distortions of time and space in Pound's poem are contrasted in the poet's mind to the artificial paradise of dope and help explain the sudden shift in register from the visionary to Pound's racialist, conspiratorial outlook, when he turns abruptly from St. Teresa to attacking Semites, "their villain the grain god" (87/593).

Martinelli told Bukowski that Pound's lament in Canto 92, "Le Paradis n'est pas artificiel / but is jagged / For a flash / for an hour / Then agony / then an hour. / Then agony" (92/640), was written "when the cruel Miz Martinelli was his beloved & she was out … down in Spade-town …. turning on … and sweet gramps was locked up inside St. Liz … longing to protect his fragile butterfly" (Moore 2001: 87). Martinelli's reading of Canto 92 is convincing; it recalls Pound's lines that directly precede the lines she remembers in her letter:

But in the great love, bewildered
    farfalla in tempesta
under rain in the dark:
        many wings fragile
Nymphalidae, basilarch, and lycaena,
Ausonides, euchloe, and erynnis (92/639)

"Farfalla" is butterfly; the names in the final lines are the Linnaean names of butterfly families. Sheri is the fragile butterfly in need of solid food, the sustenance of poetry, not dope.[6] She accepted the name then chided Pound for asking a "butterfly to do the work off a [sic] the milk wagon horse ... and because she realizes how good you are & what a drag that joint must be ... she trys [sic] and because she is a butterfly & don't move the wagon very fast ... you give her hell" (SM to EP 8/25/1956).[7]

Poetry, Pound told Martinelli, is like a pyramid: "Think of pyramid, SOLID, it does not wobble" (EP to SM 1/15/1958). Pound was explicit with Sheri that poetry was not dope—poetry was not a way to get off, not Baudelaire's artificial paradise. In a note that Sheri preserved dated "Dec. 17, 1957 9:30 p.m." continuing a conversation they must have been having earlier that day, Pound wrote her "NO, damn it, it is NOT dope. The construct, image, verse, does NOT poison, it does NOT have distressing after effect. It stays SOLID, 2000 years something still there." And this afterthought: "NOT dope it is FOOD" (12/17/1957).[8] Alas, for all of her goddess-like virtues, Martinelli was no solid pyramid or pyramidal fulcrum but "tender as a marshmallow." As "Flora Castalia," goddess of inspiration, she was the delicate flower of the Castalian spring (93/652).

Before moving to Washington to be near Pound, Martinelli crashed at John Kasper's place and sometimes slept in the back of the Make It New. Pound wrote to her at Kasper's and then at the bookshop on Bleecker St., where she painted in the back. Kasper reported on a show of her work there at the beginning of May 1954 (JK to EP 4/1954).[9] The confluence of Martinelli's successful painting and her troubles with heroin seem to have triggered Pound's massive epistolary offensive in May. "Sir," Kasper reported, "your letters are the most wonderful counsel for her, and I beg you to keep writing every day. She is very upset when she doesn't hear from you. [I]t often makes the difference for the day" (JK to EP 6/7/1954). When Martinelli was strung out or tempted back to drugs, Kasper and friends would search her out and rescue her whether she wanted rescue or not. Before she moved down to Washington (where she shared an apartment for a time with Dave Horton [Moore 2001: 16] and later Bill McNaughton [Moody 2015: 316]), Kasper would drive her down on his regular trips between "the Needle and the Dome," the Empire State Building and the Capitol.

Pound's love for Martinelli, cloaked in extravagant, paradisal language, is one half of the Sheri Cantos; the other half is political, where Pound's racial metapolitics, coded in Aesopian language, breaks through the erotic shimmer, the "lux in diafana" of the goddess, with irruptions of racism. Canto 93 is certainly the climax of the Sheri Cantos, but their love is posed against those

Semitic "Hyksos, butchers of the lesser cattle" (93/648, 643). The poet's dissident economics comes in too: Shakespeare and Dante "mentioned the subject" of "distributive justice" and usury, Pound insists as the canto moves on, but "the lit profs discuss other passages in abuleia" (93/647). Pound is determined to steer his beloved toward his way of seeing that justice is done and how the world might be saved from those destructive children of Moses, but "Without guides," Pound worries, "having nothing but courage / Shall audacity last into fortitude" (93/652)? Martinelli and her friends may have the audacity to challenge the status quo, but unless they listen to the poet and ground their revolt on Pound's metapolitics—his spiritual, racial, and ethical values—their unguided efforts will dissipate into countercultural utopian dreaming.

Necessarily, Martinelli invested in Pound's agenda, not just the poetry. Pound's conspiratorial worldview deeply affected her vision of the world. Sadly, Martinelli's paradisal spirit was polluted with Pound's right-wing, racialist outlook. Insofar as Martinelli was Pound's "white Goddess," the emphasis could fall equally on "white." As she wrote Pound:

> I'm NO actress
> I live /
> and do my job /
>   which is: BEING A WHITE FEMALE WHO IS CRAZY ABOUT HER
> GODS HEROS
> HER ANCESTORS ARTS & CRAFTS
> IN A WORLD
> THAT IS OUT TO MURDER PRECISLEY THAT.[10]

"[A]nd" she added, "for six years of love of the ONE white man in the world ... she inherited the smear" of anti-Semitism (see Moore 2001: 137). Writing to Bukowski on December 15, 1960, Martinelli complained:

> I got so sick of them bleeding heart white apologists saying "white" soupremacy that I finally wrote a letter to der hediterr & told him that one is NOT "white" one IS WHITE & not about to feel any guilt for it [...] not natural; moral; or ethical to make it legal to banish the song of the nightingale because the crows caw & hawk / [...] and I am bored with it / MOCKING MY OWN SKIN OR MY MAW OR PAW OR MY TRADITIONS & MY CULTURE OR MY RACE ... DEGRADING MY RACE OR MY SEX OR COLOUR OR GOD AIN'T GONNA ELEVATE THE NIGGERS OR US EITHER (Moore 2001: 120–1)

She concluded her letter by advising study of Frobenius (Moore 2001: 121), "Frobenius" having become a sign meaning something like "Afrocentricity" in the St. Elizabeths circle: "Frobenius" will hip Afro-Americans to their real African heritage so they will leave white folks alone with theirs.

We know it was Martinelli who forwarded "Alfalfa Bill" Murray to Pound and thus got him interested in Waddell. She would have read Waddell with excitement given her life-long identification with Isis and Egypt: "i come out of egypt & return there," she wrote to Bukowski, and claims that it was "sheri at st. liz that got the hieroglyphics into the cantos" (Moore 2001: 215).[11] Her letters to Pound are often decorated with Egyptian hieroglyphic animals. Insofar as she "was born OUTSIDE of CLASS … SEX … OR POLITICS. I SEE what I SEE. I AM as I AM" (SM to EP 5/1/1957),[12] as she says in the letter cited earlier, Martinelli partakes of the androgynous spirit of the princess Ra-Set whose boat "moves with the sun" of Cantos 91, 94, and 98. Having absorbed Waddell, there would be no racial problem here (not that it could occur on this metaphysical plane)—Isis too is a white goddess, albeit of the heavens, not the sea—Isis is "my Lady of the Skye" (Moore 2001: 215). Significantly for Pound's project, Isis wears a throne on her head. Insofar as Martinelli is Isis, she is a none-too-firm supporter of the throne, and Pound wishes a throne that will not "sqush"—this connection underwrites Pound's worries about Martinelli's psychological softness, her vulnerability to alcohol and drugs.

Martinelli stands for a white-goddess complex in the poem; she is Leucothea and Isis; she is also the supportive and inspiring "Sibylla" of Canto 90, as well as "Isis Kuanon" (90/626). "Quan yin is one of the many names of my Goddess," she explained to Bukowski (Moore 2001: 120). It was as Leucothea, the white goddess, that she rescued the drowning poet. "Leucothea had pity," Pound writes, "mortal once / who now is a sea-god" (95/667) helping him reach the land of the Phaecians—the *paradiso terrestre* that was to focus *Thrones*. Once metaphorically ashore, Marcella Spann, Martinelli's successor as lover and inspiration, became the Nausikaa who could lead him to the utopia of Phaecia. Unlike Odysseus, Pound would have liked to marry Spann and once in Italy even proposed to her (Moody 2015: 451).

Hurt and angry as she was by Pound's rejection of her and his return to Italy with her rival, Marcella, and his wife, by October 1958 Martinelli was already forgiving Pound, admitting that "I love you still {and hate you also} & miss you much … [T]here is no one to talk to on my level but you … and without your further sticking by me I'll die" (SM to EP 10/11/1958, p. 3). In spite of everything, Martinelli remained his determined disciple, proselytizer, and purveyor of his racial politics: "Now the only one still carrying on your job is me," she would write on October 11, 1958.

In a 1956 letter Sheri had chided Pound that "as soon as this stupid race war is settled & everybody is exactly the same color.... then to their amazement they will wake up & discover that half of them are women.... and then the sex war will begin" (SM to EP 8/25/1956, p. 2). By 1960, she takes a slightly different view with Bukowski, suggesting that Pound may have influenced her about the coming race war between the other races and whites. "The communists are forcing the race war to 'divide' and weaken us / what the divine intelligence is doing I can but surmise and look at the real world" (Moore 2001: 124).

Martinelli's surmise should be familiar by now: "Nature does not begin the process of decay until the tree has fallen," she begins:

> Nature does not allow any order to stand that is UNatural—the process is that the Nordic or Aryan appears with the Law & sets up shop / then the softer soul'd whites show & intermarry with the delicious coloured races or sometimes a renegade nord will take a lady of colour to bed but not to wife & then the Spies of Godtt show up because the fruit is ripe to rot which makes us blow up & the Nordic seed of the Law petrifies in the memory cells of the new Indians / & we have culture preserved until a new batch of sperms arrive capable of continuing culch ... The East Indians have perfectly petrified Aryan Law but they are not capable of furthering it—they preserve the seed and it will bloom again. (Moore 2001: 124)

But Martinelli thinks that somehow real poetry will survive till the next cycle of culture, when the New India under Aryan Law arrives (Moore 2001: 53). This by now familiar eugenic nightmare echoes Hitler, Waddell, Murray, Bilbo, Kasper, and Pound.

In December 1958 Martinelli complained to Pound in a doggerel squib that purported to be an "exclusive interview with BooVOOdoo" about how "[t]he California mind-state is paralyzed by Zen Bud[d]hism":

ZEN BOO VOO DOO
"Zen BooVoodoo vot did you do?"
    Zen I took oveh the Federal Reserve"
"an' ZEN booVOOdoo vot did you do?"
    Zen I took oveh the Supreme Court
"an' ZEN booVOOdoo vot did you do?
    ZEN I chost took OVEH"

Despite the irregular quote marks, we are overhearing a conspiratorial dialogue. The Yiddish dialect marks Martinelli's awareness of a connection Pound makes between what he calls "the Bhud rot" (99/717), the state of the Warren Court, and the Jewish conspiracy—or as Martinelli calls them here, echoing *The Protocols*, "the Sa[n]hedrin, and 'Zionist Overlords.'"[13] Turning serious, Martinelli finds this conspiracy was very much in evidence "SINCE DREW PEARSON PRINTED RED SMEAR AGAINST JOHN KASPER" who had been arrested in Tennessee on charges of sedition and suspicion of conspiring to bomb schools there. Kasper's relationship to Pound had already been exposed by the *New York Herald* (see *JK & EP* 177–81), but Pearson had further compromised them both in his syndicated column. Martinelli's letter is a direct response to a Pearson article, written just weeks earlier. She continues:

> sent on more Drew p.[Pearson] will send it to admiral C[rommelin] he might use it—Dr. Giovanni[ni] very dead set against Kasp—I hold my old opinion that he is druvvvvvv onward..& none of these white want to be stirred—they HATE him was'nt [sic] the henemy—because he forces sides—they runnin' like insects ... I don't like it here—but I'm NOT about to apologize for being white OR baby-sittin' with you OR meeting Kasp![14]

This letter also reveals Martinelli as the link to the San Francisco poetry scene: "Chap here says: 'tell Pound IF he wants to write ANY kind of answer to his critics—re. John Kasper OR anything else.I'll publish it / ' or if Pound wants anything published I'll do it / his name is L. Ferlinghetti City Lights Books etc" (SM to EP 12/19/1958). Ferlinghetti, like his fellow publisher and poet Peter Russell in England,[15] was hoping that Pound might distance himself from Kasper. Martinelli would have expected just the opposite. She was John Kasper's good friend, and she knew that Pound neither disapproved of his agitation nor believed the charges against him were real but rather thought they were a frame-up by the usual suspects—the actual or metaphorical Elders of Zion. As with Russell, Pound never responded to this offer, nor to a letter sent by Ferlinghetti himself offering to publish him.[16]

Despite the failure of a Pound/Ferlinghetti alliance, Martinelli placed her mimeographed *Anagogic & Paideumic Review* for sale in City Lights, publishing in it such poets as Bukowski, Bob Kaufman, Clarence Major, Charles Richardson, and others. By 1960 she would announce to Bukowski that she was the "Queen of the Beats" (Moore 2001: 54).

Despite her explicit "Poundian" racial politics, the poets Martinelli were most drawn to in San Francisco were Bob Kaufman and Allen Ginsberg. Biracial, half-Jewish Kaufman—whom she called Bomkoff—was a special favorite: in a letter to Pound she called him "[t]he most intelligent person in San Francisco" (5/3/1960, p. 4), though she admits that while "his mind is lively ... the reds got it ... one wd have to work like mad.. & anyhow I ain't IN love with him..I'm saying he loves my spirit..he has yet to direct any but the kindest & most loving words to me" (8).[17]

She praised Allen Ginsberg repeatedly to Bukowski, much to Bukowski's annoyance. In January 1961, Martinelli told Bukowski that she found Ginsberg "more of a man right at this moment on earth ... than any white christer walkin' / sittin' / standin' / layin' [livin'?] or dead except Ezra Pound" (Moore 2001: 162). She admired "Howl" because "it IS a HOWL from HELL" (Moore 2001: 113). Bukowski was almost pathologically allergic to any kind of "poetic" grandstanding or artistic posing, believing that "[a] poet should hang alone" (Moore 2001: 108). When he wondered if Ginsberg's much publicized visit to Castro's Cuba wasn't "going too far out" (118) and felt that he would suffer for it as a poet, Martinelli concurred.[18] Then she reflected:

> I KNOW that the Zionists are not going to & NEVER had ANY intention of ever allowing the American Jews to rule / so any effort [like Ginsberg's] on the part of any American to help destroy the existing order shall be wasted effort as far as he is concerned because Jew or no Jew he is now an American & nobody likes any of us ... only the niggers got any support back home / even the jews were betrayed ... paid for Israel and got Zion ... their old lag ... so Allen doth not betray the anglo-saxon order ... with that Castro visit ... he betrays his own people unless he is a Zionist and I do not know & gorHELLUPme I don't wanna know (Moore 2001: 112)

Ginsberg can be a Jew and a good American so long as he is not in the power of the Zionist Overlords. If Israel is the dream of the Jewish people, "Zion" is the coercive project of the elders and their scheme for the destruction of the metapolitical order, for which reason they "support the niggers" in their fight for civil rights they don't know how to use. As she says in a letter to Pound,

> The Negroes have not as yet proven even a small capacity to USE their liberty.
> In fact they notorious for the
>   MIS-USE   of it /
> Former plantation slaves—present narcotic slaves OR
>   Baptist church slaves /
> And those lovely blacks who returned to Liberia is it? / One saw them stroll across the cinema screen—
>   In THAT climate—top hats / ties / gloves / tails
>   Slaves imitatin' the master /
> The black serves to retain the lost white cultures / same's the Jap retains the Chinese / like body cells /
>   holdin' the pattern until [it] is

again necessary for it to re-appear /
Dante's 500 [years] / homer over 2000 [years]
Bun [Pound] shootin' for at LEAST 2000 / [years]
Ezra Pound remains the ONLY white skinned person (besides his "immediate family") who is UNapologetic about the color of his pink skin. (SM to EP 12/19/1958)[19]

Aside from a depressing glimpse into a racial essentialism learned from Pound, this statement about unchanging high-cultural forms, bequeathed to the world by the beneficent Aryans and retained by cultureless *Untermenschen* only capable of imitation, when coupled with the one about Ginsberg and the Zionists quoted earlier, suggests the contradictions within Martinelli between vision and politics that make her a "right-wing muse." Yet, as Martinelli admitted ruefully to Bukowski in the same letter about Ginsberg, she was at that moment the doting lover of a much younger Jewish man, nineteen-year-old Ernie Walker, while remaining more or less happily married to her Chinese American husband Gilbert Lee: "Gib is a Slant & Ernie is a Jew … I am some 'racist' Buk … a disappointment to all Zion" (Moore 2001: 114). Like her friend Kasper—who himself later married a Vietnamese woman and whose best employee and close friend at the Make It New Bookshop was Florette Henry, an African American—Martinelli is far too American, in all the best sense of that besmirched and misunderstood word, to "Maintain antisepsis" (94/655) as Pound wished and to live by the racial categories he had taught her. In a letter of 1962 to Pound she closes with "gratitude for this much / chance to know the Terror. // If you had not liberated me, how would I ever have realized what it was that I caused you to feel in all my ignorance?" (SM to EP 7/4/1962); thanks to Pound, her imagination had been initiated into knowledge, and the Muse had been freed to become what some might call a frightened crank and others a "child of Ovid," high priestess in the cult of Pound.

* * *

The snarky article in *The Nation* by David Rattray, a seventeen-year-old Dartmouth undergraduate, called "A Week-end with Ezra Pound" (*The Nation*, November 16, 1957, pp. 343–4) showed the poet amongst his acolytes, including Martinelli and her "huge eyes like a cat" (qtd in Moore 2005: 14). It reached H.D. in Switzerland, when it was brought to her by her psychiatrist, Erich Heydt (Doolittle 1979: 5). Encouraged by Heydt and Norman Holmes Pearson, H.D. began to write *End to Torment: A Memoir of Ezra Pound*, published posthumously in 1979.

Feeling a kinship with Martinelli, in whom she recognized herself, H.D. opened a correspondence with Martinelli that lasted till H.D.'s death. H.D.'s care and attention meant the world to Sheri and encouraged her through dark times on the West Coast. After H.D.'s death, Sheri dedicated two issues of her mimeographed *Anagogic and Paideumic Review* to H.D. (May and June 1970); both exist among the Martinelli papers at the Beinecke. The May issue opens with a quotation from Edgar Cayce, the American mystic, from his *Story of Creation*, Chapter III, "The Fire Races," p. 23:

> all people, regardless of colour, are one blood & members of the "perfect race." Colour of the race merely adapted one to the conditions which were to be met, & symbolized the chief attribute of people of that race. In the white race, sight or seeing, was predominant or emphasized; in the red, feeling or emotion, in the yellow hearing and in the brown, the emphasis is on the sense of smell.[20]

"H.D. is the perfect girl of the white race," Martinelli begins. I'd like to suggest that Cayce's more benign—or at least less fraught—racial theories, which seem to stem less from Agassiz than from Helena Blavatsky's taxonomy in *The Secret Doctrine*, may be where Martinelli's views come to rest. Obviously, this polygenetic position remains full of problems, as the hierarchy of races keyed to the senses is a subtle argument for white superiority, since sight is the most culturally privileged sense and smell the least. But as the title of her review reminds us, we are to read Cayce's text anagogically, as Dante taught; that is, "above the senses," as what is signified here "gives intimation of higher matters belonging to the eternal glory" (qtd in Adams 1971: 121). Martinelli reconciled Pound's metapolitics and her personal life. Anagogically.

Notes

1. In Canto 95, following *The Odyssey*, Leucothea is Ino, daughter of Cadmus, who appears to Odysseus as a sea bird (*Od.* V. 266–368; Terrell 1984: 587). The notebooks suggest that Pound was also Cadmus, who late in life became a blue serpent. He is figured as the wise "natrix" or water-snake (91/636) and the "blue serpent" who "glides from the rock pool" in Canto 90 (90/626–7). Thus, Leucothea, daughter of Cadmus, is a daughter of Ovid—Martinelli herself.
2. To be fair, Martinelli contested this reading in a conversation with Steven Moore (see Moore 2005: 19).
3. Martinelli insisted in letters to Pound that the pot was planted, the charges a frame-up (see Moore 2005: 19).

4   See Henderson (2010: 370–2).
5   *Natural Philosophy of Love* 155; see Terrell (1984: 496). In Canto 25, Pound recounts a similar vision, of the sculptor who sees "the form in the air" before getting to work; "he sees the in and the through / the four sides" (25/117), much as Michelangelo seems to have seen the slaves he was liberating from the stone in his awe-inspiring unfinished sculpture.
6   See *Paradiso* 17 where Cacciaguida compares Dante's poetry to "life giving nutriment": "Chése la voce tua sarà molesta / nel primo gusto, vital nodrimento/ lascerà poi, quando saràdigesta" (*Par.* 130–2). One also thinks of William Carlos Williams's contemporary work "Asphodel: That Greeny Flower" (1955), where he concludes that "men die miserably every day / for lack of what is found there" in the "despised" form of poetry (Williams 1963: 318).
7   Beinecke YCAL MSS 899, Box 12, folder "Pound, Ezra 1958."
8   Beinecke YCAL MSS 899, Box 12, folder "Pound, Ezra 1957."
9   Beinecke YCAL MSS 43, Box 26, folder 1128.
10 Beinecke YCAL MSS 43, Box 33, folder 1390.
11 On December 7, 1958, Bill McNaughton wrote Pound: "the goddamned Waddell was given to me by someone, I think Sheri, because she thought it was 'interesting.' Well, I never read the book, I never even opened it, because from what I see Waddell is an insane old bore" (Beinecke YCAL MSS 43, Box 32, folder 1339).
12 Beinecke YCAL MSS 43, Box 33, folder 1390.
13 The connection between Indian religion and the Jews is made obliquely in *The Protocols*, with a reference to "Vishnu, in whom is found [our kingdom's] personification—in our hundred hands will be, one in each, the springs of the machinery of social life" (*Protocols* 205).
14 Beinecke YCAL MSS 43, Box 33, folder 1393.
15 Just after the poet's release, Peter Russell wrote Pound: "I read an article [...] which said that you supported Kasper in his anti-negro activities? I really can't believe this to be true. The impression given is that you are not only anti-semitic (I think I understand your position on this score and I would defend you from the accusation of real anti-Semitism) but that you are also anti-negro. I hope you aren't going to put your head into another hornet's nest over this score. The days of race discrimination before the law are I hope almost over, and if you start supporting some crazy hysterical diehards, I reckon you'll deserve any trouble you get into. But I'm sure you don't. But it might be wise to keep track of the accusations against you, and issue a public statement before the press gets a knife under your ribs again. ... Waal, its mighty nice to have a grandpa out of detention!!!" (PR to EP 5/5/1958; Beinecke YCAL MSS 43, Box 45, folder 1979).
16 Beinecke YCAL MSS 43, Box 33, folder 1392.
17 Beinecke YCAL MSS 43, Box 33, folder 1393.

18 Jack Kerouac, too, was irritated by Ginsberg's "pro-Castro bullshit" (Kerouac to John Clellon Holmes 12/11/1963; see Kerouac 2000).
19 Beinecke YCAL MSS 43, Box 33, folder 1393.
20 Beinecke YCAL MSS 868, Box 12. Cayce's *Story of Creation* is brief, some fifty-four pages. I have been unable to to find an original date of publication.

8

Apollonius of Tyana

Just when he was most gone on Sheri Martinelli, Pound was reading Murray, Waddell, Boris de Rachewiltz's Egyptian translations, and Philostratus's biography of Apollonius of Tyana. His August 1954 letters to Olivia Agresti are full of all these figures (see letters 81–6 in *EP/ORA*). Moreover, as we have seen, Pound injected this intense Aryanist ideological concoction into the sequence of cantos, 90 through 95, that are otherwise his love poems to Martinelli—his white goddess and muse.

We first meet Apollonius of Tyana, a Greek philosopher of the Pythagorean school, in Canto 91, which is a love poem opening with old-fashioned music and Provençal, imitating a troubadour's love song: "with the sweetness that comes from my heart" (91/630). As a tradition of interpretation from Forrest Read to Timothy Materer has pointed out, the context is alchemical: "that the body of light come forth / from the body of fire." The context is also erotic and refers to Martinelli, as usual through the synecdoche of her striking eyes: "And that your eyes come to the surface / from the deep wherein they were sunken, / Reina" modulating to "Thus Undine came to the rock, / by Circeo" and

> Thus Apollonius
>   (if it was Apollonius)
> & Helen of Tyre
>   by Pithagoras [sic]
>   by Ocellus
> (pilot-fish, et libidinis expers, of Tyre[)] (91/630)

An undine is actually a type of sea-nymph, but here it represents Martinelli, who is likened to an undine in Cantos 91 and 93 (91/630, 93/643) and whose eyes were such an important part of her self-projection and muse-like influence. This poem is the second in the run of Sheri Cantos (90 to 95) celebrating the love between poet and muse. So, what is Apollonius, a celibate, ascetic Pythagorean philosopher of the first century, doing here, particularly in the company of

Helen of Tyre, slandered by Christian apologists as a prostitute, regardless of the fact that she and her mentor forgo sex? It seems that Pound's parenthetical doubt is warranted, for it was not Apollonius whom Pound should have recalled but Simon Magus, whose connection to Helen of Tyre is part of his legend. Simon is the very type of magician excoriated by the church fathers just as Apollonius was in "The Treatise of Eusebius" which accompanies F. C. Coneybeare's widely available translation of Philostratus's second-century biography of Apollonius that Pound would use in this canto and even more extensively in Canto 94.

We know that Pound heard G. R. S. Mead's lecture on Simon Magus and Helen of Tyre because a note dated 1916 in *Spirit of Romance* tells us so (*SR* 92n). Probably he'd first learned of Apollonius by reading Mead's book *Apollonius of Tyana* (1901), and he may have read his *Simon Magus* (1892), both of which are critical evaluations of these two traduced heretics from a theosophical, Gnostic perspective. He definitely reread Mead's *Apollonius of Tyana* for these late cantos, as it is a source for Canto 94, so it is intriguing that Pound seems to be unsure if Apollonius or Simon Magus is Helen of Tyre's proper partner; or, if he was unsure, that he didn't fix the poem on revision, letting his error (if that's what it was) stand.[1]

On the other hand, if Pound has *not* confused them then the Pythagorean doctrine of transmigration of souls in which Apollonius believed would seem to be in operation. Misinterpreting what is to be taken anagogically literally, Irenaeus accused Simon Magus of buying a prostitute and imprisoning her soul in her body so that it could not rise to the Father. Instead, she is forced to suffer her soul migrating into the bodies of other women, including Helen of Troy (Mead 1892: part II). So "Helen of Tyre," the bought woman, is also *all* women because Irenaeus misreads the Gnostic parable allegorically when he should be reading anagogically. Anagogically, like all women, Helen is symbolically Matter, while Simon plays the role of Mind, with "Helen" as his first thought or emanation. If Apollonius is a persona of Pound, as is commonly assumed, then Helen of Tyre personifies Martinelli, "the dope-doll" from the lower depths of Bohemia—the twentieth-century equivalent of the temple prostitute in willing thrall to a mage.[2] Theirs is a tale not of lust but of real love. Apollonius and Helen are thus "pilot-fish" swimming ahead—by a couple of millennia—of the poet and his muse/lover.

Pound converses with Philostratus's *Apollonius of Tyana* directly in Cantos 91 and 94; after that, nothing—except his name once more in Canto 101 along with Porphery and Anselm, as a builder of light. He does not reappear in Canto 97, when Pound returns to Sargon and the Abydos inscriptions where we might expect to hear of Apollonius again. In Canto 94 Apollonius ends where he begins in Canto 91, named in illuminated Neoplatonic company seemingly far from the more practical details of his civilizing mission. Still, Peter Liebregts argues that "Canto XCIV is … meant to demonstrate that the Confucius-Neoplatonic practical-metaphysical system can give rise to order and civilization by depicting through the example of one man how it had successfully gone into action in the past" (Liebregts 2004: 321). Waddell's racialism does not enter into Liebregts's account, but, as the racial dimension learned from Waddell now seems to underwrite Pound's concept of civilization, the materialist aspect of the canto needs to be conceded and considered.

In Canto 94 Apollonius of Tyana is presented the very type of the Aryan philosopher, the ultimate virtuous pagan, who worships the sun every morning, noon, and evening.[3] "Apollonius unpolluted," Pound pronounces with satisfaction (91/636)—unpolluted by toxic Semitic influences. Pound recommended Apollonius to Agresti as "that most estimable and unkikified character" (8/17/1954, *EP/ORA* 164). Casillo pointed out that Pound mistakenly associated the "Tianu" he found in Waddell with the Tyana from whence came Apollonius.[4] Thus, "From Sargon to Tyana / no blood on the altar stone" (97/700), Pound writes, creating a geographical link and a spiritual tradition against blood sacrifice. Tyana in Cappadocia is, in Waddell's view, the likely place of origin for the original Aryans; linking them with Hittites, he places the "pre-Mesopotamian capital of the 'Sumerians'" there (2013: 9). The philosopher, according to Philostratus, observes that he was descended from "the first settlers" of Tyana, although these appear to be Greeks, not indigenous people (I. I. iv. 11). Thus, the intermingling of the Apollonius material with Waddell's fantasy of the Aryan origins of Egypt on the same page in Canto 94 (94/655) only makes sense in terms of Pound's Aryanist ideology.

Working in his usual fashion of "reading through" when incorporating another text, Pound devotes most of the latter half of Canto 94 to dense pages of his notes from Coneybeare, generously larded with Philostratus's Greek. (Pound was unworried that his poem, already cryptic, might become unreadable.) Then, as Kindellan has discovered, after the *pen*^{3} 本 ideogram (root, origin, source) (94/660), Pound turns aside to William Seagle's *Men of Law* (1947) to notice Edward I of England and his partner Eleanor, probably an Aesopian nod to his relationship with Martinelli (see Seagle 1947: 135–7; Kindellan 2017: 100–101), before returning to Apollonius's trip up the Nile to conclude with a series of deliberately tautological remarks that are designed to stress racial and ethnic purity.

Like Apollonius, Pound's readers must travel the world seeking wisdom. So we follow him to India, the Red Sea, Achilles' barrow at Troy, all the way to Gades (Cadiz) Spain, where Pound interpolates "Sumerian capitals" on the columns marking the Pillars of Hercules (94/658)—thereby adding to the lore of Waddell's Phoenician seafarers. Eventually Apollonius visited Upper Egypt to instruct the locals as to the Indian (that is to say, Aryan) origins of their philosophy (94/659–60) in much the same way as Menes and Sargon had done thousands of years before and Pythagoras had done more recently. Moreover, Menes, Sargon's rebellious son, came to Egypt from the Sumerian colony on the Indus, while Apollonius, like Pythagoras, brought the philosophy he had learned from the Indian Brahmins to the gymnosophists (the naked philosophers) of Upper Egypt.

In Mead's theosophical *Apollonius of Tyana*, also a source for Pound here, Mead stresses the connection between Apollonius's philosophical school and that of Pythagoras. A lost biography of Pythagoras written by Apollonius evidently discussed Pythagoras's trip to India and return to the Hellenic world with "Indo-Aryan philosophy," the teachings of the Brahmins or "Arya" (Mead 1901: 11), in just the way Apollonius's did.

Although Apollonius is often compared to Jesus Christ, he was a very different sort. Jesus made the narrow rounds of Palestine scandalizing the Jewish ultras and mingling with ordinary folk. Apollonius travelled the earth from India to Spain up past the cataracts of the Nile into Ethiopia. He consorted with royalty and philosophers, not fanatics and fishermen. Apollonius was a guru with a worldwide reputation, while Jesus lived and died in provincial obscurity. A celibate, vegetarian ascetic, dressed in linen, Apollonius actively sought wisdom; he didn't receive it from on high. His philosophy was not at odds with any religion; wherever Apollonius travelled he sought to reform and renew the rites performed in the temples, specifically attempting to reform sacrificial rituals by substituting figures made of incense for actual animals—hence "no blood on the altars" (94/655, 97/700, 97/701). Despite the overwhelming evidence in Homer of Greek animal sacrifice, Pound chooses to follow Waddell rather than Homer, finding the offering of simple fruits of the earth, or prayer alone without material offerings, to be an aboriginal Aryan practice.

Finally, and most important, unlike Jesus Apollonius played an active role in politics, urging resistance to Nero and lending his influential advice and endorsement to would-be emperors like Vespasian (mentioned by Pound 94/659) and, in the climax of his story, confuting Vespasian's tyrannical son, the Stalinistic Domitian, at a trial in Rome itself. Rather than allowing himself to be sacrificed to redeem mankind, however, Apollonius simply "vanishes" from the imperial courtroom (II. VIII. v. 283) to reappear later amongst his friends far away (II. VIII. x. 359). This anticlimactic miracle is redeemed somewhat by Philostratus's invention of the speech Apollonius would have made had he decided to stay and face the court. Mead, for one, spends almost no time on this concocted defense of philosophy and likely believed it to be wholly the creation of the biographer (Mead 1901: 28). Pound does not cite it either, although he recommends the late books of the biography to Agresti (4/21/1954, *EP/ORA* 160).

The whole thrust of Philostratus's account is that the purpose of philosophy is to speak truth to power—in Pound's idiom, "to put ideas into action." Apollonius does not build political factions; he is "not particular about theoretical organizations," Pound says (94/659), following a passage in Mead that may have reminded Pound of his own peculiar situation. "Apollonius did not establish any fresh organization," Mead writes; "he made use of those already existing, and his disciples were those who were attracted to him personally by an overmastering affection which could only be satisfied by being continually near him" (Mead 1901: 61). This is precisely how Pound's own disciples felt about him. In May 1960, Martinelli relayed to Pound something H.D. had told her in a letter: "she knows what I now know. There is MORE adventure / In a day of Ezra Pound's conversation. / than there is in a lifetime with the Soldier type" (SM to EP 5/60)[5]—probably H.D. was comparing the poet favorably to Air Chief Marshal Hugh Dowding.

Instead of political parties, one man saying what he really thinks is the catalyst for change; although, ironically, Pound himself cloaks these thoughts discretely in Chinese and Greek, suggesting in an aside only that "V.35 [is] worth attention" (94/659). "一 | 人" [I^1 | Jen^2]—"One man" (94/659), he writes, steering us to Philostratus V. 35 (V. xxxv. 539) and to another place (V. xxxvi. 536), from which Pound provides the Greek (though not the English) to report that a philosopher "should say what he really thinks" (94/659).[6] One man to another, Apollonius urges Vespasian to be that man (V. xxxv. 549); he wants him to be a true philosopher-king. However, and disappointingly, we don't hear much in plain English about what Pound really thinks.

Pound is yet more cautious in Canto 97, where he inserts Philostratus's Greek to convey that the threat of a tyrant (this time Nero) against philosophy and truth "was thrown in my way as a touch-stone" (94/658) for philosophers. True philosophers are unimpressed by the threat of state violence, including abrupt imprisonment without trial; weaker wise men flee (I. IV. xxvii. 435). Nero set the precedent of banishing philosophers from Rome as their virtuous ways cast a bad light on his decadent excesses, although publicly he said he opposed philosophy because "he suspected its devotees of being addicted to magic" (I. xxxv. 431). In Philostratus's account, Nero wished to be an actor, not an Emperor, so he used his august position to chase boys and cast himself in theatrical entertainments all over the Empire. Pound honors the "tough guy Musonius" (91/635) (whose name may be Aesopian for Mussolini),[7] a philosopher colleague and correspondent of Apollonius (I. IV. xlvi. 459–61), who was not intimidated by Nero's *fatwa* against philosophers; nor was Apollonius. He found Nero's behavior a disgrace and said so. For this he was interrogated by the Roman authorities. Apollonius denied he was a magician or prophet; his forthright replies earned the respect of Nero's underlings, and so the philosopher avoided further prosecution (I. IV. xxxix–xliv. 441–57).

One wishes Pound had included Apollonius's reply to the "mouthpiece" of Domitian (II. VII. xxxvi. 251) who visited him in prison, hoping to get the philosopher to say incriminating things about himself or his friends. Apollonius said: "[I]f I have been cast into prison for telling Domitian the truth, what would happen to me if I refrained from telling it? For he apparently regards truth as something to be punished with imprisonment, just as I regard falsehood" (II. VII. xxxvi. 253). Pound must have thought this speech reflected his own situation, but we don't hear it, even in Greek.

If only Pound would be forthright as Musonius and Apollonius! But recall that Pound also knew Apollonius believed that the proper philosopher chooses his place and time to die (II. VII. xxxi. 239); perhaps this was not the time or place for Pound to declare his essential sanity and be tried for his life by the Eisenhower administration as Apollonius was by Domitian. Pound could tell himself that he had already spoken truth to power in the radio broadcasts. For whatever reason, Pound realized that the United States was not anxious to try him. Eustace Mullins thought we were afraid to; it would expose the corruption at the heart of the system (Mullins 1961: 336). Pound did too, writing Agresti: "Nero just as dirty a swine as Roosevelt / and Ike not half the man Domitian was," evidently because Eisenhower refused to bring Pound to trial (*EP/ORA* 160).[8] Domitian brought Apollonius to court but abandoned his examination for essentially the same reason Pound was not to be tried; he was afraid of what might come out.

If Apollonius is an Aryan paragon, an alter ego of Pound himself, as Casillo noticed (Casillo 1985: 72), Apollonius must also be anti-Semitic. Casillo noted that the pharaoh Amasis, whose soul has become trapped in the body of a lion recognized and rescued by Apollonius, was the pharaoh who "delivered Egypt from the nomadic Hyksos" (Casillo 1985: 100), the Semitic (though not Jewish) invaders of Egypt. This story is hinted at in typically cryptic fashion at the end of Canto 91: "Apollonius / who spoke to the lion" (91/636). Apollonius's affinity for anti-Semitic resistance means he has something in common with Vespasian (94/659), who, Philostratus tells us (although Pound does not), came to Apollonius for advice about whether or not to pursue the imperial purple having just put down a revolt in Palestine resulting in the deaths of some tens of thousands of Jewish rebels (I. V. xxvi. 541).[9]

When Apollonius ascends the Nile as far as the cataracts to converse with the gymnosophists, he approaches the borders of Ethiopia. He visits the Memnon colossi, statues of the pharaoh that were said to cry out at dawn when struck by the rays of the rising sun.[10] Pound's purpose of reporting on Apollonius's Nile journey might be to show that Apollonius explored and understood the origins of economics and that economic activity in its purest form is practiced in proximity to the sun—where the light is strongest—not in "darkness" (94/655). At one point, it is reported that at a certain spot the Ethiopians lay out their goods and retire. The Egyptians arrive, taking what they want and leaving equivalents of their own behind. All is out in the open. This incident looks forward to Canto 108, where Pound quotes English law that "sale must be in place / overt not in backe room" (108/789). Pound is always against any backroom dealing, which he associates with financial skulduggery, usually by Jews, as in Canto 104, with Disraeli's purchase of the majority of Suez Canal shares using Rothschild money without Parliamentary approval (104/762).

Apollonius finds the straight barter carried out on the upper reaches of the Nile a practice ranking far above the mere moneymaking of the Greeks, who take a financial view of wealth, imagining that one obol begets another (I.V. xliii. 573; 94/660), thereby valuing the exchange of money over the exchange of goods. Apollonius holds forth at length praising simple barter, concluding: "What a splendid thing then it would be, if wealth were held in less honour and equality flourished a little more"; weapons would not be forged, men would agree on the value of necessary things, not on gaining profit at the expense of others, and "the whole earth would be like one brotherhood" (II. VI. ii. 7). Pound does not repeat Apollonius but thinks what the philosopher said important enough to give us the page number in Coneybeare. More laconic, Pound renders the philosopher's praise as "The Africans have more sense than the Greeks" (94/660) because they deal in things and not abstractions, real goods on the basis of equity and not financial values based on what the market will bear. Pound is elsewhere critical of barter as an economic paradigm; he knows too well that the primal scene of barter is a commonplace in the beginnings of most economic texts, so it's possible there is an element of satire in this scene. Still, ascending the Nile means we are nearing the origins (signified by the Chinese ideogram *pen³* 本) not only of civilization but of economics too. We are in an Edenic economic zone where equivalences of value are not problematic.

If we have Coneybeare nearby, we can figure out that "AEthiops" is the "one word meaning to burn and be warm" that Pound gestures to in the canto (II. VI. v. 17n; 94/660). It comes from "aethos," to burn. The ancients reckoned the Ethiopians as those nearest the sun, which accounted for their dark color. This moment complicates any simplistic reading of Pound's racial attitudes as being in their essence anti-black; rather, like Apollonius, his views are essentially pro-ethics and "pro-white." It's worth speculating as to whether Pound might hear "ethos" near to "aethos," for fair and open barter is another way of saying justice. After all, "an eye for an eye" is a kind of barter. The idea of equivalence of value between disparate objects lies behind the notion of equity that Pound associated with agriculture. So in the lines immediately following the *pen³* 本 ideogram (root, origin, source), barter becomes the earthly paradigm, the root or origin of "thrones, / and above them: Justice" (94/660).

The scales of justice derive from Egyptian religion. In the drama of the weighing of the soul of the deceased before Osiris, a merchant's balance is used, with the soul in the scales against the ostrich feather glyph of *ma'at*, or justice. This Egyptian ideal of balanced justice, equity, carried by Christianity into the present West, is also central to Pound's image of Confucianism as "the unwobbling pivot." It signifies fair exchange: "stick to what's sold on a two pan balance," he quotes from the *Eparch's Book* in Canto 96 (96/685).

Equity, balance, justice: all one. Tautology is the figure of perfect equivalence, perfect balance. The concept emerges in the tautological presentation of the Chinese king sign on these pages. Here at last we come to language that touches on the historical crisis amidst which Pound is writing. Apollonius "wanted to keep Sparta, Sparta ... not a melting pot" (94/661). He wanted to "keep the institutions of Sparta in their original purity," which meant not mingling with other peoples and also limiting immigrants (II. VI. xx. 85). Likewise, Apollonius told Vespasian that "the king shd / be king" and that the ruler over the Greeks should be one who can speak Greek (I. V. xxxvi. 57), "as against that schnorrer Euphrates"—an opportunist philosopher and Apollonius's rival—and the pretty rhetoric of Dion, whose honeyed words, so opposite Apollonius's terse and unadorned speech, should be "set to music" (94/660). The expressions of these two are out of balance, one partial, the other florid. This is obviously Pound's way of criticizing his irresponsible contemporary poets—"Pulitzer sponges"—like Peter Viereck on the one hand, mere composers of delicate lyrics on the other, neither tendency facing what needed facing: the extinction of the American experiment as "a white man's country,"[11] Sparta.

Far from passively rendering to Caesar what is Caesar's and reserving to God what is God's, as Jesus recommended, Apollonius, philosopher and public intellectual par excellence, wished to instruct Caesar, not just to endure him. Pound had devoted himself to just this kind of pedagogy with FDR, who was to be one ideal reader of *Jefferson and/or Mussolini*, and Mussolini himself. Pound's job, then, as he saw it, was to explain one leader to the other. Much like Confucius, Philostratus's narrative can be read as a handbook for princes; no wonder that Liebregts claims Pound found Neoplatonist and Confucianist terminology "interchangeable" and virtually "synonymous" (Liebregts 2004: 10). The Emperor of Rome, no less than the Emperor of China, should also be a philosopher. Philosophy is the antidote to tyranny.

The surprise gesture to Coke, "Coke once he got into parliament" (94/661), deserves comment, given the role Coke will play in the final group of Washington Cantos. Unsupported, the line doesn't mean much, though in retrospect we can guess that Pound is gesturing toward the "Petition of Right." Because Pound has Coneybeare in front of him, however, it is possible that the reference to Coke is the poet's comment on these lines arguing that it is not the man who abstains from injustice that is just, but he who influences others. From this will arise a crop of other virtues, "those of the court and the legislative chamber" (VI. xi. 97).

Put plainly, Pound's essential mission has not changed. Here, he is still trying to teach "Caesar," still trying to "raise the cultural level" though his didactic cantos. But his habit of indirection, of folding up his message in esoteric envelopes and making his plain meaning literally Greek, suggests to this reader that, even if his intended audience was Sheri Martinelli, in fact Pound was intimidated by his seemingly intractable situation as a political prisoner. Here, Pound's self-censorship is almost complete; his struggle for the light is most desperate.

Notes

1 Pound mentions Mead's book to Agresti (9/17/1954, *EP/ORA* 164). The phrase "Daughter of a sun priest in Babylon" (94/659) is a reference to the antecedents of the Empress Julia Domna, the philosopher-empress and "guiding light of the

[Roman] Empire during the reigns of her husband Septimus Severus and her son, Caracalla" (Mead 1901: 26). Julia Domna was Philostratus's patroness and commissioned Apollonius's biography. This genealogical information is not in Philostratus, nor in Mead exactly, although Terrell cites Mead in his note. Mead reports that Julia was "the beautiful daughter of Bassianus, priest of the sun at Emesa" (1901: 26), not Babylon—a curious mistake by Pound, given his use elsewhere of Babylon as synecdoche for the Jewish Power (see *Pisan Cantos*, 74/457, etc.). However, Pound is here under Waddell's influence, and Waddell insists on "the total absence of Semitic dynasties in Mesopotamia and Babylonia until after the Kassi Dynasty about 1200 B.C." (Waddell 2013: 429). So for the moment Babylon meant an Aryan, not a Semitic, civilization. Pre-Semitic Babylon worshipped the sun god Shamash. Shamash ("of fine Aryan type": Waddell 2013) can be seen conversing with Hammurabi about his epoch-making law code on the famous stele where the laws are inscribed—the earliest legal text. Pound would have seen this picture in William Seagle's *Men of Law: from Hammurabi to Holmes* (1947), a "dominant intertext" for the latter pages of Canto 94 (Kindellan 2017: 100–101) as well as in Waddell's *Makers*, where it is the final plate (pl. xxiv).

2 Kindellan quotes from an "extraordinary" 1959 Martinelli letter to Norman Holmes Pearson entitled "The tao of canto 90" : "the year is 1954 around easter-tide; the scene is on the lawn of St. Liz—Merlin the Magician is being held political prisoner by the High Priests of Black Magic—with his magical powers Merlin the High Priest of White Magic has called into being a female: created by love out of love" (qtd in Kindellan 2017: 104n).

3 A useful overview of current scholarship on Apollonius is *Theios Sophistes: Essays on Flavius Philostratus' Vita Apollonii*, by Kristoffel Demoen and Danny Praet (Brill: Leiden & Boston, 2009). Philostratus's book is viewed by some as a novel, by others as the biography of a philosopher/magician. There is a long scholarly tradition of comparisons between Apollonius and Jesus. There seems to be controversy over the extent to which Apollonius's travels and miracles were merely conventional. A recent new translation of *Philostratus: The Life of Apollonius of Tyana* (Christopher P. Jones [Cambridge: Harvard University Press, 2005]) is the subject of a detailed, informative, and very tough review by Gerard Boter and Jaap-Jan Flinterman. See *Bryn Mawr Classical Review*, 2005.09.62.

4 Waddell thinks "Tianu" means "the Western Sunset Land," "Land of the Lions," apparently "Syria-Phoenicia" (2013: 315), which doesn't seem very close to Cappadocia in Central Anatolia (see also Waddell 1930: 97, 195). Casillo's is by far the most interesting reading of the role of Apollonius in *The Cantos*. Noting the link to Apollo, the sun god, Casillo traces an Aryanist tradition of sun worship and solar heroes—like Heracles—to which Pound's work is attached. Pound is placed, persuasively, in an intellectual tradition to which Nazism also belonged— the very tradition Viereck labels "metapolitical" in his book. It includes Thaddeus

Zielinski's *La Sybille: Trois essais sur la religion antique et la christianisme* (1924), Alfred Rosenberg's *Der Mythos des 20. Jahrhunderts* (1930), Houston Stewart Chamberlain's *The Foundations of the 19th Century* (2 vols.), to which Rosenberg's *Mythos* is explicitly a continuation, and Arthur de Gobineau's *Essay of Human Inequality*, translated (in part) in 1856 by two Americans, Josiah C. Nott and Henry Hotze, both ardent white supremacists and proslavery men. Nott was influenced directly by Samuel Morton, whose biased studies of human crania proving "negro inferiority" had such a decisive effect on Louis Agassiz (see *JK & EP* 64–7). Gobineau, who served the French government in Persia, also wrote a book about translating cuneiform texts. It would be interesting to learn if his work influenced Waddell.

5   Ezra Pound papers, Beinecke YCAL MSS 43, Box 33, folder 1392.

6   Pound's Chinese source for "one man" in the *Rock-Drill* Cantos—appearing in 85/567, 86/583, 89/620, and 94/659—is "i jênn iuên" (85/567), from Shu, the History Classic, given as a source for Canto 85 by Pound himself (85/579 n.). It is also known as *Shang Shu* or *The Books of Shang*. The passage comes from Shang Shu, Book V. T'ae-Kea, Part III [Tai Jia III]. In Legge's translation, "一 人 元" is "Let the one man be greatly good." The whole sentence reads, "Let the one man be greatly good, and the myriad regions will be rectified by him." (AH)

7   Musonius, "the man with the spade" (94/659) to whom Pound does homage in Canto 91 and in Canto 97), was put into a labor camp by Nero and set to work on the Corinth canal in much the way Soviet convicts were used to dig the Baltic–White sea canal in the 1930s, where some 25,000 prisoners died.

8   Pound's view may be "because Domitian acquitted Apollonius ... of sedition, whereas, Eisenhower left Pound in custody" (Henderson 2010: 352).

9   Pound does not use Apollonius's opinion of the Jews as having "long been in revolt not only against the Romans, but against humanity; and a race that has made its own a life apart and unreconcilable, that cannot share with the rest of mankind in the pleasures of the table nor join in their libations or prayers or sacrifices, [they] are separated from ourselves by a greater gulf than divides us from Susa or Bactra or the more distant Indies" (V. xxxiii. 541).

10 Philostratus mentions only one statue, but the Romans had repaired the second statue by the time he wrote. The statues actually portray Amenhotep III and still stand today. Incidentally, the many portraits of Amenhotep show him to be a person whose appearance most would call "African."

11 Pound wrote Agresti on August 12, 1954: "the alleged literati write what will sell NOT what wd / function for sanitation" (*EP/ORA* 167).

9

Canto 97

Nummulary Moving toward Paradise

"If a penny of land be a perch
                that is grammar /
        nummulary moving towards prosody" (97/685)

Canto 97 falls naturally into two parts, so it's worth wondering why these aren't two cantos instead of one; and, since it *is* one poem, just what the relationship between the two parts is. In a recent essay, Roxana Preda has provided a useful metaphor—the two halves of Canto 97 are like two sides of the same coin: "one side is stamped with the face of the emperor and establishes the coin with relation to land, grain, silver; the face is 'historical' and asserts the power relations in a certain period of history."[1] This corresponds to the first half of Canto 97, loaded as it is with political, economic, and, specifically, monetary history. The reverse "points to a different order," that of "sacerdotal authority, they contain religious symbols and expressions of cultural value: the face of a god, the symbol of the cross, the insignia of a culture" (*G* 41). If Preda is right, this reverse side of the coin and second part of the canto is its metapolitical dimension.

    The first part of Canto 97 is the historical obverse; that's the history of monetary systems, courtesy of Alexander Del Mar. The canto divides just where Preda says it does with the lines "New fronds / novelle piante" (97/695; see Figure 9.1).

    The Italian leads us to the last stanza of the final canto of Dante's *Purgatorio*, XXXIII, where, as Preda points out, Dante, having bathed in the river Eunoe where one's good deeds are remembered, feels "reborn, a tree renewed, in bloom / with newborn foliage, immaculate, / eager to rise, now ready for the stars" (*Purgatorio* XXXIII 143–4; *G* 41); ready, that is, to cross into Paradise. The

> "This coil of Geryon" (Djerion) said Mr Carlyle,
>   in Congress,
>   who later went to the Treasury,
> New fronds,
>
> novelle piante 新
>
>   what ax for clearing?
> 親 *ch'in*¹   旦 *tan*⁴   親 *ch'in*¹
> οἶνος αἰθίοψ the gloss, probably,
> not the colour. So hath Sibilla a boken ysette
> as the lacquer in sunlight ἀλιπόρφυρος

Figure 9.1 Canto 97/695.

ideogram *hsin*¹ 新 means "make it new" or renew to Pound; it is part of his "make it new day by day, make it new" slogan. In *Jefferson and/or Mussolini* it had a specific political valence: "It shows the fascist ax for the clearing away of rubbish" (*J/M* 113). *Hsin*¹ 新 also has a family resemblance to the Social Credit logo, which shows a man "striking at the root" of a tangled bush with an axe (see Figure 9.2). Quoting Thoreau, the slogan below the logo says: "There are thousands hacking at the branches of evil to one who is striking at the root."[2]

As the poet had hoped to convert Mussolini to his variant of Social Credit, his "Volitionist economics," *hsin*¹ 新 probably meant both to him. The meaning of true sovereignty has been established in the first half of the canto; the second part will put it on a proper metapolitical, Aryan, basis.[3] The next three ideograms— ch'in¹ 親 tan⁴ 旦 ch'in¹ 親—means something like a new dawn for the people to grow; even, to push a little, "renaissance." Pound is not just talking about himself but cultural renewal. It seems that the rest of the canto is set up to introduce a *paradiso terrestre*.

Figure 9.2 American Social Credit Movement logo, Beinecke.

Canto 97 Obverse: History as a Monetary System

While reading Alexander Del Mar in the 1950s Pound came upon the "Nummulary theory" of value. "Value is not a thing," Del Mar reasons, "nor an attribute of things; it is a relation, a numerical relation, which appears in exchange. Such a relation cannot be accurately measured without the use of numbers, limited by law and embodied in a set of concrete symbols, suitable for transference from hand to hand. It is this set of symbols which, by metonym, is called money" (Del Mar 1983: 7–8). In short, "Money is a Measure and must of necessity [be] an Institute of Law" (Del Mar 1983: 8). This theory of monetary value means that the ratio of value between coins within the same monetary system is legislated. If money is a measure, it can never be a commodity—any more than miles or kilograms can become commodities (see *SP* 293).

To issue money is to assert control over the value of things. This is the true nature of sovereignty. The all-wise creator's plan for a perfectly ordered universe expresses a perfect hierarchy of value. In his essay on Mencius, "Mang Tsze," Pound had written: "Civilization consists in the establishment of an hierarchy of values" (*SP* 104). The emperor, a metapolitical entity for Pound, is a philosopher-king who stands ideally for order and benevolence on earth, sitting on the pinnacle of value, maintaining this hierarchy. By controlling the currency, he controls the signs of value in the world. A major theme in the Washington Cantos is establishing a proper scale of values, with ratio and "proportion" (90/625).

Pound realized that a currency based on anything that could be commodified, such as gold, could not maintain a stable system of value; it would fluctuate. *The basis of currency must not be convertible into currency.* It must not be for sale, in a world where almost everything is. Only the sacred—insofar as it remains sacred—is not for sale. Only the Temple—however defined, or delineated—is *Temenos*. "The Temple is holy *because* it is not for sale" (97/696; my emphasis). The phrase "The temple is not for sale," or sometimes just the temple sign that Pound saw in Sargon's seal, is, ominously, the signature of sacred Aryan primacy. It pervades Canto 97 and reappears in Canto 100 (100/741).

Real money is always, at least nominally, issued by the state and based on the credit of the state. The state's credit is based on the power of its people, the state's total productive potential. But Pound understood, decades before most economists thought it was important, that total productive potential is ultimately based on the abundance of nature. That abundance, in turn, is the expression of sacred energies and, in Pound's view, a divine will with a plan. As we've seen, this is why Pound's is ultimately a metapolitical vision with a sacred dimension. Without that sacred dimension, all that's left is capitalism, an unsustainable theory and practice directed by the "hoggers of harvest," practicing the technologies of dispossession.

"Sovereignty inheres in the power to issue money," Pound wrote in a note published in the first issue of *The European* (March 1953), a Rightist venue that would eventually publish Canto 101 in 1959. "The sovereign who does not possess this power is a mere rex sacrificulus, non regnans." He continued, "In a republic, where the citizen has rights and responsibilities, the citizen who will not inspect the problem of monetary issue is simply not exercising his functions as a citizen"; the citizen is sacrificed to become a mere consumer. Pound concludes by saying with rare cogency: "To be distracted by questions of administrative forms, race hatreds, man hunts, or socialisation of everything but the national debt, is merely swallowing sucker-bait" (*SP* 322).[4] As opposed to the sacred gold coin issued by the sovereign pontiff, secular money is issued by banks in the form of debt. John Randolph railed against this now universal practice: "Nation silly to borrow its own" and pay interest on it (87/589, 89/612). The absurdity of the state borrowing its own money, the value of which is determined by bank rates controlled by boards of private bankers, is one of the puzzling facts of our economic system. This is why Pound finds the foundation of the Federal Reserve under President Wilson in 1913 one of the great economic crimes and why Wilson is vilified in *The Cantos* and elsewhere (see Marsh 1998: 74–8). This is why setting Eustace Mullins to write his exposé *The Secrets of the Federal Reserve* (1952), which has become a right-wing classic, was a postwar priority of the poet's.

Del Mar published *The History of Monetary Systems* in 1895 at the height of Populist agitation against the Gold Standard. The next year William Jennings Bryan's "Cross of Gold" speech at the Democratic Convention at Chicago won him the nomination for president. Monetary "theory" was at its height. Gold Bugs denounced "Free Silver"; learned tomes proliferated over the problematic of "bi-metallism"—on whether both gold and silver could coexist as media of exchange. "In view of the existing monetary conflict," Del Mar began, "the reader should be led to enquire whether this is a 'monometallic,' or 'bimetallic' work, the answer is, it is neither." The terms are misleading, Del Mar argued, because both theories "imply that money consists of metals and that this is what measures value. The implication is erroneous; the theory is physically impossible" (Del Mar 1983: 7). Del Mar's project was a direct intervention into the hottest political issue of the day. He proposed: "Money is perhaps the mightiest engine to which man can lend an intelligent guidance" (Del Mar 1983: 5; qtd in 97/690), but the guidance Americans were getting was anything but intelligent; instead, they got partisan polemics disguised as science.

Like Brooks Adams's *Law of Civilization and Decay*, one of Pound's valued sources, which was printed the same year, the *History* is a pessimistic tale of cultural decline. Del Mar does not use Adams's idiom of physics, but his view is similar. The course Del Mar charts is an exemplary pessimistic narrative of modernity, expressing what Max Weber would later call "the desacralization of the world." The history of monetary systems is the history of the decline of sovereignty as expressed in the abandonment of the sacred prerogative to coin gold. This was first held by the temple priests, one reason why the "temple is not for sale." In the West the coining of gold became a monopoly of the sovereign pontiff in Rome. Then the prerogative was lost to the grasping, secular Caesars: "Gold was under the Pontifex / Caesar usurped that" (89/622). "Pontifex maximus" means the supreme priest. The term "pontiff" survives to this day to describe the pope—a sacred figure to some—but his sacred sovereignty has been usurped by the secular; he is only "maximus" to a (nominally) universal church.[5]

Eventually, due to the overwhelming importance of trade with the Orient, including the highly profitable trade of European silver for Indian gold, Rome built Constantinople at the nexus of exchange. In the seventh century the sovereignty of the Eastern Empire was challenged by the Muslim caliph Abd-el-Malik, who first coined gold without imperial permission—which is why Pound uses him in Canto 97 (97/688). In the West the sacred monopoly was maintained by the Byzantine emperors until 1204, when the city was looted during the Fourth Crusade led by the Venetians. After "Dandolo got into Byzance," as Pound notes (97/691), the sacred aura was lost, and European kings began immediately to issue gold coins for the first time in thirteen centuries.

The final period of economic degradation is Private Coinage, starting in the seventeenth century when kings ceded the prerogative of issue coins to goldsmiths, banks (like the Bank of Amsterdam and the Bank of England), and finally, in the nineteenth century, to private companies like the East India Company. By the time Del Mar was writing, nations had ceded their sovereignty (their right to issue money) to a few private bankers who maintained the International Gold Standard for their private gain (Del Mar 1983: 370). Del Mar is "against usury / and the degradation of sacraments" (92/641).

We come now the "Nummulary theory" of value, which Pound will cite as "moving toward" a theory of prosody. "Value is not a thing," Del Mar reasons, "nor an attribute of things; it is a relation, a numerical relation, which appears in exchange. Such a relation cannot be accurately measured without the use of numbers, limited by law and embodied in a set of concrete symbols, suitable for transference from hand to hand. It is this set of symbols which, by metonym, is called money" (Del Mar 1983: 7–8). The "Greek and Roman republics" called money "nomisma and nummus," respectively, "because the law (nomos) was alone competent to create it" (Del Mar 1983: 8). In short, "Money is a Measure and must of necessity [be] an Institute of Law" (Del Mar 1983: 8). The nummulary theory of monetary value means that the ratio of value between coins within the same monetary system is legislated and therefore fixed. Ergo: money cannot be a commodity—gold money cannot be leveraged against silver coin.

"Nummulary theory" brings the discourse of law and the discourse of money intimately together. As Nicholls points out, the Roman gold/silver ratio of 12:1, which lasted twelve hundred years, "[lies] behind the mass of local detail in the poem, almost like a Platonic form" (Tryphonopoulos & Adams 2005: 47) on which Pound can found his poem. Pound desires to "lay down the law," just as the state does when it dictates the value of money. Following Del Mar from Canto 89 (89/614) onward, Pound insists on "sovereignty / i.e. the power to issue" (103/752); it is a phrase repeated insistently in his letters of the early 1950s, most famously in a letter to W. C. Williams (11/13/1956), reprinted in *Paterson* Book V: "That sovereignty inheres in the POWER to issue money, whether you have the right to do it or not" (Williams 1963: 216).[6]

In the absence of anything acknowledged as universally sacred, Pound thought local credit based on local agricultural produce might suffice. Pound wrote Agresti: "No freedom (locally) without local control of money OR local control of exchange value in some form issued against locally produced food" (*EP/ORA* 54). Pound is not thinking about sacred currency here because there is no imperium to underwrite it; rather, he's imagining local issues, based on "work done." This is Gesellite "*Arbeitswert*" as issued in Wörgl, Austria, in the 1930s, the Island of Guernsey in the nineteenth century, and various other places since, with some success. Popular sovereignty is the power to establish an order of value by issuing currency based on social labor locally accounted for.

The relative value of currency is determined by law, not nature. There is no "intrinsic value" to the so-called precious metals, except in their usefulness as material, not money. Historically, the power to establish monetary value has required a legislated ratio of the value between gold and silver. The Roman ratio was 12:1 silver to gold. But in India and China silver was valued much higher than in Europe, at between six or seven units to one of gold. From ancient times through the nineteenth century a determinative fact of world history was the profitable shipment of silver to India in exchange for gold; Marx talks about it, as do Brooks Adams and Fernand Braudel. Del Mar: "Since the Julian era, in whatever country the ratio of 12 prevailed, that country may be safely regarded as having been first under Roman-pagan, and afterwards Roman-Christian domination; in whatever country west of India the ratio of 7 or 6 1/2 prevailed, it may be regarded as having been under Moslem influence"; because the Moslems traded more heavily with India than with largely Christian Europe, "it might also be concluded that wherever any intermediate ratio between 6 1/2 and 12 prevailed, the place was at or near the frontier-line between spheres of Roman and Moslem influence" (Del Mar 1983: 140), for example the Baltic area where an 8:1 or "octonary" ratio prevailed (97/693).

Pound realized that Del Mar had devised a credible measure for much of world history—and all the more so as Del Mar underlines his thesis in terms that harmonize wonderfully with Agassiz's teaching about inspired creation and intelligent design:

To those to whom the ratio of value between the precious metals appears due to any other circumstance than the arbitrary laws of national mints, or to those whose attention to the history of this recondite subject has now been drawn for the first time, the ratio may seem a strange and inadequate criterion of political or religious domination; but *it is precisely in such obscure relations between great and little things than an all-wise Creator has sheltered the truth of history from man's destructive powers.* The forgery of books, the defacement of monuments, the perversion of evidences, the extermination of non-conformists, the invention of fabulous cosmogonies and superstitious fictions—all are made in vain to conceal or crush the truth so long as a blade of grass or a breath of air remains on earth to reveal it; for *all Nature is united in a mysterious harmony*, and to even approximately master one branch of science is to gain a key which, with patience and industry, may eventually unlock for us all the others. (Del Mar 1983: 140–1; my emphasis)

It is strange that Del Mar, who has been teaching us that the value of money is legislated, not intrinsic, should invoke Agassiz's god without much irony. "The all-wise Creator" of harmonious Nature is also the sheltering cherub of true History, protecting truth from the obscurantist and destructive powers who would falsify it by preserving the traces and "obscure relations" between great and little that reveal what really happened. The "ratio" of value between gold and silver is a more than adequate criterion for measuring "political or religious domination." No attempt to black out or "conceal or crush" this truth can ever succeed. Del Mar makes this very Poundian argument as part of a demonstration showing that otherwise-mysterious ratios of value between gold and silver extending over many centuries reveal lasting cultural influences. The impact of Muslim influences on France, for example, are to be found in "Merovingian coinages," rather than the victory of Charles Martel over the Moors at Tours (Del Mar 1983: 140). Furthermore, these ratios have a sacred character, as "the Moslem coinages, like the Roman and Byzantine, were employed as a means of disseminating religious doctrine" (Del Mar 1983: 140). Canto 104: "Gold was in control of the Pontifex / [the ratio was] standard at Byzance / and El Melek / until 1204" (104/764), the time of Abd-el-Malik (97/688).

Pound realized that these semi-sacred, imperially authorized ratios, enduring centuries, had a negative analogue in interest rates on loaned money. The rate of usury had also a metaphysical—and, ultimately, a demonic and destructive—character. He wants us to believe that the sixteen beneficent maxims of *The Sacred Edict* were "bitched by an (%) interest rate" (98/712). Throughout, Pound wants to "compel the reader's attention towards some larger, universal conflict of good and evil that relates to the ambiguous functions of precious metals"

(Nicholls 2004: 236). Everything that Pound means by "the blackout of history" was done "to conceal or crush the truth so long as a blade of grass or a breath of air remains on earth to reveal it" (Del Mar 1983: 141). Nature against unnatural blackout: that's Del Mar speakin', not Pound. And we know Pound read this particular paragraph because he cites other language from this page in Canto 97, in this case one of his enigmatic lines of "right naming": "barleycorn, habbeh, tussuj, danik, one mithcal" (97/688); in Del Mar it reads "96 barleycorns=48 habbeh=24 tussuj=6 danik=1 mithcal," recording the ratios of "the earliest Moslem system of coinage" (Del Mar 1983: 141). Pound chose to use this rather than the "Poundian" passage above it. Perhaps is it more important for Pound to establish sovereignty—to, in effect, "issue currency" like the mithcal and its derivatives—than to buttress his argument about the blackout of history. Curiously tautological, "Mithcal" means "any weight with which one weighs"— i.e. the weight of a dinar coin (Del Mar 1983: 141), which itself symbolizes "the standard," or the unit of measure. Yet, break it down and we find ... barleycorns. The ideal unit of measure is based on the abundance of nature.

Let's go further: it should be axiomatic that value is to money as meaning is to language; insofar as money is a measure, so must nummulary "move toward prosody," the measured language of poetry. Pound told Agresti: "Money is an articulation. Prosody is an articulation of the sound of a poem" (7/5/1951, *EP/ORA* 68). Again, we return to "If a penny of land be a perch / that is grammar." As Pound learned from Del Mar, "the division of moneys into weights and measures ... is to be found in all the kingdoms which grew up from the Roman provinces; for the custom is as ancient as the Empire itself" (Del Mar 1983: 213–14). In England, pounds, shillings, and pence were also measures of land, with a penny equaling a perch, or 160th part of an acre, as the penny was 160th part of the mark of account (Del Mar 1983: 213). If a penny of money is also a perch of land (about four-and-a-half square feet), that is grammar because it establishes the correct "'is' of equivalence"—measure is not abstract but attached to what is measured, the world. "Prosody," Pound wrote Michael Reck in 1955, "the total sound of the poem, 2 lines or 200 cantos" (Reck 1967: 186); measure is to prosody as grammar is to syntax. Likewise, if the weight of a barleycorn be the smallest unit of Muslim currency, then the Confucian/Jeffersonian "agrarian" strand running through all *The Cantos* suddenly reemerges in coinage. All four of the foundational discourses of *Thrones* are brought together: money, law, land, and language. This may help explain the occasional references to Pythagoras in these cantos. He's the caelator's (stone carver's) son ending Canto 107 (107/783). The great (Egyptian-educated) geometer is all about ratios.[7]

Nicholls suggests that "the idea of *ratio* is so important" to *Thrones* because

> it supports a kind of abstract thinking ... Ratio does more than "rhyme" in Pound's thinking with the principle of "right reason" adduced in earlier parts of the poem, and connoting balance and equity; less obviously it also announces an ideal of absolute identity which the centrifugal movements of *The Cantos* had quite consistently refused ... Pound's use of the ratio form exemplifies a desire, increasingly powerful in these last Cantos, to abolish social complexity in the name of some sovereign act of performative utterance. (Nicholls 2004: 239–40)

Pound's presentation of Confucian edicts, Byzantine admonitions, and Coke's legal opinion in these poems certainly shows his desire to imitate "performative utterance," while his commitment to the ideal of "absolute identity" explains his racial essentialism (not his *racism*: ideally, every race has its proper place in the cosmic scheme). The presentation of Del Mar on money with an emphasis on sacred ratios speaks to his desire to make "money talk"—but talk rationally, not to speak the demonic, coercive language of usury. Regardless, Pound's utopian cantos will be founded on ratios derived from these foundational discourses; *Thrones* have four legs to stand on. For a moment, Pound squares the epic circle and controls his poem.

Canto 97: Reverse

Roxana Preda sees the second part of Canto 97 as a "ceremony," a "ritual" meant as a quintessence of Pound's "holy beliefs about life, art, money and government. Pound's temple is dedicated to the sun and the ceremony he officiates will start at dawn and end at sunset" (*G* 41). This solar rite describes an arc from sunrise *tan* (the dawn) to sunset, "the sun's car thrown into the sea" at evening at the end of the canto (97/699, 703). What's left out of her account is the ritual's overtly Aryan expression and its fairly explicit erotic content because the sacred reverse of Canto 97 is a "Sheri Canto"—that way paradise lies.

The last pages of Canto 97 are a phantasmagoria of Sheri-talk, Waddell's Aryanism, and sun worship. Having seemingly rejected the sublunary world and crossed to paradise, it is striking—but, in light of their sexual relationship, unsurprising—that Pound returns to the paradise we have visited before, the carnal paradise of Venus. If Canto 97 describes a ritual, it is shared with Martinelli. She is generally conceded to be "Sibilla" who "hath ... a boken ysette" (97/695), i.e. *La Martinelli* (1956), for earlier Sheri had appeared under cover as the Sybil in the story of Merlin (91/633). This part of Canto 97 expresses a paradisal Martinelli motif present from Canto 90 extending at least as far as Canto 102. Here, we find her epithet (besides "Sybil"), "Kuanon"; the obsession with eyes; the extensive dwelling on the exact hue of what Moore takes to be her "russet-gold" hair (Moore 2005). This may be a way of saying "sherry," the Spanish wine, as a play on Sheri's name. We also find what we now know to be her words, the unspoken "From the colour the nature" of Canto 90, with the remainder voiced here "& from the nature the sign" (90/625, 97/695); all of this speaks to Martinelli's presence here as a fellow celebrant.

This ceremony is set in May "when crocus is over and rose is beginning" (97/701), the lovers' season. These Italian lyrics—Terrell suggests they are based on some popular song—must be intended for Martinelli's ears.

> Luce benigna, negli occhi tuoi,
> > Quel che voglio io, to vuoi?
> > > Tu vuoi? (97/700)

"Kindly light what is in your eyes / is what I want / you too? You want it?" It would be unreasonable not to take these lines as a lover's query. We know how much holy power Pound attributes to sexual joy; we know the power of Sheri's eyes. No, you "can't move 'em with a cold thing like economics" (see 97/698), but Pound could move a woman with hot words like these.

The lines dated May 4 that undoubtedly refer to Martinelli and Dorothy, respectively—"mid dope dolls and duchesses / tho orfener I roam"—are part of a ballad Pound wrote for Martinelli titled "Voice of Experience" that has been found in her papers decorated with her "drawing of a naked female torso" (Kindellan 2017: 106).[8] That intimate, erotic poetry is found in the midst of this none too solemn ceremony says volumes about Pound's paradise. That "May 4th. Interruption" (97/700) which breaks up the love lyrics to Sheri in Italian and the lines from "Voice of Experience" seem to point to some private event. Furthermore, the poet's admonition, against "running wode in job hunting / this is NOT good" (97/701), echoes a major theme in his 1954 letters to Martinelli, when he is trying to persuade her to come to Washington.

Massimo Bacigalupo was attentive to the erotic dimension of the latter half of Canto 97 in his intense close reading of the whole poem in *The Forméd Trace* (1980: 348–70). Much has come to light since that time that confirms most of his intuitions about the canto. Pound's real ideology is Aryan and erotic at once: "you will certainly not convert them / if you remove the houris from Paradise," Pound winks (97/698). We find this erotic strand associated with the Lombards, who come from the north, from as far away as Upsala (Uppsala, Sweden!), where there was a "golden fane" (97/701), according to Migne (see Terrell 1984: 625). Properly Swedish or not, these Lombards are accompanied by Nordic gods: first Woden, who is not named in the canto but who did "gallant deeds," and Fricco, i.e. Frigga (or Frigg) "the Beloved," Woden's consort and a fertile goddess of love, whom Migne chastely calls "peace." With them are more familiar Greek divinities: Priapus, the (male) god of desire, and—finally—Venus herself, "Dea libertatis" goddess of liberty, goddess of release in every sense. What are we to make of this potent Nordic and erotic combination, unless it is some invocation of love, desire, and gallant deeds, not against enemies, as Migne would have it, but the liberating deeds of a lover? Knowing that he and Martinelli were enjoying a fulfilling sexual relationship, it is hard not to see this as Pound's sly confession. He is priapic Woden and she the beloved Frigg and Venus.

Later, when going through various recensions of Roman dictionaries found in *Migne's Patrologia* (G 47), it is telling that Pound lands on Greek words for "masculine," "manly" ("being less elegant"), and "feminine" (97/702), suggesting that he's still preoccupied with the sexual dimension of this ritual. "All this came down to Leto (Pomponio)" (97/702): Pound wants us to think he has the obscure medieval lexicographer in mind, which has led to extended commentary about Pound's intense preoccupation with right-naming and the proper definition of words—an interest that is hard to square with the poetry he actually wrote. Nonetheless, Pound's clarification about which Leto is meant suggests that the better-known Leto also crossed Pound's mind here. She's the goddess associated with childbirth and fertility beloved of Zeus and pursued relentlessly by jealous Hera. Martinelli, then, is probably linked to Bernice (sic)—i.e. Berenice, the mythical Egyptian queen who sacrificed a lock of her lovely, long (some say blonde) hair for her husband's safe return from battle against the (Semitic) Syrians. If Pound remembers that Berenice may have been blonde, she may be linked in his mind to those "pre-Dynastic" Aryans, those "Goths," of which Waddell and Murray wrote and to whose work Sheri introduced him.

In the next pages, the poem descends as deep as it will ever go into the archaeological Aryan fantasy world of Waddell, with the Aryan "Aswins drawing the rain cloud," who Waddell imagines as "horsemen of the sun" (1980: 9) and the "Sumerian" glyph complex, already discussed, that is supposed by Waddell to be the Aryan "Sargon's Sumerian inscription as Pharaoh at Abydos" (Waddell 1930: 19; 94/655, 97/699) that existed "a thousand years before T'ang," the founder of China's oldest dynasty c. 1766 BC (97/699). As discussed, Pound gives us his date in Canto 94: "somewhere about 2 7 0 4" (94/655), which is the date of Pharaoh Menes's accession to power in Egypt, according to Waddell

(1930: x) in order to establish Aryan priority, without which civilization could not occur. If we are reading a solar ritual, then Aryan priority and white supremacy are basic to the rite.

Clearly the Aryans have a special relationship with *kosmos*; no wonder Waddell's Aryans are sun-worshippers, as is Pound. There is a clear distinction made in these pages between the state of affairs "neath the moon, under Fortuna" under the sign of luck (96/676; see also 97/696), where financial manipulation, stock gambling, and the production of prices for profit is the order of the day rather than goods for the general welfare—"Consumption is still done by animals," including humans, Pound reminds the economists, drily (97/700). This world of speculation, of probabilities, and of pure luck is contrasted with the realm above, the realm of the Sun, where is order: "above the Moon there is order / beneath the Moon, forsitan [perhaps]" (97/697). In Waddell's fantastic view, Semites are moon worshippers, Aryans worship the sun. The temple sign that Pound abstracted from Sargon's seal, which appears four times in Canto 97, is linked to Stonehenge, a sun temple. Aryans write from left to right, where Semites write from right to left, in "the sinister direction of the Moon-cult of their Mother-goddess, as opposed to the sun-rise right hand." In a moment of outrageous special pleading, Waddell goes so far as to claim that various Aryan royalty—Cadmus himself and the "Indo-Aryan Emperor Aoka" are his examples—choose to write against their natural grain for the convenience of their Semitic subjects (Waddell 2011a: 16).

Preda does acknowledge that "anti-Semitic sentiment" emerges "in a thread of its own" in Canto 97 (*G* 46), but it is much more than that; anti-Semitism is actually constitutive of Pound's paradise ("maintain anti-sepsis, / let the light pour" [94/655]) in the sense that Semites could never exist there; indeed, the poem shows over and over again that they are trying to destroy it.[9] I fear that is the radical meaning of the closing line of *The Cantos*, "to be men, not destroyers" (117/823).

This "racial" line of commentary runs close to Casillo's reading in *Genealogy of Demons*, but it seems worth revisiting. In the 1980s Casillo was working against a critical consensus that Pound was a benign and even transcendent genius, the view so compellingly put forth by Hugh Kenner in the *Pound Era*. Then, there was a need to correct the record; Casillo used Canto 97 among others to show that Pound's views did not change after World War II or as the result of his incarceration. Casillo argued correctly that "Pound's poetry and correspondence ... provide abundant proof that his anti-Semitic cultural mythology persisted after the war" and that it "was highly imprudent for Pound to express overtly many of his political and cultural views" (Casillo 1988: 95). These truths were not welcomed at the time; they remain unpalatable, but they should no longer be controversial. Our understanding of Pound is different now. Following in Casillo's footsteps, as I do here and as I warned in the Introduction, does not mean that I aim to prove Pound's anti-Semitism. Long ago proven, Pound's anti-Semitism is no longer a provoking question. What does interest me is his Aryanism. Pound is "pro-sun," as he says in Canto 96. (Although, to be sure, he is complimenting the Persian, therefore Aryan, King Chosdroes for exterminating "all Asia," including those Avars who made a desert of Europe—a fairly transparent Aesopianism for the current Soviet menace.) Overall, though, I believe Waddell is used for a *constructive* purpose as far as Pound is concerned. Waddell's is the buried historical counternarrative: our true history. Pound is lifting the blackout, so he has to maintain a constructive attitude, which is not easy for him to sustain.[10] He has been engaged, in these late cantos, in constructing a temple that transcends commodity exchange; it "is not for sale." If, as Preda plausibly argues, we are being treated to a sacred ceremony expressing Pound's "holy beliefs" within this sacred ground, this "Temenos" (97/701), what we are getting is some kind of Aryan religion. Pound all but declares that only through such a racialized ceremony can we glimpse paradise.

Just what sort of paradise is this? Is it experienced through mystical, Aryanist solar ritual? How does that square with the intensely personal and erotic dimension of this part of the poem? Above all, how does it connect to the first half of the poem, that reading-through of Del Mar? There is no satisfactory answer; perhaps Canto 97, like Canto 94, which is also infused with Aryanist metapolitics, is a kind of lecture demonstration, ginned up for Martinelli's benefit. The first half of the poem is the lecture on Del Mar's *Monetary Systems*, just as in Canto 94 Pound lectured on Philostratus's *Apollonius*. Rhetorically, then, Pound is the teacher, Martinelli the student. In the first half of Canto 97 he instructs her; in the second, he delights her. The rhetorical teacher/student relationship might be the other side of the muse/poet relation. The Muse inspires, but she has no specific ideological content. As she inspires, the poet enlightens, filling her with his agenda, inspiring her, in turn, to give her own art a sun-wise turn.

Notes

1   Roxana Preda, "Gold and/or Humaneness: Pound's Vision of Civilization in Canto XCVII," *Glossator* 10 (2018): 27–49.

2   Gorham Munson to Ezra Pound, September 5, 1939. The slogan is a quote from Thoreau's *Walden* (2008: 55). In the letter, Munson regrets not being able to see Pound off on his return to Italy because he had to go to Washington on Federal Writers' Project business. Director of the American Social Credit Movement, Munson regrets that a "Big Bertha book" has yet to be written on US money politics along the lines of Willis A. Overholser's *Short Review and Analysis of the History of Money in the United States* (1936), a pamphlet pushed by Pound. Munson would supply the big book himself with his *Aladdin's Lamp* (1945). Beinecke YCAL MSS 43, Box 33, folder 1201.

3   See Casillo (1988). He definitely associates the ax hidden in the *hsin* ideogram with the Fascist ax, reading it as an Aesopian substitution; "The presence of tan (the dawn sign) in conjunction with *hsin* (the axe) signifies a secret doctrine or 'arcanum' known only to the initiated and cast in mythical form to save the visionary from persecution … The axe also has a major symbolic significance in relation to Mussolini's clearing of the Pontine marshes … Like Sargon, Mussolini is an axe worshipper, having chosen the bound rods and axe (*fasces*) as symbol of his power and authority. Mussolini's worship installs him within Pound's royal chronology, the long tradition of Aryan kings" (Casillo 1988: 104–105).

4   Kasper was certainly distracted by race hatred (see 12/6/1956, *EP/ORA* 15). As for socialists: "Another Meridiano come, a bit dull. Will NONE of these well intentioned socialoid nuts EVER understand that to 'control the econ / forces and equate 'em to needs of nation' is O.K. but that to try to do it by socialization of EVERYTHING to anything save money issue is like trying to run a locomotive from the cowcatcher or from under the wheels" (10/28/1948, *EP/ORA* 15).

5   Since its founding in 1942 the Vatican Bank has been involved in questionable corrupt activities, including funding the exfiltration of Nazi war criminals, CIA clandestine operations, the P2 Lodge Scandal, and money laundering. Numerous exposés have appeared. It's a pity Pound didn't know about this criminal organism. More recently the massive LIBOR scandal and, currently, Deutsche Bank money-laundering and Wells Fargo mortgage fraud confirm in spades Pound's view of banks and bankers.

6   In this letter Pound mentions Del Mar, whom he was reading in November 1956. See *Pound/Williams* (1996a: 302–303, 304n).

7   "Pythagorean tuning" was the prevailing musical mode in Europe until the sixteenth century. Pound was well-versed in medieval music. It occurs to me that Pythagorean ratios may well provide a key to Pound and paradise that his words don't.

8   Another erotic poem to Martinelli, called "Honi Soit" ("Honey Swat"), is similarly decorated. Kindellan writes that "Martinelli's drawing is accompanied by the following marginal note: 'Maestro wrote this to make a "chune" [tune], dated "1955

or thereabouts" when Canto 97 was being composed.'" Kindellan adds: "There exists a manuscript version of this poem too. Written on the inside of an envelope from Martinelli to Pound, dated October 7, 1955, it is covered with drawings of parted female lips" (Kindellan 2017: 106). Relying in part on suggestions I seem to have given him that I now regret, Kindellan does not care to speculate on "collaborations of a more corporeal kind" (Kindellan 2017: 107), but, in light of the testimonials published by Steven Moore, Martinelli's decorative collaborations seem further proof of their enthusiastic fleshly communion.

9   An undated note preserved by Martinelli warns her: "as far as the k / they will Judas you EVERY time. / and spend and SPEND to prevent your painting madonnas and holy pictures" (YCAL MSS 868, "Pound, Ezra fragments").

10 Pound told Agresti that "the sonsZOV destroy all copies of Del Mar and Waddell" (7/2/1955, *EP/ORA* 195).

10

Pound's Agrarian Bent

Physiocracy against Degradation

Notorious for his interest in money and sustained attacks on finance capitalism, Pound is less recognized for his attention to the productive side of the economy, agriculture. Yet, early and late, Pound can fairly be called an agrarian who believed that the family farm, the homestead held in freehold, is the basis for any civilized society and a sane, sustainable economy. "The Occident is based on the homestead," Pound claimed in a 1942 radio broadcast, "... the civilization of the whole western world comes up from the soil, and from the personal responsibility of the man who produces things from it" (6/19/1942, Doob 1978: 176). In a 1952 letter to Olivia Agresti, Pound suggested that an Agrarian party be started in Italy "to be called AGRARI having *NO institutional program* / nothing that could connect them with any political -ism." Nonetheless, he outlined an Agrari program starting "with slogan alberi e cisterni [trees and cisterns] then proceeding to include aqueducts / bonifica [land reclamation]," then promoting "soy beans, peanuts (for fodder) maple trees and kudzu, for ground cover to prevent soil erosion" (*EP/ORA* 93; Pound's emphasis). In his final manifesto—"Program in Search of a Party," sent to Dave Horton in 1958–9—Pound urged "[t]hat the health dept. should pay some attention to quality of food ... the history of agriculture, ... the value of rye as against wheat."[1]

Since the 1930s, influenced in part by Paul de Kruif's *Hunger Fighters* (1928), Pound had been a persistent advocate for healthy nutritional food, recognizing that the adulteration of food for profit was a classic symptom of and perfect metaphor for Usura, the metaphysical dimension of usury economics, a life-denying, profit-seeking ethos that is in every sense "contra naturam"—against nature, which is the ongoing life process, the abundance, the source of everything. "With usura sin against nature, / is thy bread ever more of stale rags / is thy bread dry as paper, / with no mountain wheat, no strong flour" (45/229); Canto 45 says it all. As he wrote in *Meridiano di Roma* in September 1940: "the agricultural morality remains. The grain is and remains sacred" (qtd in Nicholls 2014: 10). But in 1957 Pound was complaining to Norman Holmes Pearson about "French bakers bypassing yeast to save time / and bread ruined / diseased sponge sold in cellophane" (5/24/1957),[2] adding that the French do complain about it, suggesting that some agricultural morality remains, at least in France. Perhaps we can say that usury is to economics as Usura is to the economy of nature, i.e. ecology.

The late cantos abound in wheat imagery. In the spring of 1957 Pound was reading *The Sacred Edict*. In Cantos 98 and 99, the latter mostly written at one go in a notebook in March,[3] we find: "Without grain you will not eat" (98/712); "Food is the root / Feed the People" (99/715); and "There is worship in plowing / and equity in the weeding hoe" (99/731). Following up, still paraphrasing *The Sacred Edict*, he writes: "keep mind on the root; / Ability as with grain in the wheat-ear / Establish the homestead / ... Sow to the very corner" (99/724). The true heartland is the homestead, the family farm. Like the grain in wheat, ability is innate potential. But it needs cultivation and careful breeding, as wild grasses were anciently cultivated and gradually bred into nutritious wheat. A few pages later we read: "The State is corporate / as with pulse in its body" (99/727), "pulse" meaning both heartbeat and grain. Later on, we learn "strength of men is in grain" (106/772) and "wheat was in bread in the old days" (107/783).

In Canto 99 Pound defined the state as "order, inside a boundary" (99/728). Following the sage advice of *The Sacred Edict*, Pound realized that protecting the boundary, the wheat fields, and the homestead requires a system of dykes and drainage: "Dykes for flood-water, / someone must build 'em; / must plan 'em" (99/727). Proper drainage is a concern in the Washington Cantos, as the references to the ancient "cunicoli"—a prehistoric drainage system discovered in Italy by Giulio Del Pelo Pardi and cited in three cantos (101/744, 103/752, 116/815)—show.[4] "Take care of the body as implement," Pound quotes; "It is useful / to shield you from floods and rascality" (99/726). Explicitly agricultural, the implications here are eugenic. The flood is an inundation from outside, threatening pollution of the "Ancestral spring making breed, a pattern" (99/727) because "the whole tribe is from one man's body / what other way can you think of it?" (99/728). Following Agassiz as well as eugenic "laws of nature," Pound worried that racial "mongrelization" implied the end of civilization as such. He may have remembered Hitler's warning in *Mein Kampf*: "All who are not of good race in this world are chaff" (1999: 296).

Pound's agrarian bent is the product of American populist politics descended from the Farmer's and People's Parties of the late nineteenth century, themselves the political offspring of Thomas Jefferson and the French physiocrats, Mirabeau and especially its inventor, François Quesnay. Quesnay's intellectual ancestor was a geographer named Rousselot de Surgy, from whom Quesnay plagiarized extensively in writing his Confucian *Le despotisme de la Chine* in 1767 (Maverick 1946: 127–8). De Surgy, in turn, must have profited from *Confucius Sinarum Philosophus*, a translation of Confucius prepared by the Jesuit Mission in China in 1687, among whom was Prospero Intorcetta, the Sicilian Jesuit. Pound knew who Intorcetta was and appreciated his importance as a transmitter of Confucius to the West. He recalled Intorcetta's portrait, seen in Sicily, in Canto 104 (104/762), where he is positioned in close proximity to Comte Mirabeau, an important French physiocrat. Complaining of historical ignorance, Pound wrote Agresti about "lack of knowledge of sequence / Kung / Intorcetta /, Leibnitz, Voltaire, Leopoldine reforms, 1776" (4/3/1954, *EP/ORA* 145). Like the Leopoldine reforms, the American Revolution was informed by Confucian political economy in the guise of physiocracy. It was Mirabeau who called Quesnay "the Confucius of Europe" (Meek 1963: 18–19) in reference to Quesnay's invention of the science of economics (Gay 1977: 349), which became physiocracy. Quesnay had already constructed his famous *Tableau économique* (1758), the first econometric model, before publishing his praise of China as a rational, agricultural empire (Fox-Genovese 1976: 74).

To my astonishment the first translation into English of *Le despotisme de la Chine* was done by Lewis Maverick, in his book *China: A Model for Europe* (1946).[5] Maverick was an important correspondent and informant of Pound in 1957; he is mentioned by name in Canto 105 (105/770). "Maverick just as good as his book," Pound wrote with obvious satisfaction to John Theobald in August of that year, "even apparently willing to enter into conversation with other denizens" (8/3/1957, *EP/JT* 64). Maverick's *Economic Dialogues in Ancient China: Selections from the Kuan-tzu*, a collection of thirty-two essays attributed to Kuan-Chung,[6] is a main source for Canto 106. Pound learned of Maverick's work through Tze-Chiang Chao, a translator of Tu-Fu and a reader at the Make It New Bookstore, where he mingled with Pound's younger followers, including David Wang, Sheri Martinelli, Florette Henry, and John Kasper. Chao had written on ancient Chinese monetary theory and in December 1956 suggested Pound find "a copy of Kuan-Tzu, the greatest economist China has ever produced" (*EPCF* 167), which led Pound to Maverick's book. In a letter written the next summer Chao informed Pound that he (Pound) had already encountered Kuan-Tzu in Confucius's *Analects*, where he is praised for unifying and rectifying the empire (6/16/1957, *EPCF* 169; see also *Con.* 257). There, Pound had rendered his name Kwan Chung and had Confucius remark that but for him "we'd be wearing our hair loose, and buttoning our coats to the left," a line rendered "But for Kuan Chung we would still dress as barbarians" in Canto 106 (106/773). Chao translated Confucius's meaning for Pound more soberly, as "without benefiting from Kuan Tzu ... [China] might have been subjugated by a foreign race" (12/24/1956, *EPCF* 168), which is likely what Pound means in his canto.

Unfortunately, Pound does not seem to have known Maverick's earlier translation of Quesnay. If so, he would have been struck by Maverick's opening sentence: "On reading the ancient Chinese philosopher Mencius, I realized how strongly his writings resemble those of the physiocrats of eighteenth century France" (Maverick 1946: 111). No wonder, then, that Maverick's edition includes generous "Selections from the Book of Mencius," on pages 65–79. The parallels are indeed remarkable; the circle of influence from Confucius and Mencius to the French Enlightenment to Pound and back again is complete. "*The Book of Mencius*," Pound wrote in 1942, "is the most modern book in the world" (*SP* 288).

Quesnay was a well-regarded Enlightenment *philosophe*, and physiocracy, if controversial, was well respected by a host of eighteenth-century luminaries, including Adam Smith and Grand Duke Leopold II of Tuscany, who is celebrated in *The Cantos*. Turgot, the French monarchy's last best hope, was influenced by physiocracy. The Dauphin, the French King's brother, was friendly with Quesnay and imitated the Chinese emperors by, if not plowing the first furrow, at least allowing himself to be shown holding a small model plough in his hands. Maverick notes that "another European prince of more robust character, the Emperor Joseph of Austria, used a full sized plow" in direct imitation of the Chinese emperors in 1769. This piece of political theatre is recorded in Cantos 86 and 89 (86/585, 89/621). Physiocracy was well-known to Benjamin Franklin and Thomas Jefferson, who were friends with Pierre Samuel Du Pont de Nemours, author of a book on physiocracy and protégé of Quesnay as well as negotiator of the treaty of 1783, in which France recognized the United States.[7] Lastly, Hector St. John de Crèvecoeur, French author of *The American Farmer* (1783) and another correspondent of Jefferson's, was much influenced by physiocracy. Pound must have run across Quesnay's name in his reading;[8] unaccountably, he does not notice Quesnay by name in *The Cantos* or anywhere else I have been able to discover.

Quesnay published his treatise on China in four issues of the journal *Ephemerides*. The first three parts are copied from Rousselot's history and include, among much Confucian material, the plowing emperor and the sixteen maxims of *The Sacred Edict* that Pound would cite in Canto 99 (Maverick 1946: 196–8). Part four is addressed to contemporary economic problems in France and proposes a physiocratic political economy based on a "Natural Order," with "Natural Laws" established by the "author of nature" (Maverick 1946: 265). They are those physical and moral laws "most advantageous to the human race" (Maverick 1946: 264). "These fundamental laws," Quesnay writes, "which were not at all of man's asking, and to which all human power must be subjected, constitute the natural rights of men, dictate the laws of distributive justice," establish the armies to assure the protection of the nation against "unjust encroachments of external or internal powers against which it must protect itself," and finally "establish the public revenue in order to provide all of the necessary funds for security, good order, and the prosperity of the state" (Maverick 1946: 265). This is a metapolitics. "These natural and fundamental laws of the body politic" are maintained through a "guardian authority established by the nation"—for China, the Emperor; for France, the monarchy.⁹

Following Quesnay, Du Pont wrote: "The science of economics is nothing but the application of the natural order of government to society." Peter Gay comments: "Economics was, therefore, more than a mere science of wealth; it was the science of social justice" (Gay 1977: 351)—a science guaranteed to be aligned with natural reason. This vision of a guardian authority in harmony with nature and man prompted the properly problematic slogan "legal despotism" (see Gay 1977: 494–5) but brings us close to Pound's similar metapolitical views on authority. If the state is properly constituted and the moral laws followed, perhaps by taking Confucius's advice, the supreme authority will be prevented from becoming tyrannical by nature itself. The holder of executive power must realize that his own best interest is the same as the Empire's because "the laws of nature impose themselves with such force that no rational man can refuse their assent" (Gay 1977: 495).

Pound's metapolitical thought is strongly Confucian. By exposing Confucian affiliations within French physiocracy, we can shed light on an important tension, if not contradiction, in Pound's thinking about political economy: his respect for law and representative government on the one hand and his need for some guardian authority "willing the national good," responsible for the whole people, on the other. As an agrarian populist in need of an enlightened despot, Pound recurs to "natural law," or the laws of nature, i.e. metapolitics, to justify his politics. This contradiction repeats in a twentieth-century key the unresolved tensions the physiocrats discovered as they attempted to adapt their concept of natural law to actual political economy. Only an advisor to semimythical

Chinese emperors, I Yin,[10] the first exemplary person we meet at the opening of *Rock-Drill*, Canto 85, succeeded in doing this:

> Our dynasty came in because of great sensibility
> All there by the time of I Yin
> All roots by the time of I Yin (85/563)

I Yin is a persona of Pound himself, another more recent advisor imparting timeless Confucian truths. The emperors allegedly succeeded because they recognized that "[o]nly the most absolute sincerity under heaven can effect any change" (*Con.* 95) and convinced a few people to act on that principle. This advice is a quintessence of Pound's dissident metapolitics. Change in this case would not mean deviating from the course of nature but changing *back* to the *chung yung* or middle path; this is why we turn "conversation towards justice" (99/724). Once on the middle path, political faction would disappear and class struggle would not exist. Class collaboration and social harmony would prevail. Distributive justice would underwrite social justice. Social justice, in turn, would be guaranteed economically by the rational laws of nature.

In accordance with the laws of nature, the physiocrats believed that all wealth came directly from the earth, quite in accord with *The Sacred Edict*, which states "wealth is produced by nature" (Baller 1979: 61). The source of wealth was cultivated land; wealth itself, the "net product," was agricultural produce. Farmers were the sole productive class and "agriculture the supreme occupation, not only because its produce was primary on the scale of wants and always in demand, but also—and mainly—because it alone yielded a disposable surplus over new cost" (Meek 1963: 20). "Productive" to the physiocrats meant productive of a net product; all other occupations, manufacture, and commerce were, by contrast, "unproductive and sterile" (Meek 1963: 20). As for finance, Quesnay argued against "the trivial and specious science of financial operations whose subject-matter in only the money stock of the nation and the monetary movements resulting from traffic in money, in which credit, the lure of interest … bring about a sterile circulation" (Kuczynski & Meek 1972: 21–2). In 1942 Pound asserted, "Money converts itself into foodstuffs, or 'develops' (or degenerates) as credit" (qtd in Nicholls 2014: 11). He told Agresti: "Grain supply depends on work and nature / money supply on the issuers" (1/7/1949, *EP/ORA* 32). True credit, as opposed to bank credit, rests in the abundance of nature realized in agricultural output—including prospective production; "The true basis of credit … is, the abundance, or productivity, of nature with the responsibility of the whole people behind it" (*SP* 309). Pound was already in the physiocratic tradition when he wrote in 1914: "The artist is one of the few producers. He, the farmer and the artisan create wealth; the rest shift and consume it" *(LE* 222). Quesnay was more rigorous; probably associating artisanal production with luxury goods, he chastised "the third estate"—"predominantly artisans, manufacturers and tradesmen who scorn the husbandman" and mislead the nation into monopolies, exclusive privileges, profit taking, and trade wars (Maverick 1946: 269). But as Adam Smith noted, under a properly physiocratic regime the third estate could serve a useful purpose even if not increasing the net product and thus remaining technically unproductive (see Gay 1977: 352).

However, if finance is sterile, it is not inert; finance is, to the physiocratic mind, literally counterproductive, a "cult of sterility" destroying "the mystery of fecundity" (*SP* 287). The financier/usurer is a destroyer of natural value in the service of private profit; the financier is "the hogger of harvest" opposed to the local farmer who nurtures natural abundance: "Said Baccin: 'That tree, and that tree, / Yes I planted that tree'" (88/601).

In contrast to the financial destroyers, who confuse profit for wealth, the physiocrats used two telling words for wealth: "jouissance" or "utilité." The physiocratic idea of wealth referred to "things which satisfy in a direct manner the general human demand for food, raiment and shelter. It is much nearer nature's gifts and the bodily needs of man than that which the urbanized man conceives as wealth" (Beer 1939: 140). Quoting Mencius, Pound stresses use value: "Let it be seen that the people USE (caps. mine) their resources of food seasonably" (*SP* 103; Pound's emphasis). Physiocrats were oriented toward values-in-use rather than values-in-exchange, life-sustaining satisfactions rather than profit. This sense of *jouissance* is indicated in the American Declaration of Independence drafted by Jefferson, which famously calls for "Life, Liberty and the Pursuit of Happiness."[11]

Pound's political economy is grounded on specific agricultural practice. "Mang Tsze" shows how Mencius's well-field system—eight fields surrounding a ninth communal field centered by the communal well—is based directly on arable land from which all wealth was created. "It is nature, the actual existence of goods, or the possibility of producing them that really determines the capacity of a state" (*SP* 282). It is on this "material basis" (*SP* 300), the nine-field system of fields arranged like a tic-tac-toe board, that the superstructure of Confucianism was raised. Pound's political philosophy is sited there, too.

In November 1937 Pound wrote to C. H. Douglas that he was reading Mencius "looking at the original text not merely the translation" (*EPEC* 209). This suggests that he was reading the second volume of Legge's *Chinese Classics*

(1893). Significantly, when Pound explains Mencius's system in his 1938 essay, he explains it not in terms of social credit, but in terms of Italian Fascist practice; the nine-field system predicts the Italian *amassi*, or communal granaries: "The earlier *politica* or *amassi* was as follows: in a square divided in nine equal parts, the central one was cultivated by the eight surrounding families and its produce went to the administration, this was commuted to ten percent ... In irregular country a just equivalence of what would be equal measuring of flat acreage" (*SP* 105). The nominal 10 percent is a tithe, not a tax, a share of production, not a lien against it. "Tax as a share of something produced," Pound repeats in Canto 99 (99/726; see also 99/718, 99/725). Writing in August 1939 to Jorian Jenks, the principal British fascist writing on agriculture, Pound observes that "[Fascist Minister of Agriculture Edmondo] Rossoni rightly said that amassi showed a way to a completely new method of taxes"; that is, Pound argues, "TITHES, considered [good by] Mencius who found fixed charge evil" (*EPEC* 224). Pound is emphatic in "Mang Tsze" in justifying Mencius's 10 percent tithe: "In the conditions of 500 and 400 B.C. if you cut the tithe lower that 10 per cent you could live only as the 'dog and camp-fire people'. If you raised it above 10 per cent for traders and people in the centre of empire and above the NINE FIELDS share system for rurals and border folk, you would have tyranny" (*SP* 103).

Naturally, the tenth must be collected after the harvest is in, not beforehand. In "Mang Tsze" Pound takes up the tax question explicitly, quoting "'nothing is worse than a fixed tax.' A fixed tax on grain is in bad years a tyranny, a tithe proper, no tyranny" (*SP* 103). "Mencius distinguishes a tax from a share," Pound explains; "he is for an economy of abundance" (*SP* 100). This remark illuminates the lines Pound inserted late into his composition of Canto 105: "A tenth tithe and a circet of corn" (105/771)[12] placed alongside the names of Admiral Crommelin and General del Valle, both states' rights extremists violently against racial integration (and mentors to Pound's disciples John Kasper and Dave Horton, respectively). *They* would uphold a just tax system and, in so doing, follow Mencius and (through him) Confucius. Pound continued to cite Mencius as late as 1959, showing that practical social justice "should consist in a share of the available products" (*SP* 323).

In late 1957, Pound promoted an agrarian party in the United States. The Wheat in Our Bread (WHIB) party is closely linked to Kasper's white nationalist program as the proper and sincere expression of agrarian and racial virtue (see *JK & EP* 205–13). WHIB's rather unwieldy and mysterious name was an example of Pound's Aesopian language to give away "nothing that could be construed as connecting to any 'ism.'" Its name was inspired by the British right-wing publication *Housewives Today* that Pound received, which promoted organic farming and demanded that the government put wheat vitamins back in their bread.[13] As I have detailed elsewhere, in 1957 Pound wrote to Jack Stafford his thoughts on the "laws of nature," race, and "wheat in bread" in a "Note Against Degradation." "We want pure food," the poet opined, "wheat in bread, time given for yeast to function i[n] making bread" (9/25/1957).[14] Although no official manifesto or party platform has been found, it is plausible that the full "Note Against Degradation" (see *JK & EP* 155–6) approximates the platform of the WHIB party. If so, this plank speaks to its agrarian, physiocratic aspect.

Of course, WHIB was a white nationalist, segregationist, states' rights party too, the immediate goals of which would have been compatible with the Seaboard White Citizens' Council to whom it was announced. The sole public report of the WHIB organizational meeting came from the muckraking gossip Drew Pearson, who, probably relying on illegal FBI surveillance tapes, predictably called WHIB "Nazi-like" (see Pearson B17). No doubt he wanted to emphasize WHIB's racist aspects, but in another sense he wrote better than he knew, for Hitler in *Mein Kampf* argues, in a physiocratic vein strikingly reminiscent of Thomas Jefferson, that "preserving a healthy peasant class as a foundation for a whole nation can never be valued highly enough ... A solid stock of small and middle peasants has at all times been the best defense against social ills such as we possess today." It "is the only solution which enables a nation to earn its daily bread within the inner circuit of its economy." When domestic agriculture is prospering, "[i]ndustry and commerce recede from their unhealthy leading position and adjust themselves to the framework of a national economy of balanced supply and demand" (Hitler 1999: 138). Compare Jefferson in *Notes on the State of Virginia* (1787):

> Those who labour in the earth are the chosen people of God, if ever he had a chosen people, whose breasts he has made his peculiar deposit for substantial and genuine virtue. It is the focus [i.e. hearth] in which he keeps alive that sacred fire, which otherwise might escape from the face of the earth ... [G]enerally speaking, the proportion which the aggregation of the other classes of citizens bears in any state to that of its husbandmen, is the proportion of its unsound to its healthy parts. (Jefferson 1984: 290–1)[15]

Agrarian, peasant parties, and even the organic food movement have a long history of right-wing affiliations, stretching deep into the nineteenth century.[16] The Nazi slogan "Blut u. Boden" [blood and soil] stems from polemics justifying the proto-Nazi *Artamen*, a back-to-the-land movement in eastern Germany in the 1920s. Heinrich Himmler made his Nazi bones in this area, and the Argentine-born Nazi Richard W. Darré—who became Reich minister of food and agriculture (1933–42) and author of *Das Bauerntum als Lebensquell der Nordischen Rasse* (1927) and *Neuadel aus Blut und Boden* (1930)—gave blood and soil a broad ideological underpinning. Fortunately, Pound was unaware of these writings.

The Soil Association in Britain during the 1950s is an example of this nexus, as was the Melbourne *New Times*, with which the young Noel Stock was affiliated. This provided an Australian outlet for Pound et al. informing readers about the Jew/Commie conspiracy along with organic farming practices.[17] Just down the road from where I write, the Rodale Institute, well known for its men's health and sport magazines, has long promoted organic farming while supporting the right-wing anti-fluoridation campaign.

Through his correspondent Beatrice Abbott, an avid gardener, Pound was apprised that fluoridated water was a Communist scheme to stupefy the masses; he will mention water fluoridation occasionally in letters. Kasper included an article on fluoridation in his *Clinton-Knox County Stars and Bars* (February 1957) titled "Clinton Water Now Has Rat Poison (Fluorine)" by "T. H. Benton," likely Kasper himself. The article notes that water fluoridation is not something voted on by citizens but is imposed on local water companies by shadowy federal agencies. He quotes a local resident (who might also be himself): "First they slip the niggers in the schoolhouse, then they put rat-poison in the water without letting the people know or even vote on it." Current agitation about GMOs, ubiquitous in organic food circles, takes a similar line and feeds on similar fears. Anxiety about environmental degradation has structural similarities to those of Pound and his friends. The natural order of things is under threat.

So Pound was technically correct when he reassured young William Cookson that "'Wheat in Bread' seems nearer to Soil Association movement in Britain than to a howl for white supremacy" (1/10/1958; qtd in Moody 2015: 390); but as the Soil Association was, at that time, a revenant fascist group led by Jorian Jenks, this disclaimer means less than one might at first think. Explicit white supremacy no, but racialist politics yes; call it the Blood and Soil Association. Let each race rise to its own height, as Kasper had put it in his *New Amsterdam News* letter, but those heights should never be the same.

In 1920s Italy, while Hitler and Darré were writing, Mussolini's "Battle for Grain" deployed high tariffs on grain imports and subsidies to support the Italian peasantry and economic autarky. In the manner of the Chinese emperors and Emperor Joseph before him, Mussolini showed himself cutting grain and operating FIAT tractor ploughs. Praise of agriculture as the core of economic autarky and concern for the smallholder are aspects of fascism that are too easily forgotten but which resonated with Pound's Confucian/Jeffersonian outlook.

But what of Pound's demand in "Note Against Degradation" for "pure food, wheat in bread, time given for yeast to function i[n] making bread"? Kasper himself clarified some of what it meant at a sentencing hearing in Knoxville three weeks after forming WHIB. Kasper accused the judge of abetting a genocide of the white race by upholding the law on school integration, told him he had learned much from Ezra Pound, and argued that all he, Kasper, had tried to do was "give more light" to "increase the intelligence" of Americans, as the American people, so it seemed to him, were "starving for mental nourishment, mental nutriment. Our bodies are well taken care of, but we are dying in our heritage of history" (Kasper 1957b: 10). This idea that Americans were starving for their true history, currently being rewritten by Jewish Communists, was congruent with Pound's notion of what his cantos were doing—feeding the people. "Nutrition" serves as one of Pound's master metaphors for content. As he reiterated forcefully to Sheri Martinelli, poetry is "NOT dope it is FOOD."[18]

Wheat in Bread is also the nutritious ideological content of Pound's *Cantos* and other writings. In Canto 45 it is suggested by the "strong flour" and "mountain wheat" that Usura renders scarce. In Canto 80, written at Pisa, Pound imagined himself as a shepherd "to take the sheep out to pasture / to bring your g. r. [gentle reader] to the nutriment / gentle reader to the gist of the discourse / to sort out the animals" (80/519–20)—the sheep would separate from the goats depending on how they responded to Pound's poetic fodder. Instructing Dallam Simpson on the content of Simpson's *Four Pages* in 1948, Pound insists: "Confucius and Gesell were SEED god dammit SEED" (Moody 2015: 291). These seeds were to sprout into a Confucian hybrid using Pound's Gesellite economic mechanism to escape the debt/tax system. By 1957 there was a Jeffersonian slant involving the states' rights/racial angle; Stafford suggests that, in the 1950s, Pound's "policy was to get the Southern farmers to support his programme of monetary reform after attracting them by his 'states' rights' stand and his racial views which evolved from his theories of culture" (see *JK & EP* 158; Stafford 1969: 60).

When trying to explain, to Olivia Agresti, Kasper's arrest in Tennessee for speaking out against school integration, Pound told her: "Kasper defeated same as South was in 1864, cause mind was diverted from money and taxes, customs, onto local issue having no broad or defensible theoretical basis save in nature itself" (12/6/1956, *EP/ORA* 236).[19] He said something similar to David Wang: "Unfortunate that J. K. shd / be on local line, not on universal slogan." What Kasper gets "diverted FROM," Pound insists, "is issue of money. & tax SYSTEM"

(*EPCF* 181–2). Evidently, unlike Pound, who seeks to redress corruption at the top by focusing on issues of sovereignty, especially monetary issue and unfair taxation, Kasper had chosen the wrong ground for any successful resistance to racial integration. As Pound told Wang: "K / probably in ERROR mixing with ignorant / which is different from the crowd" (9/27/1957, *EPCF* 194) so he was bound to be defeated, just as the South had been a century earlier. The ignorant have not "mobilized their intelligence," he explained to Wang, "all the mutt can object to is AMOUNT of taxes," as very few will understand anything more; "the secret doctrine is not necessarily secret NOT from desire to monopolize it" but because people cannot see the bigger picture of sovereignty, coinage and the basic infamy of the tax system—as a system (*EPCF* 190, 182).[20]

Pound was released from St. Elizabeths in April 1958 and returned to Italy in May. Canto 107 ends on an elegiac note: "Wheat was in bread in the old days" (107/783). This implies that the US Constitution once meant something but is now adulterated. It means that the basis of the state—any state, China, Italy, the United States—is in agriculture. The extent to which agriculture is neglected and mere trade promoted, especially the sterile shiftings of financial paper (such as now passes for "wealth management"), predicts the ruin of the state. "Don't burn to abandon production and go into trading," Pound warns in Canto 99; don't "Dig up root to chase branches" (99/730). An economy based on money values also means obfuscation of history and literature and the consequent degradation of textbooks, a theme in Pound's letters to John Theobald, Norman Holmes Pearson, and Harry Meacham in the last years of the poet's confinement. In textbooks, what aliment is permitted is adulterated by "slop," from which extracting intellectual nutriment is impossible, except by "a gift of GAWD to their instructor" enabling him to "dissociate the pewk / from the punkins" (9/11/1957, *EP/JT* 84). His attempt to remedy this situation in his collaboration with Marcella Spann is *Confucius to Cummings*, a poetry anthology designed to "arouse curiosity, not kill it and this *without implying false values or false views of proportion*" (*Con. to Cum.* vii; my emphasis). Knowing true values must lead readers back to the earth and the laws of nature.

Preceding any concept of Left or Right, physiocracy and Confucianism are merely in accordance with "Nature." Nature does not ally itself with the Left or even democracy. The family farm stands in resistance to collectives as Rome (that is, "civilization") resists Babylon (i.e. Semitic excess and barbarism).

Homestead versus kolschoz
Rome versus Babylon (103/752)

We might add to this equation producers versus destroyers of production: those Portuguese (actually Dutch) uprooting spice trees to create scarcity and so drive up monetary values noticed in *The Cantos* (89/616, 92/642). Thinking along with Pound, we'd need to add Mencius versus Marx and, more painfully, racial segregation versus mongrelization; all of these must be upheld or degradation follows, as history showed.

Notes

1 Marsh (2011: 212). See Beinecke YCAL MSS 43, Box 19, folder 854.
2 Norman Holmes Pearson, Beinecke YCAL MSS 899, Box 79, folder "Pound, Ezra 1957."
3 Beinecke YCAL MSS 43, Box 120, folder 4975, Notebook 107 Marzo 14 April. See Baller (1979: 3–19); 99/720–8.
4 Giulio Del Pelo Pardi is directly in the physiocratic tradition. His *For World Peace* (1923) was translated by Pound's friend at Catholic University, Giovanni Giovannini, and printed by John Kasper's friend Paul "Pablo" Koch in 1955 with a more-or-less Confucian "Preface" probably by Pound or composed under his direction. "Agriculture," Del Pelo Pardi writes, "satisfies the elemental needs of life, and it is man's most permanent material possession & his only real wealth. Agricultural products have intrinsic value. This is particularly true of wheat, which has always been the mystical & symbolical expression of life, the basis of prosperity of peoples in peace & of resistance to war" (17). Del Pelo Pardi's son Tommaso, who visited Pound at St. Elizabeths in 1953, and Boris de Rachewiltz edited Giulio's *Agricoltura e civiltà* (1923) (Turin: Boringhieri, 1971). This work argues a direct connection between a philosophically superior culture and its agriculture.
5 Maverick was an authority on the physiocrats. See Lewis A. Maverick, "Chinese Influence upon the Physiocrats," *Economic History* 3 (February 1938): 54–67; and "The Chinese and the Physiocrats," *Economic History* 4 (February 1940): 312–18. (AH)
6 In fact, the authorship of the text was disputed: there may be as many as four authors. The text appears to have been assembled between 700 and 300 BC (see reviews). Maverick himself suggests the book was composed between 330 and 300 BC (1946: 14).
7 The text is *Physiocratie: Ou Constitution Naturelle du Gouvernement le plus Avantageux au Genre Humain* (1768). Du Pont later edited *Ephemerides*, the journal that published Quesnay's book *Despotisme de la Chine*.
8 Pound probably knew of Quesnay through either or both of the following writings of H. G. Creel: *Confucius, the Man and the Myth* (New York: The John Day Co.,

1949), which mentions Quesnay on numerous pages; and Creel's "The Master Who Lighted the Way in China," *New York Times Sunday Magazine*, August 28, 1949, pp. 15–16, 18, which mentions Quesnay on p. 18 (see Henderson 2010: 60).

9   "The authority must be unique and impartial in its decisions and operations, and be united under a head who alone holds executive power, and the power of compelling all citizens to the observance of the laws, of assuring the rights of all against all, of the weak against the strong, of preventing and suppressing unjust encroachments, usurpations and oppressions by internal and external enemies of the kingdom" (Maverick 1946: 268).

10 I Yin is the same as Y Yin who figures just pages later (85/566–7). Further confusions: Terrell says that I Yin literally means one who rules—an odd name for a minister (Terrell 1984: 467)! In the event, Terrell tells us that I Yin or Y Yin was "chief minister to Ch'eng T'ang 1766–1753 B.C. first emperor of the Shang dynasty" (Terrell 1984: 467) and steers us to Pound's translation of the *Analects* (*Con.* 248). Cookson adds that this person is Tching Tang, he who opened the copper mine in Canto 53 (53/264) and became the "make it new" emperor (53/265).

11 I'm reminded of John Ruskin's concept of wealth and its opposite, "illth."

12 A "circet" is a gift of grain or produce from a farmer to a local church.

13 Drew Pearson, "The Washington Merry-Go-Round. Kasper Meeting Here Described," *Washington Post*, December 1, 1958, p. B17.

14 Jack Stafford, Beinecke YCAL MSS 43, Box 49, folder 2190.

15 As I noticed in *Money & Modernity*, this passage draws freely on one by Cicero in *De officiis* that turns up in a note to the "third edition" of Quesnay's *Tableau économique* (1758) where Jefferson might have seen it. See Marsh (1998: 15, 246n); and Kuczynski and Meek (1972: 15, 22–3n).

16 A recent book in German, *Braun Ökologen; Hintergrund u. Strukturen am Beispiel Mecklenburg-Vorpommerns* (Rostock: Heinrich Böll Stiftung, 2012), shows that the connection is still strong, even in German territory.

17 A neat summary of English right-wing "blood and soil" ideology: "International forces, almost always described as Jewish, were conspiring to rob Britain of her fertility both in the sense of the condition of the soil, but also of her 'manhood.' The country could starve either by the workings of international trade, through another war or by having lost her capacity to use her own soil. When war did actually break out, the resulting mechanisation of British agriculture merely served to intensify those feelings. The Right 'viewed the land as a fundamental resource, not only for the production of food, but as a locus of values and ways of seeing and thinking worthy of preservation' and increasingly came to consider that post war agriculture would intensify production methods and produce poorer food as a result" (David William Hargreaves, "Ill Fares the Land? The Concept of National Food Self Sufficiency in Political Discourse 1880–1939" [M.Phil, University of Bradford, 2012], pp. 212–14). (AH)

18 Sheri Martinelli papers, Beinecke YCAL, MSS 899, Box 12, folder "Pound, Ezra 1957."
19 Pound knew that the Confederacy surrendered in 1865, not 1864. But he believed that the South was defeated by its debts as much as on the battlefield. He blamed Jewish Judah Benjamin, the CSA Secretary of the Treasury, as the nefarious agent of international usury out to sabotage the new nation.
20 Pound had hinted darkly at some higher purpose to Kasper's agitation in a letter to Bo Setterlind as well. See *JK & EP* 156.

11

The Coke Cantos 107–109 as an Argument for the Defense

At the 2015 International Pound Conference at Brunnenburg, Mary de Rachewiltz made an intriguing observation about the last line of Canto 100, "Jan. 1, '58" (100/742), suggesting that it was on that date that Pound decided he must get out of St. Elizabeths under any conditions. He would forgo a trial and accept conditions that would allow his release, even as a nonperson. The date is late for Canto 100, which had been written by then, and, appended as it is to the end of the poem, it suggests a late addition.[1] Intriguingly, January 1, 1958, is just days after Pound finished drafting the Coke Cantos—December 28, 1957—and days before he turned his attention to Catherine Drinker Bowen's biography of John Adams, *John Adams and the American Revolution* (1952), on which he was taking notes until March 9, 1958.[2] If Mary's conjecture is correct, then that date might mean that Pound felt he had completed his brief for release; that in the Coke poems he had sketched in canto form the arguments that needed to be made about his case regarding misprision of treason, *habeas corpus*, the Petition of Right and its basis in the Magna Carta, and, finally, the right to trial by a jury.

It is more or less agreed that the Coke Cantos and perhaps *Thrones* as a whole are concerned with justice and law, specifically law founded on right reason and local custom ("consuetudines" [105/768]); e.g. the "Common Law." In a recent essay, Kristin Grogan speaks for most when she says the Coke poems are concerned with "English legal history" (*G* 329). *Thrones* culminates in the three cantos praising Coke because he fought for the common law derived from the English root: "our PIVOT"—the Magna Carta (107/779).

Parliament's victory in achieving Charles I's assent to the Petition of Right is the climax of this group of poems and, in the view of some, the culmination of Pound's epic altogether. Charles's endorsement occurred "in June [June 6, 1628] and toward twilight" (108/784), at 4 p.m., details supplied by Pound's reading of Coke's biographies—Catherine Drinker Bowen's *The Lion and the Throne* (1957) and *Edward Coke: Oracle of the Law* (1929) by Hastings Lyon and Herman Block.[3]

Peter Makin sums up: "The story implied by Cantos CVII–CIX is of how Sir Edward Coke (lawyer, Chief Justice, and now Member of Parliament) humbled tyranny with law" (Makin 1985: 283). Bacigalupo comments: "Pound closes *Thrones* with a final textual persona of a lawgiver, choosing for once a subject not eccentric—in fact the very origins of English and American legislation, and of the antiauthoritarianism by which this is marked" (Bacigalupo 1980: 444). No one quite concedes that Cantos 107 through 109 work as poems, but they are strong evidence of Pound's sudden elated confrontation with the actual work of the great Coke, whose authority he had long accepted through his reading of Jefferson and Adams.

Pound's turn to Coke was more than historical curiosity, more even than a timely addition to the paradisal curriculum of *Thrones*; it was personal. Pound soon realized that Coke spoke directly to his own legal predicament. Reading Coke for himself instantly made him Pound's advocate. To Pound, Coke's writing must have seemed like a key to open his prison's doors. For the prisoner long confined, what is paradise but the physical freedom to come and go as one pleases?

Pound had been preparing for Coke for weeks before he sat down with the actual *Institutes*.[4] He was looking into Lyon's and Block's Coke biography as early as mid-September, judging from a citation noticing "p.314+" in a meditation on the dangers of the royal prerogative under Charles I that Pound dated September 15.[5] Page 314 and following in Lyon and Block deal with the Parliamentary struggle against the Crown to successfully obtain the Petition of Right that may be said to culminate the authorized *Cantos*. The Petition of Right is shown to have evolved over discussions concerning the rights of *habeas corpus* (Lyon & Block 1929: 314–21).[6] The Commons argued that "no freeman be committed without due cause shown; that every one, however committed, had a right to habeas corpus; and that, if no legal cause of imprisonment appeared, he was to be bailed or released" (Lyon & Block 1929: 317–18).

The situation the Petition of Right was to remedy was Pound's own. Was he not arbitrarily imprisoned without trial or chance of legal redress? That Pound identified his own situation with such a prisoner is suggested by these November 1957 lines in Notebook 111 that cite Lyon and Block's biography:[7]

Stands mute
    not guilty p. 232
...
3 months to habeas
Till 18 B under Churchill the sow-face
Act xxv. 25 (see 107/775)

On page 232 of *Edward Coke: Oracle of the Law* we are in the midst of the trial and execution of Richard Weston—part of the Overbury/Somerset purge of 1615. Thomas Overbury, courtier, poet, and writer, had died while imprisoned in the Tower; there was suspicion he had been poisoned by his keepers. Eventually a vast plot was exposed implicating James's sometime favorite Robert Carr, now Earl of Somerset, and his wife Frances Howard. The scandal, too involved to go into here, was investigated and prosecuted by Coke (see Lyon & Block 1929: 210–38). The accused poisoner had at first refused to go to trial; such refusal was, Coke was prepared to charge, tantamount to a confession of guilt. Threatened with torture and a terrible humiliating death, Weston pled not guilty and threw himself on the mercy of the court, which duly found him guilty of treason and sentenced him to be hanged—the easier death. Lyon and Block comment in words excerpted by Pound for recalling his own situation when he stood mute before the bar in the winter of 1945. "Fortunately the situation was left open to be provided for much later by the humane statute under which a plea of **not guilty** is entered for the prisoner who **stands mute**" (Lyon & Block 1929: 232). This is how Pound "pled" on November 27, 1945, in the District of Columbia District Court, Judge Bolitha J. Laws presiding.

These lines from the Notebook do not exist in the published poem, but a cryptic version of the remainder survives in Canto 107: "3 months to *habeas* / B.18" (107/781). "3 months to *habeas*" refers to the steadfast resistance of Parliament to King Charles's attempt to usurp the liberties of the Commons, which resulted, ultimately, in the Petition of Right; while "B.18" refers to the notorious British Defense of the Realm Article 18B, which resulted in the internment without any due process of individuals deemed disloyal or profascist in England during World War II. Among them were many of Pound's correspondents: the lively Sir Barry Domvile,[8] Sir Oswald Mosley, Raven Thomson, Arnold Leese, and others. Their situation, imprisonment without trial for an unstated term, predicted Pound's own.

As is well known, Coke's *Institutes* had been brought to Pound's attention by Moelwyn Merchant, who was doing research at the Folger Library; the books themselves were supplied by Professor Giovanni Giovannini on October 30, auspiciously the poet's seventy-second birthday (see Moody 2015: 408–409; Kindellan 2017: 142).[9] The *next day* Pound was writing John Theobald excitedly about having "got the full sense of clarity an hour or two ago" (10/31/1957, *EP/ JT* 111), recommending that, should Theobald find himself teaching English prose, he might "LOOK at some Coke or Blackstone, and lay off the Miltosh and pewkery and etc."—the verbose and contorted English derived, as Pound saw it, from the King James Version of the Bible, which had "bitched our heritage" (107/777), literary and otherwise.

Pound immediately set himself to Coke's cantoization. November 2 he wrote Mary that the Coke Cantos "were intended to be 'paradisal' and linked him to Dante: '72 years to get to him, exactly when needed fer canto 107 or wotever, or 108. Parad[iso] X'" (qtd in Kindellan 2017: 142). The three Coke Cantos, 107 through 109, were drafted in a rush less than two weeks after Pound's first look into the *Institutes*. Notebook 111 (#57) is filled up with Coke material. Notebook 112 (#58), which begins November 8, 1957, is titled "Coke."[10] As Moody reports, "from that day he filled [the] entire notebook with notes and drafts for all three Coke Cantos" (Moody 2015: 409). Virtually all of Cantos 108 and 109 are verbatim from this notebook with very few changes, save a transition piece cut from after the end of 108 to 109 (pages 29–31). "It seems likely they were all in draft by Dec. 29th," Moody says, though to him they remain notes that don't cohere (Moody 2015: 406, 409). Kearns judges that "Pound had not lived long enough with his materials to have developed a sure feeling for them" (Kearns 1980: 224). Given this headlong composition from material scarcely assimilated in the poet's head, much less well digested on the page, the Coke Cantos are best read as a single, tripartite poem. "What carries us through these pages" is not an argument but "their energy, wit and nobility of spirit" (Kearns 1980: 224). What carries us through, I suggest, is Pound's sudden resolve to be free, no matter what.

Despite what he wrote Mary at the outset of his engagement with Coke, that the Coke material would become "paradisal," what if, in the ensuing weeks, the Coke Cantos went a different direction; what if they are *not* ultimately the paradisal culmination of Pound's epic, as Pound initially hoped and is generally assumed, but, rather, a swerve away from it? What if they are Pound's brief for the defense, a bid for, and justification of, his release from St. Elizabeths? *Thrones* is prison literature by a man arguably betrayed by his lawyer, his publisher, and even his wife; a man sentenced to perpetual confinement unless he bestirred himself on his own behalf (Moody 2015: *passim*). He knew that others—Archibald MacLeish, his daughter Mary, and his personal lawyer Robert Furniss—were at work on his behalf, but Pound wanted to contribute to his own cause. Naturally he would have preferred his case to be decided on its merits in a court of law, not by some psychiatric diagnosis. He realized that the others, notably Furniss, were working along different lines that eventually proved successful; the government would drop his case for failure to prosecute, *nolle prosequi* ("nol pros"). But this required psychiatrists to attest that he was "incurable," meaning release into permanent exile as a nonperson, legally incompetent, tainted with the diagnosis of insanity and under the control of his "Committee," Dorothy: free, yet not free.

Pound wrote Mary in late October 1957 before receiving the Coke that he had "96/106 'Thrones' in rough draft, dunno how much needs correcting, and a few lines of 107" (qtd in Kindellan 2017: 142). Kindellan wonders if this means that "Pound may have conceived of *Thrones* as effectively ending with Canto 106," which suggests that "the so-called Coke Cantos of 107–109 represent a fairly late addition to the volume as a whole, and may originally have starter the next sequence" (Kindellan 2017: 142). Typically, Pound published a decad of cantos at a time, so a version of *Thrones* running from 96 to 106 would make sense. Markedly "paradisal," Canto 106 had closed with a sigh after a series of passionate prayers to a number of goddesses, Circe, Athena, and Aphrodite among them, but it ends on a melancholy note: "The sky is leaded with elm boughs" (106/775); the poet looks out at the St. Elizabeths elms through glass;[11] he is inside, confined; the feminine figures are out there, free, divine, and untouchable. Had this line ended *Thrones*, we'd look at the book very, very differently, as a kind of prisoner's prayer and lament.

But because Pound had received that timely gift of Coke, Canto 107 opens in quite a different key, a key of hope: "The azalea is grown while we sleep / in Selinunt / in Akragas / Coke Inst 2" (107/776). Setting aside the obscure references to Sicily,[12] it is clear that the poet has discovered Coke's second *Institutes*. Commentators generally take the flourishing azalea as the "organic" growth of the English Common Law (Cookson 2001: 252; Hickman in *G* 318). There is the suggestion throughout the Coke Cantos that the law is, or should be, a well-tended garden.[13] As it has no obvious referent, "Box hedge, the garden in form" (107/780) could refer to Coke's book. Later, Pound notices the "500 mulberries" planted by Robert Cecil, Coke's patron, at Hatfield, a detail he got from Bowen (1957: 331–2). He must have liked the mulberries for their connection to China, silkworms, and *The Sacred Edict* (98/712), but he may also be symbolizing the state as a flourishing, well-tended garden or orchard.[14] Coke and Iong Ching (Yong Zheng), the Emperor who promulgated *The Sacred Edict*, are linked at the end of Canto 108 as responsible statesmen. "Coke, Iong Ching / responsabili" (108/790), urging irrigation projects, the repair of bridges, and civic planning—in a phrase, "setting their lands in order" by codifying laws.

From the beginnning of Canto 107, another hopeful sign is that Pound has chosen new, powerful legal representation in the "oracle of the law" Sir Edward Coke, "the clearest mind ever in England" (107/778). Coke's authority is rooted "in that Charter" (107/777), the Magna Carta, and certified by his profound knowledge on the Common Law as ratified by the *Institutes of the Lawes of England* (1628–44). In evoking Coke, Pound is effectively laying Coke's magisterial volumes on the defendant's table and claiming his rights as a citizen, patriot, and defender of the US Constitution, which, as everyone knows, descends directly from the Magna Carta, Thomas de Littleton, Coke, and, through them, John Adams and Thomas Jefferson, Pound's heroes all.

If the Coke Cantos are in fact an argument for the defense, then the climactic moment is the acceptance and ratification of the Petition of Right, June 7, 1628, by a reluctant King Charles I, celebrated on the first page of Canto 108 (108/784). The Petition of Right is a monument to the Rule of Law asserting against arbitrary tyranny, *habeas corpus*, among other human rights. According to sources Pound knew well, the Petition of Right evolved from lengthy debate concerning the rights of *habeas corpus* (Lyon & Block 1929: 314–21; Bowen 1957: 478–503). The petition confirmed the fundamental rights of Englishmen; in Catherine Bowen's words:

> About this petition there was no fine language, no conscious "poetry" or philosophical argument concerning freedom and the soul of man. Penned by lawyers, it spoke the plain language of the common law: a practical instrument to keep innocent men out of prison, to relieve them if put there arbitrarily and to give each subject, whether innocent or guilty, his chance at trial. (Bowen 1957: 498)

The situation the Petition of Right was drafted to remedy was Pound's own. Was he not arbitrarily imprisoned without trial or chance of legal redress? Denial of *habeas* is clearly a major issue in Pound's case that the poet felt keenly and wished to bring to public attention in his poem. As he complains in Canto 109, "Nor can the King create a new custom / in the fine print" (109/792). By "King," Pound suggests executive power; the "new custom" may well gesture to the newfangled practice of remanding political dissidents to perpetual confinement in mental institutions. Pound did have a jury trial on his sanity, but not on the treason charge brought formally against him. Moody has argued persuasively that even the sanity trial was a sham, with the jurors having little choice but to follow the unanimous testimony of a team of psychiatrist experts working simultaneously for the defense and the prosecution in Pound's case (Moody 2015: 167–92). During Pound's confinement, the Alaska Mental Health Enabling Act (1956) had been proposed, which designated a vast tract of the sub-arctic territory (some 1,000,000 acres) for psychiatric cases under federal care. Pound's friends, including the DAC and John Kasper, testified against this psychiatric Siberia in

Congress, with special reference to Pound, arguing that the reservation might well be used for political prisoners—Moscow-style. Such an extrajudicial option, which under the terms of the proposal would have permitted the admission of mental patients before any judicial review and dispensed with the requirement that patients even be present for a judicial hearing, might well have constituted a kind of "fine print," resuscitating in the jargon of psychology extinct forms of oppression like the infamous *lettres de cachet* of the Stuart period, and so undercutting Constitutional guarantees of due process. Writing pseudonymously in *New Times*, Pound announced: "Jury System in Danger."[15]

Canto 109 takes up this question of trial by jury. "Jury trial was in Athens," Pound notes darkly on its last page (109/794), implying that it is not in Washington, D.C. In 1945, Pound had no jury trial pursuant to his indictment, only on the question of his sanity. Juries show up on the first page of that canto also, where the poet observes that men at the time of Edward Confessor "could not have been / 'excused jury service' / had there been no juries in his, the Confessor's time," i.e. the eleventh century (109/791). An admonition against packing juries Pound found in Coke is mentioned in Canto 108 as well (108/788). On November 29, 1957, Pound wrote Norman Holmes Pearson, citing Coke re: juries: "Coke Institutes, Part 2. Articuli super Chartas that they shall put in those inquests and juries such as be next neighbours, most sufficient, and least suspicious [,] if sherrifs [sic] don't[,] they, the sher / git attachment lying against 'em" (11/29/1957).[16] The same piece, "Coke on Principles," that first mentions Lyon and Block begins "Jury trial / from Athens. By majority" and continues "Nature of jury, Peers. i.e. capable of understanding the issue Vicinage, capable of understanding the circumstances."[17] Clearly, trial by jury was on the poet's mind.

The substance of Pound's complaint is that he is being held without due process or jury trial indefinitely in contravention of *habeas corpus*, the most basic of human rights, guaranteed by the Petition of Right and the Bill of Rights. But *why* is he being held? The Coke Cantos try to answer that question too.

Pound argues that he is being held for trying to prevent World War II. Pound never changed his view that the war was an Anglo-Jewish war against civilization, i.e. Europe (and Japan).[18] The poet, like Edward VIII, had tried to stop it. This is why King Edward, who managed to delay the catastrophe, gaining "three years peace" (106/775), had to be ousted (109/793); why Presidents Fillmore, Pierce, and Buchanan were forgotten; and why Pound had to be shut up. Likewise, Siger of Brabant (a figure we can read as Aesopian for Pound himself), mentioned in Dante's *Paradiso* and cited in Canto 107[19] as one of the lights of Paradise, was traduced and reviled on earth for his lectures arguing "for truths that won him envious hate" during his lifetime (107/776; see *Paradiso* X. l. 136). Coke, too, suffered the royal displeasure because he would not sell out his principles to the interest of King James; like Pound he spent his seventieth birthday imprisoned for treason (Bowen 1957: 454–7).

Early in November 1957, Pound acquired a copy of Catherine Bowen's brand-new *The Lion and the Throne* (1957), her award-winning biography of Coke, probably through Dave Horton. By November 17, Pound was quoting Bowen on "misprision of treason" to Harry Meacham. Coke's *Third Institutes*, which Pound had not yet seen for himself, turned out to be most relevant to his own case:

> p. 219 Catherine Bowen's "The Lion and the Throne" has the following quote.
> "When one knowest of any treason or felony and concealith (sic) it," Coke later wrote, "this is misprision of treason, the offender to be imprisoned for life, to forfeit all his goods, debts and duties forever, and the profit of his lands during his life." Coke adds that "by the common law, concealment of high treason was treason." (11/17/1957, Meacham 1967: 70)

"This re / trial of Walter Raleigh," Pound explained. Coke was among the prosecutors at that trial and later claimed, disingenuously, that he thought Raleigh would somehow be sentenced only for the misprision, not for treason proper, which is what happened. Pound is obviously using the quote as his own defense. He had always considered Roosevelt and the nest of Soviet spies FDR called his administration the real traitors in his case. He told Meacham that General del Valle, war hero and super-patriotic head of the DAC, "is on record that what I did was for the good of the country" (Meacham 1967: 70). Far from betraying the United States, Pound had been blowing the whistle on the real traitors who were bent on involving the USA in a European war against its real interests and the good of civilization generally; had he not done so, he believed, he would have been guilty of misprision of treason by concealing what he knew. A much fuller rendition of this passage would lead off the essay collection *Impact* (1960b: vii–viii), edited by his then-disciple Noel Stock. A typed sheet quoting Coke at length on misprision of treason was sent to Norman Holmes Pearson (and likely others). "RUB in Coke on Misprision / say E.P. had no RIGHT to keep quiet," he told Pearson just before his release (EP to NHP 3/26/1958).[20] Oddly, although Pound did not hesitate to point out the parallels to friends and correspondents, he says nothing quite as explicit in these poems—the self-censorship pointed out by Peter Nicholls seems to have tied his tongue. Clearly, this passage would have been the very citadel of Pound's defense had he ever been brought to trial on treason charges.

When I claim that in Cantos 107 through 109 Pound is making an argument for his defense, I do not mean that he made his case in the form of a legal brief. Rather, the argument is an important strand in a complex and too often incoherent outpouring impelled by his decision to be free, no matter what, and that his paradise is a dream of freedom. Coke and the "Coke Cantos" are "paradisal" because Coke's work points the way to the poet's release. For all of his years in Europe, Pound was proudly, self-consciously American. He was an extreme patriot. In his own mind, all of his political agitation had been to expose the real traitors—the international Jewish conspiracy. His obsession with Thomas Jefferson and John Adams is an expression of patriotism, as was his Quixotic trip to the United States in 1939. So is his life-long critique of America astray, betrayed by finance capital. Naturally, part of his defense against the treason charge was to assert his American roots.

The Connecticut Charter

Commentators seem baffled by the inclusion of "The Connecticut Charter" (1662) in Canto 109. In his recent *Glossator* discussion, Alex Niven assumes that the Charter functions as a link between English and American law: "Pivoting on this legal vignette," Niven writes, "the canto has crossed the Atlantic to discover the continuation of its legal tradition in the foundational roots of the United States" (*G* 363). In an important note pointing toward David Ten Eyck's book on the Adams Cantos, Niven speculates that "the passage may well have been part of an aborted attempt to initiate a new 'American section' of these Cantos that never materialized." Here he follows Ten Eyck's suggestion that the *Charter* "was intended as a bridge to a more extensive return to American themes" (*G* 364; see also Ten Eyck 2012: 147). Pound uses the Connecticut Colonial Charter in much the same way he uses the Magna Carta "as a foundational text on which to build a just society" (Ten Eyck 2012: 145). This interpretation leads Niven to posit that Pound imagines the unlikely Charles II as "a judicious ruler" (*G* 364).

In these cantos, the Connecticut Charter is accompanied by obscure references to the legendary exploit of Pound's ancestor Joseph Wadsworth who in 1662 spirited away the precious document from the Royalist Sir Edward Andros to hide it in the famous "Charter Oak" till the danger was past. Years later, in 1715, Wadsworth was publicly recognized for this daring patriotic act: "'In grateful resentment to Wadsworth, 20 shillings'" (109/793, 111/802).[21] This colorful episode from Pound's "family annals" is described briefly in Pound's autobiographical "Indiscretions" (P&D 6). There, Pound presents the episode as an "embarrassment to legitimist tyranny" (P&D 6) that is ultimately properly understood and rewarded—a situation like his own in the 1950s.[22] The inference must be that the Charter serves an autobiographical, even polemical, function in Canto 109. Relevant as this must be to the biographer, even Moody fails to mention Wadsworth and the Charter or even to try to discuss Canto 109 in his otherwise exhaustive biography. That's odd, because the whole point, for Pound, of inserting the Charter into the final canto—and thus into *The Cantos* as a whole—is to assert his bona fides as a descendant of the oldest colonial New England stock, to show he is as American as the Adamses themselves.

If Pound were only interested in asserting the strong links between English common law and its American offshoot, he should have returned to John Adams. Indeed, as Ten Eyck well knows, Pound toyed with this idea in the pages of notes he took on Catherine Drinker Bowen's *John Adams and the American Revolution* (1950) that Ten Eyck prints as Appendix E of his book (Ten Eyck 2012: 185–93), although Ten Eyck does not quite indicate Pound's source text (Ten Eyck 2012: 210n). Pound even wrote Bowen a fan letter about her *John Adams*, accompanied by a copy of *Rock-Drill* and the Connecticut Charter, as though presenting his bona fides as a poet and an American: "As far as I am able to learn you[r] Adams is worth all the, i.e. more than all the American history being revealed at present in the beaneries," he wrote Bowen.[23] Bowen's biography of Adams even ends with a gesture toward "Coke on Littleton" that Pound had used in the Adams Cantos. On April 5, 1958, Bowen returned the compliment re: *Rock-Drill*: "I am reading it and rereading, with excitement and pleasure … what a super p. 75."[24] Any reader as familiar with John Adams as Pound could supply a dozen better bridges than the obscure Connecticut Charter written by Connecticut Governor John Winthrop and the British executive. Almost any of Adams's major texts—*Thoughts on Government* (1776) or *The Constitution of Massachusetts* (1780), to name two—could show the continuity between the English and American legal traditions better than the Connecticut Charter does.[25]

No, the Connecticut Charter is included into Canto 109 because of its autobiographical force, not its historical importance. On November 23, Pound wrote Pearson: "NHP / I cd / cert USE ten or more copies of the Conn. charter. And should be grateful for Bates." Albert Carlos Bates's *Charter of Connecticut: A Study* (1932)[26] was sent along promptly. Pound's reply shows its real significance was in family lore:

Charter Oak / recollections / for N. H. P. / re A.C. bates Vol. on Con. Charter (1932)

> Childhood memory of engraving stile ottocento / Capn. Wadsworth entering room to steal charter.Embellished story that he swept out the candles on table with swish of his cloak.
> Recollection that this illustrated school book o[f]. say 8th grade, but it may only have been in Wadsworth family, 250 th anniversary celebration, where I believe it can now be found
> around 1893, [I] was taken to look at a large stump (presumably oack [sic]) with a young tree growing out of it. this was said to be THE oak.
> Nothing in Bates wd / rule out a new shoot having risen from the stum[p] at that time.
> yu [sic] can draw yr / own conclusion re / effect of family tradition, emphasis, pen yeh. etc. (EP to NHP 12/15/1957)[27]

The hidden agenda of the Charter is to show that Pound himself is such a shoot risen from the old Wadsworth stump.[28] This covert autobiographical sprig is part of a pattern in these Washington Cantos. Recall that in Canto 88 John Randolph is introduced in such a way as to highlight his connection to St. George Tucker, Dorothy's maternal great-grandfather (88/599). The moment is a shout-out to Dorothy but also a subtle reminder that Pound really believed that, as he said in *Indiscretions*, he could "write the whole history of the United States" from his family annals (*P&D* 6).

Pound and Catherine Drinker Bowen

The profound effect of Catherine Drinker Bowen's biography of Coke on Pound is well known, but the influence of her John Adams biography hasn't garnered much attention because the extensive notes he took on that book did not result in any cantos. As mentioned, January 1958 found Pound reading Bowen's *John Adams and the American Revolution* with growing excitement. In fact, his poetry notebook of the period shows that he was drafting a new section of John Adams Cantos based on Bowen's book.[29] In the midst of his enthusiasm, on February 3 he could contain himself no longer: "Dear Mrs. Bowen," he typed, "I have held off writing you up to page 291 of your J. Adams. … The coincidence in citations between my verse on J. A. published in '39 and yours in '49 indicate a certain agreement in our criteria of values."[30]

Bowen's focus was on the younger John Adams—her tale ends with the Declaration of Independence in 1776 and Adams aged forty, while Pound's ten "Adams Cantos" ranged far beyond. But Bowen begins her book with one of

Pound's favorite bits of Adams: "The revolution was in the minds and hearts of the people … in the course of fifteen years before a drop of blood was shed at Lexington" (Bowen 1950: xiv). Pound, whose Adams Cantos had made little impression on the wider world, had been using the passage for years. He paraphrased it in Canto 32 and more fully in Canto 33 (33/161) published as early as 1931. He repeated it in Canto 50, composed in the summer of 1936, well before he decided to devote a decad to Adams, in *Cantos LII–LXXI* (1940), his last-ditch effort to prevent the United States from entering the war in Europe.

But what was it about page 291 in Bowen's biography that prompted Pound to turn to his typewriter? On that page, John Adams is deep in the crisis brought on by the Stamp Act of 1765—the crowning insult of several British measures, including the Revenue Act of 1764, which interfered with the profitable Triangle trade, and a Currency Act that forbade the printing of paper money in the colonies—a measure particularly resented by Pound; he devotes a long page to it in his *Economic Nature of the United States* (1944; *SP* 137–8). Finally, the Proclamation of 1763 (part of the settlement of the long war between England and France called in the United States "the French and Indian War" of 1754–61) forbade Americans to migrate across the Allegheny range. The Stamp Act was, Adams wrote in his diary, "[t]he enormous engine fabricated by the British Parliament for battering down all the rights and liberties of America" (qtd in McCullough 2001: 62). The Stamp Act required that government-issued stamps be bought and affixed to "every commercial and legal document—newspapers, ships' clearance papers, wills, deeds, college diplomas, marriage licenses" (see Bowen 1950: 252), and all to pay for the expenses incurred by subsidizing an occupying force of 20,000 British troops forced on the restive colonies. Nothing could have been better calculated to unite the American colonies in resistance. John Adams was at the forefront. The event provoked his first extended work of political and legal theory, "Dissertation on the Canon and Feudal Law (1765)," prompting the deathless cry "No taxation without representation." When the Stamp Act went into effect November 1, 1765, it sparked a boycott of public business, including closing the courts, since lawyers refused to purchase the stamps. It did more than that, indicating plainly a crisis of authority within the British Empire noted by Bowen on her page 291:

> This business of the courts was only one phase, one facet of a great constitutional question: the question of allegiance, sovereignty, the limits of the realm, the basic relation of colonies to mother country … If the King kept the courts closed, it was a removal of the King's protection from the people. Protection and allegiance

were reciprocal. If protection were removed, would not the people remove their allegiance also? Where would such a horrid doctrine terminate? It would lead to treason! And there was no precedent, no guide to look to. (Bowen 1950: 291)

Surely, these lines were taken by Pound as relevant, obliquely, to his own predicament, entering his thirteenth year of confinement, still untried, convicted of nothing, and, in his own mind at least, one whose loyalty to his mother country had been put into question, not by his own actions but by the high-handed machinations of the Roosevelt administration and its usurocratic successors.

Dave Horton, knowing Pound's interest in Coke's *Institutes*, probably brought *The Lion and the Throne* and Bowen to Pound's attention. In that first letter to Bowen Pound wanted her to know that "Mr. Horton within days of seeing you[r] Lion and Throne set to preparing a new edtn / Coke Institutes II (the Magna Carta chapter)" (EP to Bowen 2/3/1958), though in his next letter Pound had to confess to Bowen that "'Dave' has no capital and could only proceed at the rate of two pages per day, no telling when it might be available" (EP to Bowen 3/18/1958). Not soon: the work would eventually appear two years after the poet's death as *Coke on Magna Charta: Selections from Coke's* Second Institutes, offset from the 1797 edition (Coke 1974).

Earlier we saw Pound's transcription of Bowen on misprision of treason in his letter to Meacham. He had obviously seized on this concept as the justification for his behavior during the war. It appears that Pound also mentioned misprision to Bowen directly, although no letter is in the Beinecke file to show it. Bowen treated the subject with tact when she wrote to Pound on April 5, 1958, just days before his unexpected release:

About Coke and misprision of treason. I wonder if he really said he expected Ralegh [Raleigh's own spelling] to be convicted only of Misprision. I can't believe it. I did not enjoy writing about those treason trials, Essex, Ralegh, Gunpowder, though Essex I did not mind so much because I did not like him. But with Ralegh and G-pow[d]ers I was wading in blood and treachery, and my boy Coke did not play a pretty part, did he. (Bowen to EP 4/5/1958)

When it came to the Coke Cantos, Pound was not interested in openly pursuing the dark, more questionable side of Coke's prosecutorial career so he does not mention his role as prosecutor and attorney general for the Crown. For her part, Bowen does not bring up measures Coke recorded against the Jews, but Pound did, citing Coke *Second Institutes* on this matter on "15 000 three score," referring to numbers of Jews banished by Edward I (108/785), and he uses

Coke citing Bracton to obliquely endorse the prohibition of selling land to Jews (107/779), as commentators Bacigalupo, Casillo, and P. D. Scott have noted.[31]

In what I take to be an unsent letter to Bowen, Pound closed with remarks showing how he applied Coke to current events. He claimed: "We are under something worse than King Charles, and the forced loans are not even for the benefit of the governmental authority but [a set] of irresponsible enemies."[32] The reference to King Charles and the forced loans is to the Five Knights jailed in 1627 for refusing to pay unsanctioned levies ordered by the King in an attempt to bypass Parliament; it is an Aesopian allusion most probably to US assistance to the United Nations and its affiliates. Bowen in particular recounts vividly Charles's strenuous and illegal attempt to raise funds via "forced loans" throughout the country without any authorization by Parliament to support an equivocal policy in Europe (see Bowen 1957: 476–86). To Pound, Charles's tyrannical levies were analogous to current US policy, which obliged the United States to fund the United Nations with taxpayer dollars. Sited in New York (the capital of international usury), the UN was best positioned to subvert the United States, while we paid for it—an article of faith of the American Right to this day.

Pound uses Coke to support his typically American right-wing views, including the eugenic threat posed by racial integration authorized by the Warren Court that I quoted at the beginning of this book:

> [It r]emains to be seen whether we have the stuff in us that our English [f]orebear had in the days of Coke and Selden, or whether we have [b]een miscegenated, bastardized, mixed and brain washed until we can [n]o longer resist executive, quasi-[r]oyal encroachments or the [c]orruption of jus [sic] judges working to uproot all our heritage.[33]

The mention of judges points unmistakably to the Supreme Court, which to Pound authorized much of what was wrong with the United States.[34]

"Eisenhower Warren, Warren Eisenhower," Pound muttered to himself in another unsent undated letter or meditation regarding Bowen's book: "Every appointee of Roosevelt, ever[y] man smuggled onto the Supreme Bench" to "declare anything he, (Roosevelt) does constitutional," he wrote, remembering Senator Wheeler in 1939. He added, "Milton Ike and the palace guard Loathe the word Coke the instant they have any inkling of its meaning" and "you have confreres"—perhaps those on the court?—"who babble of international responsibilities as if they could be anything but rot and corruption if they fail to guard inherited and legal right inside our own country."[35] Milton Eisenhower, the brother of the president, was himself president of The Johns Hopkins

University at the time. Perhaps he would be responsible, in Pound's mind, for a curriculum where Coke was not valued, or repressed. It is all part of the general drift into autocracy, abetted by the betrayal of the courts, which had "resolved" the great constitutional question of the relationship of the states to the federal government in a series of disastrous decisions subverting the US Constitution and decades of precedent.

Pound's radical Right politics are likely what shut down his epistolary relationship with Bowen. As was his wont, Pound began to impose on Bowen with his usual hobby-horses. On August 13, 1958, Pound wrote Bowen from Brunnenburg: "there is need of new and vigorous work on the Constitutional Convention" (EP to CDB 8/13/1958).[36] "I have never seen anything dealing WITH THE ABSOLUTE SURRENDER OF ALL REAL POWER BY THE INDIVIDUAL STATES. They confirm it in section 8, clause 5 or Art 1. and surrender ignominiously in the fine print. section 10 ... " That is, the real power of the individual states is surrendered to Congress and the federal government by granting it the power to "[c]oin money and regulate the value thereof" (US Const. Section 8, clause 5), a surrender confirmed in Section 10 where it is written, "No State shall coin money; make any Thing but gold and silver Coin a Tender in payment of Debts" (US Const. Section 10, Para. 1). Pound was incensed by these clauses because they stood in the way of establishing "local control of local purchasing power" through innovations like Gesellite scrip, as Pound recommended in *Virginians On Guard!* (1956). Pound had marked his moment of appalled (and *belated*) discovery in Canto 100: "Oh GAWD!!! that tenth section ... / 'any portion of ... ' DAMN IT" (100/735). This surrender was compounded by the creation of the Federal Reserve Bank in 1913, which took the power to create money and to regulate its value out of control of Congress and put it into the hands of a consortium of private banks and bankers where it remains today.

On December 8, 1958, in her last letter to the poet, we find Bowen defending the Warren Court to Pound: "US reaction always 'Kill the Umpire!' ... We can't have federalism without an umpire. Me, I think the Supreme Court has done and is doing a superb job." Pound's reply to this letter marks the end of their correspondence:

You can't dodge the whole problem of REAL sovereignty, or the Court's
betrayal of all of us, by not resisting the betrayal of Dec. 23, 1913 [i.e. creation
of Fed. Reserve.]
       Disraeli's double OX [double cross] of parliament etc. Can I
persuade you to read some history, such as Del Mar or Benton

> Randolph has been done. Raliegh was on to something :
> Genova having "nothing left but her usury".
> C[harles] F[rancis]. Adams may have covered up something {r.e. J.A.} It was Jackson the bank tried to kill. (EP to CDB, 12/17/1958)

Disraeli's double cross of Parliament in arranging to borrow Rothschild money to purchase Suez Canal Company shares without Parliamentary approval is a recurrent theme in *Thrones*. In Pound's reading, this bloodless geopolitical coup, generally hailed as a masterstroke not unlike Jefferson's Louisiana Purchase, put the United Kingdom into the hands of Jewish usurers (104/762). By bypassing Parliament (which was not in session when the opportunity presented itself), Disraeli behaved much the way King Charles had with his extraparliamentary levies. The incident explains somewhat Pound's admonition against backroom dealing in the obscure "HORSFAIRE" section at the end of Canto 108 (108/789–90). Ambassador Charles Francis Adams was the editor of his grandfather's papers "and one of the invisible heroes of *The Cantos*" (Ten Eyck 2012: 56); his motive for covering something up must refer not to John Adams but to John's son (and Charles's father), John Quincy Adams, who lost his 1828 reelection as president to Pound's hero, Andrew Jackson. Pound spent time on John Quincy Adams in Canto 36 and tried there to belittle him and to portray him as an eccentric figure, friend of the Bank of the United States and inimical to the glorious epoch of Jackson and Van Buren that Pound so admired. The inference Pound wanted Bowen to draw seems to be that John Quincy Adams was pulling strings behind the scenes during "the Bank War."[37]

Although the reasons Pound may have decided not to pursue a reprise of John Adams to end his cantos can't be known for sure, if he had followed Bowen's narrative arc he would have ended with poetry celebrating American Independence. The last notes taken from Bowen's *John Adams* in Pound's Notebook come from Bowen's final pages, 604 and 605:

> endowed by their Creator
> with sart'n
> Otis this writ against

These notes record Bowen's rendition of Abigail Adams hearing her old acquaintance Tom Crafts read the Declaration of Independence from the Massachusetts State House balcony in Boston on July 19, 1795. The dialect touch is Bowen's (1950: 604), not Abigail Adams's, who described the scene plainly to John in a letter dated July 21, 1776. Mrs. Adams records only that "When

Col. Crafts read from the Belcona [balcony] of the State house the proclamation, great attention was given to every word" (Adams & Adams 1976: 148). Pound delighted in dialect and pounced joyfully on Bowen's elaboration with thoughts of using it in his poem. In her version, Bowen next situates John Adams in Philadelphia City Tavern in a reverie, recalling his old mentor James Otis, now old and mad, speaking out in court against the notorious "Writs of Assistance" back in 1760. These were general search warrants that might result in the seizure of goods (often, to be sure, contraband) that colonial merchants felt were their own. "*This writ is against the fundamental principles of English law! An act against the constitution is void!*" Otis claimed. And then Bowen turns Adams's mind to Coke, as she must have turned Pound's: "How far, John wondered now," how far had he gone with Coke on Littleton, that expert on real property, "—how far with Sir Edward Coke? How far with the law, with right and wrong, with sinning and learning" (Bowen 1950: 605)? In Canto 63 Pound had already cited "Coke upon Littleton"—Coke's extended commentary on Thomas de Littleton's treatise *Tenures* that are part of his *Institutes* (63/352; see Terrell 1980: 276). Pound recounts Adams remembering his mentor's, Jeremiah Gridley's, advice that "you must conquer the INSTITUTES" in Canto 63 (63/352). Ten Eyck concurs with Peter Makin in finding Coke a major theme in the Adams Cantos (Ten Eyck 2012: 82), because Coke is a major influence on Adams's life and career.

Coke and his *Institutes* close *Thrones* for more personal reasons. The right reading of the Magna Carta and the tradition of English jurisprudence lights Pound's road out of the bughouse to freedom from incarceration. For all of their "kidells and skarkells" and archaic, "auncient" language, the "Coke Cantos" are not driven by antiquarianism but by Pound's situation. This realization sheds light on two other problems in these cantos.

Four Acres

In their *Glossator* essays, both Kristin Grogan and Alex Niven pause over the Coke's "Stat. de 31 Eliz" that ends Canto 108 and continues into Canto 109. This is the "Statute of 31 Elizabeth Cap. 7 concerning Cottages and Inmates"—a title that must have struck inmate Pound of St. Elizabeths. Niven quotes it fully, noting that "Pound picks freely from pages 736 to 745 of the second *Institutes* as he underlines his central argument: that the new buildings carefully specified in the statute 'have been provided with appropriate breathing space' (the crucial 'four acres of ground' already alluded to in Canto 108) because of the just legal precedents set down to guide their construction." Niven notes that "curtilagia teneant means literally 'cottage dwellers'"—quoted from Coke's page 736—and that "enough land about each of them" (109/791) is Pound's paraphrase of "for every cottage four acres" spelled out in Canto 108 (108/790; see G 356).[38] Niven suggests that Pound is thinking of city planning and finds a timely interest in "Coke's blue-print for a well-ordered, well-planned city" (G 358).

It is true that Pound had thought long and hard about the well-ordered *polis* and the ideal "four-gated" city: "the whole creation concerned with 'FOUR,'" he insists at the close of Canto 91 (91/636). And by 1957 he had heard something of Frank Lloyd Wright and utopian Taliesen West in Arizona through his friends Ralph and Lorraine Reid.[39] But a development of cottages on four-acre lots is not a city but a very spacious suburb. Probably, the four-acre plan speaks to a dream of freedom for the poet, who felt keenly the close quarters of his confinement. In a 1957 piece, "ADLAI and ALASKA," on the Alaska Mental Health Bill—written for, but never published in, the DAC's newsletter, *Task Force*—Pound shared his thoughts on improving mental hospitals. Pound never complained about conditions at St. Elizabeths, but his suggestions indicate the unpleasant, claustrophobic realities of hospital life:

> There are, we take it, few "mental hospitals" that would not be vastly improved by the dismissal of psychiatrists, and turning over the therapy to the medical staff, a saving to the tax payers but probably slow of attainment in that it would conflict with the vested interest. In the mean time one might apply at least the humanity reserved for animals in the modern zoo. That is the lions and tigers can get out onto the terraces, the elks have a paddock. Asylums could be built with southern exposure, the vilest cases could have access to individual porches, those with milder bewilderments to general porches and those needing exercise to areas surrounded by a high wire fence when not fit to be at large on the whole grounds, allowing all, in suitable degree, to get from stuffy interiors into god's open atmosphere, whether in their own state or in the drear wastes of Alaska.[40]

His visitors were betimes appalled at the veritable bedlam inside Pound's locked ward, which the poet seemed to withstand with truly Confucian patience (see Marsh 2011: 204–205).[41] The dream of four blessed acres that haunts Cantos 108 and 109 should be read against the poet's days and nights of confinement among the incontinent and insane. This suburban ideal (somewhat reminiscent of his boyhood Wyncote) is what freedom from the hospital looked like to Pound.

If we read Cantos 107 through 109 as Pound's brief for his defense, it must be confessed that such a reading leaves much in these cantos out of the picture. Yes, there is a great deal of English legal history here, if fitfully presented, and yes, the paradisal imperative, the "persistent awareness" of a divine, metapolitical order aligning *polis* and *kosmos* that the poet felt so strongly regardless of his personal situation, is clear in the many quotations from Dante's *Paradiso* X and wistful lyrical trills: "Clear deep off Taormina / high cliff and azure beneath it" (109/794). But looked at from ground level, as it were, they just as clearly express Pound's desperate desire to *get out* into the open air and daylight.

Notes

1   Kindellan argues that Canto 100 had been in the works since at least 1942 (Kindellan 2017: 182) once one factors in the earliest fragments and latest addenda. The version we have seems to have been ready by mid-August, 1958 (Kindellan 2017: 204). Canto 100 was published in the *Yale Review* of December 1958 (Gallup 1983: 349).

2   David Ten Eyck has made available these notes in "Appendix E" to his important book on Pound and Adams. Despite the title "Unpublished notes on John Adams and the American Revolution in the *Thrones* Poetry Notebook," Ten Eyck doesn't seem to realize that these notes derive *directly* from Bowen's book (see Ten Eyck 2012: 185–93, 210n).

3   Lyon and Block's contribution to the Coke Cantos is not well known, but many of the lines of 107/781—about the Dutch weavers in Norwich (Lyon & Block 1929: 18), the whores hanging about Westminster (1929: 31), the use of grain for food only (1929: 187), and the question of burning heretics (1929: 188)—come from their *Oracle of the Law*. Their book quotes extensive passages from contemporary documents, much more so than Bowen, who is a master of indirect discourse.

4   Pound was clearly researching the law both for his own case and for his poem. The same piece, "Coke on Principles," that first mentions Lyon and Block begins with lines about juries. Further down the page Pound mentions "[Henry Sumner] Maine," likely a reference to Maine's legal classic *Ancient Law: Its connection with the early history of society, and its relation to modern ideas* (1861). Pound reckoned he could summarize what he needed from Maine "in ½ page." In the end, he doesn't seem to have used Maine at all (Beinecke YCAL MSS 43, Box 83, folder 3642).

5   Beinecke YCAL MSS 43, Box 83, folder 3642.

6   In an addendum to the untitled note vilifying the Warren Court that I have quoted previously, Pound writes: "vid. Lyon and Block: Edward Coke Houghton Mifflin 1929 p. 316+"; these are pages devoted to the discussions leading to *habeas corpus* and the Petition of Right.

7   Notebook 111, August–November 1957, in Beinecke YCAL MSS 43, Box 122, folder 4979.

8   Domvile recounts his experience of denial of due process and his service "on board His Majesty's the stone frigate" Brixton Hill Prison 1940–3 in *From Admiral to Cabin Boy* (1947). Domvile writes that he expects his book to be suppressed; Pound confirms this impression by quoting his correspondent Ingrid Davies in Canto 102: "'The libraries' (Ingrid) 'have no Domvile.' Jan 1955 / as was natural" (102/749).
9   Pound wrote to Pearson on September 23, 1957, that "Merchant" was "doing apparently INTELLIGENT job of {Law} in Shx / reading Coke, a week after I eggzorted G[iovanni].G[iovannini]. to being [sic] me C[oke]. on Littleton." "Coke on Littleton" is the first part of Coke's *Institutes* (Beinecke YCAL MSS 899, Box 79, folder "Pound, Ezra 1957").
10 Beinecke YCAL MSS 43, Box 122, folder 4980.
11 The elms reoccur amidst totems of Sheri Martinelli in Canto 116: "Twice beauty under the elms— / To be saved by squirrels and bluejays" (116/816).
12 No treatment of Canto 107 can fail to mention David Gordon's "Edward Coke: The azalea is grown" *Paideuma* 4(2 & 3) (Fall–Winter 1975): 223–99. Through what I would call "creative philology," Gordon is able to integrate all of the farflung references, including to Sicily, in this rebarbative canto. For all of that, Gordon's extraordinary work appears to supplement, rather than explicate, the poem. It's not quite credible to this reader.
13 A traditional trope—consider the Gardener's speech in Shakespeare's *Richard II*, Act III, scene iv. l. 1892f: "Go bind up yon dangling aprickoks" etc.
14 Even so, the gardens of Hatfield were achieved by enclosing "the common pasture" (107/782), which does make one think of the common law, so there may be a counter-current to any easy allegorical symbolism.
15 "17 Jury System in Danger," *New Times*, April 20, 1956, p. 6. (AH)
16 Norman Holmes Pearson Papers, Beinecke YCAL MSS 899, Box 78, folder "Pound, Ezra to NHP 1957."
17 Beinecke YCAL MSS 43, Box 83, folder 3642.
18 At the outbreak of the war, Pound wrote to both German and US correspondents, including Representative Jerry Voorhis (Republican, California) to this effect (see Marsh 2011: 152–3).
19 Siger, not "Sigier," as Pound has it (107/776).
20 Norman Holmes Pearson papers, Beinecke YCAL MSS 899, Box 78, folder "Ezra Pound, 1958."
21 Fittingly, the Charter Oak appeared on a commemorative US quarter dollar in 1999.
22 In that same passage Pound refers to the revolutionary hero Israel Putnam, also of Connecticut, who prudently drove 130 sheep up to Boston in June of 1775 to relieve the British siege there. Pound noted the incident again in his jottings from Bowen's *John Adams* (see Ten Eyck 2012: 187; Bowen 1950: 443).

23 Although Pound turned away from the John Adams material he was finding in Bowen, he continued to be interested in her work. In Notebook 114 he wrote: "there are serious characters / Rock-Goullart-Catherine Bowen / here are Thrones" (Notebook 114, p. 8).

24 Canto 91/635.

25 That said, the "Connecticut Charter" of 1662 does "incorporate" (a key term in Pound's political vision) the Connecticut Colony and establish a "Body politique" (109/793) with representative local government.

26 Cited by Ten Eyck (2012: 146).

27 Beinecke YCAL MSS 899, Box 78, folder 3433.

28 Otherwise, Pound is careful to hide the Wadsworth connection, which links him directly to his maternal ancestor, the poet and Dante translator Henry Wadsworth Longfellow, arguably the best-known (and best-loved) nineteenth-century American poet. Perhaps Longfellow's fame is precisely the reason Pound avoids mentioning him directly as family in *Indiscretions* (*P&D* 6). Likewise, Pound excises Longfellow's attendance at Hawthorne's funeral in Canto 103 (103/752), though he is present in Pound's source text, Roy Nichols's *Franklin Pierce* (1931: 525).

29 Notebook 113 (#59), December 28, 1957, Marzo '58, pp. 39–56, Box 122, folder 4981.

30 Beinecke YCAL MSS 43, Box 5, folder 231.

31 Casillo's long note pp. 360–1 is instructive (though confused by typos). See Scott (1990: 52). Incidentally, Pound's imitation Elizabethan ballad on "Gondomar" and King James suggests that Pound thought the Spanish ambassador, Count Gondomar, was Jewish. Terrell thinks Elizabeth's unlucky and traduced physician Roderigo Gomez, supposedly a marrano, is meant; but Pound may have taken the hint about the ambassador from Bowen, who comments on Gondomar's "Sephardic" dark looks (Bowen 1957: 348).

32 Beinecke YCAL MSS 43, Box 5, folder 231.

33 "Coke on Principles," Beinecke YCAL MSS 43, Box 83, folder 3642.

34 Pound's letters to Norman Holmes Pearson are full of grumblings and mutterings in this vein: "while bastardization, mongrelism rages elsewhere, no sense of race / no sense of eugenics" etc. (EP to NHP 8/23/1957, YCAL MSS 899, Box 78, folder "Pound, Ezra to NHP 1957").

35 Beinecke YCAL MSS 43, Box 5, folder 231.

36 Bowen would later write that "vigorous work on the Constitutional Convention" in *Miracle in Philadelphia: The Story of the Constitutional Convention* (1966). Though Bowen does not mention Pound in her preface, it is fair to wonder if he may have helped provoke that excellent book.

37 See Marsh (2005).

38 Niven notes that "curtilagia teneant" is quoted from Coke, page 736. Coke's subject is cottagers and their cottages and curtilage, which is the attached piece of land, "foure acres of ground at the least" (Coke 737), spelled out in Canto 108 (108/ 790, Niven *G* 356) as "for every cottage four acres," Pound paraphrases this in Canto 109 as "enough land about each of them" (109/ 791) (AH).

39 Ezra Pound papers, Beinecke YCAL MSS 43, Box 44, folder 1874. Ralph and Lorraine Reid met Frank Lloyd Wright on July 1, 1957. Lorraine Reid told Wright about Pound's situation and sent the architect *Women of Trachis* and D. D. Paige's *Selected Letters of Ezra Pound*.

40 Beinecke YCAL MSS 43, Box 66, folder 2850.

41 "Bedlam"—a contraction of "Bethlehem"—simply means "madhouse" and is derived from St. Mary of Bethlehem in London, which, like St. Elizabeths centuries later, presented a scene of indescribable confusion and uproar.

12

Pound at Colonus

The Poet as Oedipus

"The visit to Ezra was awesome," Robert Lowell wrote to James Laughlin on August 31, 1966, having seen Pound in Venice; awesome "and rather shattering, like meeting Oedipus—he said, I began with a swelled head and am ending with swelled feet." Lowell reports that Pound said "many other things, then stretches of long silence ... [H]e has a nobility that I've never seen before, the nobility of someone, not a sinner, but who has gone astray and learned at last too much." When Lowell tried to flatter the old man as one who had entered Purgatory, the elder poet would have none of it; Lowell felt "he'd been talking cant when I tried to cheer him." Pound had "no self-pity, but more knowledge of his fate than any man should have" (Lowell 2005: 473).

Later Lowell would distill his memories of Pound into a short poem that would appear in *Notebook 1967–68* and, slightly revised, in *History* (1973):

Ezra Pound

Horizontal on a deckchair in the ward
of the criminal mad ... A man without shoestrings clawing
the Social Credit broadside from your table, you saying,
"... here with a black suit and black briefcase; in the brief
an abomination, Possum's *hommage* to Milton."
Then sprung; Rapallo, and the decade gone;
and three years later, Eliot dead, you saying,
"Who's left alive to understand my jokes?
My old brother of the arts ... besides he was a smash of a poet."
You showed me your blotched, bent hands, saying, "Worms.
When I talked that nonsense about Jews on the Rome
wireless, Olga knew it was shit, and still loved me."
And I, "Who else has been in Purgatory?"

You, "I began with a swelled head and end with swelled feet." (Lowell 1975: 140)

As his letter to Laughlin shows, Lowell was one survivor who could understand Pound's jokes; the Kenyon PBK classics major knew that Oedipus means "swollen foot" and that, however slyly, Pound acknowledged his tragic role, brought upon him by his overweening ambition to save Europe and write the modern epic.

Lowell himself was no mere tourist of purgatory. Imprisoned as a "fiery catholic C.O." during World War II in protest of the firebombing of German cities, he had some experience as a political prisoner, having served a year and a day at Danbury Federal Prison in Connecticut—a fact he mentioned in a note to Pound before the first of many visits to the older poet at St. Elizabeths (Lowell 2005: 70–1). As well, locked as he was into chronic bipolar suffering, Lowell had extensive experience with a variety of mental institutions. And like Pound he had translated Greek tragedy, although he worked with Aeschylus, not Sophocles.[1] Perhaps that's why, when he puts on the Dantescan persona in his poem, he puts it on with a twist, making the Italian poet's first-person/third-person exchanges into an intimate second-person address. Equal to equal.

When Donald Hall met Pound in Rome in 1960 to conduct his famous interview for the *Paris Review* he was greeted by a shattered poet. In his memoir Hall also likens Pound to Oedipus. Where he had "feared what would answer my knock" would be "madness, rebuff, cruelty, arrogance," he found a lonesome old man who "as he spoke … separated his words into little bunches, like bursts of typing from an inexperienced typist: 'You have driven—all the way—from England—to find a man—who is only fragments'" (Hall 1992: 181). Writing of Pound's 1963 interview with Grazia Livi, printed in *Epoca*,[2] it seemed to Hall that Pound "spoke with the tragic energy of a defeated king, like Oedipus the victim of his own errors—fallen, lamenting his smallness in the center of a stage that he dominates" (Hall 1992: 249). Hall cites Canto 115, where Pound wrote of Wyndham Lewis that "he chose blindness / rather than have his mind stop"—so did Oedipus. But after such knowledge, what forgiveness? Pound found himself in the poet's version of Oedipus's blindness, captured by silence. He worried to Livi that "words have become empty of all meaning" (Hall 1992: 248). Unable to believe in coherence—unless in the form of a tragic destiny, as fate—Pound found "neither life nor death the answer" (115/814).

This image of Pound as a contemporary Oedipus helps us get the most out of the haunted photographs Richard Avedon took of the poet with William Carlos Williams shortly after Pound's release from St. Elizabeths and immediately before his embarkation for exile in Italy. By all accounts, the visit was awkward for both old friends. In this well-known sequence we sometimes see Pound hovering behind Williams, and in one close-up we see the grizzled poet with shirt open and eyes squeezed shut, as though blind, like Oedipus, especially as in *Oedipus at Colonus*. There Oedipus appeared to his doomed son Polyneices as "that man lost among strangers … his eyeballs blind, his clothing in squalid rags, his hair tossed by the wind" (Yeats 1952: 353). This translation, by Yeats, is one Pound owned.

Yeats rightly thought a good deal of his version, though Pound's copy of the play is unmarked and may never have been read. However, Pound undoubtedly read the letter "To Ezra Pound" that accompanies the "packet" which serves as introduction to his revised *A Vision* (1937),[3] a book that "announced a new divinity" (Yeats 1966: 27). There, Yeats refers to the charged moment of Oedipus's return to earth's womb, quoting from his own translation. For Yeats, Oedipus's death signifies the end of the Homeric age; he sees him "totally separate from Plato's Athens, from all that talk of the Good and the One, that cabinet of perfections" (Yeats 1966: 28). Oedipus ends as a chthonic figure, whose death is a *hieros gamos*, a return to the mothers, the Furies. When he goes to join them at the end of the play, when he dies and is apparently swallowed by the earth, Oedipus climbs the hill of Demeter, Persephone's mother. There, in Robert Fagles's version, "the lightless depths of earth [burst] open in kindness to receive him" (Fagles 1984: 381) as Oedipus descends to the sources of poetic power. But Yeats quotes his own translation in "A Packet for Ezra Pound," speaking frankly of the "foundations of the earth … riven to receive him, riven not by pain but by love" (Yeats 1952: 360). These highly sexual (and Eleusinian) images of a *hieros gamos* between Oedipus and his mother earth recall the "connubium terrae" of Canto 82. It is hard to think of Oedipus's death at Colonus and not think of Pound's Canto 83, where the infant wasp

>   goes amid grass-blades
>   greeting them that dwell under XTHONOS XΘONOΣ
> OI XΘONIOI;   to carry our news
>   εἰ χθονίους   to them that dwell under the earth,
> begotten of air, that shall sing in the bower
>   of Kore,   Περσεφόνεια
> and have speech with Tiresias, Thebae (83/553)

Yet these lines refer back to Canto 1 and Odysseus's speech with Tiresias; it is not a reference to Sophocles.[4] It seems doubtful that Pound had the fate of Oedipus uppermost in mind when he wrote them. Still, the *meaning* of this journey under the earth is the poetic meaning of Oedipus's death in the sacred grove of the Eumenides; it is a return to the sources. I speculate that this famous moment in *The Pisan Cantos* colors Lowell's and Hall's reading of Pound as Oedipus.

Their reading of Pound as Oedipus is put into doubt by the lack of any other reference by Pound to Oedipus (there is an offhand reference in Canto 74 [74/459]) and by Pound's own reading of himself as an Orestian figure. He can be glimpsed as Orestes in *The Pisan Cantos*, in *Rock-Drill*, and more clearly as Elektra in his strange and inspired translation of Sophocles' play.⁵ But it is the nature of tragedy that the hero does not choose it—tragedy seeks him out—so at Pisa Pound may have wished to play Orestes and yearned, as he does implicitly in Canto 82, for the merciful judgment by Athena, whose vote breaks the jury's deadlock over Orestes' fate in Aeschylus' *The Eumenides*. The pardon of Orestes by Athena is also alluded to in Cantos 87 and 89 where "Ἀθήνη swung the hung jury" (87/591, 89/621).

This matters because the acquittal of Orestes requires the transformation of the Furies into the Eumenides, or "the kindly ones." As it happens, they abide under the sacred grove at Colonus where Oedipus goes to die and where Sophocles himself was born. The Furies' unique conjoining of fury and forgiveness, of sacred rage and divine justice, makes them a potent myth of poetic power and inspiration. Robert Lowell's translation obliquely Freudianizes the Furies as "the mind of the past," as *repressed*, tamed, and driven underground to become a source of lyric fertility (Lowell 1978: 122, 123). In his version of *The Eumenides*, called *The Furies*, Athena charges them to forgo hate and to "sing of the land, the Aegean, / mild breezes airing / a landscape shot with sunlight / human seeds, all things that grow" (Lowell 1978: 124).

Oedipus becomes tragic through his resistance to, and forced acceptance of, the dimension of vision—represented first by Tiresias and later by himself. In seeing what Tiresias sees—"the Truth"—Oedipus blinds himself in remorse for his crimes. The tacit link to Pound's silence is clear. If Oedipus blinds himself because of what he has done, so Pound chose silence for what he had said. So, at any rate, goes the conventional narrative, but it is just as likely that Pound did not choose silence at all—that, as he said, it captured him.

If Pound did think of himself as a kind of Oedipus, does it mean that he knew too much about his own fate; or that he saw himself as the victim of his own errors? At the end of Yeats's *Sophocles' King Oedipus* (1928), Oedipus discloses himself to the people as who he really is: not a king but, as Yeats stresses in his translation (suiting his own mythology), a blind beggar. Yet the man who knows too much is full of questions: "Where am I?" he asks. "Where am I going? Where am I cast away? Who hears my words?" (Yeats 1952: 325). That's Yeats's version; Robert Fagles has Oedipus say, "where's my voice"? (Fagles 1984: 239)—a translator's choice closer to my interest in Pound's silence. These questions can be answered in part by going to the sequel, *Oedipus at Colonus*.

After blinding himself, Oedipus sets out in penitential wandering, a kind of *dromena*, led by Antigone, his eldest daughter, which ends some years later in the grove dedicated to the Furies in a suburb of Athens. Colonus is a place of dense poetic fullness, where, in Fagles's deliberately allusive language, "the nightingale sings on, / her dying music rising clear, / hovering always, never leaving, / deepest green" (Fagles 1984: 326). (Fagles can't resist mainlining English literature into the veins of Sophocles.) However problematic his word-echoes are, they serve my purpose because they underline that, by the time he has arrived at Colonus, the disgraced King of Thebes has become, in effect, Tiresias: outcast, seer, *and* poet. In the twentieth century, thanks to Pound's reworking Eliot's *Waste Land* to make Tiresias the device that holds the poem together, Tiresias speaks not as a seer but as the poet of witness—in spite, or rather because, of his blindness. So, in the end Oedipus is seer and poet, too. As with Milton, in his sublime "Hymn to Light" at the opening of Book III of *Paradise Lost*, the shutting out of nature's light by blindness allows the celestial light, vision, to shine inward, purging the poet's mind of the "mist" of the vegetative world "that I may see and tell / of things invisible to mortal sight" (l. 54–5).[6] The blind poet sees invisible reality—including the future—not the "real world" of mere appearances.

We know Oedipus has come to the place where he will die, so the tragedy of the last Oedipus play is muted; much more resonant is its uncanny exaltation. Oedipus goes to his death reconciled to the gods, and we feel that, however darkly, the universe coheres. The action of the play seems incidental, consisting of efforts by his son Polyneices and Creon to recruit Oedipus for their local political advantage. Oedipus spurns them, cursing with Lear-like passion. When Creon kidnaps his daughters, Antigone and Ismene, King Theseus of Athens easily gets them back; it's a mere subplot to remind us how powerful Theseus, the Athenian, is. That incidental problem solved, Oedipus can now go to his death.

The parallels I wish to draw—and that I think Lowell and Hall were half-consciously drawing in comparing Pound to Oedipus—are not hard to find. Pound's return to Italy was to be a return to the sources of his poetic power.[7] There, having finally understood himself, he could finally get *The Cantos* together and finish his poetic task in a state of visionary insight. So the younger generation of poets hoped and believed that Pound had repudiated politics and his political Klan—Kasper and co.—who distracted him while he was in custody. Perhaps, insofar as the younger men, Lowell and Hall, tried to help, they both attempted to play Theseus …

… but one doesn't want to push the parallels too far. For there are ironies as well; the return has not been productive. Pound is blocked, all but speechless.

Far from finding himself attuned to the gods, he is at odds with them, in Hell on earth. Perhaps the faithful younger poets merely wish to elevate Pound to a tragic status by exaggerating his visionary dimension. And yet there were the drafts and fragments (some of which had been written before Pound's release, or, like "Addendum for C," even earlier). When Hall saw them, he read them in "awe turning to elation." They were the best cantos since the *Pisans*, he thought: "they returned to lyricism and to personal vulnerability, his own life and his own concerns surfacing through the details of history" (Hall 1992: 223–4). The divine fire still burned, if fitfully.

The poets made sense of Pound's increasing estrangement from language and loss of confidence in his poem—of his evident defeat—by likening him to Oedipus after he had solved Laius's murder and therefore entered the mystery of his own being. Pound's silence, as it stole upon him, is a tragic analog to Oedipus's blindness. But there is one big difference: Oedipus willed his blindness—"the hand that struck my eyes was mine, / mine alone—no one else— / I did it all myself" (Fagles 1984: 241; and see Yeats 1952; 325). Yet it is not clear that Pound chose silence; there is the late remark to Dominique de Roux: "I did not enter into silence, silence captured me" (Tytell 1987: 336). He told Grazia Livi: "[A] strange day came and I realized that I did not know anything, indeed that I did not know anything at all. And so words have become empty of all meaning" (qtd in Hall 1992: 248).

More than depressed, Pound seems in Hall's harrowing account to be afflicted by an almost uncontrollable mood disorder,[8] in which, with horrible irony, he is seized by that condition of abulia against which he spent his life railing. Hall correctly notes that these seizures are attested as far back as his internment at Pisa; he sees in Pound "energy and fatigue in constant war; fatigue continually overpowering energy, only for energy to revive itself by a fragile and courageous effort of will." The "fatigue seemed more than physical; it seemed abject despair, accidie, meaninglessness, abulia, waste" (Hall 1992: 197). These assaults of mood might appear several times in an afternoon. Thinking about Pound as a kind of Oedipus, we see the connection between psyche and fate, blindness and vision, silence and insight.

String out a parallel something like this: as soon as Oedipus learned of the prophecy made about him, he lived his life in such a way as to preserve himself, protect his family, and prevent the foredoomed tragedy. Yet it was because of his leaving home to avoid any contact with his supposed parents that he found himself at the meeting place of three roads where he was assaulted by the stranger, Laius, thereby activating the tragic prophecy. Later, when Thebes is visited by a plague because Laius's killer has not been brought to justice, Oedipus uses his heroic will to truth and powers of riddle-solving to find the killer, thereby bringing on the tragedy he had done everything to avoid. He then blinded himself. After wandering a long time, he came to the place of his death and found himself transformed from political outcast to seer and poet.

Similarly, Pound sought through his poem, *The Cantos*, to preserve cultural coherence and prevent the collapse of Western civilization. For him the place where the three roads meet is the poem. But the poem is under constant assault from within and without by hostile cultural, historical, religious, and even unconcious forces. The poem is always in-resistance-to, defensive, alert, combative. The struggle between darkness and light, between Babylon and Apollo, Semitic nomad and Aryan farmer, Usura and natural ethics ("ethics is from agriculture"), which structures the poem, reflects at the level of culture the struggle of energy against fatigue (abulia) he feels within himself. "Not lie down," Pound exhorts himself and his readers at the end of Canto 97—like a marathoner sensing the end of the race (97/703).

Pound told Hall that *The Cantos* were to be the "tale of the tribe," the poem including history, perhaps a coherent global epic. But, as he admits, he is not a demigod; just as he cannot make his life cohere, full as it is of "errors and wrecks," so he cannot make the poem cohere, which means he cannot make history coherent.

> Tho' my errors and wrecks lie about me.
> And I am not a demigod
> I cannot make it cohere. (116/816)

"Coherence" is the key term in Pound's *Women of Trachis*, when, at the climactic moment, the demigod Herakles announces: "SPLENDOUR IT ALL COHERES" (Pound 1957: 50)—the line for which Pound thinks the play was written;[9] certainly it is the line for which the play was translated. The actor's "mask of agony" is removed; he turns to the audience in "the make-up ... of solar serenity" (1957: 50). Burning as he is in a napalm shirt, Herakles is nevertheless serene. The contrast between this unconcealment of serenity within Herakles' physical agony reflects Pound's own stubborn faith in a coherent and essentially benign universe. This is reflected in the difference between Herakles' inner serenity and outward agony. This same difference lies near the heart of Pound's tragic position and why he can be justly compared with Oedipus.[10] But just because the universe *does* cohere, even if his notes do not, the problem is not in the universe but in himself. Pound is not a demigod; he is a human being.

And just because he believed the universe coheres, Pound had long postponed imposing coherence on his poem—*The Cantos* always seemed to Pound a work-in-progress. That is why we still have a provisional title "Drafts of XXX Cantos," even for the first, most textually stable group of poems. At some point, at his leisure, Pound planned to put the whole thing together, make it coherent. At various times Pound thought the moment had come. Around 1940, Pound contacted George Santayana in Rome, hoping for some kind of tutorial in philosophy. After the war, Pound must have felt that *The Cantos* would have to wait until he had completed his translations of Confucius, including the Odes. Then the hospital became an intoxicating space in which the poet compensated for his loss of liberty by imagining he exercised power as an "unacknowledged legislator" and authority on the Constitution to extreme elements of the political Right and reveled in playing teacher to numberless young poets, seekers, and sycophants. Finally, his release to Italy should have provided the time to bring *The Cantos* together.

When Pound thought he had failed to create a coherent poem, as he had failed earlier to prevent the Second World War, he had found himself "like an ant from a broken anthill / from the wreckage of Europe, ego scriptor" (76/478). His incarceration was equivalent to Oedipus's unrecorded wanderings. So the return to Italy and romantic Brunnenburg may well have seemed at first like finding sanctuary. There he could complete his work.

Ensconced in Brunnenburg with Marcella and his daughter, Pound started to do just this, sitting down with Mary to make glosses as to who was speaking when in the cantos and trying to reconcile the printed cantos in English to Mary's improved and updated Italian version. Mary was to play Antigone to Pound's Oedipus—the helpful, dutiful Antigone of *Oedipus at Colonus*—and Brunnenburg was to be the sacred grove of poetic abundance, as it is in the play. As its name suggests, the castle would tap sacred sources—*Brunnen*—to become a Castalia of the Muses: "Many springs are at the foot of / Hsiang Shan" (112/804), Pound wrote, hopefully, looking up at the Mutspitze. But the old man was not a demigod, and he could not make it cohere. Mary is eloquent about the problems of having such a father in *Discretions*: "blinded by his glory," she recalls, "I did not see all his needs. The family had been trained for a demigod, and as such he came" (de Rachewiltz 1975: 305). Mary was expected to be her tragic father's shelter, to help him be "the lovable human being he is"—almost as though Pound himself had forgotten how to be human.

Besides, the castle was too cold; years of institutional steam heat had sapped Pound's tolerance for winter's damp (Moody 2015: 451). Moody's biographical work and Marcella Spann Booth's reflections show Pound found himself in an untenable and "tragic" dilemma: in love with Marcella, in legal thrall to his wife, and for both of these reasons alienated from Olga. Estrangement from Olga meant that he could not get to Venice, in so many ways his point of poetic origin: "Pride, jealousy and possessiveness / 3 pains of hell," he muttered (113/807). Marcella was eventually maneuvered out of the way by Dorothy in September of 1959, and Pound, helpless and bereft, retired to Brunnenburg to die (Moody 2015: 462–3).

In a letter he wrote Elizabeth Bishop in 1963, Lowell recounts a conversation with Mary about her father's uncharacteristic despondency. "Somewhere there was an awakening from father" (Lowell leaves out the "her" from "her father"—in his case a truly Freudian slip); this was, he concluded, "not a disillusionment but a surprise" for Mary. Lowell reported that Mary had told him that

> until six years ago I never questioned one of his thoughts … When he came back we didn't know that even he couldn't do anything … [T]wo years of sitting hardly raising an arm and thinking all his contemporaries' careers had gone better than his … stopped me from translating the Cantos, saying they were no good. Do people in such a state really feel the terrible things they say? … [A]t first it was Cantos at every meal. (Lowell 2005: 417)

Mary's remarks prompted further reflection by Lowell that bears on his Oedipus comparison: "I have been thinking of the great callousness and bravado of Ezra's existence, so free[,] one might have thought[,] of most men's waverings, feelings of being a copy, of not pursuing a goal etc. Then the shell breaks and the cold air tortures the exposed flesh. The partial recovery, though the other was a recovery of humanity" (Lowell 2005: 417). In Lowell's mind Pound the demigod had seemed free of the usual anxieties about originality or doubts about his ability to pursue the supreme poem. Pound's sudden loss of confidence—the breaking of the shell of seeming; the unconcealment (to use Heidegger's vivid term) of "the exposed flesh" to the cold truth—is equivalent to an awakening and recovery of the poet's "humanity." Lowell's sentence is somewhat obscure: the breaking of the shell recovered Pound's humanity, but Lowell wants to believe that he also recovered—at least partially—*from that* and went back to being a demigod, the way Lowell imagined him. To be Pound, as to be Oedipus in Lowell's view, is to experience being human, as it were, *from the outside*—as in a visionary dream. In a 1948 letter to William Carlos Williams, Lowell reported e. e. cummings telling Pound: "You're humane without being human" (Lowell 2005: 119). Humanity is that from which Pound's shell of "callousness and bravado" had protected him. Oedipus lives a similar paradox: the truth made him *inhuman*, a monster, and yet at the same time fulfilled his tragedy by making him most human. When he exposes himself on stage in all his wretchedness, he represents the *unspeakable*.[11] He is thus prepared to become, as he becomes in the sequel *Oedipus at Colonus*, seer and poet and demigod. His mysterious death is attended by divine thunder—though his essential mortality is stressed (see Fagles 1984: 381).

Pound's alleged crimes were also unspeakable if we think of the late cantos as a coded defense and justification undertaken in Aesopian language. What Pound really wants to say, the content, must be hidden, but, as he told Hall, "The *what* is so much more important than how" (Hall 1992: 317). So the later cantos become a poem about that of which we cannot speak because the defeated Truth cannot be uttered: "It is difficult to write a paradise when all the superficial indications are that you ought to write an apocalypse" (Hall 1992: 331).

It was in this interview with Hall that Pound said many of the important things about his epic project, such as "an epic is a poem containing history" (Hall 1992: 331) and "I am writing to resist the idea that Europe and civilization are going to Hell" and "The nature of sovereignty is epic matter, though it can be a bit obscured by circumstance" (Hall 1992: 332). The conversation yields touchstone after touchstone that reflect equally on the poem and Pound's own psyche—his own sovereignty is at stake. Pound has a clear idea of what he wants to do and yet, he admits, "Okay. I am stuck …" The struggle has come up against a block. The struggle for sovereignty is also a struggle for sovereignty over himself; it goes to the heart of his Confucianism: "if a man hath not order within him, he cannot have order without him." Tellingly, he describes his poem as "the fight for light versus subconscious"—his own. In psychological terms, the fight is against his own repression, resulting in "obscurities and penumbras," and is "a bit obscured by circumstance" (Hall 1992: 333).

The necessary obscurities express the political and personal necessity of dissembling, yet they indicate to readers the need for enlightenment: "This is provisionally what I have to do," Pound told Hall, "I must clarify obscurities; I must make clearer definite ideas or dissociations, I must find a verbal formula to combat the rise of brutality—the principle of order versus the split atom" (Hall 1992: 332). Order and light go together as clarity. Clarity reveals form, is form. Form and the right "verbal formulas," Pound hopes, can "cohere" in a poem that expresses the best of Western civilization—against the unconscious, against brutality, against the Bomb, and against "the propaganda of terror and luxury" (Hall 1992: 333); in a word, against "Babylon," a metonymy increasingly used in *Thrones* (98/705, 102/748, 102/750, 103/752). Yet, despite Pound's need for clarity and definition, the poetic depths he wishes to plumb cannot be approached directly in language for political and personal reasons as well as poetical ones.[12]

It would seem that, in his teacherly effort to explain himself to Hall, Pound forgets to add something he knows perfectly well; as Heidegger says: "A poet might even come to the point where he is compelled—in his own way—that is poetically—to put into language the experience he undergoes with language" (Heidegger 1975: 59). To undergo an experience for Heidegger means "that something befalls us ... specifically, that the experience is of our own making: to undergo ... means that we endure it, suffer it, receive it as it strikes us and submit to it" (Heidegger 1975: 57). The experience Pound is having with language at this late point, 1960, after *Thrones*, with his unpublished sheaf of drafts and fragments, is the experience of blockage, or the loss of coherence. He looks into "the abyss of Nothing" (Heidegger 2000: 120), the abyss of silence where words have lost their meaning. The problem, for Pound, was the possibility that there was no coherence; that his vision of history and therefore his politics were somehow wrong and that as a result the poem was something far worse—as he said, "a botch."

Fortunately, the poem is not a quite a botch, even though it may not cohere. Its incoherence is the record of Pound's experience with language, which we experience with him as readers. Ironically, as Robert Duncan pointed out long ago and Burt Hatlen reiterates in his work, it's the very lack of coherence, its "openness," that saves *The Cantos* from its "totalitarian" pretensions to coherence.[13] But Pound could not see this, and if he had he would have rejected it; *his Cantos* are a didactic poem.

If, as Lowell wrote Laughlin, the surfeit of knowledge that Pound has is related to his fate, then that fate is bigger than Pound: it is the fate of poetry in the modern age. This comparison of Pound and Oedipus asks us to consider Pound's end less in terms of the inevitable question about Pound's "repentance" for whatever crimes or sins we think he may have committed than as the artist who, more than anyone else, took on the burden on "the enormous tragedy" of the dream of the twentieth century—not just the tragedy of the utopic fascist dream but the tragedy of so-called Western so-called civilization, which, despite Pound's best efforts to racialize the matter in the Washington Cantos, begins traditionally where *The Cantos* begin, in the Homeric poems, and which, according to many, achieved maximum depth in the Greek tragedies performed a thousand years later. This burden is the tragic burden of cultural coherence, which allows

Pound, two-and-a-half thousand years after that, to take on Sophocles' Oedipus role as the armature for his own life, as a cultural pattern and fund for poets to draw parallels from and make meanings with.

There is a further parallel between Pound's *Cantos* and *Oedipus at Colonus*. *Oedipus at Colonus* was performed for the first time in the spring of 401 BC, several years after Sophocles' death. Between the death of the playwright and the performance of his play, Athens had been utterly defeated by the Spartans. Their democracy was "replaced by a Spartan-backed reactionary dictatorship—the thirty Tyrants, who ruled by terror" (Fagles 1984: 256). By 401, however, Athens had regained some independence, the Tyrants were overthrown, and the festival of Dionysius could resume. But, as Robert Fagles writes in his introduction to the play, "it was not the same Athens; gone forever were the confidence and daring, the sense of unlimited horizons characteristic of the Periclean city." He continues:

> The audience that saw ... *Oedipus at Colonus* in 401 B.C. must have been profoundly moved, for it is among other things, a valedictory celebration of Athens as it was in its time of greatness. Sophocles must have known when he wrote it that the city was headed for defeat, perhaps destruction; in this play he brings Oedipus to Athens, or rather to the nearby village of Colonus, his own birthplace, where the blind exile from Thebes is to receive Athenian protection and, in return, guarantee victory for Athens over Thebes in some future war. That victory will be won on the site of his grave; but for that to happen, its location must remain a secret, known only to the leaders of his adopted city. (Fagles 1984: 255–6)

I propose that the readers of *The Cantos* feel much the same way. The great poem is a valedictory to "Athens," or "the idea of Europe and civilization," in a world that is going elsewhere. Just as Sophocles stages Oedipus's death at the place of his own birth, uniting his own historical beginning with a mythic end, eventually Pound sought out the place of his poetic birth, his Colonus—not Brunnenburg but Venice—as his place to die. If there is to be any victory for coherence then perhaps it took place there, a secret known only to the readers of these moving, maddening cantos.

Notes

1   Jeffrey Meyers (2011: 180) wrote that "Lowell avoided direct competition with Pound's *Propertius*" in translating that author. Perhaps this applies with the Greek dramatists as well. (AH)

2   Hall does not give a full citation. Henderson lists it as C1895 "Vi parla Ezra Pound: io so di non sapere nulla," Intervista di Grazia Livi, *Epoca*, Milan, XIV.652 (March 24, 1963): 90–3.
3   *A Packet for Ezra Pound* was originally published separately by Cuala Press in 1929. Pound would have seen it then. See the *Collected Works of William Butler Yeats*, vol. XIV, xxxii.
4   "Tiresias Thebae," quotes Andreas Divus's Latin, Englished in Canto 1 as "Tiresias Theban."
5   Another identification can be made between the poet and Herakles, the tragic hero of Sophocles' *The Women of Trachis* (trans. 1954).
6   Thanks to my colleague Jill Stephen for this suggestion.
7   For some time, it was assumed that *Thrones* was written in Italy; in fact, it was drafted out earlier, before Pound's release, and only "finalized" November 1958 in Italy (Moody 2015: 451). But James Wilhelm, in *The Later Cantos of Ezra Pound* (1977), speaks for an earlier consensus when he claims that the whole of *Thrones* was written after Pound's return to Italy. This notion of *Thrones* as a valediction is informed by the Oedipean paradigm; "This last phase of Pound's career marks still another step in his passage from youthful frenzy to quiet acceptance" (Wilhelm 1977: 5).
8   It is possible that Pound suffered from "ultra ultra ultradian mood disorder"—a little-understood and all but subclinical mood cycle of violent ups and downs occurring in cycles of twenty hours or less that is now receiving some attention in the psychological literature.
9   Pound emphasizes its importance in a complicated note, which locates the statement in an "ideogram" of allusions to his own *Elektra*, Cocteau's *Antigone*, and Mussolini's Verona speech. See *Elektra* (Pound 1989: xiv).
10 Herakles is serene. This serenity is not Nietzsche's "tragic joy," a dark Romantic reading at odds with Pound's more Stoic perspective.
11 For Oedipus and the unspeakable, see Goldhill (1986: 209–16).
12 Heidegger puts it this way: "the man who knows is not the one who blindly runs after a truth, but one who constantly knows all three ways, that of being, that of not-being and that of seeming" (2000: 120). Heidegger's adverb "blindly" refers obliquely to Oedipus, who saw when he was blind, while "the three ways" gestures toward the triple crossroads, where Oedipus met his tragic destiny and killed his father.
13 "And as we turn from Pound's political ideology to his poetry, it seems to me important to state at once that, however 'closed' and regressive the political system to which Pound committed himself, *The Cantos* remains an 'open' text. Pound's mind drove constantly toward closure. What Gertrude Stein called the 'village explainer' in Pound was (let us admit it!) always an ideologue: he wanted an Answer, and if at all possible a simple one, something that any man could get in

'one day's reading.' But Pound's poem retains as much of that quality which Keats called 'negative capability'—the capacity to 'remain in doubt, without any irritable straining after fact or reason'—as any text in our language.... In *The Cantos* Pound's 'open' poetic method tends to dissolve fascism, itself an amalgam of disparate political tendencies, back into its constituent parts. *The Cantos* may set out to affirm fascism, but in fact the poem 'deconstructs' fascist ideology; and this is, I here shall propose, a principal reason why the poem still lives" (Burton Hatlen, "Ezra Pound and Fascism," in *Ezra Pound and History*, edited by Marianne Korn [Orono, MA: National Poetry Foundation, 1985], pp. 145–72 (at 158–9). (AH)

Afterword

The book you have just read is not an attack on Ezra Pound. Throughout I have tried to show how Pound's personal situation as a political prisoner, his love for Sheri Martinelli, his right-wing politics, and his racialized metapolitics drove and impeded his ascension to the light of paradise. As in my earlier book *John Kasper and Ezra Pound*, I have tried to describe faithfully Pound's political message to his disciples at St. Elizabeths and comrades on the Right who wished to preserve a particular way of life that they saw as integral to the American Republic, namely white supremacy. In the first book, I have tried to show how this "Southern" outlook is integral to the late cantos, Pound's tale of his tribe. Showing how this perspective emerged in the cantos he wrote while incarcerated has taught me that Pound, great and ambitious poet that he was, was unequipped intellectually and spiritually for the paradisal adventure he was determined to undertake. For all of his various reading, he was unable to sustain concentrated attention on his paradisal object. He knew he needed philosophy for that; what the poet didn't realize was that he needed to be a demigod or saint as well. He settled for "Maestro" status, which might be enough for any poet of lesser ambitions. Pound's circumstances in the madhouse made any convincing ascension even more arduous. His paradise, when it revealed itself, was the paradise of any man—the ephemeral, but intense, paradise of sexual fulfillment in love and the simple wish to be free to come and go as one pleases; to be a person at liberty.

Some time ago when I was offered the opportunity to write a biography of Ezra Pound I jumped at the chance to finally "put my ideas in order" about the poet to whom I had devoted my intellectual life since my sophomore year at Bennington College. The result was *Ezra Pound* (Reaktion, 2011), a short biography that told a "sad story," as Mary de Rachewiltz told me after reading the manuscript. It is a sad story, for it is the tale of Pound's disillusionment and my own. Writing the biography of a man you have devoted your life to is like an over-prolonged goodbye. Yet our sadness is different. Pound grew disillusioned with his poem because the theory of history that sustained it was no longer credible, even to himself. The credible aspect is his powerful critique that sees history as a class struggle between a mass of debtors and a few creditors, which underwrites Pound's Jeffersonian outlook and historiography. This critique makes distributive justice history's crux by designating sovereignty as the power to establish a system of values by issuing money. But this cannot be translated into a cosmic race war between men and destroyers (117/823), Aryan and Semite, sun and moon, constructive light and destructive darkness.

The biography made me appreciate how pervasive current events were in the Washington Cantos. The cantos in *Rock-Drill* and *Thrones* contained support for states' rights ideology based on a "Southern" view of American history. In service of his view of the US Constitution, Pound became an active segregationist through his agents among his disciples: John Kasper principally but also Dave Horton, Eustace Mullins, and others. This book has made me aware that the current events were not merely events in the news but his day-to-day perceptions, his visitors, his lover, and the weather, all the usual stimuli of a good lyric poet, albeit in a highly unusual context. It's in these little things—the simple, sincere record of a human-all-too-human existence—where the beauty of Pound's late poetry lives.

From my undergraduate days I have been interested in the "American Ezra Pound," the only version of the poet I then felt I had a chance of understanding. The American Pound is inevitably the political Pound; in my scholarship I prefer to focus on history and biography. My limited learning in philosophy and my indifference to religious dogma (though not to spiritual power) means I have tended to leave the visionary poet, the esoteric, even occult Pound, out of my scholarship, although never out of my thinking.

I have been entranced by Pound since a seminar on "Yeats, Pound, Eliot" that I took sometime in the mid-1970s at Bennington College, taught by the poet Stephen Sandy. Among so much else, we read Hugh Kenner's magnificent *The Pound Era*, a book that literally changed my life and, if truth be told, gave it a direction. Kenner showed that the criticism expressed in great prose writing could be a creative act. From the beginning Pound's politics interested me, and in 1978 I wrote an undergraduate thesis directed by Phoebe Chao on Pound and Fascism called "Ezra Pound's Road to Pisa," which carried the predictable epigraph from Samuel Johnson about the road to Hell being paved with good intentions. Fifteen years later I was the student of the important Poundian George Kearns at Rutgers, completing a dissertation on the populistic Jeffersonianism of Ezra Pound and William Carlos Williams that provided the basis for my first book on Pound: *Money and Modernity: Pound, Williams and the Spirit of Jefferson* (University of Alabama Press, 1998).

Afterword

I first visited Brunnenburg in the 1990s, then spent a formative six-week NEH seminar there in 1994 directed by Tim Redman and Vince Sherry. It was there I met Burt Hatlen, who became my teacher and friend. My life then made it relatively easy to visit Dorf Tirol in the summers that followed. Perhaps it was at one of her famous teas out on the picnic table off the kitchen that Mary de Rachewiltz said to me, "In the late cantos: that's when Pound got really serious." As I had always found *Rock-Drill* and *Thrones* especially rebarbative, with their Chinese ideograms, arcane sources, and repetitive motifs and phrases, I was surprised—but also certain she must be right. I have studied those late cantos assiduously ever since. Eventually I even learned how to read them—perhaps not all of any single canto, at least without helps—but I learned the code. For these poems are written in code—actually codes—that unravel into stark binaries once one assimilates the racialized metapolitical preoccupations that underwrite it. The Aesopian language that confuses the late cantos is also personal, continuing a practice of self-concealment that Pound had used from his earliest poetry via his signature personae. So Pound the well-known antisymbolist really isn't one. There's an algebra.

Locally, the late poems are concerned with the problem of how to resist the Jewish/Communist conspiracy that is bent on destroying the American way of life; generally, these cantos show how a series of civilizations have risen and eventually fallen into racial, spiritual, and cultural decay through the romantic sensuality of the culture-founding Aryans who made them and the greedy machinations of hostile aliens—Jews latterly, but Semites before that in the time of Semitic Akkad and "Aryan" Sumer. The problem was how to maintain Sparta as Sparta, i.e. a white USA, and thus how to "maintain antisepsis" to protect the white light of cosmic reason from racial pollution. In the Far East the other culture-bearing race, the Chinese, held fast as long as they held the precepts of Confucius against the constant culture-sapping pressure of jargon-spewing Buddhists, lazy "Taozers," and, latterly, Chinese communists. In all cases the specter of race-mixing haunts Pound in these late cantos. Pound fears "the mongrelization of everything"—of the white race, of art and ideas, of the currency and of law, especially the US Constitution, which, like the temple evoked in these poems, is not for sale, though wealthy buyers persist in trying to purchase it.

Pound's anxieties were due to the immediate social, legal, and cultural context as viewed from his place of incarceration, "the bughouse," St. Elizabeths Hospital for the Insane, from the clamorous wards of which could be seen the gleaming white iron dome and Neoclassical architecture of the US Capitol. Outside was Cold War hysteria. Outside were the earthshaking decisions of the treasonous Warren Court: most radically, the overturning of that legal keystone of the American social order, *Plessy v. Ferguson*, and the "separate but equal" doctrine that underwrote Jim Crow. The *Brown v. Board of Education* decision of 1954 remains to this day a livid scar, even an open wound, across American culture, as our cities, abandoned by white flight, and our broken politics clearly show. As the first part of this project, *John Kasper and Ezra Pound*, demonstrates, Pound and his friends were shaken to the core by the *Brown* decisions.

That these late poems are really serious there can be no doubt. This is prison literature of the most serious kind. They are the work of a passionate ideologue whose notions were all too often founded on bad information distorted by his own obsessions. They are full of earnest counsel about how to save the republic by returning to the ethos of earlier times. Some of this is indigenous and Jeffersonian; much is Confucian in the broad sense, as Pound recommends the rites and edicts of Ancient China as remedies for current events; much is a disquisition on sovereignty as such, guaranteed by the exclusive right to coin money and, as a result, to literally regulate society by setting proper boundaries of weights and measures, prices and values.

A Jefferson-style republican to the core, with all the attendant racial, cultural, and economic anxieties that accompany that position, Pound is paradoxically a poet in search of an Emperor—some human, but not too human, guarantor of meanings. This contradiction was for Pound a powerful generator of poetry. Incarcerated, Pound saw himself as a kind of twentieth-century Ovid in exile. He yearned for the lost imperial cultural center as much as the Roman poet pacing the Black Sea shore. For both poets, Roma—as city and idea, as contradictory site of Republican virtue and the temptations of Imperial ambition—stood as the radiant symbol of forbidden cultural authority. As a poet, Pound could comment, critique, and advise; as a person, Pound was trying to hold on to a self beleaguered by public disgrace, fierce convictions, and private doubts. The republic he most needed to save was himself. *Rock-Drill* (1956) ends with the poet's near-drowning, his life dependent on the whim of Leucothea, significantly, the white goddess. *Thrones* (1959), the last authorized section of *The Cantos*, ends with the poet still at sea, albeit on some sort of craft, while we readers tag along uneasily in the dinghy towed astern. Just where we are going is hard to say. No landfall is in sight. *Drafts & Fragments* are at best a moving, melancholy archipelago, although Canto 110—"thy quiet house," drafted in November 1958 at Torcello with his Nausikaa, his Artemis, Marcella Spann by his side—give us an old man's paradise of simple peace and quiet.

Like others before me, my career as Pound's critic has led to disillusion. It is a road many have walked down already: Noel Stock, Robert Casillo, and Burton Hatlen, to name three. Massimo Bacigalupo and Leon Surette were perhaps always skeptics and thus had few illusions to lose. George Kearns was always reticent; if he was disillusioned, he never let on. Hugh Kenner knew all about Pound's problematic politics, but it didn't matter; to him the poetry, as poetry, was everything.

I always approached Pound as a Master. The didactic *Cantos* were a curriculum and an argument. Their content was all-important to Pound, and most of that content is a dissident politics, economics, and theory of history. Always I have tried to understand Pound's political economy as he would wish to be understood, on his own terms. This was never easy. Pound was not a "liberal": like all radicals he despised us. The late cantos are serious, but they mustn't be taken seriously as political wisdom in particular or even wisdom literature more generally. Pound's anti-Semitism was never visceral, like Eliot's or Edith Wharton's, but a sudden—if belated—realization that the Jewish conspiracy against the rest of mankind was real. Mussolini was a revelation; Pound's loyalty to Il Duce was heartfelt and never wavered; it was greater than his duty to the United States, which was already, so far as Pound was concerned, enemy-occupied territory. World War II meant the triumph of Anglo-Soviet-Jewish aggression against European and Japanese civilization. America was next. Like the FBI, Pound saw the movement for Black Civil Rights as the result of the Communist conspiracy. Its purpose was to corrupt and weaken the USA through "mongrelization" in order to make the country easy prey for a destructive usocracy. Since Pound shared the Nazi outlook that Jews and Communists were the same, the Civil Rights struggle confirmed his conspiratorial worldview. Inevitably, Pound supported segregation, because white supremacy was mandated by the cosmic order. Ezra Pound: anti-Semite, fascist, segregationist. Three strikes—you're out!

And yet I must love him, as one loves a wayward father. In spite of everything. Because of everything.

Allentown, PA, August 2019

Appendix A
A Primer of Poundian Economics

WORK is not a commodity. Money is not a commodity. The state HAS credit, and does not need to rent it from banks.

The BASIS of money [is], the abundance of nature and the responsibility of the whole people. (EP/ORA 232)

The Cantos is a global epic; if it is "the poem including history," then economic arrangements, institutions of exchange, and its language—money—are integral to any responsible history. Pound told Agresti, "Money is an articulation. Prosody is an articulation of the sound of a poem, Money ... is articulation of total purchasing power of the nation" (7/5/1951, EP/ORA 68). In explicitly making economics a theme in his epic poem, Pound was only making plain what was implicit in other epics. All epic poets are economists of a sort, some more and some less openly. Like most twentieth-century reformers of consequence, Pound is an economic determinist, believing that restructuring of economic arrangements is the surest way to reform society for the good. Pound was widely read in dissident economic theory, including Marx and Lenin, but suspicious of academic economists. Therefore, Ezra Pound is regarded as a "crank" about economic matters, especially about money.

In fact, Pound thought long and hard about economics, almost as much as he thought about poetry. Such thinking came naturally. Ezra's father, Homer, was an assayer at the Philadelphia Mint during a period when "the Money Question" was *the* issue in American politics. Seemingly abstruse questions concerning the virtues and defects of metallic and paper currency, gold and silver money, monetary signs and symbols were dinner-table conversation. Years before his celebrated conversion to Major Douglas's Social Credit, young Ezra was a Republican Progressive impressed by the reformer Teddy Roosevelt, dreaming of economic reform and limits on personal wealth. Impelled by the prolonged economic crisis of the 1930s, his readings of Confucius and Mencius, the distributive mechanism of Silvio Gesell's "shrinking money," and the so-called "New Economists" attracted to A. R. Orage's *The New Age*, Pound evolved his own syncretic economic philosophy, "Volitionist Economics," in which he tried to interest Mussolini, the Teddy Roosevelt of the Italian Peninsula.

Fittingly, Pound was most interested in the contradictory nature of money, which is the language of economic exchange. His researches into money continued, during his incarceration at St. Elizabeths, to find startling if obscure expression in the difficult late cantos, as we have seen in his "reading through" of Alexander Del Mar's *History of Monetary Systems* (1896) in Canto 97. Pound's belated discovery of Del Mar's work, a direct intervention into the monetary controversies of the late nineteenth century, brought Pound's monetary thinking full circle.

Economics had surfaced in Pound's epic long before. Canto 12 is dedicated to "money business" (12/53). In Canto 18 Kublai Khan's invention of paper money is set against war profiteering, establishing a crucial nexus in Pound's thought confirmed years later by the Social Credit adage "War is economic peace; peace is economic war." Peace is economic war because it demands relentless and wasteful competition between firms and nations fighting for trade advantages; war is economic peace because it makes unlimited demands on industry. War is the only perfect consumer. The proverb implies that sabotage is the essence of the industrial system under business enterprise and corporate finance. It is only through sabotage that sufficient profit can be extracted from an economy within which all scarcity must be artificial because the problem of production has been solved. This is "scarcity economics," and its goal is to produce scarcity in a world of abundance—a demonic reversal of the original sense of economics, which meant to husband and manage limited resources in a world of scarcity.

Social Credit is taken up explicitly in Canto 38 with the inclusion of Douglas's foundational "A + B theorem." Douglas himself appears in Canto 22 as "C.H." in a debate with John Maynard Keynes ("Mr. Bukos") and Douglas shows up again in Canto 46. Canto 33 quotes extensively from Marx's *Capital*, while Lenin surfaces in Cantos 74 and 80.[1]

Pound's obsession with a sane economics is part of his life-long antiwar stance, a fact that may startle some too eager to label Pound "fascist" and so avoid looking into his economic philosophy. To Pound, the "Anglo-Jewish war against Europe"—what we call World War II—was precipitated by a panicked reaction to fascist threats to the liberal economic system dominated by the Bank of England, the bank's subsidiary British Empire, and an international financial elite, who Pound preferred to imagine as "Jews," whether individual bankers were Jewish or not. The taint of anti-Semitism, though well deserved, has unfortunately occluded Pound's important insights into the undeniable predatory and criminal propensities of finance capitalism still much in evidence today. "The State-Finance nexus," as David Harvey calls it (Harvey 2014: 46), has many names. President Eisenhower called it "the military-industrial complex." Harvey, whose credentials as the leading expositor of Marx and *Capital* might mark him as antithetical to Pound, observes how "the privileged banking establishment has managed to monopolize everyone's credit, enabling the few to exploit the many through their partiality in allocating credit, by charging usury (disguised as 'interest') and increasingly exorbitant fees, and by rewarding politicians for their service in promoting their interests" (Harvey 2014: 48–9). Pound calls this establishment the "usurocracy"; he calls its ethos "Usura." His famous chant against "Usura" in Canto 45 is the most memorable of *The Cantos* and one of the great poems of the twentieth century. As the quote from Harvey suggests, Pound's critique from the Right has strong affinities with Leftist anti-capitalism, one reason why Lenin's *Imperialism: The Highest Stage of Capitalism* remains an important touchstone for Pound. Pound's critique of capitalism evolved over time, shaped on the one hand by historical events and on the other by his own extensive historical and economic research.

Pound is in the Jeffersonian tradition of American politics and economics. Jefferson remains a radical figure, known for his deep distrust of big government and his scorn for banks and the English financial system, which he justifiably felt had been foisted on the new American republic by his political rival, Alexander Hamilton. Jefferson had a horror of debt, which reached from the past into the present like a skeletal hand. Pound never tired of quoting from Jefferson's 1813 letter to John Eppes about the dangers of debt, with its famous phrase "The earth belongs to the living" (77/488; *J/M* 115–17; *GK* 181). Every man deserves to be born free of debt, Jefferson believed. He saw farming as the only truly productive activity, all else being merely traffic; so did Pound (*J/M* 45, 63). Jefferson saw a world of producers, farmers, and craftsmen doing immediately useful labor pitted against an exploitative commercial class who merely shifted and exchanged other people's product for their own profit. Commerce was a tyranny controlled by bank credit and disciplined by debt. Following Jefferson, Pound saw history as a class struggle between a mass of producer debtors against a clique of predatory creditors.

Pound's early economics is in the moralistic Ruskinian mode. Like John Ruskin, and all economists, Pound is interested in wealth. But, properly construed, wealth cannot be defined as money or even riches. Wealth can only be what is good for life, but most often riches tend merely to be useless goods bought with money. Money itself does not constitute riches, only the power to purchase goods—Ruskin insists we remember the literal meaning of the word. Seen broadly, wealth must include the vast commonwealth of cultural and technical achievements, among them the work of poets and artists. The cultural commonwealth is the sum of achievements as a culture. Cultural failures, among them poverty, ignorance, and war, all life-denying, obviously count against a culture's wealth. Ruskin went so far as to punningly call them "illth."

Progressive reform is very much the mood of Pound's early economics as well. No wonder, then, that he was open to the economic currents flowing through the *New Age* after arriving in London in 1908. Like Pound, A. R. Orage, the journal's visionary editor, also was formed in the John Ruskin/William Morris crucible of late-nineteenth-century economic moralism. Before publishing C. H. Douglas, Orage had written an important work on Guild Socialism, a trend within socialism that had some influence on the *corporazione* idea later adopted by Italian Fascism. Pound's close friend in the 1930s, the Hungarian intellectual Odon Por, who also wrote for the *New Age,* later promoted Guild Socialism in Italy. Por imagined in several books a linkage between Guild Socialism and Mussolini's nascent Fascism, which originally had no economic program except violent anticommunism. In the 1930s, Pound and Por helped each other; Por arranged for Pound to appear on Rome Radio, and Pound was the English translator of Por's *Italy's Policy of Social Economics 1939/1940* (1941). The thrust of Pound's early economics and curiosity about Italian Fascism shows that he was interested in improving society through a more equitable distribution of the total wealth of the community including tangible and intangible cultural assets. In Italy, Pound saw the summer concert series of modern and classical music he arranged with Olga Rudge in Rapallo in the 1930s as a distribution of cultural wealth.

Primed by Orage, by the time he met Douglas at the *New Age* at the height of World War I in 1917, Pound had become interested in the economic causes of war. It was not the clash between Teutonic *Kultur* and French *civilization* the liberal press presented; rather, its causes, strategies, and tactics were determined by obscure economic interests. C. H. Douglas, a Scottish engineer, had been running an aircraft factory since the war began. He noticed that the state could mobilize for war in ways it would never mobilize for projects under peacetime conditions. He is remembered as an economic reformer with an idea, "social credit," that deserves to be taken very seriously. Pound's reviews of Douglas's *Economic Democracy* (1920) both quote this powerful insight: "Real credit is a measure of the reserve energy belonging to a community." "Real credit" is its "social credit," in other words its productive potential, including artistic and cultural production: the "cultural heritage." Douglas observes that the "'power to draw on the productive capacity to do work is clearly subject to the control of its owners through the agency of credit.'" Thus, "'it must be perfectly obvious to anyone who seriously considers the matter that the State should lend, not borrow" from private banks like the Bank of England or quasi-private entities like the Federal Reserve, "'in this respect as in others the Capitalist usurps the function of the State'" (Douglas, qtd in *SP* 208, 211). Much later, in *The Cantos*, Pound will refer to Alexander Del Mar on just this: "The right to coin money has always been ... the surest mark of sovereignty" (Del Mar 1983: 66). When the banks control the currency—or, in modern times, credit—they call the shots, not the government, which must borrow its own money and pay interest on it, a fact recognized early on by John Randolph of Virginia and quoted in Cantos 87 and 89 (87/589, 89/612). Seen in this light, the supposed sovereignty of the United States rests with the banks represented by the unelected Federal Reserve Board, rather than elected officials or even the US Constitution.

Douglas also deserves credit as one of the discoverers of the emergent consumer culture. "The only object of production is consumption," he wrote in *Social Credit* (1924: 124), not just to make profit as Marx had shown in *Capital*. By the twentieth century the problem of production had been solved, but the problem of consumption had scarcely been formulated. It was assumed, quite falsely, that everything produced would magically be consumed. So far, war remains the only perfect consumer; no one has yet figured out how to make capitalism sustainable in times of peace. Whether the problem is called overproduction or underconsumption, the basic tension remains: productive capacity overwhelms consumers' ability to consume it. The problem is not lack of the will to buy but the means to buy with, i.e. money. Douglas defined money as "effective-demand" (1924: 149) or the power to buy, because without it no demand for goods could be fulfilled, however pressing. This contradicts one of the most famous maxims of nineteenth-century economics, "Say's Law of Markets," which states in effect that "the total supply of goods and services in a free-market economy will exactly equal the total demand during any given time period," a strange early-nineteenth-century fallacy that nonetheless withstood the pressures of economic reality for a century. Douglas's critique of Say's Law is expressed in his famous A + B Theorem, which is the heart of his analysis of what ails capitalism. It was so important to Social Credit and to Pound himself that he wrote it almost verbatim into Canto 38 (38/190). Douglas had noticed that the purchasing power distributed by his factory in the form of wages, salaries, and dividends (A) was smaller than the price of the factory's product, since the latter also included other expenditures (B)—the costs of materials and tools, interest on bank loans, depreciation of plant, logistical costs, waste and scrap. Obviously, A must be smaller than A+B. It was in practice a fraction of B, which reflected most of the cost of doing business. By Douglas's reckoning, the conclusion was inescapable: purchasing power could never keep up with prices. So far the world had made up the difference through loans against future production and by dumping abroad—which Pound (and Lenin) saw as a key cause of war. Only technological innovation and cheaper raw materials, which lowered costs of production, stemmed the rush toward permanent indebtedness and an ultimate credit crash. But technical innovation decreased the cost of labor too. Workers were displaced by machines, thereby further decreasing A, the distribution of purchasing power, even as it lowered B, production costs. Now add in the "infamy" of taxes needed to pay off loans, which further stripped consumers of purchasing power. As a result, progress causes poverty. If Douglas is right, capitalism as we know it is unsustainable unless ways can be found to augment consumer purchasing power. For the last century, this has been done via "the dole," welfare programs and food stamps (or their electronic equivalent). These demoralizing expedients are necessary because they are the only way of sustaining an economic system that impoverishes the many to enrich the few. Unless this injustice was reformed, capitalism would collapse, as it did in the 1930s, the period we call the Great Depression.

Douglas mattered because the decision by the Bank of England after the Great War to return to the financial status quo antebellum by reimposing the Gold Standard was disastrous, ultimately creating conditions precipitating the famous Market Crash of 1929. Foreseeing the disaster, Pound's correspondent Arthur Kitson (who also claimed to have invented the term "social credit") charged a "Bankers' Conspiracy" in a pamphlet of that title he sent to Pound. Later on, Kitson would also send Pound *The Protocols of the Elders of Zion*, a popular and highly toxic piece of anti-Semitism that made it clear that the bankers' conspiracy was equivalent to the Jewish conspiracy.[2] Pound doesn't appear to have read the book till World War II, but he, like Douglas, Kitson, Hitler, Henry Ford, and millions of others, believed the fable of an all-seeing, all-knowing Jewish conspiracy using universal debt as a weapon to hijack history, with Russia its first victim and the Communists as its first tools.

Immediately postwar, in 1919, England was well lubricated with money, but prices seemed high. The "high cost of living" became a journalistic byword. The return to the Gold Standard reflected the policy of the bankers to deflate the economy by withdrawing credit. This would lower prices and, as creditors, it meant their debts were worth more because each unit of money was worth more. When prices are low, a pound note buys more goods. But the contraction of the economy also meant higher unemployment just when demobilized veterans were looking for work. "Orthodox" economics had no answer for this problem—and still doesn't. The Social Credit adage "Peace is economic war; war is economic peace" captures well this dilemma of modern economies. Pound himself would state the problem in Canto 22 as a kind of philosophical dialogue between Douglas and J. M. Keynes: "And C. H. [Douglas] said to the renowned Mr. Bukos [i.e. Keynes]: / 'What is the cause of the H. C. L. [High Cost of Living]?' and Mr. Bukos / The economist consulted of nations, said: / 'Lack of Labour.' / And there were two million men out of work" (22/101–102). Keynes was not yet the famous author of *The General Theory of Employment, Interest and Money* (1936), in which he pays a handsome tribute to Douglas and Gesell, but still an "orthodox economist," which is to say he believed in Say's Law of Markets.[3] What would make Keynes a Keynesian is precisely the rejection of Say's Law.

Ironically, Pound's *Social Credit: An Impact* (1935) records the impact not so much of Douglas's Social Credit ideas, which had already made an indelible mark on Pound, but of Silvio Gesell, author of *The Natural Economic Order* (1916). Though Pound had been aware of Gesell's work since 1932, when he saw it in action in the Austrian town of Wörgl, he became more interested in Gesell's thinking when he read Hugo Fack's 1935 American edition of Gesell's book. He suddenly realized that Gesell provided a mechanism for achieving some of Douglas's goals. Pound's pamphlet is designed to bring Douglas and Gesell together and in so doing to criticize Marx, English Leftists, and American New Dealers. Pound epitomizes Douglas's economic critique of finance capitalism by stating: "WORK is not a commodity. Money is not a commodity. The state HAS credit, and does not need to rent it from banks" (*Social Credit: An Impact*, 14). This allows Pound to draw a distinction between work and labor: work is what one person does, while labor is a mass phenomenon governed by market forces. (Pound complained to Agresti about the "utter idiocy of yelling more work. [sic] as [if] the ratio of needed work were unaltered by a century and more of mechanic invention" [*EP/ORA* 33]). Pound then turns immediately to quote Gesell: "'Marx found nothing to criticize in money,'—S. Gesell" (Pound's emphasis; *Social Credit: An Impact*, 15).[4] He continues: "Many vast and heavy books have ended in muddle from failure to see that property and capital are radically different. Property does not imply the enslavement of others. There is a difference between durable and perishable goods, in fact there are all degrees of durability, from that of the fresh-plucked fruit to that of the art works of Chaldea" (*Social Credit: An Impact*, 15). The heavy books certainly include the three volumes of Marx's *Capital*, where, indeed, Marx has little to say about money. Following the classical economists Adam Smith and David Ricardo, Marx subscribes to the labor theory of value, which is measured by money. Evidently, once the true nature of money is understood, via thin pamphlets like Pound's, economics can be rendered in pithy maxims, not pages of recondite algebra or difficult economic theory.

Pound rejected the labor theory of value but believed in the value of work. Gesell's innovative "*Schwundgeld*" or "stamp scrip," based on "work done" ("*Arbeitswert*"), offered a way to monetize work without first creating debts. A kind of "work money," stamp scrip can be issued whenever and wherever work needs to be done; it never needs to be borrowed, thus putting banks out of the picture. Such scrip has emerged periodically with success in many places where a shortage of circulating currency has brought economic exchange and necessary public works projects to a halt for lack of cash.

A peculiarity of *Schwundgeld* or "shrinking money" is its virtue of losing value over time. It is purely a medium of exchange, never a long-term store of value. Gesell envisioned money the value of which would decay at a fixed rate like most of the commodities for which it was exchanged; hoarded, it should rot like so many uneaten potatoes. Pound suggested a very reasonable term of 100 months—more than eight years—until the money should be valueless; held for four years, the money would lose about half its worth (*SP* 300). Such money demands to be kept in circulation, since there is no point in hoarding it or letting banks speculate with it by alternately hoarding then investing in other sectors, often overseas. If not spent, *Schwundgeld* loses value at a fixed rate of a certain percentage per month: it "oxidizes." Gesell recommended stamps to indicate the lowered value of his money, an awkward, fiddly feature. But as David Harvey points out, with the electronic money in use today, such a regulated degradation of value could easily be managed without fuss (Harvey 2014: 35).

Pound regarded *Schwundgeld* as a temporary expedient, a "half-way house" (*Social Credit: An Impact*, 14, 20) on the way to a full Douglasite reform of the money system. But he saw it could be used to manage another result of a Social Credit economy. If the state can lend, in theory it should also pay dividends to its citizens. Stamp scrip would be a perfect medium for these dividends, which would circulate rapidly, offering a sudden stimulus to any economy.

The "infamy" of taxation is a constant in Pound's economic agitation. "Mang Tsze," his essay on Mencius, pushes for a tithing, not a taxation system. If there must be taxes, let them be taken as a small portion of what is produced, a tithe. Fixed taxes, levied without regard to production, meant ruin for producers unable for one reason or another to sell their products. "'Nothing is worse than a fixed tax,'" Pound quotes Mencius: "'fixed tax on grain in bad years a tyranny, a tithe proper, no tyranny'" (*SP* 103; 87/594). Mencius is a potent economic influence on Pound—certainly as much as Douglas or Gesell—and a constant touchstone for economic sanity and good public policy.

Pound's syncretic economic philosophy melding Douglas and Gesell, leavened with his physiocratic bias towards agrarian societies, matured in the 1930s as "Volitionist Economics." The following were its key premises:

1. All wealth is ultimately rooted in the generosity of nature.
2. The "cultural heritage" includes all the arts—the poet is as much a producer as a farmer or a machinist.
3. All history is the class struggle between a mass of debtors and a few creditors.
4. The resolution of that struggle is the understanding that:
    a) money is not a commodity; it is a means of exchange.
    b) labor is not a commodity; it is life itself.
5. Class collaboration directed by responsible individuals willing the national good by welcoming civic responsibility is the road to prosperity.

This last expresses the "volitionist" part of his program. One has to want the national good, not private profit.

Pound's title *Jefferson and/or Mussolini* neatly encapsulates Pound's political economy in the 1930s. Pound believed that Volitionist reforms steered by a genius at the top (Mussolini and/or Roosevelt) could reform capitalism and save Europe and America from financial and therefore political disaster—that is, a bankers' war against civilization. "Usurocracy makes wars in succession," he wrote in "Gold and Work" (1944); "It makes them according to a pre-established plan for the purposes of creating debts" (*SP* 338), because, under the perverse canons of value promoted by "demoliberal ideology" (*GK* 26) (the myth of the free market and "free trade," based on convertible gold), debt is equivalent to wealth. Pound foresaw that a second global war would be necessary to save the liberal economic system and wanted to forestall it. To do this it would be necessary to install "a sane economic system somewhere," anywhere, as a check on the big lie that liberal capitalism and democracy were compatible systems. Pound hoped that Fascism under the pragmatic direction of Mussolini might adopt his economic scheme and thereby take economic steps toward an ideal republic, an agrarian autarchy saturated with the wisdom of Confucius, where the classes collaborated on the social good and the economic program promoted productive labor and saw to it that goods were distributed justly.

Both in England and America the new party should be a MATERIAL PARTY with three parts to its platform:

> When enough exists, means should be found to distribute it to the people who need it.
>
> It is the business of the nation to see that its own citizens get their share, before worrying about the rest of the world.
>
> (If not, what is the sense of being "united" or organized as a state? What is the meaning of "citizen"?[)]
>
> When the potential production (the possible production) of anything is sufficient to meet everyone's needs, it is the business of the government to see that both production and distribution are achieved. (*SP* 234)

The distributive mechanism would be Gesell's "stamp-scrip." In this way, the state lends against its own credit and pays no interest to anyone. Taxes would be minimal and the state could, in principle, pay dividends to its citizens.

Pound's utopic dream was never realized; he thought Fascism "flopped" for lack of Confucian probity. Years later, incarcerated at St. Elizabeths, having translated virtually all of Confucius, Pound was still at work agitating for a sane economic system. The key was proper money. To issue money is to assert control over the value of things. This is the true nature of sovereignty. "Civilization," he had written in his essay on Mencius, "consists in the establishment of an hierarchy of values" (*SP* 90). Money, decommodified, its value established by law (not by markets), is one comprehensive way of measuring this hierarchy. Much in the Washington Cantos is concerned with establishing a proper scale of values, with ratio and "proportion" (90/625).

While reading Alexander Del Mar in the 1950s Pound came upon the "Nummulary theory" of value. "Value is not a thing," Del Mar reasons, "not an attribute of things; it is a relation, a numerical relation, which appears in exchange. Such a relation cannot be accurately measured without the use of numbers, limited by law and embodied in a set of concrete symbols, suitable for transference from hand to hand. It is this set of symbols which, by metonym, is called money" (Del Mar 1983: 7–8). In short, "Money is a Measure and must of necessity [be] an Institute of Law" (Del Mar 1983: 8). This theory of monetary value means that the ratio of value between coins within the same monetary system is legislated. If money is a measure, it can never be a commodity—any more than miles or kilograms can become commodities. As we've seen, this "Nummulary theory" brings the discourse of law and the discourse of money intimately together as a principle of cohesion in the Washington Cantos.

Notes

1. Pound's fugitive economic writings remain for the most part out of print. Fortunately, William Cookson's edition of Pound's *Selected Prose 1909–1965* contains a representative sampling of Pound's economic writing, including crucial essays like "Mang Tsze" (1938), on Mencius, which contains Pound's exposition of the "nine-field system" and his theory of taxation. *Selected Prose* samples pamphlets like "What Is Money For?" (1939), "Gold and Work" (*Oro e Lavoro*, 1944), and "The Economic Nature of the United States" (1944), as well as *ABC of Economics* (1933) and *Social Credit: An Impact* (1939). Roxana Preda's collection *Ezra Pound's Economic Correspondence 1933–1940* (2007) gathers many letters full of Pound's economic dicta also found throughout *The Cantos*.
2. Kitson referred to the *Protocols* in his book in a way that makes it clear that he saw them as prophetic of current banking: "Ample warnings of the debt-slavery which the use of gold as the basis for money inflicts have been sounded from many quarters of late years; but the most effective statement is contained in the 20th Protocols of the Learned Elders of Zion, as translated by the late Victor E. Marsden, formerly correspondent of the *Morning Post*" (Arthur Kitson, *The Bankers' Conspiracy! Which Started the World Crisis* ([London: Elliot Stock, 1933], 40).
3. David Harvey also discusses, quotes, and evaluates Gesell positively in *Seventeen Contradictions and the End of Capitalism* (2014: 35, 45).
4. This was not true, but nobody knew it until the belated release of Marx's 900-page *Grundrisse*, not published in full until 1951. English translations of Marx's German text would not be available until the 1970s. Gesell had written: "But theorists of interest have always, for the foregoing reasons, neglected to study money. Marx, for example, did not give the theory of money even five minutes as one can verify by reading his three large volumes on interest (capital). Proudhon underrated money less, and came nearest to solving the problem of interest …. Marx finds nothing to criticize in money" (Gesell, *The Natural Economic Order: A Plan to Secure an Uninterrupted Exchange of the Products of Labor, Free from Bureaucratic Interference, Usury and Exploitation*, translated from the 6th German edition by Philip Pye (San Antonio, TX: Free-Economic Pub. Co., 1929).

Appendix B
"Homage to Grandpa" by Sheri Martinelli

The Light Year, Autumn 1961

HOMAGE TO GRAMPA

"... a great stud."

excerpts from a letter
to the light year editor

by Sheri Martinelli

...
"the pressure at any point of
    (one moment .. I had to look it up ..
    Mr. Cummings teaches to quote ac-
    curately .. if one is quoting)
"The pressure at the pivotal point on which
any art changes or swings into direction is
tremendous .." ...

Ezra Pound has had TREMENDOUS PRES-
SURE put on him -- I didn't see anyone
else going into those old metal doors at
4:30 BUT him -- because the A R T changed
& the Goddess used Ezra as a pivotal point.

We live in a barbarous age - yes - but a
wonderous & exciting age for the Arts -
every day I scan our Newspapers I see evidence of the presence of Ezra Pound & what
he got born to teach us.

People no longer say: "you're ALL wet .."
they are now saying: "oh fairly .. wet .."

Thanks to dear Miles publishing Grampa's
letter - Reno said: "if you had no previous
experience with E. P. that letter would take
the enamel off your teeth .."

The Shape Changer -- and Miles will be part
of that circle of Dog Farts who smeared
Ezra. Do you WANT to spend eternity
with Dog Farts, Miles? What will happen
to your Love Reservation for we Indians?
Filled with Dog Farters like Wang?

I would very much like it if you would
acknowledge your error. Ezra Pound was

not AT St. Liz -- such talk is too fairy - fied
for Ezra - he was IN St. Liz & he was most
definately NOT a patient - he was there because of an international political situation
which has not yet been fully done with -- nor
likely to be for 2000 MORE years.

Wasn't Miles in NYC when it was the
VORTEX of the States & the town joke in
1948 ish was: "what will they do the next
time Jesus Christ comes?" and the answer
was .. "they'll declare him insane .."
            one is not saying that
Ezra IS Jesus Christ .. one is merely tie - ing
that joke up with the fact that Ezra had been
treated in the way the joke implied -- at about
the same time.

and who went for the oky - doke is you
Miles -

Ezra Pound is the ONLY man I'd ever met
-- in the full sense of being a man.
BomKoff at a different degree of it . is also
a man in the same way.

I'd like to record this fact ...
    that Ezra Pound .. agish 69 to 72 ish ..
could fuck better than any man
& that includes men of many colours ..
                    Ezra Pound is
the best fuck that ever got born & he has
the MOST adequate prick & he loveth a
woman's smell & he balls like a fierce - wild
eagle
and the ideas he flows through a woman's
mind whilst he flows through her body .. ah
that ..
    if you have ever seen the wild sea ..
how can water drops do more than awaken
a sweet ache in the spirit ..
Patient? don't be a 4 - sided square Miles -
Grampa ain't a fallen angel - he's a ballin'
angel ....

Charlie Parker reserved his rhythm for his

horn & kept his talk direct & to the point. Ezra did the same.

It is called   discipline

and I am a sorry example of the lack of it - but then . .

that is also why I got put into grampa's paradise . .

"for having such a good time" "Miz Kikz" said Arthur King --

one of the most basic differences between we all - alikes is WHAT we choose to LOVE -

Ezra Pound loved SANITY & ORDER - it

was a quaint mockery to "legally" declare him insane - it would take a most ancient soul to think of that one. I suppose one might in a high mind - state - beyond it all - say it is the precise back - wards of poetic justice - it is a terrible & awful joke because it is outrageously intelligent. Miles says he loves humanity & then with an almost invisible smear - adds to the pain & hurt of a good & benevolent man

and a great stud

and a Shape Changer - a Maker of Souls -

his gig

NO DAMAGE TO GRAMPA

"Isn't the light of E. P.,
burning for all it is worth,
secure from the dog fart dark? . . ."

Dear Sheri,

I'm happy to celebrate your love of Ezra Pound -- this love being one of the most attractive things about you, as I know you in your letters. And one of the great things about Pound, certainly, is his capacity to inspire such passionate reverence. Parts of your letter, and your fiery drawing opposite, will decorate the Light Year handsomely, perhaps even classically.

I have omitted most of your attack upon Wang and Rattray, these two Davids whom you smite in the unseemly guise of a Lady Goliath. Your natural woman's weeds become you a good deal more than the steel-breasted fustian for waging all - out literary war. I wish both of us might consecrate our energies to glorify what we love, and remember that time spent in the sickening exercise of execration is -- time spent. Whereas time taken in any healthy fulfillment of love is time divided into the sliced instant

of eternity. We now see what time is, do we not? Hatred, or the need to prevail in some way, any way, or all ways over some, any, or all other creatures, -- hatred is the thing that requires time, needs it to the damned degree of being it. In love, however, who has not discovered that not only is time consumed but obliterated?

And if your love for Ezra is ill - served by useless abuse of active detractors, then that love is sword - served when you skewer an innocent figure of speech, "poet and patient at St. Elizabeths", as arising from subtle, diabolical depths. Did you not read "in jail", "in stir", "imprisonment", "jailed on a fairy tale" -- all these sprinkled through the letters in description of Pound's impounding? At best, your railing seems impulsive fustian jesting ; at worst, compulsively unjust. Isn't the light of Ezra Pound, burning for all it is worth, secure from the dog fart dark, real or imagined? And is no heavenly body to be allowed existence except those reflecting and orbiting Grampa? Don't start another religion, Sheri. Too many men lately who change shapes as much or more than he: Miller, Eisenstein, Picasso, Stravinsky, Chaplin, Forster, D. Thomas, H. Crane, Balanchine, Owen. . . So let homage to your particular star not be demanding to the point of damage to Grampa. The heavens, even today, are bright with multitudes of stars whose light is not exclusive, but rather interlocking from begining to end, inclusive.   -- Miles

Figure B.1. Sheri Martinelli's "Homage to Grandpa" and letter to editor Miles Payne as printed with Payne's reply in *Light Year*, Autumn 1961. With thanks to Steven Moore.

Bibliography

Adams, Hazard. *Critical Theory Since Plato*. San Diego, CA: Harcourt, Brace Jovanovich, 1971.
Adams, Henry. *John Randolph* (1882, 1888). Boston, MA: Houghton Mifflin, 1888.
Adams, John, and Abigail Adams. *Book of Abigail and John*. Cambridge, MA: Harvard University Press, 1976.
Agassiz, Louis. *Gists of Agassiz*. Edited by John Kasper. Washington, DC: Square $ Books, 1953.
Bacigalupo, Massimo. *The Forméd Trace: The Later Poetry of Ezra Pound*. New York: Columbia University Press, 1980.
Baller, F. W. *The Sacred Edict of K'Ang Hsi* (Shanghai 1924). Facsimile. Orono, ME: National Poetry Foundation, 1979.
Barnhisel, Gregory. *James Laughlin, New Directions, and the Remaking of Ezra Pound*. Amherst: University of Massachusetts Press, 2005.
Beard, Charles, and Mary Beard. *Rise of American Civilization*. New York: Macmillan, 1930.
Beer, Max. *In Inquiry into Physiocracy*. London: Allen and Unwin, 1939.
Bernal, Martin. *Black Athena: The Afroasiatic Origins of Classical Civilization*. 3 vols. New Brunswick, NJ. Rutgers University Press, 1986–2006.
Bendersky, Joseph W. *"The Jewish Threat": Anti-Semitic Politics of the U.S. Army*. New York: Basic Books, 2000.
Bilbo, Theodore G. *Take Your Choice: Separation or Mongrelization*. Poplarville, MS: Dreamhouse Press, 1947.
Blevins, Jeffrey. "Pound Sign." *English Literary History* 81(4) (2014): 1327–61.
Bordewich, Fergus M. *America's Great Debate: Henry Clay, Stephen A. Douglas, and the Compromise that Preserved the Union*. New York: Simon & Schuster, 2012.
Bowen, Catherine Drinker. *John Adams and the American Revolution*. Boston, MA: Atlantic Monthly Press, 1950.
Bowen, Catherine Drinker. *The Lion and the Throne: The Life and Times of Sir Edward Coke 1552–1634*. Boston, MA: Little, Brown, 1957.
Bridson, Douglas G. "Interview with Ezra Pound." *New Directions* 17 (1961): 159–84.
Broyard, Anatole. *When Kafka Was the Rage*. New York: Vintage, 1993.
Bruce, William Cabell. *John Randolph, 1773–1833*. New York: Putnam, 1922.
Budge, E. A. Wallis. *The Egyptian Book of the Dead* (1895). New York: Dover, 1967.
Budge, E. A. Wallis. *Egyptian Religion* (1900). New York: Gramercy Press, 1968.
Carpenter, Humphrey. *A Serious Character: The Life of Ezra Pound*. Boston, MA: Houghton Mifflin, 1988.

Casillo, Robert. "Pound, L. A. Waddell and the Aryan Tradition of *The Cantos*." *Modern Language Studies* 15(2) (Spring 1985): 65–81.

Casillo, Robert. *A Genealogy of Demons: Anti-Semitism, Fascism and the Myths of Ezra Pound*. Evanston, IL: Northwestern University Press, 1988.

Chang, Carsun (Zhang, Junmai). *The Development of Neo-Confucianism Thought*. Vol. 1. New York: Bookman, 1957.

Cheadle, Mary Patterson. *Ezra Pound's Confucian Translations*. Ann Arbor: University of Michigan Press, 1997.

Chernow, Ron. *Alexander Hamilton*. New York: Penguin, 2005.

Conover, Anne. *Olga Rudge & Ezra Pound: "What Thou Lovest Well ...."* New Haven, CT: Yale University Press, 2001.

Coke, Edward. *Coke on Magna Charta*: Selections from Coke's *Second Institutes*. Hawthorne, CA: Omni Christian Book Club, 1974.

Cookson, William. *A Guide to the Cantos of Ezra Pound*. Revised ed. New York, Persea, 2001.

Cornell, Julien. *The Trial of Ezra Pound*. New York: John Day, 1966.

Coyle, Michael, and Preda, Roxana. *Ezra Pound and the Career of Modern Criticism*. Rochester, NY: Camden House, 2018.

Curtis, George Ticknor. *Life of James Buchanan*. 2 vols. New York: Harper Bros, 1883.

Dante. *Paradiso*. Translated by Robin Kirkpatrick. New York: Penguin, 2007.

De Benoist, Alain. *Aus rechter Sicht: Eine kritische Anthologie zeitgenössener Ideen*. 2 vols. Translated by Patrick de Trevillert. Tübingen: Grabert, 1983 and 1984.

Del Mar, Alexander. *The History of Monetary Systems* (1896). Orono, ME: National Poetry Foundation, 1983.

Domvile, Barry. *From Admiral to Cabin Boy*. London: Boswell Publishing, 1947.

Doob, Leonard W., ed. *"Ezra Pound Speaking": Radio Speeches of World War II*. Westport, CT: Greenwood Press, 1978.

Doolittle, Hilda (H.D.). *End to Torment*. New York: New Directions, 1979.

Doolittle, Hilda (H.D.). *Trilogy*. Edited by Aliki Barnstone. New York: New Directions, 1998.

Douglas, C. H. *Social Credit* (1924). Vancouver, BC: Institute for Economic Democracy, 1979.

Dowthwaite, James. "Revised Intentions: James Buchanan and the Antebellum White House in Canto CIII." *Glossator* 10 (2018): 215–30.

Dudek, Louis. *Dk/Some Letters of Ezra Pound*. Montreal, QC: DC Books, 1974.

Etcheson, Nicole. *Bleeding Kansas: Contested Liberty in the Civil War Era*. Lawrence: University Press of Kansas, 2004.

Fagles, Robert, trans. *Sophocles: The Three Theban Plays*. New York: Penguin, 1984.

Farley, David. "Damn the Partition! Ezra Pound and the Passport Nuisance." *Paideuma* 30(3) (2001): 79–90.

Fenollosa, Ernest. *The Chinese Written Character as a Medium for Poetry*. Edited by Ezra Pound. San Francisco, CA: City Lights, n.d.

Finkelman, Paul. "Complete Anti-Federalist" (a review). *Cornell Law Review* 70(1) (1984): 182–207.

Flory, Wendy Stallard. *Ezra Pound and* The Cantos: *A Record of Struggle*. New Haven, CT: Yale University Press, 1980.

Flory, Wendy Stallard. *The American Ezra Pound*. New Haven, CT: Yale University Press, 1987.

Fox-Genovese, Elizabeth. *The Origins of Physiocracy*. Ithaca, NY: Cornell University Press, 1976.

Frobenius, Leo. "Early African Culture as an Indication of Present Negro Potentialities." *Annals of the American Academy of Political and Social Science* Vol. 140, "The American Negro." (November 1928): 153–65.

Frobenius, Leo. *Leo Frobenius on African History, Art, and Culture: An Anthology*. Edited by Eike Haberland. Princeton, NJ: Markus Wiener, 2014

Gallup, Donald. *Ezra Pound: A Bibliography*. Charlottesville: University Press of Virginia, 1983.

Gay, Peter. *The Enlightenment: An Interpretation: Vol. II. The Science of Freedom*. New York: Norton, 1977.

Gill, Jonathan. "Ezra Pound and Langston Hughes: The ABC of Po'try." In *Ezra Pound and African American Modernism*, edited by Michael Coyle, pp. 79–109. Orono, ME: National Poetry Foundation, 2001.

Goldhill, Simon. *Reading Greek Tragedy*. Cambridge: Cambridge University Press, 1986.

Griffis, William Elliot. *Millard Fillmore: Constructive Statesman, Defender of the Constitution, President of the United States*. Ithaca, NY: Andrus & Church, 1915.

Grogan, Kristin. "Three Ways of Looking at a Canto: Navigating Canto CVIII." *Glossator* 10 (2018): 329–53.

Hall, Donald. *Their Ancient Glittering Eyes: Remembering Poets*. New York: Ticknor & Fields, 1992.

Harvey, David. *Seventeen Contradictions and the End of Capitalism*. Oxford: Oxford University Press, 2014.

Hegel, G. W. F. *Science of Logic*. Cambridge: Clarendon Press, 1975.

Heidegger, Martin. *Poetry, Language, Thought*. Translated by Albert Hofstadter. New York: Harper Colophon, 1975.

Heidegger, Martin. *Introduction to Metaphysics*. Translated by Gregory Fried and Richard Polt. New Haven, CT: Yale University Press, 2000.

Henderson, Archie. *"I Cease Not to Yowl" Reannotated: New Notes on the Pound/Agresti Correspondence*. 3rd ed. Houston, TX: CreateSpace, 2010.

Hesse, Eva, ed. *New Approaches to Ezra Pound*. London: Faber & Faber, 1969.

Heymann, C. David. *Ezra Pound, The Last Rower: A Political Profile*. New York: Viking, 1980.

Hickman, Miranda. "'The Clearest Mind Ever in England': Pound's Late Paradisal in Canto CVII." *Glossator* 10 (2018): 309–28.

Higgs, Henry. *The Physiocrats* (1897). New York: Augustus M. Kelley Publishers, 1968.

Hitler, Adolf. *Mein Kampf* (1924). Translated by Ralph Mannheim. Boston, MA: Houghton Mifflin, Mariner, 1999.

Hollis, Christopher. *The Two Nations: A Financial Study of English History* (1935). New York: Gordon Press, 1975.

Holman, Hamilton. *Prologue to Conflict: The Crisis and Compromise of 1850* (1963). Lexington: University Press of Kentucky, 2015.

Holmes, Sarah C. ed. *The correspondence of Ezra Pound and Senator William Borah*, Urbana and Chicago. Illinois UP. 2001.

Homberger, Eric, ed. *Ezra Pound: The Critical Heritage*. London: Routledge Kegan Paul, 1972.

Houen, Alex. *Terrorism and Modern Literature*. Oxford: Oxford University Press, 2002.

Howard, Alexander, ed. *Astern in the Dinghy: Commentaries on Ezra Pound's* Thrones de los cantares XCVI–CIX. *Glossator* 10 (2018).

Jefferson, Thomas. *Writings*. New York: Library of America, 1984.

Kasper, John. *Gists of Agassiz*. Washington, DC: Square $ Books, 1953.

Kasper, John. "Segregation or Death." *Virginia Spectator*. "Segregation Issue." 1957a.

Kasper, John. "Statement of Defendant Nov. 16, 1957 [sic]." 1957b.

Kearns, George. *Guide to Ezra Pound's* Selected Cantos. New Brunswick, NJ: Rutgers University Press, 1980.

Kearns, George. *Ezra Pound: The Cantos*. Cambridge: Cambridge University Press, 1989.

Kenner, Hugh. "Under the Larches of Paradise" (review of *Rock-Drill*). *Hudson Review* 9(3) (Autumn 1956): 457–65.

Kenner, Hugh. *The Pound Era*. Berkeley: University of California Press, 1971.

Kerouac, Jack. *Jack Kerouac: Selected Letters 1957–1969*. Edited by Ann Charters. New York: Penguin, 2000.

Kimpel, Ben, and T. C. Duncan Eaves. "American History in *Rock-Drill* and *Thrones*." *Paideuma* IX(3) (Winter 1980): 417–39.

Kindellan, Michael. *The Late Cantos of Ezra Pound: Composition, Revision, Publication*. London: Bloomsbury, 2017.

Kindellan, Michael. "'Tinkle, Tinkle, Two Tongues': Sound, Sign, Canto XCIX." *Glossator* 10 (2018): 83–120.

Kuczynski, Marguerite, and Ronald L. Meek. *Quesnay's Tableau économique*. Basingstoke: Palgrave Macmillan, 1972.

Lan, Feng. *Ezra Pound and Confucianism: Remaking Humanism in the Face of Modernity*. Toronto, ON: University of Toronto Press, 2005.

Leary, Lewis, ed. *Motive and Method in* The Cantos *of Ezra Pound*. New York: Columbia University Press, 1961.

Lefkowitz Mary R., and Guy MacLean Rogers, eds. *Black Athena Revisited*. Chapel Hill: University of North Carolina Press, 1996.

Lenin, Vladimir I. *Imperialism: The Highest Stage of Capitalism* (1917). New York: International Pub, 1939.

Lewis, George. *Massive Resistance: The White Response to the Civil Rights Movement.* London: Hodder Arnold, 2006.
Liebregts, Peter. *Ezra Pound and Neoplatonism.* Madison, WI: Fairleigh Dickinson University Press, 2004.
Lowell, Robert. *History.* New York: Noonday, 1975.
Lowell, Robert. *The Oresteia of Aeschylus.* New York: Noonday, 1978.
Lowell, Robert. *The Letters of Robert Lowell.* Edited by Saskia Hamilton. New York: Farrar Straus Giroux, 2005.
Lyon, Hastings, and Herman Block. *Edward Coke: Oracle of the Law.* Boston: Houghton & Mifflin, 1929.
Makin, Peter, ed. *Provence and Pound.* Berkeley: University of California Press, 1978.
Makin, Peter, ed. *Pound's Cantos.* Baltimore, MD: Johns Hopkins University Press, 1985.
Makin, Peter. "Ideogram, 'Right-Naming,' and the Authoritarian Streak." In *Ezra Pound and China*, edited by Zhaoming Qian, pp. 120–42. Ann Arbor: University of Michigan Press, 2003.
Makin, Peter, ed. *Ezra Pound's* Cantos: *A Casebook.* Oxford: Oxford University Press, 2007.
Malm, Mike. *Editing Economic History: Ezra Pound's The Fifth Decad of Cantos.* Frankfurt am Main: Peter Lang, 2003.
Marsh, Alec. *Money & Modernity: Pound, Williams and the Spirit of Jefferson.* Tuscaloosa: University of Alabama Press, 1998.
Marsh, Alec. "John Quincy Adams and/or Martin Van Buren: Canto 34 and 37." *Paideuma* 34(1) (Spring 2005): 59–88.
Marsh, Alec. *Ezra Pound: A Critical Life.* London: Reaktion, 2011.
Marsh, Alec. *John Kasper and Ezra Pound: Saving the Republic.* London: Bloomsbury, 2015.
Martin, Waldo E., Jr., ed. *Brown v. Board of Education: A Brief History with Documents.* Boston, MA: Bedford/St. Martins, 1998.
Martinelli, Sheri. Beinecke YCAL MSS 868, Box 12, several folders "Pound, Ezra."
Martinelli, Sheri. Correspondence with Ezra Pound. Beinecke YCAL MSS 43 1954, Box 33, folders 1389–1393.
Martinelli, Sheri. Correspondence with Ezra Pound. Beinecke YCAL MSS 53, Box 12, folder 277 "1962–1963."
Materer, Timothy. *Modernist Alchemy: Poetry and the Occult.* Ithaca, NY: Cornell University Press, 1995.
Maverick, Lewis. *China: A Model for Europe.* San Antonio, TX: Paul Anderson Co., 1946.
Maverick, Lewis. *Economic Dialogues in Ancient China: Selections from the Kuan Tzu.* No publisher listed, 1954.
McCullough, David. *John Adams.* New York: Simon & Schuster, 2001.
Meacham, Harry M. *The Caged Panther: Ezra Pound at St. Elizabeths.* New York: Twayne, 1967.
Mead, G. R. S. *Simon Magus.* London: Theosophical Publishing Society, 1892.

Mead, G. R. S. *Apollonius of Tyana*. London and Benares. Theosophical Publishing Society, 1901.
Meek, Ronald L. *The Economics of Physiocracy*. Cambridge, MA: Harvard University Press, 1963.
Menand, Louis. *The Metaphysical Club*. New York: Farrar, Strauss & Giroux, 2002.
Meyers, Jeffrey. "Robert Lowell and the Classics." *Kenyon Review* 33(4) (2011): 173–200.
Moody, A. David. *Ezra Pound: Poet. Vol. III: The Tragic Years 1939–1972*. Oxford: Oxford University Press, 2015.
Moody, A. David, and Joanna Moody, eds. *Ezra Pound to His Parents: Letters 1895–1929*. Oxford: Oxford University Press, 2010.
Moore, Stephen. *Beerspit Night and Cursing: The Correspondence of Charles Bukowski and Sheri Martinelli 1960–1967*. Santa Rosa, CA: Black Sparrow, 2001.
Moore, Stephen. "Sheri Martinelli: A Modernist Muse." *Gargoyle Magazine* 41 (1998) with "Homage to Grampa" (2005). stevenmoore.info/martinelli/index.shtml.
Mullins, Eustace. *This Difficult Individual, Ezra Pound*. New York: Fleet Publishing, 1961.
Murray, William H. *Adam and Cain*. Boston, MA: Meador, 1951.
Muse, Benjamin. *Ten Years of Prelude*. New York: Viking, 1964.
Muse, Benjamin. *Virginia's Massive Resistance*. Gloucester: Peter Smith, 1969.
Nadel, Ira, ed. *The Cambridge Companion to Ezra Pound*. Cambridge: Cambridge University Press, 1999.
Nicholls, Peter. "'Two doits to a boodle': Reckoning with *Thrones*." *Textual Practice* 18(2) (2004): 233–49.
Nicholls, Peter. "The elusive Allusion: Poetry and Exegesis." In *Teaching Modernist Poetry*, edited by Peter Middleton and Nicky Marsh, pp. 10–24. London: Palgrave Macmillan, 2010.
Nicholls, Peter. "Ezra Pound's Lost Book: *Orientamenti*" (draft). Personal communication, 2014.
Nicholls, Peter. "Late Pound: The Case of Canto CVII." *Journal of Philosophy: A Cross-Disciplinary Inquiry* 8(20) (Fall 2015): 1–16.
Nicholls, Peter. "Hilarious Commentary: Ezra Pound's Canto XCVIII" *Glossator* 10 (2018): 51–82.
Nichols, David A. *A Matter of Justice: Eisenhower and the Beginning of the Civil Rights Revolution*. New York: Simon & Schuster, 2011.
Nichols, Roy Franklin. *Franklin Pierce: Young Hickory of the Granite Hills*. Philadelphia: University of Pennsylvania Press, 1931.
Niven, Alex. "'To the King Onely to Put Value': Monarchy and Commons in Pound's Canto CIX." *Glossator* 10 (2018): 355–69.
Norman, Charles. *The Case of Ezra Pound*. New York: Funk & Wagnalls, 1968.
Paige, D. D., ed. *Selected Letters 1909–1941* (1950). London: Faber & Faber, 1982.
Parker, Richard. "Some contexts for Canto XCVI." *Glossator* 10 (2018): 1–26.

Pearson, Norman Holmes. Papers. Beinecke YCAL MSS 899, Box 78, folder "Pound, Ezra 1957."

Pestell, Alex. "'In the Intellect Possible': Revisionism and Aesopian Language in Canto C." *Glossator* 10 (2018): 121–61.

Philostratus, Flavius. *The Life of Apollonius of Tyana*. Translated by F. C. Coneybeare. London: Macmillan, 1912. Reprint. Desmondous, 2013.

Pound, Ezra. "Academia Bulletin Zweck." Beinecke YCAL MSS 43, Box 66, folder 2838.

Pound, Ezra. Correspondence with Catherine Drinker Bowen. Beinecke YCAL MSS 43, Box 5, folder 231.

Pound, Ezra. Correspondence with David Gordon. Beinecke YCAL MSS 43, Box 19, folder 854.

Pound, Ezra. Correspondence with T. David Horton. Beinecke YCAL MSS 43, Box 23, folder 1002.

Pound, Ezra. Correspondence with John Kasper. Beinecke YCAL MSS 43, Box 26, folders 1124–1134.

Pound, Ezra. Correspondence with Sheri Martinelli. Beinecke YCAL MSS 43, Box 33, folders 1389–1393.

Pound, Ezra. Correspondence with Norman Holmes Pearson. Beinecke YCAL MSS 899, Section V, Personal Papers.

Pound, Ezra. Correspondence with Henry Regnery. Beinecke YCAL MSS 43, Box 44, folder 1862.

Pound, Ezra. Correspondence with Ralph Reid. Beinecke YCAL MSS 43, Box 44, folder 1874.

Pound, Ezra. Correspondence with Jack Stafford. Beinecke YCAL MSS 43, Box 49, folder 2190.

Pound, Ezra. Correspondence with David Wang. Beinecke. YCAL MSS 43, Box 54, folder 2485.

Pound, Ezra. Family Correspondence. Beinecke YCAL MSS 43, Box 59, folders 2652–2265.

Pound, Ezra. Poetry Notebooks Canto 88 et seq. Beinecke YCAL. MSS 43, Box 120 (August 25–September 6, 1954).

Pound, Ezra, ed. "*Virginians On Guard!*" Seaboard White Citizens' Council. No press. 1956.

Pound, Ezra. *Women of Trachis*. New York: New Directions, 1957.

Pound, Ezra. *Pavannes & Divagations*. New York: New Directions, 1958.

Pound, Ezra. *The Confucian Odes* (1954). New York: New Directions, 1959.

Pound, Ezra. *ABC of Reading* (1934). New York: New Directions, 1960a.

Pound, Ezra. *Impact: Essays on Ignorance and the Decline of American Civilization*. Edited by Noel Stock. Chicago, IL: Henry Regnery, 1960b.

Pound, Ezra. *Translations*. New York: New Directions, 1963.

Pound, Ezra. *Selected Cantos*. New York: New Directions, 1968a.

Pound, Ezra. *The Spirit of Romance*. New York: New Directions, 1968b.

Pound, Ezra. *Literary Essays*. New York: New Directions, 1968c.
Pound, Ezra. *Confucius*. New York: New Directions, 1969.
Pound, Ezra. *Guide to Kulchur* (1938). New York: New Directions, 1970a.
Pound, Ezra. *Jefferson and/or Mussolini* (1935). New York: Liveright, 1970b.
Pound, Ezra. *Selected Prose 1909–1965*. Edited by William Cookson. London: Faber & Faber, 1973.
Pound, Ezra. *Ezra Pound and the Visual Arts*. Edited by Harriet Zinnes. New York: New Directions, 1980.
Pound, Ezra. *Ezra Pound/Letters/John Theobald*. Edited by Donald Pearce and Herbert Schneidau. Redding Ridge, CT: Black Swan, 1984.
Pound, Ezra. *Pound/Lewis: The Letters of Ezra Pound and Wyndham Lewis*. Edited by Timothy Materer. New York: New Directions, 1985.
Pound, Ezra. *Personae: The Shorter Poems of Ezra Pound*. Revised ed., prepared and edited by Lea Baechler and A. Walton Litz. New York: New Directions, 1990.
Pound, Ezra. *Ezra Pound and James Laughlin: Selected Letters*. Edited by David Gordon. New York: W. W. Norton, 1994.
Pound, Ezra. *Pound/Williams: Selected letters of Ezra Pound and William Carlos Williams*. Edited by Hugh Witemeyer. New York: New Directions, 1996a.
Pound, Ezra. *The Cantos*. 6th paperbound printing. New York: New Directions, 1996b.
Pound, Ezra. *Ezra and Dorothy Pound: Letters in Captivity 1945–46*. Edited by Omar Pound and Robert Spoo. New York: Oxford University Press, 1999.
Pound, Ezra. *Ezra Pound's Economic Correspondence*, 1933–1940. Edited by Roxana Preda. Gainesville: University of Florida Press, 2007.
Pound, Ezra, and Marcella Spann. *Confucius to Cummings*. New York: New Directions, 1964.
Pound, Ezra, and Rudd Fleming. *Elektra*. Princeton, NJ: Princeton University Press, 1989.
Preda, Roxana, ed. *Ezra Pound's Economic Correspondence*. Tallahassee: University Press of Florida, 2007.
Preda, Roxana, ed. "Gold and/or Humaneness: Pound's Vision of Civilization in Canto XCVII." *Glossator* 10 (2018): 27–49.
Qian, Zhaoming, ed. *Ezra Pound's Chinese Friends*. Oxford: Oxford University Press, 2008.
de Rachewiltz, Mary. *Discretions*. New York: New Directions, 1975.
Rainey, Lawrence. *A Poem Containing History: Textual Studies in The Cantos*. Ann Arbor: University of Michigan Press, 1997.
Reck, Michael. *Ezra Pound: A Close-Up*. New York: McGraw Hill, 1967.
Redman, Tim. *Ezra Pound and Italian Fascism*. Cambridge: Cambridge University Press, 1991.
Said, Edward W. *On Late Style: Music and Literature Against the Grain*. New York: Vintage, 2006.

Sawyer, Lemuel. *A Biography of John Randolph of Roanoke, with a Selection of his Speeches.* 1844.
Scott, Peter Dale. "Anger in Paradise: The Poetic Voicing of Disorder in Pound's Later Cantos." *Paideuma* 19(3) (1990): 47–63.
Seagle, William. *Men of Law: From Hammurabi to Holmes.* New York: Macmillan, 1947.
Sieburth, Richard, ed. *The Pisan Cantos.* By Ezra Pound. New York: New Directions, 2003.
Spoo, Robert. "Law." In *Ezra Pound in Context.* Cambridge: Cambridge University Press. 2010.
Stafford, Jack. "Ezra Pound and Segregation." *London Magazine* n.s. (9) (1969): 60–72.
Stock, Noel. "Ezra Pound in Melbourne 1953–57." *Helix* 13/14 (1983): 159–78.
Stock, Noel. *Poet in Exile: Ezra Pound.* New York: Barnes & Noble, 1964.
Stock, Noel. *Reading The Cantos.* New York: Pantheon, 1966.
Stock, Noel. *The Life of Ezra Pound.* New York: Pantheon, 1970.
Sunic, Tomislav. *Against Democracy and Equality: The European New Right.* Budapest: Arktos Media, 2011.
Taylor, Richard. "Sheri Martinelli: Muse to Ezra Pound." *Agenda* 38(1–2) (2001): 98–112.
Ten Eyck, David. *Ezra Pound's Adams Cantos.* London: Bloomsbury, 2012.
Terrell, Carroll F. *A Companion to the Cantos of Ezra Pound. Vol. I.* Berkeley: University of California Press, 1980.
Terrell, Carroll F. *A Companion to the Cantos of Ezra Pound. Vol. II.* Berkeley: University of California Press, 1984.
Thoreau, Henry David. *Walden, Civil Disobedience and Other Writings.* Edited by William Rossi. Norton Critical Edition. New York: W. W. Norton, 2008.
Torrey, E. Fuller. *The Roots of Treason: Ezra Pound and the Secret of St. Elizabeths.* New York: Harcourt Brace Jovanovich, 1984.
Tryphonopoulos, Demetres P., and Stephen J. Adams. *The Ezra Pound Encyclopedia.* Westport, CT: Greenwood, 2005.
Tryphonopoulos, Demetres P., and Leon Surette, eds. *"I Cease Not to Yowl": Ezra Pound's Letters to Olivia Rossetti Agresti.* Urbana and Chicago, IL: University of Illinois Press, 1998.
Tytell, John. *Ezra Pound: The Solitary Volcano.* New York: Anchor Press, 1987.
Van Buren, Martin. *The Autobiography of Martin Van Buren* (1920). New York: Chelsea House, 1983.
Viereck, Peter. *Metapolitics: From Wagner and the German Romantics to Hitler* (1941 rev.). New Brunswick, NJ: Transaction, 2004.
Waddell, L. A. *The Indo-Sumarian Seals Deciphered* (1925). Hawthorne, CA: Omni, 1980.
Waddell, L. A. *The Aryan Origins of the Alphabet* (1927). Reprint. Bloomfield, NJ: Read Books, 2011a.

Waddell, L. A. *Egyptian Civilization, Its Sumerian Origin and Real Chronology* (1930). Reprint. Bloomfield, NJ: Read Books, 2011b.
Waddell, L. A. *Makers of Civilization in Race and History* (1929). Reprint. Bloomfield, NJ: Read Books. 2013.
Williams, William Carlos. *Paterson*. New York: New Directions, 1963.
Wilhelm, James J. *The Later Cantos of Ezra Pound*. New York: Walker, 1977.
Yeats, W. B. *The Collected Plays of W. B. Yeats*. New York: Macmillan, 1952.
Yeats, W. B. *A Vision*. New York: Collier, 1966.
Zaibert, Leo. "Towards Meta-Politics."*Quarterly Journal of Austrian Economics* 7(4) (2004): 113–28.

Index

Chinese Characters and Phrases

一 [I¹] 153
一人 ["one man"] 153. See also "i jênn iuên"
一人元 ["i jênn iuên"] ["Let the one man be greatly good"] 159
義 [I⁴] [one of the four tuan] 12, 13, 18, 30, 31, 81
元 [yuán or yian² or iuên] 159
康 [K'ang¹] 42, 104
新 [hsin¹] 162, 175
親 [ch'in¹] 162
人 [jen²] 153
仁 [jen²] [one of the four tuan] 12, 13, 18, 30, 31, 81
仁 義 禮 智 [jen, I, li, chih] [the four tuan] 12, 13, 18, 30, 31, 81
旦 [tan⁴] 162
智 [chih⁴] [one of the four tuan] 12, 13, 18, 30, 31, 81
本 [pen³] 151, 156
禮 [li³] [one of the four tuan] 12, 13, 18, 30, 31, 81
靈 [ling²] 18, 20, 41, 103, 124
熙 [Hsi¹] 42, 104

Abbott, Beatrice 186
Abd-el-Malik 166, 168
Abel 19, 95, 96, 99, 109. *See also* Bible
"absolute politics" 18, 30
Abydos 102, 103, 106, 150, 172
Abyssinia 88, 89, 92, 93; Abyssinian 93
Academia Bulletin 76
Acheson, Dean 75
Achilles 30, 42, 50, 152
Adam 99. *See also* Bible
Adam and Cain (Murray) 78, 91, 92, 96–8, 107, 111
Adams, Abigail 208
Adams, Brooks 165, 167
Adams, Charles Francis 208
Adams, Henry 55
Adams, John 22, 193, 194, 198, 201, 202, 203, 204, 208, 209, 211, 212, 213
Adams, John Quincy 56, 71, 73, 208
Adams, Stephen J. 17, 166
Adams family 202
Adorno, Theodor W. 46
Aeschylus 216, 218
Aesopian language, and states' rights 51–76; in Canto 88's Aesopian parable of Randolph vs Clay to express opposing concepts of money 56; designed to mislead prison censors looking for evidence of Pound's basic sanity and treasonous intent 36; for family and friends in *The Cantos* 54; Lenin on 25, 37, 52–3; in the naming of Kasper's WHIB party 184; in Randolph standing in for contemporary states' rights agitators, including Pound himself 53, 54; shrouding Pound's racial metapolitics in the Sheri Cantos 138; using Belgian neutrality (1831) in Canto 103 to object to a 1955 treaty leading to Austrian neutrality 70. *See also* coded language
Africa, as the origin of economics 156; distinguished from Egypt by Eurocentrists 106, 107; seat of civilization 110; slavery in 88, 89; source of cult of Osiris 104; two different cultural styles ("Hamitic" and "Ethiopian") per Frobenius 84
African Americans, Bilbo's plan for the "voluntary" resettlement of 111; politicized by Jewish agitation 83
Africans, as agricultural and ethical 77, 87; as incapable of civilization 106; as more sensible than the Greeks 155
Afrocentricity 106, 139

Against Democracy and Equality (Sunic) 21
Agassiz, Louis 2, 77, 89, 90, 159, 167, 168
Agdu 103
Agrari 177
agrarian ideology in *The Cantos* 96, 169, 177–91
Agresti, Olivia Rossetti 4, 5, 29, 30, 40, 50, 78, 89, 90, 95–9, 136, 149, 151, 153, 154, 157, 159, 167, 169, 176, 177, 179, 182, 187
Agricoltura e civiltà (Del Pelo Pardi) 189
agriculture, African genius for 86, 87, 92; association with equity 156; as the basis of the state 188; as the core of economic autarky 186; direct connection with a philosophically superior culture 189; Jewish separation of divinity from, 96; as man's only real wealth 189; as the source of ethics 221; as the supreme occupation, 182
Agriculture for Beginners (Burkett, Hill, & Stevens) 97
Akkad 106
Akkadians 99
Aladdin's Lamp (Munson) 175
Alaska Mental Health Enabling Bill 198, 210
Alexander of Aphrodisias 126
Alexander the Great 53
Amaral, José 134
Amasis 154
Amassi 184
Amenhotep III 159
America First 28
The American Farmer (Crèvecœur) 180
American Nazi Party 76
American Revolution 55, 179, 193, 202, 203, 211
American Social Credit Movement 162, 163
Among the Himalayas (Waddell) 29
Amphion 11
anagogical poetics 124–5
anagogy 9–32; definition of 16
Analects 68, 179, 190
Anatolia 158
Anchises 132
Ancient Britain: In Light of Modern Discoveries (Del Mar) 98
Ancient Britain Revisited (Del Mar) 109
ancient history, Aryan model of 104–6

Ancient History of Western Asia, India and Crete (Hrozny) 91
Ancient Law (Maine) 211
Andros, Edward 201
Anglo-Israelism 109
Ani 103
animal sacrifice 96, 109, 152
Anselm 40, 41, 150
Antef 103, 104
anti-bank 55, 68
anti-black 146, 156
anti-Communism, of the American Right of the 1950s 3
Anti-Defamation League (ADL) 89, 90
anti-federalism 53, 55, 74
anti-fluoridation 186. *See also* water fluoridation
Antigone 219, 222
Antigone (Cocteau) 227
anti-philology 40, 42, 57
anti-Reconstruction 55
anti-Semitism, as constitutive of Pound's paradise 173; of Ezra Pound 24, 80, 81, 91, 101, 146, 173, 174; of Eustace Mullins, 3l; of L. A. Waddell 78, 81, 97; of William H. "Alfalfa Bill" Murray 97
anti-usury 19, 166
Antony 107, 108
Antony and Cleopatra (Shakespeare) 78, 107, 108
Aoka 173
Aphrodite 117, 132, 197
Apollo 158, 221
Apollonius 12, 13, 19, 34, 40, 44, 46, 96, 110, 123, 128, 149–59, 174
Apollonius of Tyana (Mead) 110, 152, 153, 158
Aquinas, Thomas 11, 28
Ara 79, 104
Arbeitswert 167
Aristotle 41
Arlington, Virginia, School Board 70
Arnaut Daniel 45, 123, 127
Artamen 185
Artemis 39, 129, 130
Arya 17, 30, 152
Aryan model of ancient history 104–6
The Aryan Origins of the Alphabet (Waddell) 100, 110

Aryanism, of Agassiz 24; of Adolf Hitler 24, 80, 85, 92, 141; of Bedrich Hrozny 91; of John H. Harvey 91, 102, 105; of John Kasper 141; of L. A. Waddell 24, 40, 78, 79, 80, 81, 82, 91, 97, 99, 100, 101, 102, 103, 104, 105, 106, 108, 109, 110, 141, 151, 152, 158, 170, 172, 173; of Pound's metapolitics in the late cantos 3, 13, 17, 18, 36, 77, 78, 79, 80, 81, 82, 85, 87, 91, 95, 96, 97, 100, 101, 102, 103, 104, 106, 107, 108, 123, 141, 149, 151, 152, 154, 158, 164, 170, 171, 172, 173, 174, 175; of Pound, threatened by hostile Semitic pressure 3; of Theodore G. Bilbo, 105, 141; of William H. "Alfalfa Bill" Murray 91, 98, 102, 105, 107, 108, 141, 172

Aryan-ness, as the measure of civilization 80

Ash, Lady (Queen) 102, 103

"Asphodel: That Greeny Flower" (Williams) 146

Aswins 172

Athena 106, 110, 120, 197, 218

Athens, as signifying "the idea of Europe and civilization" in *The Cantos* 226; jury trial system 199

Ausonides 137

Austrian Independence Treaty 69–70; right-wing opposition to ratification of 70

Austrian neutrality 70

Autobiography (Van Buren) 56, 73

Autobiography (Williams) 132

Avedon, Richard 216

Axis 2, 30, 67, 79

Babylon, Apollo versus 221; metonym for "the Jews" and therefore financial scheming 65, 67, 158, 224–5; Rome versus 65, 68, 188

Baccin 183

Bacigalupo, Massimo 19, 29, 38, 50, 57, 80, 120, 122, 123, 127, 171, 194, 206

Badiou, Alain 18, 30

Baller, F. W. 12, 31, 42, 43, 182, 189

Bank of Amsterdam 166

Bank of England 166

The Bank of the United States 55, 208

Bank of the United States (Benton) 55

"the Bank War" 53, 56, 73, 208

Baraka, Amiri 6

Barkun, Michael 110

Barnard, Mary 98

Barnhisel, Greg 79

barter 155, 156

Baruch, Bernard 28, 88, 89, 90

Bassianus 158

bastardization 28, 32, 82, 85, 86, 109, 206, 213

Bates, Albert Carlos 202, 203

"Battle for Grain" 186

Baucis 115

Baudelaire, Charles 138

Beamish, H. H. 97, 98

Beard, Charles 61, 74

Beard, Mary 74

Beards, the 74

Beatrice 117, 131, 134, 186

Beats, Martinelli as Queen or Mother of 30, 136, 142

Beecher, Henry Ward 62, 69, 74

Beer Hall Putsch 128

Beethoven, Ludwig von 25, 46

Behe, Michael 91

Belgian neutrality 69, 70

Belmont, August 49, 67, 68

Benét, Stephen Vincent 59

benevolence, contested by capitalist materialism ("Usura") 19; the domination of, as the leading theme of Cantos 90–95, 19; one of the Confucian "four tuan" 30

Benjamin, Judah 191

Benoist, Alain de 18, 20–2, 31, 32

Benton, Thomas Hart 33, 40, 53, 55, 56, 59, 72, 73, 186, 207

Benton Award 56–7

Berenice 172

Bernal, Martin 104, 105, 106, 110

Bible 54, 95, 99, 196. *See also* Abel; Adam; Cain; Eve; Exodus; Genesis; Jehovah (JHV, JHWH); King James Version; Luke, Gospel of; Matthew, Gospel of; Moses; Old Testament

Bilbo, Theodore G. 82, 91, 105, 107, 111, 141

bi-metallic, versus monometallic 165

Bishop, Elizabeth 223

Black Athena Revisited (eds. Lefkowitz & Rogers) 110
Black Athena: The Afroasiatic Origins of Classical Civilization (Bernal) 106
black-out 17, 49, 51, 169, 174; Byzantine history as part of 40; imposed by the usurers and the Jews 40; Randolph, Alexander the Great, and Antoninus Pius as victims of 53
Blackstone, William 54, 195
Blavatsky, Helena 11, 145
Block, Herman 193–5, 198, 199, 211
"blood and soil" ideology 185, 186, 190. *See also* "Blut u. Boden"
blood sacrifice 96; rejection of 96, 151, 152; Semitic penchant for 19
"Blut u. Boden" 185, 186. *See also* "blood and soil" ideology
Boas, Franz 111
Boldereff, Frances 110
Bollingen Prize 5; controversy 18, 30
Bonaparte, Napoleon 69
Bonifica 177
The Book of Coming Forth By Day (Budge) 103
The Book of the Falcon (Frederick II) 110
Booth, Marcella Spann 11, 114, 130, 131, 140, 188, 222, 223; cantos for (Cantos 110, 113) 130
Borah, William 93
Boter, Gerard 158
Bowen, Catherine Drinker 193, 197, 198, 200, 202–9, 211–13
Boxer Rebellion 79
Bracton, Henry de 206
Brahmins 152
Brancusi, Constantin 85
Braudel, Fernand 167
Braun, Eva 128, 190
Brennan, William 71, 114
Bridson, D. G. 25, 26, 66
Bristowe, Ethel Susan Graham Paterson 109–10
Britain, fertility of, attacked by a conspiracy of international forces 190; origins in colonization and civilization by Aryans, predominantly Phoenicians 100, 103
British Union of Fascists Quarterly 85

Brixton Hill Prison 212
Brooks, Preston 62, 63, 65
Brown II 10, 24, 53, 64, 76
Brown, John 74, 75
Brown v. Board of Education 2, 10, 24, 53, 58, 59, 63, 64, 77; as the anti-segregation decision 71; as judicial usurpation leading to a "mongrelized" USA 24; as the rejection of white supremacy as an ideology 2; as the triumph of tyrannical federal power over local custom 2
Broyard, Anatole 114, 135
Bruce, William Cabell 72, 73
Brunnenburg 100, 193, 207, 222, 223, 226
Brut (Layamon) 98, 126
Bryan, William Jennings 165; "Cross of Gold" speech 165
Buchanan, James 40, 57, 58, 60, 63–5, 70, 75, 199
Buckley, William F., Jr. 70
Buddhism 17, 43, 141
Budge, E. A. Wallis 103, 104
Bukowski, Charles 30, 114–16, 120, 121, 124, 131, 133, 135–7, 139–44
Bundy, Cliven 3
Bundy Ranch standoff 3
Bunting, Basil 47
Burbank, Luther 98
Burns, Anthony 60
Bush, Ronald 34
Butler, Nicholas Murray 68, 69
Byzantine coinages 166, 168
Byzantine history, as part of the black-out 40

Cacciaguida 146
Cadiz, Spain 152
Cadmus Bookshop 122, 145, 173
The Caged Panther: Ezra Pound at St. Elizabeths (Meacham) 53
Cain 19, 95–111. *See also Adam and Cain* (Murray), Bible
Calhoun, John C. 59, 72
Callimachus 127
capitalism, structural contradictions of 36
Caracalla 158
Carnegie Endowment for Peace 58, 68, 69
Carpenter, Humphrey 114
Carr, Robert 195
Carver, George Washington 87

Casillo, Robert 49, 71, 80, 81, 91, 100, 101, 108, 110, 151, 154, 155, 158, 173–5, 206, 213
Castro, Fidel 143, 147
Cavalcanti, Guido 45, 118–20, 123, 126
Cayce, Edgar 145, 147
Cecil, Robert 89, 197
Central Intelligence Agency (CIA) 175
Cerinthus 117
Ch'eng T'ang 190
Chamberlain, Houston Stewart 159
Champetier, Charles 20
Champollion, Jean-François 105
Chang, Carsun 16
Chao, Tze-Chiang 179, 180
Charles I 27, 193, 194, 198, 206
Charles II 201
Charlotte Court House 56, 73
Charter Oak 201, 202, 212
Charter of Connecticut: A Study (Bates) 202
cheng ming, as contradicting the ideogrammic method 44. *See also* "right naming"
Ch'eng T'ang (Tching Tang) 101, 102, 172, 190
chih[4] [智] [one of the four tuan] 12, 13, 18, 30, 31, 81
ch'in[1] [親] 162
China 29, 31, 66, 78, 79, 87, 91, 102, 157, 167, 179–81, 188, 190, 197
China: A Model for Europe (Maverick) 179
Chinese, as a culture-bearing race 3, 77, 78, 79, 86, 108
Chinese Civil War 37
Chinese Classics (Legge) 183
Chosdroes 174
Christian Book Club of America 109
Christian Identity Movement 95, 109
Christianity, as a "Jew religion" 19–20
Churchill, Winston 194
Cicero, Marcus Tullius 190
Circe 197
City Lights Bookstore 30, 142
Civil Rights Act of 1965 27
Civil Rights movement 81, 82; as premised on racial equality 82
Civil War 24, 56, 58, 59, 63, 64, 67, 74, 75; as caused by economic anarchy stirred up by profit-seeking Jews 67; as caused by "issuers" or "[t]he intrigues of interested cliques" 56, 63; as caused by Northern aggression 75; as caused by northern financial machinations, not slavery, 56; slaves as red herring to explain cause of 63
civilization, measured by its Aryan-ness 80; threatened or lost by racial integration 78, 80, 107
Civilization or Barbarism: An Authentic Anthropology (Diop) 110
Clay, Henry 54, 56, 59, 73, 78
"Cleaners Manifesto" 47, 48, 50
Cleaners Press 47
Cleopatra 78, 107, 108
Clinton, Tennessee 78, 186
"Clinton Water Now Has Rat Poison (Fluorine)" ("T. H. Benton") 186
Clinton-Knox County Stars and Bars (ed. Kasper) 186
Cocteau, Jean 227
coded language, concealing resistance to the racial integration of schools and the inevitable "mongrelization" of society 52; to express Pound's theories of states' rights and segregation in the Washington Cantos 24; for the expression of ideas too dangerous for Pound to express openly 26, 37; in the *trobar clus* operating in the "Sheri cantos" 45; in *trobar clus* of troubadour poetry 35, 45, 122, 125. *See also* Aesopian language
Coke, Edward 11, 14, 23, 28, 32–4, 40, 49, 157, 170, 193–203, 205–7, 209, 210–13; on misprision of treason 200; on Principles 32, 199, 211, 213
"Coke Cantos" (107–9) 11
Coke on Magna Charta: Selections from Coke's Second Institutes (Coke) 205
Cold War 1, 37
Colonus 217–19. *See also Oedipus at Colonus* (Sophocles)
Coltrane, John 46
Commedia (Dante) 15, 34, 51. *See also Paradiso* (Dante); *Purgatorio* (Dante)

Committee to Restore the Constitution (Roberts) 3
Companion to the Cantos (Terrell) 12
Compromise of 1850 58–60, 63, 67, 74
Coneybeare, F. C. 12, 46, 150, 151, 155–7
Confederacy 191. *See also* Civil War
Confucianism 3, 16, 18, 23, 34, 40, 44, 50, 156, 183, 188, 224; as "the unwobbling pivot" 156
Confucius 4, 6, 11, 12, 16, 19, 20, 23, 28, 32, 39, 43, 68, 78, 79, 81, 87, 91, 103, 104, 107, 108, 123, 126, 130, 157, 179–81, 184, 187–89, 222
Confucius Sinarum Philosophus (Confucius, tr. Intorcetta *et al.*) 179
Congress of Vienna 69
Connecticut Charter 49, 201, 202, 203, 213
Connecticut Colony 213
Conover, Anne 49
Constitution. *See* United States Constitution
The Constitution of Massachusetts (Adams) 202
Constitution of Virginia, efforts to revise 54
Constitutional Convention 207, 213
Cookson, William 21, 43, 66, 84, 91, 119, 186, 190, 197
Cornwallis, Charles 54
Corti, Egon Caesar 49
Couvreur, Séraphin 31
Coyle, Michael 7, 21
Crafts, Tom 139, 208, 209
Crash of 2008 73
Cravens, Margaret 132
Creel, H. G 189, 190
Creon 219
Crèvecoeur, Hector St. John de 180
Crommelin, John 3, 109, 142, 184
The Cross and the Flag (ed. Smith) 82, 98
"Cross of Gold" speech (Bryan) 165
Cuala Press 227
cult of Osiris 104
cult of Eleusis 126
Cummings, E. E. 107, 126, 130, 188, 223
Cunard, Nancy 132
cunicoli 178
Cunizza 127, 128, 131
Curtis, George Ticknor 58, 60, 61, 75

Cyprian 96, 118
Cythera (Kuthera) 127

D., H. *See* H.D.
Danbury Federal Prison 216
Dandolo, Enrico 166
Daniel, Arnaut *see* Arnaut Daniel
Dante Alighieri 6, 11, 13, 15, 16, 28, 29, 34, 45, 50, 113, 117, 118, 123, 126, 127, 128, 133, 139, 144, 145, 161, 196, 199, 211, 213; Dantescan 216
Danton, George 52
Darré, Richard W. 185, 186
Das Bauerntum als Lebensquell der Nordischen Rasse (Darré) 186
Dauphin. *See* Louis, Dauphin of France
Davenport, Guy 51
Davies, Donald 33
Davies, Ingrid 132, 212
De officiis (Cicero) 190
Declaration of Independence 183, 203, 208
Dedalus, Stephen 22
Defence Regulation 18B 194, 195
Defenders of the American Constitution (DAC) 3, 57, 198, 200, 210
defenestration 75, 76
Del Mar, Alexander 12, 13, 29, 40, 48, 58, 61, 98, 161, 163, 165–70, 174–6, 207
Del Pelo Pardi, Giulio 178, 189
Del Pelo Pardi, Tommaso 189
del Valle, Pedro 184, 200
Demeter 217
Demetrius 107
Democratic Party 27, 63, 75
Demoen, Kristoffel 158
Le despotisme de la Chine (Quesnay) 179, 189
Deutsche Bank 175
Diafan 119, 120
Diana 39, 126
Dion 156
Dionysius 226
Diop, Cheikh Anta 106, 110
Discretions (Rachewiltz) 222
Disraeli, Benjamin 37, 155, 207, 208
"Dissertation On the Canon and Feudal Law (1765)" (Adams) 204
"distributive justice" 139
District of Columbia 60. See also Washington, D.C.

District of Columbia District Court 195
Divine Comedy (Dante) 15, 34, 51
Divus, Andreas, 227Domitian 152, 154, 159
Domna, Julia 157, 158
Domvile, Barry 195, 212
"Donna mi Prega" (Cavalcanti) 45
Doob, Leonard 25, 66, 177
Doolittle, Hilda. *See* H.D.
dope 98, 114, 136–8, 171, 187; as an artificial paradise 137; as a Jewish/Communist plot 136; as a major theme in the Washington Cantos 114, 136; as poisonous in contrast with the solidity of poetry 138, 187. *See also* drugs, heroin, marijuana
Douglas, C. H. 183
Douglas, Stephen A. 59, 61, 63, 64, 75
Dowding, Hugh 153
Dowthwaite, James 57, 58, 65, 68
Drake, Francis 129
drugs, as part of a wider conspiracy to stupefy and control the masses 136. *See also* dope; heroin; marijuana
Du Bois, W. E. B. 111
Du Pont de Nemours, Pierre Samuel 180, 181, 189
Duchamp, Marcel 120
Dudek, Louis 71
Duggan, Laurence 75
Dulles, John Foster 69–70
Duncan, Robert 225
dynastic race hypothesis 104, 106

East India Company 166
Eaves, T. C. Duncan 56, 57, 64, 68, 73, 74
Economic Dialogues in Ancient China: Selections from the Kuan-tzu (Maverick) 179
The Eddas (tr. Waddell) 98, 100
"Edict of Expulsion" (Edward I) 38
The Edinburgh Companion to Ezra Pound and the Arts (ed. Preda) 132, 134
Edward I 38, 151, 205
Edward VIII 59, 63, 64, 199
Edward Coke: Oracle of the Law (Lyon & Block) 193, 195, 211
Edward the Confessor 199
Egypt 13, 50, 78, 79, 91, 99, 101–8, 110, 140, 151, 152, 155, 172

The Egyptian Book of the Dead (tr. Budge) 104
Egyptian civilization 104, 105, 106; founded by a "dynastic race" of non-Africans (Petrie) 104, 106; founded by white people (Bilbo) 107; Sumerian origin of (Waddell) 100, 102
Egyptian Civilization, Its Sumerian Origin and Real Chronology (Waddell) 100, 102
Egyptians 103–6, 110, 118, 155
Eisenhower, Dwight 37, 52, 71, 154, 159, 206
Eisenhower, Milton 206
Eisenhower administration 154
El 99
Eleanor 151
Elektra 218
Eleusinian mysteries 132
Eleusis, cult of 126
Eliot, T. S. 11, 215
Elizabeth I 129, 209, 213, 223
End to Torment: A Memoir of Ezra Pound (H.D.) 144
England, Jews banished from 38; purchase of Suez Canal shares 37
English Common Law 14, 193, 197, 198, 200, 202, 212; links with its American offshoot 202
The Enneads (Plotinus) 16; "On Intelligible Beauty" (*Ennead* V.8) 16
The Eparch's Book (Leo the Wise) 40, 156
Ephemerides 180, 189
Epoca 216, 227
Essay of Human Inequality (Gobineau) 159
Essex, Robert Devereux, 2nd Earl of 205
Etcheson, Nicole 75
Ethiopia 89, 152, 155
eugenics 2, 77, 98, 107–11, 141, 178, 206, 213
The Eumenides (Aeschylus) 218
Eunoe 161
Europe, China as a model for 179; exhausted by war 46; Pound's ambition to save 216; Pound's remedy for the cultural threat to 23; Talleyrand and Metternich's reconstruction of 58; a wheat god as the salvation of 109
The European 164
European New Right (ENR) 18, 20–2

"European renaissance," as a lifelong
project of Pound's 22–3; saner
economics and Confucius as the
path to 22; the ENR's project for 22
Eusebius 150
Eve 99. *See also* Bible
Evola, Julius 22, 32
evolution, Agassiz not a believer in 77;
denied by William H. "Alfalfa Bill"
Murray 98; Pound not a believer in
2; versus "intelligent design" 2
Exodus 99. *See also* Bible
Ezra Pound and the Cantos: A Record of Struggle (Flory) 113
Ezra Pound Encyclopedia 17
Ezra Pound Institute of Civilization 76
Ezra Pound: The Critical Heritage (ed. Homberger) 33, 36
Ezra Pound's Adams Cantos (Ten Eyck) 201, 202, 208, 209, 211, 212, 213
Ezra Pound's Fascist Propaganda 1935–45 (Feldman) 4

50 Poems (Bunting) 47
Faber & Faber 57
Fagles, Robert 217–20, 224, 226
family farm, versus collectives 188
Fang, Achilles 30, 42, 50
Farley, David 25, 32
Farmers' Alliance 96
Farmer's Party 178
fascism 23, 24, 29, 30, 35, 80, 81, 83, 98, 186, 228
Fasti (Ovid) 133
Faulkner, William 83
Federal Bureau of Investigation (FBI) 27, 185
Federal Reserve Bank 3, 207; creation of 207; exposé of authored by Eustace Mullins 3, 165; founding of as a great economic crime 165
Federal Reserve Board 88
Feldman, Matthew 4
Fenollosa, Ernest 43, 44, 62
Ferlinghetti, Lawrence 142
Fielding, Henry 73
Fillmore, Millard 57–62, 64, 74, 199
finance, as sterile but not inert 182, 183, 188
finance capitalism 3, 19, 23, 66–7, 177, 201; Pound's sustained attacks on 177. *See also* loan-capital

Fine Gael 22
First Dynasty of Egypt 102
"Five classics" 12
Five Knights 206
Fleming, Floyd 92
Flinterman, Jaap-Jan 158
Flora Castalia 39, 115–17, 119, 127, 138
Flory, Wendy 113
Folco de Marseille (Folquet) 128
Foote, Henry 59
Forché, Carolyn 6
Forgotten Kingdom (Goullart) 11, 98
The Forméd Trace: The Later Poetry of Ezra Pound (Bacigalupo) 29, 80, 171
Fortune 88
The Foundations of the 19th Century (Chamberlain) 159
Four Books (Confucius) 12
Four Pages 47, 187
the four tuan 12, 13, 18, 30, 31, 81
Fourth Crusade 166
Fox-Genovese, Elizabeth 179
Frankfurter, Felix 28, 88
Franklin, Benjamin 180
Franklin Pierce: Young Hickory of the Granite Hills (Nichols) 58
Frederick II 110
"Freedom Now or Never" (anon.) 77, 87–90
French, William 137
"the French and Indian War" of 1754–61 204
French Enlightenment 180
French monarchy 180
French physiocracy 4, 179, 181
French revolution 22
Freud, Sigmund 76; Freudian 121, 223; Freudianizes 218
Frigga (Fricco or Frigg) 172
Frobenius, Leo 41, 84, 88, 89, 139, 140
From Admiral to Cabin Boy (Domvile) 212
Frost, Robert 9
Fugitive Slave Law 60, 63, 74, 75
the Furies 217–19
The Furies (Lowell) 218
Furniss, Robert 27, 196

Gaddis, William 114
Gallagher, Patrick 40
Gallup, Donald 76, 211
Galton, Frances 107, 110

Gargoyle Magazine 115, 132
Gay, Peter 179, 181, 183
Gea 116
"Gea Mater" (Martinelli) 124, 127
Genesis 95, 96, 99. *See also* Bible
Genlis, Stéphanie Félicité, comtesse de 69
genocide of the white race 187
Geryon 15
Gesell, Silvio 187
Gesellite 61, 167, 187, 207
Ginsberg, Allen 136, 142–4, 147; left-wing politics of 136
Giovannini, Giovanni 26, 40, 142, 189, 195
Gists from Agassiz (Agassiz, ed. Kasper) 2, 77, 89
Glossator 15, 29, 34, 38, 39, 42, 43, 46, 49, 57, 58, 161, 170, 172, 173, 174, 193, 201, 209, 210
Gobineau, Arthur de 159
Gold Standard 165, 166
Goldsmiths 166
Gomez, Roderigo 213
Gondomar, Diego Sarmiento de Acuña, 1st Count of 213
Gonne, Maude 22
Gordon, David 34, 87, 212
Gothic Ripples (Leese) 98
Goths 99, 102, 104, 106, 172
Goullart, Peter 11, 29, 98, 213
grain, as a pervasive theme in the Washington Cantos 4, 178. *See also* "Battle for Grain"; wheat imagery
grain god 96, 137
grain sacrifice, versus blood sacrifice 19, 96
Gramsci, Antonio 21
Grant, Hugh G. 74
Grant, Madison 98, 108
Grant, Ulysses S. 74
"Greater Liberia Act" (Bilbo) 111
Greece, free of Semitic or African influences on its pre-Classical culture 104; lost as a civilization through race mixing 107; viewed since the Enlightenment as the origin of civilization 105
Greenwich Village 37, 98, 114
Gridley, Jeremiah 209
Griffis, William Elliot 58, 59, 61, 62, 74
Griffith, Arthur 22
Grogan, Kristin 15, 29, 193, 209
Grosseteste, Robert 119, 132
Guanyin. *See* Kuanon (Gwanyin, Guanyin, Kuan yin, Quan yin)
Guernsey 167
Guide to Ezra Pound's Selected Cantos (Kearns) 31
Gunpowder treason trial 205
Gwanyin. *See* Kuanon (Gwanyin, Guanyin, Kuan yin, Quan yin)
Gymnosophists 152, 155

habeas corpus 14, 193–5, 198, 199, 211
Hall, Donald 14, 23, 57, 216, 217, 219–21, 224, 225, 227
Hamilton, Ian 119
Hammurabi 158
"Hand and Soul" (Rossetti) 29
Hargreaves, David William 190
Harper's Ferry 75
Harvey, John H. 91, 97, 98, 99, 102, 105, 109
Hatha Yoga 81
Hatlen, Burton 225, 228
Hawley, William 42
Hawthorne, Nathaniel 67, 109, 213
Hayne, Robert Y. 72
H-bomb 122, 224
H.D. 128, 132, 144; as the Dryad-type 128
Heath, Percy 114
Hegel, Georg Wilhelm Friedrich 18, 30, 31
Heidegger, Martin 23, 223, 225, 227
Helen of Troy 150
Helen of Tyre 128, 129, 149, 150
Henderson, Archie 25, 37, 49, 87, 89, 93, 109, 137, 146, 159, 190, 227
Henry, Florette 136, 144, 179
Henry, Patrick 74
Hera 172
Heracles 158
Herakles (*Women of Trachis*) 221, 227
herders, versus farmers 95
The Heritage of Britain (Harvey) 91, 98
heroin 114, 136–8; use of by Martinelli 114, 136, 138; addiction to by William French's wife 137. *See also* dope; drugs; marijuana
Heydon, John 12, 122
Heydt, Erich 144
Heyman, Katherine 132
Hickman, Miranda 197

Hillyer, Robert 5
Hilton, James 11, 29
Himmler, Heinrich 185
Hindu, genius for tolerance 86, 92
Hiss, Alger 28, 75
history, Aryan model of 104–5; as a Jeffersonian class struggle between a clique of creditors and a mass of debtors 28–29, 36; as a recurring cycle of Aryan priority, miscegenation, and consequent racial degradation 78, 80, 107, 108, 141; as a struggle between virtuous Aryans (culture-builders) and devious Semites (destroyers) 17, 36, 78, 85, 95, 101, 135, 139, 188, 221; as racial and economic parables featuring virtuous Aryans and devious Semites 17
A History of the Ancient Near East Circa 3000–323 BC (Van de Meiroop) 110
History of Egypt (Petrie) 106
History of Monetary Systems (Del Mar) 12, 13, 40, 165
Hitler, Adolf 2, 17, 24, 58, 66, 77, 78, 80, 84, 85, 90, 92, 105, 128, 141, 178, 185, 186
Hitler's Table Talk (Hitler) 66
Hollis, Christopher 37, 49
Holman, Hamilton 74
Holmes, John Clellon 147
Holmes, Sarah 93
Holy Guide (Heydon) 12
Homer 77, 96, 105, 121, 144, 152; Homeric 113, 217, 225
homestead 65–68, 76, 177, 178, 188; as the basis for any civilized society and a sane, sustainable economy 177; versus *kolschoz* 65–8, 76, 188
Hoover, J. Edgar 27
Hopkins, Harry 28, 80, 91, 206
"Horse on Fire" (Bukowski) 133
Horton, T. David 3, 27, 47, 56, 70, 76, 82, 87, 136, 138, 177, 184, 200, 205
Hotze, Henry 159
House Un-American Activities Committee (HUAC) 28
Housewives Today 185
Howard, Frances 195

Howl (Ginsberg) 143
Hrozny, Bedrich 91
Hsi^1 [熙] 42, 104
Hsi, K'ang 42, 104. See K'ang^1 Hsi^1 [康熙]
Hsiang Shan 222
hsin^1 [新] 162, 175
The Hudson Review 9, 49, 55, 124
Hughes, Langston 85
Hui 68
The Human Plant (Burbank) 98
Hunger Fighters (de Kruif) 177
Hyksos 139, 155
"Hymn to Light" (Milton) 219

I^1 [一] 153
I^4 [義] [one of the four tuan] 12, 13, 18, 30, 31, 81
I Ching 12
"i jênn iuên" [一人元] ["Let the one man be greatly good"] 159
I Yin (Y Yin) 31, 182, 190
Ibsen, Henrik 46
ideogrammic method 39, 43, 44; versus "precise terminology" 44
Imagism 48
Imperial Fascist League (IFL) 97
Imperialism: The Highest Stage of Capitalism (Lenin) 52, 69
Indo-Aryan 152, 173
The Indo-Sumerian Seals Deciphered (Waddell) 100
Ino 122, 145
Institute of International Education 75
Institutes of the Lawes of England (Coke) 40, 194–200, 205, 209, 212
"intelligence," cosmic order in earthly nature (Agassiz) 82
"intelligent design" 2, 77, 167
International Gold Standard 166
Interposition, doctrine of 54, 72, 73
Intorcetta, Prospero 179
Introduction to Metaphysics (Heidegger) 23
Iong Ching (Yong Zheng) 197
Irenaeus 150
Isis 113, 116, 140
Ismene 219
Italy 11, 29, 66, 113, 131, 140, 175, 177, 178, 186, 188, 216, 219, 222, 227

Jackson, Andrew 53, 56, 71, 73, 208; attempted assassination of by the Bank of the United States 208
James I 195, 200, 213
Jameson, Frederic 17
Japan, Matthew Perry's "opening" of 62
Jarrell, Randall 33
Jefferson, Thomas 4, 10, 21, 22, 24, 53–5, 70, 72, 76, 157, 162, 179, 180, 183, 185, 190, 194, 198, 201, 208
Jeffersonian concept of money 56
Jeffersonian interpretation of the United States 56
Jeffersonianism 23, 24, 29, 35, 36, 53, 54, 73; practiced by John Randolph 53, 54, 56; as practiced by Thomas Hart Benton 56; in Pound's politics 23, 24, 29, 35, 36, 54, 55, 78, 169, 187
Jehovah (JHV, JHWH) 20, 96. *See also* Bible
jen² [人] 153
jen² [仁] [one of the four tuan] 12, 13, 18, 30, 31, 81
jen², I⁴, li³, chih⁴ [仁 義 禮 智] [the four tuan] 12, 13, 18, 30, 31, 81
Jenks, Jorian 184, 186
Jenner, William Ezra 70
Jesus Christ, as not a Jew for the Christian Identity Movement and for Dallam Simpson 95
Jewish conspiracy 67, 85, 142, 201; countered by a benign conspiracy of creative intelligence 85
Jewish/Communist conspiracy, acting through the Warren Court 28, 52; desirous of destroying the white race and the "American way of life" 52; determined to subvert and subjugate the United States 1; to end segregation in the public schools 24, 26, 27; exposed by the Melbourne *New Times* 186; manifested in the Civil Rights struggle 1; menacing the United States from within 83; Roosevelt as the figurehead of 37
Jim Crow 27, 41, 59, 64, 78, 82, 97
Joan of Arc 117
John Adams and the American Revolution (Bowen) 193, 202, 203

John Birch Society 49
John Kasper and Ezra Pound: Saving the Republic (Marsh) 3, 54, 57, 61, 84–6, 90, 92, 98, 136, 142, 159, 184, 185, 187, 191, 212
John Randolph (Adams) 55
Jones, Christopher P. 158
Joseph II (Emperor Joseph of Austria) 180, 186
Joyce, James 22
Judaism 19, 78, 95
jury, right to trial by 193, 199; Coke on 199; in Athens 199

Kahal 95–106
K'ang¹ [康] 42, 104
K'ang¹ Hsi¹ [康熙] 42, 104
Kansas-Nebraska Act 61, 63, 64, 75
Karlgren, Bernard 31
Kasper, John 1–4, 10, 18, 24, 27, 37, 40, 47, 54–6, 76, 77, 82, 83, 84, 86, 87, 89, 90, 92, 97, 98, 109, 110, 132, 136, 138, 141, 142, 144, 146, 175, 179, 184, 186–8, 189, 190, 191, 198, 219; distracted by race hatred 175; suspected of conspiring to bomb schools in Tennessee 142
Kassi Dynasty 158
Kati 103, 104, 110, 118
Kaufman, Bob 30, 136, 142
Kearns, George 18, 19, 31, 34, 41, 196
Keats, John 228
Kenner, Hugh 9, 29, 34, 41, 49, 80, 173
Kentucky Resolutions of 1798 and 1799 24, 53, 72; as a "recipe for disunion" (Washington) 24
Kerouac, Jack 147
Khaiti (or Khati or Khatti or Catti) 104
Kilpatrick, James J. 24, 53, 54, 56, 70, 72
Kimpel, Ben 56, 57, 64, 68, 73, 74
Kindellan, Michael 34, 39–43, 46, 50, 51, 57, 74, 91, 97, 110, 117, 119–24, 129, 130, 136, 151, 158, 171, 175, 176, 195–7, 211
King James Version 196. *See also* Bible
Kirk, Russell 72
Kirkpatrick, Robin 133
Know-Nothing Tea Party Movement 3
Koch, Paul "Pablo" 189
kolschoz (kolkhoz), versus homestead 65–8, 76, 188

Kore 217
Korean War 37
Korn, Marianne 228
kosmos 39, 173; and polis 1, 15, 18, 20, 211
Kossuth, Lajos 62, 69
Kruif, Paul de 177
Ku Klux Klan (KKK) 3, 82, 219
Kuanon (Gwanyin, Guanyin, Kuan yin, Quan yin) 113, 116, 140, 171
Kuan-Chung (Kuan Chung, Kwan Chung) 179, 180
Kuan-Tzu (Kuan-Chung) 179
Kuang-Tzu 40
Kuczynski, Marguerite 182, 190
Kung. *See* Confucius
Kuthera Aphrodite 117
Kutik, Ilya 38

labor theory of value 36
LaDrière, Craig 40
Lagia 134
Laius 220, 221
Lan, Feng 39, 41, 42, 50
Lane, Helen S. 70
L=A=N=G=U=A=G=E poetry 6
Laomon's 126
The Late Cantos of Ezra Pound: Composition, Revision, Publication (Kindellan) 40
Late Style (Said) 24
The Later Cantos of Ezra Pound (Wilhelm) 227
Lattimore, Richmond 120
Laughlin, James 51, 79, 215, 216, 225
The Law of Civilization and Decay (Adams) 165
Lawrence, David 88
Laws, Bolitha J. 195
Layamon 98
Layamon's Brut (Layamon) 98
Leary, Lewis 71
Leaves of Grass (Whitman) 74
Lee, Gilbert 130, 134, 135, 144
Leese, Arnold 97, 98, 195
Lefkowitz, Mary R. 106, 110
Legge, James 19, 31, 41, 79, 183
Lehman, Herbert H. 89, 90
Lehman banking family 90
Leibnitz, Gottfried Wilhelm 179

Leihkapital 58, 65, 66, 69. *See also* loan-capital
Lenin, Vladimir 25, 37, 52, 67, 69
Leo the Wise 40
Leopold II of Tuscany 180
Leopoldine reforms 179
Leto, Giulio Pomponio 172
Leucothea (Leucothae) 10, 117, 121, 122, 130, 131, 133–5, 140, 145
Lewis, Wyndham 25, 97, 216
Lhasa and Its Mysteries (Waddell) 29, 98
li^3 [禮] [one of the four tuan] 12, 13, 18, 30, 31, 81
LIBOR scandal 175
Liebregts, Peter 16, 23, 29, 30, 57, 117, 119, 127–9, 133, 151, 157
The Life of Apollonius of Tyana (Philostratus, tr. Coneybeare) 12, 40, 46, 149, 150, 151, 153, 154, 157, 158, 174
The Life of James Buchanan (Curtis) 58, 75
"light philosophy" 17, 119; versus the Hebraic black-out 17
Light Year (ed. Payne) 115
Lincoln, Abraham 75, 76
Lindbergh, Charles 28
ling^2 [靈] 18, 20, 31, 41, 103, 124; translated by Pound as "sensibility" 18, 20, 31, 41, 182
Linnaeus, Carl 6, 138
The Lion and the Throne (Bowen) 193, 200, 205
Little Rock, Arkansas 78
Littleton, Thomas de 198, 202, 209, 212
Livi, Grazia 216, 220, 227
loan-capital 23, 58, 65, 66, 67, 68. *See also* Leihkapital
Lohbeck, Don 82
Lombards 23, 40, 171, 172
Longfellow, Henry Wadsworth 76, 213
Loseff, Lev 38
Lost Horizon (Hilton) 11
Louis, Dauphin of France 180
Louisiana Purchase 208
Lowell, Robert 215–19, 223, 225, 226
Lowells (Massachusetts family) 55
Luce, Henry 88
Luke, Gospel of 127. *See also* Bible
"Lux in diafana" (Martinelli) 117, 124
Lyon, Hastings 193–195, 198, 199, 211

McCarthy, Joseph R. 3, 10, 28, 37, 66, 67, 70; McCarthyism 5, 71; McCarthyite, 67MacLeish, Archibald 196
Macmillan, Harold 70
McNaughton, Bill 3, 47, 48, 66, 136, 138, 146
McPherson, Douglas, *pseud. See* Paige, D. D.
Madison, James 53, 54, 72, 98, 108
Madonna Giovanna 119
Magna Carta 14, 193, 197, 198, 201, 205, 209
Magus, Simon 128, 150
Maine, Henry Sumner 211
Major, Clarence 30, 136, 142
Make It New bookshop 18, 37, 97, 136, 138, 144, 179
Makers of Civilization in Race and History (Waddell) 30, 97, 100
Makin, Peter 10, 34, 44, 45, 57, 123, 126–8, 133, 134, 194, 209
Malone, George W. 70
Mandate of Heaven 20
Mang Tsze. *See* Mencius (Mang Tzu)
Manheim, Ralph 32
Manifesto for a European Renaissance (de Benoist & Champetier) 20
Manis 106
marijuana, Martinelli arrested for possession of 136. *See also* dope; drugs; heroin
Marsh, Alec 73, 76, 85, 165, 189, 190, 210, 212, 213. See also *John Kasper and Ezra Pound: Saving the Republic* (Marsh)
Martel, Charles 168
Martinelli, Ezio 114, 135
Martinelli, Sheri (Shirley Burns Brennan) 11, 14, 16, 19, 27, 29, 30, 33–5, 39, 45, 49, 73, 81, 82, 97, 113–17, 119–45, 146, 149–51, 153, 157, 158, 170-2, 174–6, 179, 187, 191, 212; cantos for (Cantos 90–95, 97, 102), 33, 45, 113ff.
Marx, Karl 90, 167, 189
Mason-Dixon Line 27, 64
Massime degli antichi Egiziani (Rachewiltz) 97

"massive resistance" 10, 24, 53, 59, 72
Materer, Timothy 12, 13, 137, 149
Mathews, Robert Henry 43
Mathews' Chinese-English Dictionary (Mathews) 43
Matthew, Gospel of 49. *See also* Bible
Matthiessen, F. O. 76
Maud, Ralph 110
Maverick, Lewis A. 179, 180, 189
Maximus (Olson) 110
Mays, David John 72
Meacham, Harry 53–5, 70, 188, 200, 205
Mead, G. R. S. 110, 150, 152, 153, 157, 158
Meador Books 97
Mediterranean 78, 87, 91, 100, 108
Meek, Ronald L. 182, 190
Mein Kampf (Hitler) 2, 77, 178, 185
Memnon Colossi 155
Memoirs of the Prince de Talleyrand (Talleyrand) 57, 58, 69
Men of Law: from Hammurabi to Holmes (Seagle) 151, 158
Mencius (Mang Tzu); 4, 11, 66, 87, 101, 103, 104, 108, 123, 164, 180, 183, 184, 189; "nine field" system 66, 183, 184
Menes 102, 103, 106, 152, 172
Mensdorff, Albert 58, 63, 67–9; Mensdorff Letter 58, 63, 67–9
Mentor 120
Merchant, Moelwyn 195, 212
Meridiano di Roma 175, 177
Merlin 136, 158, 170
Merovingian coinages 168
Mesopotamia 17, 81, 99, 101, 102, 158; Mesopotamian 105
Metamorphoses (Ovid) 115
metapolitics 1, 9, 16–22, 30, 77, 80, 81, 86, 87, 103, 108, 135, 138, 139, 145, 174, 181, 182
Metapolitics: From Wagner and the German Romantics to Hitler (Viereck) 17–18
Metapolitik 18, 30
Meyer, Eugene 88
Meyers, Jeffrey 226
Michelangelo 146
Middle Kingdom 78, 87
Migne, Jacques-Paul 172

Millard Fillmore: Constructive Statesman, Defender of the Constitution (Griffis) 58
Milton, John 206, 215, 219
Minos 103, 106
Mirabeau, Honoré Gabriel Riqueti, comte de 179
Miracle in Philadelphia: The Story of the Constitutional Convention (Bowen) 213
miscegenation 28, 78, 108, 206
misprision of treason 193, 205; Bowen on 200; Coke on 200
Missouri Compromise of 1820 63
Il mistero dell' amor platonico del medio evo (Rossetti) 133, 134
Mithra 95
Mnuchin, Steve 73
Modern Jazz Quartet 114
Molotov, Vyacheslav 69
Mommsen, Theodor 66
money, as based on the credit of the state 164; called "nomisma and nummus" by the Greek and Roman republics 13, 166; Congressional surrender of power to create and to regulate value of 207; credit as the future tense of 48; issuance of as characterizing sovereignty 13, 61, 163, 164, 166, 167; Jeffersonian concept of 56, 73; as the language of capital 36; local control of as the basis of local freedom 167; as a measure (Del Mar) 163, 166; quantity theory of, supported by Del Mar and Pound 29; the value of as legislated, not intrinsic (Del Mar) 168
mongrelization 32, 52, 82, 91, 107, 109, 111, 178, 189, 213; as leading to loss of civilization 107, 178, 189; as leading to racial degeneracy 108; object of the Jewish/ Communist conspiracy 27, 70, 90; stemming from the *Brown* decisions 24, 52 as weakening the United States domestically and internationally 32
Monna Vanna 119
Moody, A. David 4, 16, 34, 46, 57, 74, 113–15, 117, 123, 137, 138, 140, 186, 187, 195, 196, 198, 202, 222, 223, 227
Moore, Steven 30, 115, 116, 120, 121, 124, 130, 131–45, 171, 176
Morgenthau Plan 28
Morse, Samuel 62
Morton, Samuel 159
Moses 135, 139. *See also* Bible
Moslem system of coinage 166-9
Mosley, Oswald 195
Mozart, Wolfgang Amadeus 6, 137
Mullins, Eustace 3, 30, 37, 40, 71, 75, 76, 154, 165
Multan 102
Munson, Gorham 175
Murray, William H. "Alfalfa Bill" 78, 81, 82, 91, 92, 96–100, 102–9, 111, 140, 141, 149, 172
Musonius 154, 159
Mussolini, Benito 21, 22, 24, 76, 88, 89, 93, 154, 157, 162, 175, 186, 227; Verona speech of 227
Myrdal, Gunnar 111
Der Mythos des 20. Jahrhunderts (Rosenberg) 159

Na Khi 6, 13, 40, 98
The Nation 144
National Association for the Advancement of Colored People (NAACP) 89, 90
National Geographic 29
The National Review 70
National Socialism 66
National States' Rights Party 3
Nausikaa 130, 131, 140
The Negro's Place in Call of Race (Murray) 97
mongrelization 32, 52, 82, 91, 107, 109, 111, 178, 189, 213; as leading to loss of civilization 107, 178, 189; as leading to racial degeneracy 108; as weakening the United States domestically and internationally 32; object of the Jewish/Communist conspiracy 27, 70, 90; stemming from the *Brown* decisions 24, 52 16–20, 23, 29, 30, 40, 57, 117, 133, 151, 157
Nero 152-4, 159
Neuadel aus Blut und Boden (Darré) 186

neutrality. *See* Austrian neutrality, Belgian neutrality
The New Amsterdam News 86, 186
New Deal 25, 97
New Right. *See* European New Right (ENR)
New Times (Melbourne) 2, 7, 47, 70, 76, 91, 186, 199, 212
New York Herald 142
New York Times 88
New York Times Sunday Magazine 190
Ni Houlihan, Kathleen 22
Nicholls, Peter 12, 16, 17, 29, 34, 38, 44–7, 49, 50, 58, 166, 169, 170, 178, 182, 200
Nichols, Roy Franklin 58, 62, 63, 66, 67, 71, 75, 76, 213
Nietzsche, Friedrich 227
Nile, as near origins of civilization and economics 156; site of straight barter found by Apollonius 155
Nin, Anaïs 114, 134
nine fields share system 66, 183, 184
Niven, Alex 201, 209, 210
Norman, Herbert 76
Notes on the State of Virginia (Jefferson) 185
Nott, Josiah C. 159
Nous 128, 133
"Nude Descending a Staircase" (Duchamp) 120
nullification 24, 54, 73
Nullification Act (South Carolina) 73
nummulary theory of monetary value 163, 166

Obama, Barack 32
Occident, based on the homestead 177
Ocellus 17, 149
Odlin, Reno 16, 108
Odysseus 10, 120–2, 140, 145, 217; *The Odyssey* (Homer) 34, 120–2, 145. *See also* paradiso terrestre, Phaecia
Oedipus 215–27
Oedipus at Colonus (Sophocles) 217, 218, 222, 224, 226
Old Testament 39; as Jewish propaganda 99. *See also* Bible
Olson, Charles 6, 110
"one man" [一人] 153. *See also* "i jênn iuên"

Orestes 218
Osiris 104, 156; cult of 104
Otis, James 208, 209
Overbury, Thomas 195
Overholser, Willis A. 175
Ovid 46, 115, 133, 135, 144, 145

P2 Lodge Scandal 175
A Packet for Ezra Pound (Yeats) 227
Paideuma (Frobenius) 41, 84
Paideuma (journal) 32, 76, 108, 212
Paige, D. D. 92, 214
Papyrus of Ani 103
paradise, anti-Semitism as constitutive of Pound's 173; as beyond Pound's grasp 6; dope as an artificial 137, 138; as a dream of freedom 14, 194, 201; erotic nature of Pound's 11, 14, 121, 128, 170, 171; as eternal truth 15-16; glimpsed through a racialized ceremony 174; as a man's good nature (Kati) 103; as a paradise of books 11; Richard St. Victor on the splendors of 126; Siger of Brabant as one of the lights of 199
Paradise Lost (Milton) 219
Paradiso (Dante) 146, 196
paradiso terrestre 23, 51, 124; as a contradiction 14, 17; introduced in Canto 97, 162; the land of the Phaecians as 122, 130–1, 140. *See also The Odyssey* (Homer), Phaecia
Paris Review 23, 216
Parker, Charlie 114
Parker, Richard 76
Paterson (Williams) 167
Patrologia (Migne) 172
Paul the Deacon 40, 58
Pauthier, Guillaume 41
Payne, Miles 115
Pearson, Drew 142, 185, 190
Pearson, Norman Holmes 5, 7, 82, 91, 92, 97, 109, 136, 144, 158, 178, 188, 189, 199, 200, 202, 203, 212, 213
Pearlman, Daniel 34
pen[3] [本] 151, 156
People's Party 178
Perón, Evita 128
Perry, Matthew C. 62
Persephone 118, 217

Pestell, Alex 15, 26, 38, 39
Petition of Right 28, 157, 193, 194, 195, 198, 199, 211
Petrie, Flinders 100, 104, 106, 107, 110
Phaecia 10, 121, 122, 131, 140. *See also The Odyssey* (Homer), paradiso terrestre
Pharisees 95
Pharos 79
Philemon 115
Philo 107, 108
philology 9, 15, 34, 35, 40–2, 57, 118, 120, 212
Philostratus, Flavius 12, 40, 46, 149–51, 153, 154, 155, 157, 158, 159, 174
The Phoenician Origins of the Britons, Scots and Anglo-Saxons (Waddell) 103
Phoenicians, claimed by Laurence A. Waddell to be Aryans and not Semites 100, 102; claimed by Theodore G. Bilbo to be Caucasians 107
physiocracy 4, 177, 179–83, 185, 188, 189
Physiocratie: Ou Constitution Naturelle du Gouvernement le plus Avantageux au Genre Humain (Du Pont de Nemours) 189
Picabia, Francis 46
Pierce, Franklin 40, 57, 58, 60, 62–68, 75, 199, 213
the Pillars of Hercules 152
Pius, Antoninus 53
Plato 217; Platonic form 166
Plessy v. Ferguson 64
Plotinus 16
Pocahontas 55
The Poetry of Ezra Pound (Kenner) 29
polis 6, 19, 20, 210; and kosmos 1, 15, 18, 20, 211
Polyneices 217, 219
Pomponio 172
Pontifex 165, 168
"popular sovereignty" 60, 61, 63, 64, 75
Populism 55, 91, 96
populist politics 178, 181
Porphery 150
Poseidon 121
Pound, Dorothy 54, 55, 70, 71, 127, 130, 132, 136, 171, 197, 203, 223; as Committee of the person and estate of Ezra Pound 70, 197

Pound, Ezra. *Groups of cantos*: Adams Cantos 201, 202, 203, 204, 209; "Aryan" Cantos (94 and 97) 96, 98, 100; Benton (Thomas Hart) cantos (88–9) 33, 52, 55, 56, 57, 59; *Cantos LII–LXXI* 204; Coke Cantos (107–109) 11, 14, 28, 33, 34, 193–214; *A Draft of XXX Cantos* 222; *Drafts & Fragments* 109; Martinelli (Sheri) cantos (90–95, 97, 102), 33, 45, 113ff.; *The Pisan Cantos* 5, 46, 65, 108, 127, 158, 217, 218, 220; "Sacred Edict cantos" (98–9), 11, 12, 178; *Section: Rock-Drill* (85–95) 1, 4, 6, 9–14, 18–20, 23, 31, 33, 34, 40, 41, 49, 52, 54, 57, 74, 79, 101, 103, 108, 113, 114, 124, 135, 182, 202, 218; Spann (Marcella) cantos (110, 113) 130; *Thrones* (96–109) 1, 4, 6, 9–17, 23, 33, 34, 36, 38, 40, 42, 44, 46, 48, 49, 52, 57, 66, 74, 79, 98, 104, 108, 111, 113, 114, 116, 118, 119, 122, 131, 140, 156, 169, 170, 193, 194, 196, 197, 208, 209, 211, 213, 225, 227; Washington Cantos (*Rock-Drill* and *Thrones*), passim. *Individual cantos*: Canto 1, 77, 78, 217, 227; Canto 6, 127; Canto 7, 25; Canto 18, 76; Canto 19, 68, 76; Canto 23, 132; Canto 25, 117, 146; Canto 28, 49; Canto 29, 119, 122, 127; Canto 32, 22, 204; Canto 33, 22, 204; Canto 34, 73; Canto 36, 126, 208; Canto 37, 73; Canto 38, 69; Canto 45, 177, 187; Canto 49, 137; Canto 50, 22, 204; Canto 53, 190; Canto 63, 209; Canto 72, 81; Canto 74, 51, 108–9, 127, 158, 218; Canto 76, 69, 90, 222; Canto 78, 127; Canto 79, 46; Canto 80, 187; Canto 82, 217, 218; Canto 83, 217; Canto 85, 12, 18, 20, 30, 31, 35, 39, 41, 46, 50, 81, 85, 103, 124, 182, 190; Canto 86, 12, 19, 37, 64, 180; Canto 87, 40, 84, 90, 113, 126, 137, 165, 218; Cantos 88–9, 33, 52, 55, 56, 57, 59; Canto 88, 12, 13, 33, 52, 54, 55, 56, 57, 59, 71, 86, 183, 203; Canto 89, 12, 15, 33, 52, 53, 55, 56, 57, 59, 64, 73, 165, 167, 180,

189, 218; Cantos 90–95, 11, 19, 113, 114, 117, 122, 123, 124, 135, 149; Canto 90, 9, 11, 19, 34, 55, 71, 115, 117, 118, 119, 120, 122, 126, 127, 128, 130, 133, 140, 145, 158, 164, 171; Canto 91, 13, 31, 39, 117, 120, 122, 123, 126, 127, 128, 129, 140, 145, 149, 150, 151, 154, 155, 159, 170, 210, 213; Canto 92, 13, 119, 128, 137, 166, 189; Canto 93, 4, 17, 41, 96, 103, 104, 117, 118, 119, 121, 124, 127, 138, 139, 149; Canto 94, 12, 18, 19, 44, 46, 81, 96, 98, 100, 102, 103, 105, 106, 113, 116, 123, 140, 144, 150, 151, 152, 153, 155, 156, 157, 158, 159, 172, 173, 174; Canto 95, 9, 19, 30, 120, 122, 129, 133, 140, 145; Canto 96, 9, 10, 44, 156, 173, 174, 210; Canto 97, 12, 13, 15, 17, 29, 44, 46, 48, 78, 85, 95, 96, 98, 100, 102, 103, 106, 109, 113, 120, 136, 150, 151, 152, 153, 159, 161–76, 221; Cantos 98–9, 11, 12, 178; Canto 98, 12, 17, 29, 42, 104, 109, 134, 140, 168, 178, 197, 225; Canto 99, 12, 13, 16, 17, 20, 29, 31, 41, 42, 43, 78, 83, 130, 141, 178, 181, 182, 184, 188, 189; Canto 100, 13, 25, 36, 37, 38, 42, 51, 52, 53, 56, 65, 67, 71, 73, 98, 164, 193, 207, 211; Canto 101, 58, 150, 164, 178; Canto 102, 113, 120, 171, 212, 225; Canto 103, 46, 51, 56–70, 74, 75, 167, 178, 188, 213, 225; Canto 104, 13, 20, 37, 46, 49, 76, 109, 128, 155, 168, 179, 208; Canto 105, 2, 13, 24, 29, 40, 41, 46, 98, 108, 179, 184, 193; Canto 106, 13, 20, 98, 178, 179, 180, 197, 199; Cantos 107–109 (Coke Cantos), 11, 14, 28, 33, 34, 193–214; Canto 107, 6, 14, 38, 46, 47, 48, 53, 108, 169, 178, 188, 193, 194, 195, 196, 197, 199, 200, 206, 211, 212; Canto 108, 15, 29, 38, 155, 193, 196, 197, 198, 199, 205, 208, 209, 210; Canto 109, 48, 49, 64, 196, 198, 199, 201, 202, 209, 210, 211, 213; Canto 110, 130; Canto 111, 201; Canto 112, 109, 222; Canto 113, 130, 223; Canto 115, 216;

Canto 116, 15, 178, 212, 221; Canto 117, 14, 51, 92, 119, 173.; *Works other than cantos*: "ADLAI and ALASKA" 210; *Analects* (Confucius, tr. Pound) 68, 179, 190; "L'Aura Amara" (Arnaut Daniel, tr. Pound) 127; "Ballatetta" 118; *Canzoni* 118; "Chung Yung, The Unwobbling Pivot" (Confucius, tr. Pound) 31, 45, 79; "Coke on Principles" 32, 199, 211, 213; *The Confucian Odes* (Confucius, tr. Pound) 12, 42, 45, 222; Ode 242 [3.I.8] 31; *Confucius* (tr. Pound) 10, 14, 16, 18, 19, 31, 45, 68, 79, 179, 182, 188, 190, 202; *Confucius to Cummings* 107, 130; *The Economic Nature of the United States* 204; *Elektra* (Sophokles, tr. Pound) 218, 227; *Ezra Pound and James Laughlin: Selected Letters* 130; *Ezra Pound/Letters/John Theobald* 15, 17, 86, 179, 188, 195; *"Ezra Pound Speaking"—Radio Speeches of World War II*, 25, 66, 177; *Ezra Pound's Chinese Friends* (ed. Qian) 18, 30, 31, 50, 179, 180, 188; *Ezra Pound's Economic Correspondence* (ed. Preda) 183, 184; "Four Steps to the Bughouse" 24–6; *Guide to Kulchur* 21, 22, 31, 85; *Homage to Sextus Propertius* 226; "Honi Soit" (Pound) 175; "I Cease Not to Yowl"; *Ezra Pound's Letters to Olivia Rossetti Agresti* 4, 6, 20, 28–30, 39, 40, 50, 78, 87, 89, 90, 92, 95–9, 136, 137, 149, 151, 153, 154, 157, 159, 167, 169, 175–7, 179, 182, 187; *Indiscretions* 54, 202, 203, 213; *Jefferson and/or Mussolini* 19, 21, 22, 68, 76, 162; "Jury System in Danger" 199, 212; *Literary Essays* 119, 120, 183; *La Martinelli* (intro. Pound) 113, 170; "Mang Tsze" 164, 183, 184; "Note Against Degradation" 85, 87, 185, 187; notebook 107, 29, 189; notebook 111, 194, 196, 211; notebook 112, 39, 196; notebook 113, 111, 213; "Organic Categories" (J.V. [*i.e.*, Pound]) 84; *Pavannes &*

Divagations 54, 202, 203, 213; *Personae: The Shorter Poems of Ezra Pound* 103, 118; *Pound/Lewis. The Letters of Ezra Pound and Wyndham Lewis* 97; "Program in Search of a Party" 177; Rome Radio broadcasts 25, 66, 177; *Selected Letters of Ezra Pound* (ed. Paige) 214; *Selected Prose 1909-1965* (ed. Cookson) 85, 126, 127, 164, 180, 182–4, 204; *The Spirit of Romance* 45, 115, 122, 126, 150; "Terra Italica" 126, 127; "The Tomb of Akr Çaar" 103; untitled note vilifying the Warren Court, 27–8, 206, and addendum 211 n.6; "Values" 85; "Voice of Experience" 171; *Women of Trachis* (Sophokles, tr. Pound) 214, 221, 227
The Pound Era (Kenner) 9, 173
Pound in Purgatory: From Economic Radicalism to Anti-Semitism (Surette) 49
Prabbu of Kopt 103
Praet, Danny 158
Preda, Roxana 7, 15, 21, 29, 132, 134, 161, 170, 173, 174
Presley, Elvis 82
Priapus 172
"principles of '98" 24
Proclamation of 1763 204
producers, versus destroyers of production 189
Prologue to Conflict: The Crisis and Compromise of 1850 (Holman) 74
Prometheus 4
proslavery 59, 63, 64, 159
pro-Southern 55
The Protocols of the Elders of Zion 7, 90, 98, 142, 146
Provençal, influences throughout Cantos 90–95, 122, 123, 125, 127, 149
Purgatorio (Dante) 161
Putnam, Israel 212
Pythagoras 149, 152, 169; Pythagorean 134, 149, 150, 175

Qian, Zhaoming 42
Quan yin. *See* Kuanon (Gwanyin, Guanyin, Kuan yin, Quan yin)
Quesnay, François 179–83, 189, 190
Quest Society 45, 122

Ra, Sun 106
Rabaté, Jean-Michel 120, 121
race, Agassiz's views on 77; civilizations as the product of (Bilbo) 107; as the determinate factor in human potential and development 105; eugenic attitude toward 107, 109, 213; Pound's thoughts on 109, 185, 213
race war 74, 141
Rachewiltz, Boris de 78, 97, 100, 103, 106, 110, 149, 189
Rachewiltz, Mary de 49, 91, 97, 123, 124, 193, 196, 197, 222, 223
racial amalgamation 27, 82, 83, 108
racial equality 82; as a "disease of thought" 77, 86; as leading to the "mongrelization" of society 52
racial integration of public schools, eugenic threat posed by 206; "Interposition" as part of the South's resistance to 54; as leading to the genocide of the white race (Kasper) 187; as leading to racial amalgamation and the end of white supremacy 27, 52, 82, 92; mandated by *Brown v. Board of Education* 2, 10, 59, 78; "massive resistance" to throughout the South through an appeal to states' rights and "local customs" 10, 24, 52, 53, 58, 59; opposed by John Crommelin 184; opposed by John Kasper 187, 188; opposed by Pedro del Valle 184; opposed by Pound 206; social implications of 82; supported by Herbert H. Lehman 90 as a threat to the race-integrity of white people and to civilization 78; violence accompanying 59
racial mixing 1–3, 77, 82, 83, 85–6, 98, 107; *Brown v. Board of Education* opening the door to 2, 77, 82, 83; as causing the fall of the early Aryan nations 107; as contrary to the divine plan 2; as an object of the Jewish/Communist conspiracy 1; loss of civilizations through 107
racial taxonomy 2, 10, 77–8, 79, 84–7, 90;

as a major strand in the late cantos 79; synthesized by Pound from his understanding of Agassiz and Frobenius 84
Rahab 128
Raleigh, Walter 200, 205, 208
Randolph, John, of Roanoke 51–6, 71–3, 127, 164–5, 203, 208; Charlotte Court House resolutions (1833) 56, 73; duel with Secretary of State Henry Clay 54, 56, 73; Jeffersonian politics of 54, 56; opposition to the state borrowing its own money from banks 164–5; states' rights creed of 53, 55; as a victim of the historic "blot-out" 53
"Randolph of Roanoke" (Whittier) 71
Ra-Set 39, 116, 129, 134, 140
Rattray, David 113, 144
Read, Forrest 149
Reck, Michael 50, 169
Reconstruction 24, 55
Red Scare 5
Redman, Tim 92
Reed, Ishmael 106
Regnery, Henry 72
Reid, Lorraine 210, 214
Reid, Ralph 210, 214
The Reign of the House of Rothschild 1830–1871 (Corti) 49
Republican Party 52, 63, 75
Rich, Adrienne 6, 7, 25, 46
Richard II (Shakespeare) 212
Richard St. Victor 118, 126
Richardson, Charles 30, 142
Richmond News Leader 53
"right naming" 44, 169; Pound's intense preoccupation with 172. See also *cheng ming*
The Rise of the House of Rothschild 1770–1830 (Corti) 49
Roberts, Archibald 3
Rock, Joseph 11, 29, 40, 98, 213
Rocke, Cyril 89, 92, 93
Rockwell, George Lincoln 76
Rodale Institute 186
Rogers, Guy MacLean 106, 110
Roman coinages 166–8
Roman Empire 66, 158; longevity based on settling veterans on the land 66

Rome, as epitome of "civilization" 67, 188; lost through race mixing 107; versus Babylon 65, 68, 188
Rome Radio broadcasts 2, 18, 25, 26, 30, 65, 66, 67, 154, 177
Rooming House Madrigals: Early Selected Poems 1946–1966 (Bukowski) 133
Roosevelt, Franklin D. 25, 26, 27, 28, 37, 48, 50, 52, 65, 97, 154, 157, 200, 206
Roosevelt, Theodore 74
Roosevelt administration 3, 66, 205; as the real traitors who involved the USA in World War II 200
Rosenberg, Alfred 110, 159
Rossetti, Dante Gabriel 29
Rossetti, Gabriele 133, 134
Rossoni, Edmondo 184
Rothschilds, August Belmont as agent for 67; money financing Disraeli's extraparliamentary purchase of Suez Canal shares 37, 155, 208
Rousselot de Surgy, Jacques-Philibert 179, 180
Roux, Dominique de 220
Rudge, Olga 49, 131, 132, 215, 223
Ruskin, John 91, 190
Russell, Peter 142, 146
Russia 23, 32, 37, 52, 66, 67, 70, 90
Russian revolution 66

The Sacred Edict (Kuang-Tzu 康熙, tr. Baller) 11, 12, 29, 31, 40, 42, 43, 83, 110, 168, 178, 181, 182, 197
Sahara Desert 106
Said, Edward 24–5, 35, 45, 47
St. Elizabeths Hospital 1, 2, 9, 14, 16, 23–6, 28, 38, 40, 46, 51, 53, 55, 56, 80, 82, 84–7, 89, 92, 108, 114, 118, 124, 136, 137, 140, 158, 188, 189, 193, 196, 197, 209, 210, 214, 216
St. Teresa 137
Sandomirskaja, Irina 38
Sanhedrin 142
Santa Teresa 137
Santayana, George 19, 222
Sapientia, Lady 119, 126
Sargon 13, 85, 100, 101, 102, 106, 109, 110, 150–152, 175; Sargon's seal 78, 95, 100–2, 164, 173

Sargon the Magnificent (Bristowe) 109–10
"Scandal of the Assumption" (the "Compromise of 1790") 61
Scheiwiller, Vanni 113
school integration crisis 77. See also *Brown II*; *Brown v. Board of Education*; racial integration of public schools
Schmitt, Carl 50
Schuyler, George 111
Schwartz, Delmore 36
scientific racism 18, 77
Scott, Dred 75
Scott, Peter Dale 206, 213
Seaboard White Citizens' Council (SWCC) 54, 83, 87, 90, 92, 185
Seagle, William 151, 158
secession of the Southern states (1861) 24
The Secret Doctrine (Blavatsky) 145
segregation 2, 24, 27, 71, 74, 83, 86, 87, 89, 91, 92, 189
"Segregation or Death" (Kasper) 83, 86, 89, 92
segregationism 1, 3, 4, 10, 24, 26, 71, 76, 185
Selden, John 28, 206
Seminole War 74
Semites, bent on destroying Pound's paradise 173; denied by Waddell as capable of civilization 81, 99, 158; the grain god as the villain of 137; versus Aryans 17, 78, 101, 221
Senate Joint Resolution 3 (Virginia) 72, 73
Setterlind, Bo 191
Severus, Septimus 158
Seward, William 59
Shakespeare, William 78, 108, 139, 212
Shamash 158
Shang dynasty 12, 102, 190
Shangri-La 11
Sharrock, Roger 109
Shelley, Percy Bysshe 6
Sheppard, Kathleen 110
Short Review and Analysis of the History of Money in the United States (Overholser) 175
Shu Jing [*Book of Documents*; *Shu, the History Classic*; *Shang Shu*; *The Books of Shang*] 12
Shun 20

Sibilla, as code for Martinelli 170
Sibylla, as code for Martinelli 126, 140
Sicily 179, 197, 212
Sickles, Dan 67, 68
Sieburth, Richard 34
Siger of Brabant 199, 212
Simon Magus 128, 150
Simon Magus (Mead) 150
Simpson, Dallam (Dallam Flynn, L. C. Flynn) 47, 50, 95, 187
Simpson, Wallis 64
Sims, Thomas 60, 75
Sinn Féin 22
slavery 56, 59, 60, 62–4, 67, 68, 74, 75, 88, 89, 127
Smith, Adam 180, 183
Smith, G. L. K. 82, 97, 98
Smith, Marvin 75
Social Credit 109, 162, 163, 175, 184, 215
socialism, Pound's opposition to 29, 175
socialization, 175, as a distraction 164
Soil Association 186
Somerset, Robert Carr, Earl of 195
Sophocles 216–19, 226, 227
Sophocles' King Oedipus (Yeats) 218
South (US) 2, 3, 24, 54, 55, 58–60, 63, 67, 68, 74, 75, 79, 97, 187, 188; defeated by its debts 191; Jim Crow racial segregation in 27; Northern aggression against as precipitating Civil War 75; race war in 74; resistance to integration of 10, 24, 54
"The Southern Manifesto" 74–5
sovereignty, decline of with the abandonment of the sacred prerogative to coin gold 165; inhered in the power to issue money 13, 61, 163, 164, 165, 166, 167, 169, 188, 207; of the states 53, 54, 56, 59, 72, 73. See also "popular sovereignty"
Soviet collective farm 65, 67
Soviet land policy 66
Spain 24, 67, 68, 152
Spanish 67, 68, 171, 213
Spann, Marcella. See Booth, Marcella Spann
Sparta 44, 156, 157
Spoo, Robert 26

Stafford, Jack 85, 185, 187, 190
Stalin, Joseph 28
Stamp Act of 1765 204
stamp scrip 207
State Department 25, 66, 75; as a nest of traitors and spies 67
states' rights 3, 10, 24, 26, 51–76, 184, 185, 187
States' Rights Council 74
Stein, Gertrude 227
Stevenson, Adlai 210
Stewart, Potter 71
Stock, Noel 1, 7, 15, 34, 47, 51, 66, 70, 86, 97, 98, 109, 186, 200
Stoddard, Lothrop 98
Stonehenge 173
Stoner, J. B. 3
Stowe, Harriet Beecher 74
Stresino, Edward 136
Strike 3, 47, 66, 67, 70, 76
Stuart monarchy 48, 108, 199
Sturgis, Kentucky 78
Suez Canal 37, 155, 208
Suez Crisis 37
Sulmona 46
Sulpicia 117
Sulzberger, Arthur Hays 88
Sumer 78, 79, 98, 99, 107
Sumeria 102
Sumero-Akkadian culture 91
Sumner, Charles 38, 62, 65, 67, 211
sun worship 101, 110, 173; Aryanist tradition of 158, 173, 174; in Canto 96, 174; in Canto 97, 170
Sun-God 101
Sunic, Tomislav 21, 32
Supreme Court 2, 10, 25, 28, 52, 53, 77, 88, 141, 206, 207; reorganization bill of 1937 (packing the Supreme Court) 25–6, 52. *See also* Warren Court
Surette, Leon 4, 49
Swabey, Henry S. 97, 109
Swedenborg, Emanuel 118
Sweeney, James R. 72
Swift, Wesley 109
Sybil 116, 170, 171
La Sybille: Trois essais sur la religion antique et la christianisme (Zielinski) 158–9

Tableau économique (Quesnay) 179, 190
Taft, William Howard 74
Take Your Choice: Separation or Mongrelization (Bilbo) 82, 91, 107, 111
Talleyrand-Périgord, Charles Maurice de 57, 58, 69, 73, 74
Talmud 27, 28
tan[4] [旦] 162, 170, 175
tax, nothing worse than a fixed 184; versus a tithe or a share 184
taxonomy of races. *See* racial taxonomy
Taylor, Richard 115, 124, 132
Taylor, Zachary 59, 60
Telemachus 120, 121
temple, as the signature of sacred Aryan primacy 164; not for sale 11, 13, 85, 164, 165, 174; *Rock-Drill* as about the construction of 13; sign derived from the hieroglyph for Sargon 85, 100, 101, 173
Ten Eyck, David 201, 202, 208, 209, 211–13
Tenures (Littleton) 209
Terrell, Carroll 12, 43, 56, 57, 63, 66, 69, 71, 74, 118, 123, 126, 145, 146, 158, 171, 172, 190, 209, 213
Theobald, John 15, 17, 51, 86, 179, 188, 195
Theseus 219
Thomson, Alexander Raven 195
Thoreau, Henry David 162, 175
Thoughts on Government (Adams) 202
Thrones, money, law, and sovereignty as braided discourses in 13; money, law, land, and language as the foundational discourses of 169. *See also* Pound, Ezra
Tianu 151, 158
Tibet 29, 40, 78, 79, 98
Tiresias 217–19, 227
Tom Jones (Fielding) 73
Torrey, E. Fuller 114
Touré, Askia 106
Townsman 109
treason, Coke imprisoned for 200 (misprision of, 193, 200); Pound's indictment for 13, 26, 46, 71, 198, 200, 201 (misprision of, 193, 200, 205); Raleigh sentenced for 200

Treasury Department, allegedly Communist-infested 28
"The Treatise of Eusebius" 150
trial by jury 199
"trobar clus" 35, 45, 122, 123, 125
Troubadours 34, 35, 45, 118, 122, 123, 126, 128, 149. *See also* trobar clus
Troy 91, 99, 150, 152
Trump, Donald 73; Trumpism 27; Trumpist 3, 32
"The Truth about Abyssinia, by an Eye Witness" (Rocke) 89
Tryphonopoulos, Demetres 4, 17, 166
Tsiang, Hiuen 101, 102, 110
tuan. *See* the four tuan
Tucker, St. George 54, 55, 203
Tu-Fu 179
Turgot, Anne Robert Jacques 180
Twanghi 91, 102
Tyana 12, 34, 40, 46, 110, 149–52, 158; alleged place of origin for the original Aryans 151
Tyrants 226
Tyre 128, 129, 149, 150
Tytell, John 220
Tze-Kung 68

Uncle Tom's Cabin (Stowe) 74
United Nations 206
United States, as the heir of the tradition of English law 14, 201; betrayed by finance capital 201; called "Baruchistan" by Pound 90; the Civil Rights struggle as an effort to "mongrelize" 70; Jeffersonian interpretation of 56; Pound's 1939 visit to 25, 74, 201; an object of subversion and subjugation by the Jewish/Communist conspiracy and its fronts 1, 24, 26, 27, 83; Pound's 1945 return to 26; subverted by the UN 206; threatened with destruction by the federally mandated integration of schools 53
United States Constitution 1, 3, 24, 26, 27, 29, 32, 53, 57, 58, 60, 64, 74, 81, 83, 90, 188, 198, 207, 222; bastardization of 32; betrayed by the courts 207; betrayed by the creation of the Federal Reserve Bank 207; interpreted by Buchanan, Pierce, and Fillmore as strictly limiting federal power 64; judicial usurpation of 24; objections to by Patrick Henry 74; rejected as a binding contract by the Kentucky and Virginia Resolutions of 1789 and 1799 24, 53; states' rights interpretation of 53; subverted by Jewish front organizations like the NAACP 90; under attack by the Communist Warren Court 27, 83
"Ursula benedetta" (Martinelli) 117, 124
Uruk 110
USSR. *See* Russia
Usura, the adulteration of food as a practice of 3, 177, 187; as the metaphysical dimension of usury economics 177; as a weapon of finance-capitalism 19
usury, Judah Benjamin as an agent of 191; mentioned by Dante 139; mentioned by Shakespeare 139; opposed by Del Mar 166; the rate of 168

Valli, Luigi 134
Van Buren, Martin 53, 56, 73, 208
Van de Mieroop, Marc 110
Vatican Bank 175
Venice 215, 223, 226
Venus 13, 113, 127, 130, 170, 172
Vespasian 44, 152, 153, 155, 156
Vienna 58, 68, 69, 76
Viereck, George Sylvester 30
Viereck, Peter 5, 17, 18, 19, 22, 30, 157, 158
Villiers, George, 1st Duke of Buckingham 27
Virginia 10, 24, 53–6, 70–4, 83, 89, 92, 185; Constitution of, efforts to revise 54
Virginia Resolutions of 1798 24, 53, 72; as a "recipe for disunion" (Washington) 24
Virginia Spectator 83, 89, 92
"Virginians On Guard!" (Kasper) 2, 10, 54, 61, 75, 207

Voice of America 66
"Volitionist economics" 162
Voltaire (François-Marie Arouet) 179
von Freytag-Loringhoven, Elsa 120, 132
von Metternich, Klemens 58, 69
Voorhis, Jerry 212

Waddell, Laurence A. 24, 29, 30, 40, 78–81, 91, 96–110, 140, 141, 146, 149, 151, 152, 158, 159, 170, 172–4, 176
Wadsworth, Joseph 48, 49, 76, 201–3, 213
Walden (Thoreau) 175
Walker, Ernie 144
Walluschnig, Dotto Aldo 49
Walz, Jay 75
Wang, David 92, 110, 179, 187, 188
Warren, Earl 27, 28, 52, 71, 206
Warren Court 2, 9–32, 37, 52, 53, 83, 141, 206, 207, 211; *Brown* decision 2, 206; defended by Catherine Drinker Bowen 207; as a front for a Jewish/Communist cabal 26, 27, 28, 52, 83; rejection of white supremacy by 27; vilification of by Pound 27–8, 207, 211. *See also* Supreme Court
wars, causes of 69; fomented by financial speculators so as to create debts 58
Washington, Booker T. 89, 92
Washington, George 24, 74
Washington, D.C. 9, 11, 50, 90, 114, 136, 138, 171, 175, 199. *See also* District of Columbia, St. Elizabeths Hospital
Washington Post 88
The Waste Land (Eliot) 219
water fluoridation, as a Communist scheme to stupefy the masses 186; John Kasper on 186
Weber, Max 165
Webster, Daniel 59
Welles, Sumner 38, 65–7, 75, 76; Toledo speech of 65–6
Wells Fargo mortgage fraud 175
Wen 45
Western civilization, *The Cantos* designed to express the best of 224; *The Cantos* designed to prevent the collapse of 221; the twentieth-century tragedy of 225

Western Islands Press 49
Weston, Richard 195
wheat imagery 178, 188. *See also* grain
Wheat in Our Bread Party (WHIB) 184, 185, 187
Wheeler, Burton Kendall 25, 27, 28, 52, 206
WHIB Party. *See* Wheat in Our Bread Party (WHIB)
White, Dexter 27, 28, 136, 137; as a Soviet agent 28
white supremacy 2, 3, 10, 27, 77–93, 97, 108, 159, 173, 186; as a corollary of Aryan priority 108; rejection of by the Warren Court 2, 27
as a slogan of the Democratic Party, 27
Whitman, Walt 74
Whittier, John Greenleaf 71
Who's Who 96
Wilhelm, James J. 57, 227
Williams, William Carlos 6, 120, 132, 146, 167, 175, 216, 223
Wilson, Woodrow 74, 88, 165
Windeler, B. C. 137
Winters, Yvor 33
Winthrop, John 202
Woden 99, 172
Wolverine (warship) 61
Wörgl, Austria 167
World War I 23, 25, 103
World War II 13, 23, 30, 40, 90, 173, 195, 199, 205, 216, 222; as an Anglo-Jewish war against civilization 199; international bankers as true victors of 90; Pound detained for trying to prevent 199; Pound's effort to prevent US entry into 204; Pound's failure to prevent 222
Wright, Frank Lloyd 210, 214
Wright, Jay 46, 106
Wright, Richard 111
"Writs of Assistance" 209

xreia 41

Yale Review 33, 211
Yao 20
Yeats, Georgie 12
Yeats, William Butler 21, 22, 217, 218, 220, 227

Yggdrasil (Ygdrasail) 9, 115
Yockey, Francis Parker 30
Yong Tching (Iong Ching, Yong Zheng) 110, 197
yuán [yian² or iuên] [元] 159

Zaibert, Leo 20

Zen Buddhism 141
Zeus 172
Zielinski, Thaddeus 158–9
"Zion" as the project of the Elders of Zion 143
"Zionist Overlords" 142, 143
Zukofsky, Louis 85

www.ingramcontent.com/pod-product-compliance
Lightning Source LLC
Chambersburg PA
CBHW072125290426
44111CB00012B/1787